END TIMES AND 2019

The End of the Mayan Calendar and the Countdown to Judgment Day

David Montaigne

Adventures Unlimited Press

Other Books by David Montaigne:

Nostradamus, World War III

END TIMES
AND 2019

David Montaigne

Endtimes and 2019

by David Montaigne

ISBN: 978-1-935487-92-0

Published by:
Adventures Unlimited Press
One Adventure Place
Kempton, Illinois 60946 USA

auphq@frontiernet.net

www.adventuresunlimitedpress.com

10 9 8 7 6 5 4 3 2 1

END TIMES AND 2019

The End of the Mayan Calendar and the Countdown to Judgment Day

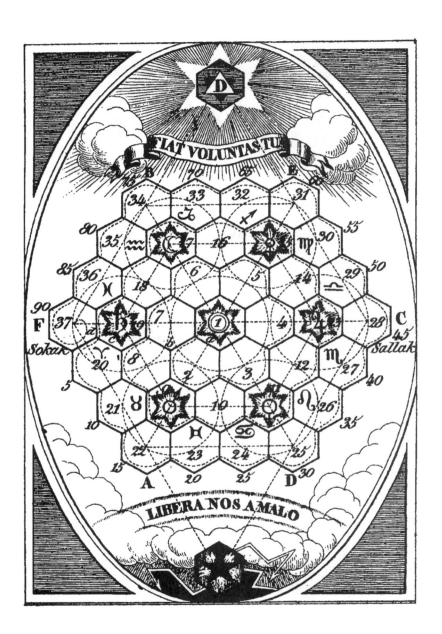

Contents

My last trip to Jerusalem in 2010—with enough knowledge and wisdom to have a much better idea of what I was looking for.

Introduction

Calculating Dates
for the End Times

A Naval Intelligence officer once told me: "I know a coded book when I see one. And *the Bible is a coded book*." That conversation may have planted the seed in my mind which eventually grew into questions, research, and roughly fifteen years later, the sudden mental breakthroughs that clarified how I would correctly interpret prophecy. Before those insights, despite studying many sources of prophecies on end times events including the Bible, the Mayan calendar, psychics like Nostradamus and Edgar Cayce, and the temples, texts, and myths from Egypt and India and other ancient cultures—I couldn't see any unifying conclusion. Different sources didn't seem to be saying the same things.

It seemed obvious that unless they were all in agreement, most of these sources must be wrong. Anyone who values the wisdom of ancient civilizations must wonder why every culture has different beliefs. Agnostics doubt anything requiring divine revelation. Christians often assume that if prophecies do not agree with the Bible, they can't be right. But if there is a single future to foresee, all valid prophecies should tell us the same things about the end of the world.

Eventually I realized that many sources are telling us the same stories; that many "different" prophecies are really in agreement. It took years for me to determine which cultural differences were important and how to recognize crucial similarities. It was like watching half of a foreign film before realizing it is probably the original version of a movie I already knew.

For most readers any comparison of varied sources of prophecy is like the fable of the blind men and the elephant. Several men who are either blind or in the dark each touch one part of an elephant (without knowing what it is) and compare notes. Of course after feeling a tusk, a leg, an ear, the belly, and the tail, they are in complete disagreement over the details and argue about the unknown thing between them. A king explains that they are all correct; that they have unrelated descriptions because they are touching different parts of an elephant.

Modern readers may best recognize the version by the 19th century poet John Saxe, which concludes that the blind men:

> *Rail on in utter ignorance*
> *Of what each other mean,*
> *And prate about an Elephant*
> *Not one of them has seen.*

But just as the blind men all contemplated and described the same elephant, different cultures are often telling us prophecies about the same future events. There is a way to understand and reconcile every valid source of end times prophecy. *It requires two simple keys.* The first key is realizing that different cultures all tell us stories which are meant to be understood from an astronomical point of view. The night sky is like an enormous clock, and ancient cultures describe unique arrangements of heavenly bodies to show us when future events will occur. The second key to understanding end times prophecy is discovering any particular culture's grand climax event and interpreting it astronomically.

Christianity's climax event—*the filter through which the Bible's end times prophecies should be viewed—is an ancient Jewish wedding ceremony* between Christ and His bride. Bible prophecy is much easier to understand if we shift our focus from events in ancient Israel and direct our attention to the future wedding in the sky. No religious beliefs are necessary to understand that the Bible has encoded astronomical information detailing the timing of an apocalypse in our near future. This is not to say that the traditional understanding of the Bible is wrong or irrelevant—but

14

the astrotheological[1] interpretation of the wedding ceremony is what will give us the clearest timing of future events.

The Bible has an end times message for us if we accept that it describes a Jewish wedding ceremony with astronomical bodies as the main characters. The ancient Maya tell a similar story and the end of the Mayan Long Count ("Calendar") on 12/21/2012 is the exact start of the Bible's seven-year tribulation—because both cultures were focused on the same astronomical events.

Many people know the Mayan Long Count ends in 2012 but few realize the Maya described the positions of astronomical bodies at the end of the world, and the that positions described for the planets are not accurate for 2012. They do match what will be seen in December 2019. The seven transitional years in between worlds can be viewed as the last years of the current world (as Christianity views the Tribulation) or as the first years of the new world (as the Maya view them.) Either way, *the end of the world as we know it* is imminent.

There is evidence that the Bible points to end times events in 2012, with far more drastic events seven years later in 2019. My astronomical perspective let me know what to look for, but with the book of Daniel and a good background in Middle Eastern history, anyone can follow Daniel to three specific points thousands of years in his future. Two of them, 1948 and 1967, are now in our past. They are the most important dates in the history of the modern State of Israel; the year it became an independent nation, and the year the Israelis took over control of Jerusalem. The third year Daniel leads us to is 2012, and the events that are set to begin then are by far the most important.

There are similar warnings from Egypt, India, and other cultures. Seven years after 12/21/2012, a cataclysmic pole shift will begin on 12/21/2019. The earth's surface features are going to change dramatically, and most people will die. Judgment Day comes seven days later as the pole shift ends on 12/28/2019. This may not be what you were taught in Sunday school, but hundreds of Bible passages supporting this interpretation point to these dates.

It may seem unlikely that so many unique prophecies from around the world are really describing the same events. We have been conditioned by more than a thousand years of Rome's efforts to mask the similarities and emphasize the uniqueness of Christianity. But we can just as easily reverse the process; looking past the foreign names which the main characters have in different cultures, we can appreciate that they have distinct motivations because the main event can be anything from a wedding ceremony to winning a ball game.

After finally understanding that many sources of prophecy are essentially saying the same things—my next task was to compare specific similarities between prophecies for confirmation. The obvious starting point was to compare the Mayan concept of the end of the world with Bible prophecies, for although the Bible stands out for having dozens of divinely inspired prophecies—the Mayan Long Count ending in 2012 has the most clearly defined timing. It didn't take long to realize that the Bible's Book of Daniel also points to 2012. Deeper analysis was necessary to match astronomical details to specific days in 2019.

Despite finding clear evidence of these dates, there is strong resistance to the idea that anyone can know when Jesus will return or that we can deduce when Judgment Day will be. Most people think we are not supposed to know specific timing for such things. This problem began with a minor translation error in Matthew 24:36. Understanding this correctly is extremely important, for if the common misunderstanding were correct, it would rule out calculating the dates of future events. Let's look at several versions of what Jesus told us in this verse:

"But of that day and hour no one knows, not even the angels of heaven, nor the Son, but the Father alone." (New American Standard Bible—NASB)

"But of that day and hour knoweth no man, no, not the angels of heaven, but my Father only." (King James Bible—KJB)

"No one knows about that day or hour, not even the angels in heaven, nor the Son, but only the Father." (New International Version—NIV)

16

"But of that day and hour no one knoweth, not the angels of heaven, but the Father alone." (Douay-Rheims American Edition (DRA)

Almost every American who reads that verse in their Bible believes that no one can know when the end will come. But a little investigation quickly shows that one crucial word in that sentence was not quite translated properly from Greek to English. The Greek word "οιδεν" ("oiden") is mistranslated as "knows." It is actually a *past tense* verb which literally means "he has seen" (and understood in his mind.) When Christians today read "no one knows" most assume no one knew then, no one knows now, and no one will ever know - when in reality Jesus was merely saying that the timing of such events *had not been known* at that point in time, on the 11th of Nisan, 33 A.D. "Concerning that day and hour nobody has known" is how this reads in accurate translations of the verse, as in Young's Literal Translation.

If anyone had wanted to discuss the future date of my wedding before I got engaged and planned it I could only have made vague estimations, and my likely response would have been "We don't know the date yet." Such an answer would have implied that my wedding would eventually take place and that at some point I would know. Jesus did the same thing in Matthew 24:36 when asked about the timing of his own future wedding (and related future events.) He told us "No one has known," which merely specifies that no one knew (in the past) up to that point. But a lack of knowledge in the past does not preclude future gains in knowledge. No one had known how to build a nuclear submarine then either.

Is it presumptuous to assume that we could know this timing today when Jesus himself did not know it? Not at all. Jesus required a lack of omniscience and omnipotence for his experience in human form. As we are told in Philippians 2:7, Jesus "emptied himself" of aspects of his divine nature in order to fully experience human nature. God does not sleep (Psalms 121: 2-4)—but Jesus slept. (Mark 4:38) God does not weep, or experience hunger, thirst, or fear—but Jesus did. God himself does not die—but Jesus had to die for our sins, and he had to do it in human form, willingly choosing to temporarily take on many human limitations. Pope John Paul II commented on Christ's apparent lack of omnipotence in Matthew 24:36 on March 3, 1999 and said: "This is an indication of the 'emptying of himself' proper to the Incarnation, which conceals the eschatological end of the world from his human nature."

Despite not knowing the day or the hour at the time He was quoted in Matthew 24:36, Jesus gave a very different answer after He was resurrected—for He had paid the bride price (arranged to be married) through death and had returned without the limitations of mortals. When His disciples asked Him about the timing of future events in Acts 1:7, Jesus replied: "It is not for you to know times or epochs which the Father has fixed by His own authority." (NASB)

(Unless otherwise noted Bible quotations from this point forward will all be from the New American Standard Bible. There are slight differences between translations, as with the epochs, seasons, dates, and moments which the NASB, KJB, NIV, and DRA translations mention in the verse above—but such variations do not affect our comprehension of a passage. Rest assured this author is comparing many Bible translations and when necessary others will be quoted— but not for every verse.)

In Acts 1:7 Jesus does not deny knowing the timing himself, as he did before the resurrection in Matthew 24:36. This implies that he does know—and that the knowledge is available at the right time. At one point this information was not meant for Jesus to know; at a later point, he did know. In biblical times, it was not meant for mankind to know. Jesus told his followers the information was "not for you."

It is meant for us to know now, in the early 21st century. With apocalyptic events set to begin in 2012, time is fast running out to reveal hidden things before they happen. And the Bible tells us repeatedly that everything which starts off misunderstood, hidden, or veiled, will eventually be clarified, understood, and revealed. The word "apocalypse" literally means "the lifting of the veil" and as we approach the end times we should expect that everything will be revealed to the masses. God wants us to know and understand everything he does. I asked Tim LaHaye (author of the very successful Left Behind series) about this after meeting him at a book signing. He did not seem overly concerned with the timing of such events, as he believes those who have truly accepted Jesus will not be "left behind" here to witness them—but he agreed that "it is possible that we will know the timing of such events better—more accurately—as the end approaches."

Some Bible verses that let us know all will be revealed include Amos 3:7 "Surely the Lord GOD does nothing Unless He reveals His secret counsel To His servants the prophets." Mark 4:22 tells us "For nothing is hidden, except to be revealed; nor has anything been secret, but that it would come to light." Luke 8:17 is very similar: "For nothing is hidden that will not become evident, nor anything secret that will not be known and come to light." As Gerald Flurry writes: "God speaks in coded language. Then when the time is right, He breaks the code. God reveals all of His truth."[2] In Daniel 12:4 that prophet clarifies that he must "make secret the words and seal up the book, until the time of [the] end. Many will rove about, and the [true] knowledge will become abundant." God has secrets which are only revealed near the end of these events. Some believe that the existence of computers and astronomical software have only recently allowed us to "break the code" and that this itself was anticipated. We should not rule out the possibility of learning the day and hour as they approach.

This interpretation of Matthew 24:36 is also supported by an understanding of ancient Jewish wedding ceremonies. Let us look beyond the one step of paying the bride price to understand additional restraints on wedding dates that are crucially important in our quest to understand the timing of events at the end of days. After an ancient Jewish bridegroom paid the bride price and after offering a cup of wine signifying his covenant with the bride, the groom would go to his father's house and add on to it, building one or more new rooms for himself and his bride to live in. The bride would still be at her father's house waiting for her future husband to come get her. She had to watch and be ready because she did not know how long it would be before her bridegroom would return. He could not tell his bride how long it would take him to finish building a place for her, because the final say on the completion of the new living quarters was not up to him. The son would build the room for his bride, but it was his father who would eventually say, "it is done, it is time to get your bride." The bridegroom did not know when his father would consider the work sufficiently finished, and neither did the bride.

At the time Jesus was quoted in Matthew 24:36, not only was He in human form, having emptied Himself of many divine abilities, but He had not yet even paid the bride price, let alone proceeded to His Father's house in the heavens to start preparing a place. By telling us that only the Father knows such things, and not the Son, Jesus was indirectly acknowledging that no bridegroom would be in a position to tell us when his father would consider the new living space finished, when the process had not yet been started. More importantly, Jesus told us these events could not happen before He went to His Father's house. Most people seem content to be told that no one knows the timing, without making the connection that Jesus was linking the timing of the end with the rituals of a wedding. But astronomically, Jesus has been at His Father's house for several years already, and we should all be very interested in His progress.

As I learned of more symbolic references to His Father's house (and many other things) I started to suspect that it should be possible to figure out the exact timing of events like the Second Coming and Judgment Day. The more research I did, the more I started to view the Bible from the perspective that there are two main messages. There is the obvious and easily understood spiritual message on the surface, and a deeper layer of veiled astronomical messages that few people will notice.

Some researchers use the Hebrew term "pesher" when describing more than one layer of meaning. Literally, the word "pesher" means nothing more than "interpretation." This is how it is used for its single mention in the Bible, in Ecclesiastes 8:1 "Who is like the wise man and who knows the interpretation of a matter?" But the Dead Sea Scrolls emphasize a more specific use of the word, not just as an interpretation but as a solution, as if solving a code or a cipher or a hidden double meaning. The Essenes who wrote commentaries two thousand years ago felt that Bible passages often went beyond the surface interpretation meant for those of ordinary mental capacity, and concealed additional truths and messages for the wise and initiated.

These hidden messages are not meant for everyone. The spiritual messages are the only ones most people need. Eternal salvation is easy to understand, and fortunately one can have faith in a heavenly reward and live life accordingly without knowing the less obvious details of exactly how and when God intends to wrap up this system of things. Christianity does not require understanding how the universe operates… or terminates.

But despite a lack of obvious clarity on some topics, they are not unknowable. Jesus repeatedly tells us that while there are many people who only understand the most literal interpretations of the Bible there are some who completely understand deeper layers of meaning. So with the impression that I generally understood the central religious/spiritual messages in Christianity, it seemed like it was time to pay more attention to Hebrews 6:1 "leaving the elementary teaching about the Christ, let us press on to maturity." I was convinced the Bible tells us everything I could hope for, if I would just look for the clues.

1 Thessalonians 5:1-4 "Now as to the times and the epochs, brethren, you have no need of anything to be written to you. For you yourselves know full well that the day of the Lord will come just like a thief in the night (for most people) …destruction will come upon them suddenly like labor pains upon a woman with child, and they will not escape. But you, brethren, are not in darkness, that the day would overtake you like a thief."

This indicates that those who truly understand the Bible are enlightened—"in the light"—not in darkness of misunderstanding—and that such enlightened Christians will not be surprised by the timing of events. It seems to tell these "brethren" or "brothers" that they are wise and initiated into a deeper understanding than the rest of us. Paul and other writers of the gospels often go out of their way to make sure we pay attention with phrasing like that of Romans 11:25 "For I do not want you, brethren, to be uninformed of this mystery—so that you will not be wise."

Of course wise brothers already understood Christ's teachings on a deeper level because they had previously learned to read and understand similar astronomical messages written into the Old Testament, "The Book of the Dead," the "Pyramid Texts" and "Coffin Texts" from Egypt, India's "Rig Veda," and in classical Greek stories like "The Iliad" and "The Odyssey." As Plutarch said centuries before Christ: "the mystic symbols are well known to us who belong to the brotherhood."[3] The brotherhood understood the importance of astronomy. They understood why ancient cultures were obsessed with keeping track of the positions of various heavenly bodies.

The Bible tells us directly, very early on in Genesis 1:14, that "God said, 'Let there be lights in the expanse of the heavens to separate the day from the night, and let them be for signs and for seasons and for days and years.'" We are told, even commanded, to look at the lights in the sky and use them as signs for timing future events. Psalms 19:1-2 clarifies "The heavens are telling of the glory of God; And their expanse is declaring the work of His hands. Day to day pours forth speech, And night to night reveals knowledge." We are told that the heavens are God's speech to us, His message, and that through these heavenly bodies He "reveals knowledge." The Dead Sea Scrolls also contain astronomical texts about the "royal science" including a "horoscope written in code" and a "true predictor of destiny."[4]

Sir Issac Newton was one of the greatest astronomers who ever lived, so it is no surprise that he aimed to decipher the Bible's code and become one of the wise brothers who understood its hidden astronomical messages. Newton studied alchemy, sacred geometry, and records of Atlantis. He was influenced by the Rosicrucians and was probably one of the earliest members of the Masonic United Grand Lodge of England. John Maynard Keynes once said of Sir Issac Newton "He looked at the whole universe and all that is in it as a riddle, as a secret which could be read by applying pure thought to certain evidence, certain mystic clues which God had laid about the world to allow a sort of philosopher's treasure hunt to the esoteric brotherhood… He regarded the universe as a cryptogram set by the Almighty… By pure thought, by concentration of mind, the riddle, he believed, would be revealed to the initiate."[5]

Unfortunately we are not all initiated into a brotherhood that teaches us how to understand such things, and Newton never did come up with a specific date. But we are all expected to study the Bible and gain wisdom. If we don't, we will live in mental darkness and will not be ready for the end times. Revelations 3:3 tells us "*if* you do not wake up, I will come like a thief, and you will not know at what hour I will come." This implies that those awake will know the hour. We won't know the timing—*unless* we learn more and wake up.

God wants us to use our brainpower to analyze things and understand His ways. Proverbs 25:2 says "It is the glory of God to conceal a matter, But the glory of kings is to search out a matter." This flat out tells us that God enjoys hiding clues and watching us solve His riddles. John 5:20 tells us Jesus "has given us understanding." Newton was one of the most intellectually capable minds in recent centuries, a master of physics and astronomy, and he felt it was worth devoting many years of his time and effort to studying and understanding the Bible, especially if unraveling the timing of biblical prophecies. Newton's essay "Observations upon the Prophecies of Daniel, and the Apocalypse of St. John" was published after his death in 1727. He had never completely narrowed down his timing for the Second Coming or Judgment Day to his satisfaction, but the range of dates he focused on is in the 21st century.

The year 2060 is often cited since its 2003 discovery in Newton's final notes; but in other sections (amongst his 4,500 pages of comments and calculations on timing such prophecies) he gave ranges of dates that he felt limited the fulfillment of the end times and these ranges rule out 2060. In reality Newton was "constantly reappraising the date at which the Day of Judgment would come, seeing it as an event that was preordained but at the same time one whose date humans might deduce."[6] Ancient Jews must have agreed that this was possible (but undesirable) for they warned that "he who announces the Messianic time based on calculation forfeits his own share in the future."[7]

Long ago, the ancient priests seemed to have a better understanding of how God handles such things, but eventually the focus on this wisdom was lost. Jesus once said to other allegedly learned rabbis: "although you ought to be teachers in view of the time, you again need someone to teach you from the beginning the elementary things." (Hebrews 5:12, NWT) There is a forgotten category of secret knowledge—a certain astronomical context in which we are supposed to understand the timing of certain events.

Daniel 12:10 says "those who have insight will understand." But for many others "while seeing, they may see and not perceive, and while hearing, they may hear and not understand." (Mark 4:12) Jesus gives us many illustrations, metaphors, analogies, and parables. For those who have insight, and know what angle to interpret them from, the messages are clear. Most will not understand. A very small group of people have been told how to interpret these messages. In Matthew 13:11 Jesus tells his disciples "To you it has been granted to know the mysteries of the kingdom of heaven, but to them it has not been granted."

Consider the example of Noah. In his day it was the unrighteous who did not know when judgment was coming. Noah, who was righteous, was told exactly when the judgment was coming. We have been told that this is going to happen again. Matthew 24:37 tells us that "the coming of the Son of Man will be just like the days of Noah."

Another way of looking at this was explained by Jason Hommel (author of the web site at http://www.Bibleprophesy.org) in an email he sent out on 5/23/11: "We should never say, 'we will never know when the Lord will return', because not knowing is a punishment for not watching and a punishment for being an evil servant of the Lord." He pointed out Revelation 3:3 "If therefore thou shalt not watch, I will come on thee as a thief, and thou shalt not know what hour I will come upon thee." He noted Luke 12:39 "And this know, that if the goodman of the house had known what hour the thief would come, he would have watched, and not have suffered his house to be broken through." He also mentioned Matthew 24:48-50 "But if that evil servant shall say in his heart, My lord delayeth his coming; And shall begin to smite his fellowservants, and to eat and drink with the drunken; The lord of that servant shall come in a day when he looketh not for him, and in an hour that he is not aware of." Hommel concluded: "If not knowing the time of the Lord's return is a specific punishment that applies to those who "shall not watch", or the "evil servants", then it seems this punishment could not apply to God's good servants who are watching."

Of course before we can watch we have to know what we are watching for. We have to understand there is a layer of hidden astronomical messages woven into the Bible's central religious messages—and that we can use it to accurately date the timing of prophesized events. I am not trying to downplay the importance of the Bible's spiritual message. I would rather know I am saved than merely know when I will die. But the well-understood core teachings of Christianity have been handled in other books already. The limited scope of this book is to focus on future events and the astronomical approach for dating them.

Without initiation into the secret mysteries, I had to study for many years before making the necessary connections. Claiming that I have achieved insights which even great minds like Isaac Newton failed to grasp may seem outrageously bold, but I am not claiming to be his intellectual superior. I have astronomical software and the internet at my disposal; Newton did not. Even with such advantages I needed almost twenty years to piece things together. This book is my attempt to bring you up to speed in a single day.

To reach that goal, the fruits of many years of research—a massive amount of evidence and analysis have been organized under one title. My friend Andrew, the first person to read my rough copy, used the phrase "information overload" to describe one section. But he agreed that it would be wrong to deny readers any of the accumulated evidence. You deserve the chance to assess this information. Much of it simply wasn't readily accessible to everyone. Some of it has been purposefully hidden from the general population. Follow along and I will guide you through Bible prophecy, Mayan culture, world mythology, and many other topics that should reveal what lies in store for us in the near future. Some of the information may be familiar already, especially if you have read the Bible. My role is to guide your perspective as you read it again, for as Hebrews 2:1 hinted, "We must pay much closer attention to what we have heard." After you have paid attention to the facts from a new perspective, you should understand why I conclude that Judgment Day is December 28, 2019.

It feels ironic that only after discovering a veiled astronomical method of dating events did I realize that there are references right out in the open that Bible scholars can use to reach the years 2012 and 2019. In later chapters we will unlock the hidden messages and show that the wedding ceremony in the sky verifies the more open interpretation and adds more detail. But even without reading between the lines and unveiling mysteries once reserved for the initiated, we can look at the history of the Jewish people and show that various prophecies occurred as written, at times that would have been predictable.

In Chapter One we look first at historical events which have already occurred. This first chapter should prove that Bible prophecy has been valid up through the twentieth century; that it led us to 1967 and is currently pointing to 2012 and 2019. The next four chapters give a clear background on the Maya, world mythology, geology, and astrophysics and how they also point to events in the Bible that will happen very soon. By Chapter Six we can use the information from these other related topics to come back to the Bible and reevaluate it from a more enlightened perspective.

(Endnotes)

[1] I first saw the word "astrotheological" used by S, Acharya. *Suns of God: Krishna, Buddha and Christ Unveiled*. Kempton, IL: Adventures Unlimited Press, 2004, p. 11

[2] Flurry, Gerald. *Ezekiel: The End-Time Prophet*. Edmund, OK: Philadelphia Church of God, 2002 p. 52

[3] Hall, Manly P. *Freemasonry of the Ancient Egyptians*. Los Angeles, CA: Philosophical Research Society, 1937, p. 48

[4] S, Acharya. *Suns of God: Krishna, Buddha and Christ Unveiled*. Kempton, IL: Adventures Unlimited Press, 2004, p. 518

[5] Keynes, J. M. "Newton the Man" in *Newton Tercentenary Celebrations*. London: The Royal Society, 1947, p. 29

[6] White, Michael. *Isaac Newton: The Last Sorcerer*. Cambridge, MA: Da Capo Press, 1999, p. 158

[7] Singer, Isidore. (Editor) *A Descriptive Record of the History, Religion, Literature, and Customs of the Jewish People from the Earliest Times to the Present Day, Volume 5*. New York: Funk and Wagnalls, 1906, p. 211

CHAPTER ONE
SUCCESSFUL BIBLE PROPHECIES
THAT LEAD US TO MODERN TIMES

There are many successful Bible prophecies detailing events which have already come to pass. The three covered in this chapter lead us to important events in 1948, 1967, and 2012. They establish that we should take Bible prophecy seriously and that 2012 is an important date for end times events in the Bible, not just regarding the Mayan calendar.

The Servitude of the Nation:

In Jeremiah 25:11, the prophet told us that the Jewish people's rebellion against God's wishes would cost them a severe punishment. "This whole land will be a desolation and a horror, and these nations will serve the king of Babylon seventy years." The Jews would spend seventy years in captivity in Babylon.

At the time this captivity began, the region had been chaotic for many years as various empires fought for domination. An alliance of Medes and Babylonians defeated the Assyrians at Nineveh in 612 B.C. The Egyptians sent armies to assist the Assyrians and help defend them against Babylon, but Assyria was soon crushed anyway. Egyptian forces then rushed into what is now Israel and Syria in an attempt to take over the western parts of the Assyrian empire before Babylon consolidated all of it. The Jewish kings generally allied with their more culturally similar brethren in Egypt every time the Egyptians were strong enough to advance, but the Babylonians repeatedly defeated the Egyptians, and did so decisively in the battle of Carchemish in 604 B.C. The Jews were punished every time they rebelled against Babylon and were recaptured. The Babylonians took Jerusalem, and exiled thousands of prisoners back to Babylon, six separate times from 606 to 584 B.C.

The seventy years of punishment began with the first batch of prisoners taken to Babylon in 606 B.C. Daniel and Ezekiel were the most prominent Jewish prophets during what is known as the Babylonian Captivity, but it was about 150 years earlier that the prophet Isaiah told us how the captivity would end.

Isaiah 44:26-45:1 tells us of Jerusalem:

"'She shall be inhabited!' And of the cities of Judah, 'They shall be built.' And I will raise up her ruins again…. 'It is I who says of Cyrus, 'He is My shepherd! And he will perform all My desire.' And he declares of Jerusalem, 'She will be built,' And of the temple, 'Your foundation will be laid.' Thus says the LORD to Cyrus His anointed." In 537 B.C., after seventy years in captivity, the Persian King Cyrus conquered Babylon and freed the Jews to return to their homeland and rebuild the Temple in Jerusalem. Readers may notice only 69 years from 606 to 537 B.C. but the ancient Middle East used a 360-day per year calendar for many things and the Jews were no exception. When Bible prophecies mention "years" they mean "years" of 360 days. Seventy of these shorter "prophetic years" or "biblical years" had passed, despite the passage of a mere 69 solar years of 365.242 days orbiting our sun.

But the servitude did not end in 537 B.C. Shortly after being freed to return to Jerusalem, the prophet Ezekiel warned the Jewish people that because Israel still did not repent and obey God, there would be greater punishment. He wrote in Ezekiel 4:4-6 "lie down on your left side and lay the iniquity of the house of Israel on it; you shall bear their iniquity for the number of days that you lie on it. For

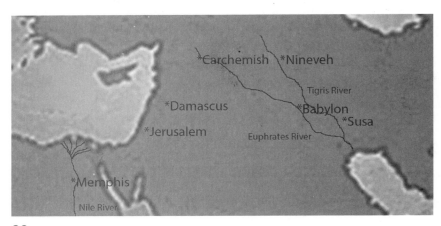

I have assigned you a number of days corresponding to the years of their iniquity, three hundred and ninety days; thus you shall bear the iniquity of the house of Israel. When you have completed these, you shall lie down a second time, but on your right side and bear the iniquity of the house of Judah; I have assigned it to you for forty days, a day for each year."

According to these words, Israel would not be free until after 430 years of God's punishment known as the "Servitude of the Nation." Seventy years of atonement had already been suffered in Babylon, so 360 years remained. As the Jews who returned to Israel in 537 B.C. refused to repent of their sins, Israel remained under the rule of foreigners from Persia, Greece, Egypt, Syria, and Rome. 360 more "years" brought them to the year 182 B.C. but Israel never became free and independent. What happened?

Perhaps the answer is in Leviticus 26:27-28: "Yet if in spite of this you do not obey Me, but act with hostility against Me, then I will act with wrathful hostility against you, and I, even I, will punish you seven times for your sins." Atonement which could have ended in 360 years was multiplied still further—seven-fold—to 2,520 years. Starting in 537 B.C. and adding 2520 prophetic years of 360 days, the allotted time equals 907,200 days. This brings us to 1948 when the modern nation of Israel was born.

This alone is rather amazing, and lends further credence to using a 360 day biblical prophetic year over the solar year when a Bible prophet specifically gives a time frame in years. But looking for even greater accuracy, deducting 907,200 days from modern Israel's birth on May 14, 1948 (The fifth day of the month Iyyar of the year 5708 in the Hebrew calendar) brings us back to the fifteenth day of the month of Av in the year 3224. This is less than a week after the anniversary of the destruction of the Temple.

Jews celebrated a holiday known as Tisha B'Av (the 9th of Av) and started a long fast in memory of the destruction of the Temple. It is possible that Cyrus' government officials noticed this fasting, ascertained the reason for it, and suggested that Cyrus declare a rebuilding of Jerusalem and its Temple. Cyrus may also have been quite pleased to learn of the Jewish prophecy that a king named Cyrus would free them from captivity after 70 years. He was apparently quite happy to oblige and fulfill his role as God's anointed one. If the process of his decision-making took six days from the start of the fasting, then the imperial decree to rebuild was exactly 907,200 days before the modern state of Israel was officially created in 1948, when rule by foreigners—the Servitude of the Nation—was finally over.

Desolation of the Holy Place & foreign rule for 2300 evenings and mornings:

Daniel gave us two completely different ways to reach the year 1967 from different events. In Daniel 8:13-14 he wrote: "'How long will the vision about the regular sacrifice apply, while the transgression causes horror, so as to allow both the holy place and the host to be trampled?' He said to me, 'For 2,300 evenings and mornings; then the holy place will be properly restored.' 'How long will the vision be of the constant [feature] and of the transgression causing desolation, to make both [the] holy place and [the] army things to trample on?' So he said unto me: 'Until two thousand three hundred evenings [and] mornings; and [the] holy place will certainly be brought into its right condition."

We may understand this better if we backtrack slightly to Daniel 8:3-14. Daniel gives us a fantastic description of the coming of Alexander the Great:

"A ram which had two horns was standing in front of the canal. Now the two horns were long, but one was longer than the other, with the longer one coming up last. (The ram symbolizes the Persian Empire, which early on was a union of Medes and Persians, until the Medes were absorbed into the Persian Empire.) I saw the ram butting westward, northward, and southward, and no other beasts could stand before him nor was there anyone to rescue from his power, but he did as he pleased and magnified himself.

While I was observing, behold, a male goat was coming from the west over the surface of the whole earth (The goats coming from the west represent the Greeks) without touching the ground; and the goat had a conspicuous horn between his eyes. (Alexander) He

Statue of Alexander the Great in Alexandria, Egypt

came up to the ram that had the two horns, which I had seen standing in front of the canal, and rushed at him in his mighty wrath. I saw him come beside the ram, and he was enraged at him; and he struck the ram and shattered his two horns, and the ram had no strength to withstand him. So he hurled him to the ground and trampled on him, and there was none to rescue the ram from his power. (Alexander completely destroyed the Persian Empire.) Then the male goat magnified himself exceedingly. But as soon as he was mighty, the large horn was broken; (Alexander died at age 33 just after conquering all the way to India) and in its place there came up four conspicuous horns toward the four winds of heaven. (Four of his top generals divided his empire amongst themselves.)

Out of one of them came forth a rather small horn…. and it removed the regular sacrifice from Him, and the place of His sanctuary was thrown down. And on account of transgression the host will be given over to the horn along with the regular sacrifice; and it will fling truth to the ground and perform its will and prosper. Then I heard a holy one speaking, and another holy one said to that particular one who was speaking, "How long will the vision about the regular sacrifice apply, while the transgression causes horror, so as to allow both the holy place and the host to be trampled?" He said to me, "For 2,300 evenings and mornings; then the holy place will be properly restored."

The passages above seem to describe Alexander the Great very well. But some people would suggest that even if we interpret the 2300 evenings and mornings of Daniel 8:14 as 2300 years of gentile (non-Jewish) rule over Jerusalem, we have no reason to automatically start with the beginning of Greek rule. There were foreign forces occupying the land from Egypt, Assyria, Babylon, Persia, Greece, Rome, Byzantium, Arabia, Turkey, and Great Britain over the course of Jewish history. There were even brief moments of Jewish independence. But since Daniel had just described Greek civilization's victory over the Persians right before mentioning the 2300 evenings and mornings, Daniel probably did intend us to start with Greek rule of the Holy Land. Luke 21:24 clarifies that this long period of foreign rule over Jerusalem by non-Jews was definitely well under way in Jesus' day: "Jerusalem will be trampled under foot by the Gentiles until the times of the Gentiles are fulfilled." Just when is this appointed time fulfilled?

A blog with Christian perspectives on the Old Testament and current events written by Dr. Claude Mariottini sheds additional light on this prophecy. He had been sent an anonymous manuscript with a title beginning "Daniel Unsealed" and was reviewing that unknown author's thoughts. (This manuscript is probably the same one now self-published with a longer title under the name Dan Bruce.) Dr. Mariottini wrote that the unknown author felt the 2300 evenings and mornings should be viewed not as days but as Passover holidays, which are described with evening and morning rituals in Exodus 12: 6-10. In all probability the evenings and mornings are properly interpreted to mean Passovers, and Jerusalem is certainly the holy place, its right condition being unity under Jewish rule, especially Jewish rule over the Temple Mount.

The easiest thing for us to do, with the wonderful aid of hindsight, is to start with the Israeli takeover of Jerusalem in June of 1967, and look back 2300 years for any historical event in which the city's Jews yielded control to a foreign power. It is well documented that shortly after the Battle of Issus in November 333 B.C. Jerusalem welcomed Alexander the Great and his armies into the city.

The Roman historian Flavius Josephus wrote that the Temple's high priest, Jaddua, had a dream telling him to greet Alexander in front of the Temple. When they met, Alexander showed the priest great reverence, and his officers asked him why, as a conquering king, he showed such respect to Jaddua. Alexander allegedly said: "I did not adore him, but that God who hath honoured him with his high priesthood; for I saw this very person in a dream, in this very habit…. having seen no other in that habit, and now seeing this person in it, and remembering that vision, and the exhortation which I had in my dream, I believe that I bring this army under the divine conduct, and shall therewith conquer Darius, and destroy the power of the Persians, and that all things will succeed according to what is in my own mind."[1]

Jaddua took Alexander into the Temple and showed him prophecies which seemed to foretell his arrival: "And when the book of Daniel was shewed him, wherein Daniel declared that one of the Greeks should destroy the empire of the Persians, he supposed that himself was the person intended; and as he was then glad….offered sacrifice to God, according to the high priest's direction."[2]

In Jerusalem there is a 1/50th scale model reconstruction of the Second (Herod's) Temple.

This event fits very nicely, 2300 years before the reunification of Jerusalem. But was this clear enough to be understood before 1967, without the benefit of hindsight? Yes it was. Two centuries ago, Adam Clarke spent forty years writing an extensive commentary on the Bible. He specifically mentions the prophecies in Daniel and wrote: "Unto two thousand and three hundred days— Though literally it be two thousand three hundred evenings and mornings. Yet I think the prophetic day should be understood here, as in other parts of this prophet, and must signify so many years. If we date these years from the vision of the he-goat, (Alexander's invading Asia,) this was A.M. 3670, B.C. 334; and two thousand three hundred years from that time will reach to A.D. 1966, or one hundred and forty-one years from the present A.D. 1825."[3]

Clarke may not have been clear on the timing of Alexander's entry into Jerusalem, as he dated from the Battle of Granicus in 334 B.C., instead of the later and more decisive Battle of Issus. He still managed to predict the future reestablishment of Jewish control of Jerusalem within one year of the event in 1967, over 140 years prior to it actually happening, based on Daniel's prophecy.

Readers may notice that in an earlier example of Bible prophecy regarding the Servitude of the Nation, 2,520 years passing required biblical years of 360 days to "make things fit" the interpretation to reach 1948, whereas the 2,300 years before 1967 have to be literal solar years of 365.242 days. Some would undoubtedly say "you can't have it both ways" and that when the Bible says "years" it must be one way or the other. But Daniel did NOT write of years, he wrote of 2300 evenings and mornings, and he probably used that odd phrase just to make sure we would interpret it as Passovers, which occur not every 360 days, but once every 365.242 day solar year.

Some skeptics have another bigger problem with accepting the timing of events in the book of Daniel—they don't believe Daniel existed at all. They feel that his alleged prophecies of Alexander the Great defeating the Persians, of the breakup of Alexander's empire—and of other prophecies we haven't even discussed, like the pillaging of the Temple by the Seleucid King Antiochus—were far too accurate to be legitimate visions. One popular theory is that someone living during the time of Antiochus made up the prophecies and falsely attributed them to Daniel, who they say never existed in the sixth century B.C. But there are many flaws with this idea.

In 1 Maccabees 2:60 (Catholic Bibles like the DRA include Maccabees and other books Protestant Bibles consider non-canonical so this is not in the NASB, NIV, or KJB) Daniel is listed as one of the Jewish people's great ancestors—and they would not have included him with Abraham and Joseph and David if his persona was recently fabricated. Ezekiel 28:3 describes the prince of Tyre, stating: "You are wiser than Daniel; There is no secret that is a match for you!" As Daniel had been known as the wisest of the wise men of Babylon, and able to interpret the hidden and secret meanings of dreams, this is obviously a comparison to the Daniel some argue did not exist until long after Ezekiel. Jesus also refers to Daniel in Matthew 24:15, and tells readers to consider Daniel's description of an abomination regarding the future. Some would argue that the description of events applies to the destruction of the Temple in 70 A.D. and not the times of the end... But we must also consider that in addition to Daniel's descriptions of events in the 6th, 4th, and 2nd centuries B.C. being "too good to believe," his prophetic accuracy seems to be on target for 1967 as well. Jesus did not view Daniel as a fictitious character describing events after the fact—and no one will claim that the Book of Daniel didn't exist until after the events of 1967.

With the two prophecies already covered we have come to 1948 and 1967, the most important dates in Israel's modern history and the most important dates for biblical prophecies which have already occurred in modern times. Obviously the world did not end in 1967, but there are other prophecies with shorter timelines to add onto this pivotal date of 1967, and they will bring us to 2012 and 2019. Before proceeding on to them, we can verify the crucially important 1967 date as a starting point for the shorter time frames. The prophet Daniel gave us a second method of reaching 1967, but this time frame must start with the Babylonian destruction of the Temple happening in 584 B.C.—and the proof that 584 B.C. is the correct year will require some effort.

The Babylonian conquest of Jerusalem and destruction of the Jewish Temple:

Jeremiah 52:4-5 tells us the Babylonians laid siege to Jerusalem in the ninth year of Judah's King Zedekiah's reign, with the siege lasting two years until Zedekiah's eleventh year. Jeremiah 52:12-16 tells us that it was in the nineteenth year of Babylon's king Nebuchadnezzar's reign that destruction befell Jerusalem. We also know that Jews commemorated this event with a day of mourning on Tisha B'Av—the ninth day of the fifth month. This seems very precise, and one would think there must be a clear correlation to a certain day for this event in our Gregorian calendar. But there are many complicating factors, and neither the day nor the year are entirely agreed upon.

There is a little confusion about the day in question. Tisha B'Av means the ninth day of the month of Av. Jeremiah 52:12 clearly tells us that Babylonian forces entered Jerusalem on the tenth day of the fifth month. We must remember that unlike the modern reckoning of days beginning at midnight, the Jews began a new day at

Jews worship at the only remaining part of the last (Herod's) Temple, the Wailing Wall or Western Wall in Jerusalem, as seen on the Sabbath at night.

sunset. It is also relevant that the destruction of the second Temple by the Romans in the year 70 A.D. occurred late on the ninth of Av—which is why this day of mourning the Temple's destruction(s) covers what we might consider two days, the ninth and the tenth.

Worse still, in 2 Kings 25:8 we are clearly told these events occurred on the seventh day of the fifth month. Do we assume Babylonian forces entered the city on the seventh and burned the Temple on the tenth, without any clarification that there was a delay of three days between events? Do we assume one of these Bible passages must be wrong, as they describe the same events with the same words—on different days?

There is even less agreement on the year this event occurred. Unfortunately there exist huge gaps in archeological evidence in the sixth century B.C. that make accurate dating of earlier events very difficult. Most writers put the Babylonian destruction of the Jewish Temple anywhere from 587 to 582 B.C., with the majority selecting 586 B.C. For our purposes, Bible prophecy "works out right" if the destruction of Jerusalem occurred in the summer of 584 B.C. Daniel 12:4-11 tells us that "From the time that the regular sacrifice is abolished and the abomination of desolation is set up" there will be "a time, times, and half a time" followed by another period when "there will be 1,290 days." The regular sacrifice Daniel mentions is worship at the Temple, and the times are years of 360 days, making the first time frame 1260 days, each day of which should be viewed as a year. The 1290 days should be understood as 1290 years. 584 B.C. plus 1260 plus 1290 gets us (with no year zero) to the year 1967, when Israel recaptured the Temple Mount in East Jerusalem, restoring the holy site to right conditions—under Jewish rule.

But this timing requires starting in 584 B.C., while many historians believe the correct year for the destruction of the Temple is two years earlier. It will take a few pages to prove that 584 B.C. is the correct year.

As is so often the case, the best and most accurate methods of keeping time are astronomical. Fortunately the Babylonians (and a great many other ancient peoples) were obsessed with keeping track of various heavenly bodies. We have detailed records of eclipses and other events, and we know when they occurred in relation to the reigns of kings and other events. Because astronomical motions are so consistent and uniform, modern computer programs devoted to tracking these heavenly bodies can calculate ancient astronomical positions to the minute. We can use this information to help verify when the nineteenth year of Nebuchadnezzar's reign took place.

One of the most useful books on this topic is "Historical Eclipses and the Earth's Rotation" by F. Richard Stephenson. He identifies approximately 420 ancient eclipses recorded by the Babylonians, Chinese, Arabs, and Europeans, and he specifies that there are tablets in the British Museum showing eclipse records for almost every year of Nebuchadrezzar II's reign, which he definitively states began in the spring of the year we consider 604 B.C.

This being his first year, his nineteenth year would begin eighteen years later in 586 B.C. If the Temple in Jerusalem fell in the summer of what we would call 586 B.C., adding 1260 and 1290 years do not quite get us to 1967—only to 1965. Knowing that 1967 is the most important date in Jerusalem's history since the Romans destroyed the Second Temple in the year 70, it is hard to accept that Bible prophecy would get us so close (1965) without a direct hit (1967.) It would seem more likely that there may be a reason to question the 586 B.C. dating of events. Perhaps we should use modern computer programs to date the astronomical data ourselves.

The following are some of the most relevant observations from the British Museum piece known as VT 4956:

"Year 37 of Nebukadnezar, king of Babylon. Month I, (the first of which was identical with) the 30th (of the preceding month), the moon became visible behind the Bull of Heaven;…Saturn was in front of the Swallow…[The 11th] or 12th, Jupiter's acronychal rising…Month II…Saturn was in front of the Swallow; Mercury, which had set, was not yet visible…The 3rd, Mars entered Praesepe. The 5th, it went out (of it)…The 18th, Venus was balanced 1 cubit four fingers above α Leonis…Month III… the moon became visible behind Cancer… Mercury passed below Mars to the East; Jupiter was above α Scorpii."[4]

Using astronomical software like Stellarium we can determine dates for events in these extremely accurate records. The single most accurate detail of Mars crossing in front of Praesepe— the Beehive cluster of stars in the constellation Cancer—happens twice in the years in question, on May 6, 566 B.C. and on May 26, 568 B.C. But the most useful and unique facts describe Jupiter, which does not appear to move anywhere near as fast as Mars. "Jupiter's acronychal rising" means Jupiter rose just after sunset, which occurred around May 5, 568 B.C. Jupiter was above alpha Scorpii—the star Antares—for a time around June 30, 568 B.C. Jupiter is nowhere near Scorpio in 566 B.C. As further backup for establishing 568 B.C. as the year being detailed by these events in the sky, (and hence establishing it as Nebuchadnezzar's 37th year) the moon first becomes visible behind Cancer around June 20, 568 B.C.

Unfortunately for any author hoping to date the destruction of the Temple in Jerusalem to 584 B.C., these Babylonian records establish Nebuchadnezzar's nineteenth year as king was in 586 B.C. For any student of prophecy hoping to be able to add 1260 and 1290 and reach the year 1967—these astronomical records do not help that chronology. If Babylonian records of Nebuchadnezzar's 37th year begin at the Spring Equinox of 568 B.C., then the Babylonian reckoning of his first year as king started 36 years earlier in early 604 B.C., just as Stephenson said. The Babylonians would say his 19th year began in the spring of 586 B.C. on the first day of the first month of Nisan. If a Babylonian told us the Jewish Temple was destroyed in the summer of Nebuchadnezzar's 19th year, they meant 586 B.C. If this were the case, we could kiss a grand goodbye to the idea of reaching 1967 from these prophecies.

But 586 B.C. is *not* the year the Temple was burned, for it was not a Babylonian who told us this happened in Nebuchadnezzar's 19th year, it was a Jew. Any historian who simply took the year of reign from the Bible and applied it to Babylonian information would understandably, *but mistakenly*, arrive at the year 586 B.C. But Jews had a different reckoning of dating kingship, with two crucially different considerations.

Jews had a civil new year that began in the fall, so Jews dated kingship beginning on the first of Tishri, not in the spring on the first of Nisan. Eventually it became common for Jews to use the Babylonian system of dating events, but not until long after they had been taken to Babylon and re-educated in new customs. Only "with the acceptance of the Babylonian calendar the regnal year would begin in the spring."[5] This can still be "controversial—the month of the Judean regnal new year. Our reckoning is based on an autumnal calendar beginning on 1 Tishri, and not on the spring calendar adopted by many scholars and which was in general use in Babylonia."[6]

The best circumstantial evidence for Jeremiah using the old Jewish autumn reckoning is found in the book of Nehemiah. In Nehemiah 1:1 he mentions the month of Kislev (November/December) in the twentieth year of the reign of the Persian king Artaxerxes. He proceeds with a chain of events and by Nehemiah 2:1 he says "And it came about in the month Nisan, in the twentieth year of King Artaxerxes…" Nisan corresponds to March and April, so if it were still the twentieth year of reign, Nehemiah obviously did not start counting the 21st year on the first of Nisan as Babylonians would. If Jews like Nehemiah—who was born and raised in Babylon generations after Jeremiah— were still using the old Jewish autumn reckoning at least seventy years after the Babylonians destroyed the Temple, then Jeremiah, who was born and raised in Israel before the Babylonians came—would not have adopted the Babylonian method so early. He would definitely have counted a king's reign from the first of Tishri, around the end of September.

A second difference in comparison to the Babylonian perspective regards which year to start with: the one the coronation takes place in, or the next year, starting new year's day? Babylonians backdated reigns to the previous new year's day, but Jews postdated reigns up to the next new year's day. Jews would say that any year beginning with one king at the start of the new year is one of his years. They would say that the year beginning in our 604 B.C. began with Nebuchadnezzar's father Nabopolassar as king, and was one of his years. They would not count the first year of Nebuchadnezzar's reign until the next new year began with him as king. If the coronation happened shortly after the Jewish new year began on Tishri 1—with a coronation in October of 604 B.C.—then by Jewish reckoning—Jeremiah would have dated the start of the reign forward to the next new year (in September 603 B.C.) starting near the fall equinox on Tishri 1. Babylonians would have backdated to the prior Babylonian new year (in March 604 B.C.) near the spring equinox on Nisan 1. These different methods yield dates 18 months apart.

Let's consider some modern analogies that may make this easier to understand. Lyndon Baynes Johnson became president on November 23, 1963. While we would not say that 1963 was "Johnson's year" as president, (as John F. Kennedy was president until November) we would say 1963 was the first year of Johnson's presidency, even though the year began January 1 and he was not president at that time. Gerald Ford became President on August 9, 1974. While we would not say that 1974 was "Ford's year" as president, (as Richard Nixon's presidency dominated the news even beyond August) we would say 1974 was the first year of Ford's presidency—even though the year began January 1 and he was not president at that time. The exact wording matters a lot, and similar minor differences in perspective make a huge difference between Babylonian and Jewish reckonings.

Jeremiah would go from inauguration day to the following New Year's Day on the first of Tishri (around late September) and count the presidency from there. It wouldn't make too much difference in Gerald Ford's case; he would lose less than two months before Jeremiah would count him as king, moving forward a little from August 9. The Vietnam War ended April 30, 1975 with the Fall of Saigon, and Jeremiah would say this occurred in the first year of Ford's reign. In November 1975 Morocco took over the Western Sahara, the Spanish empire's last colony. Jeremiah would say this occurred in Ford's second year.

On December 10, 1964, Dr. Martin Luther King received the Nobel Peace Prize. Despite the fact that this occurred more than one year after President Johnson took office in our calendar, Jeremiah would have said this occurred just three months into Johnson's reign, because Jeremiah would not have counted late 1963, or most of 1964, up until the first of Tishri. In July 1965, the first American plane was shot down by anti-aircraft missles in Vietnam, and Johnson doubled the number of men drafted into the military every month. Despite being president for 20 months at this point, Jeremiah would have said these events occurred in Johnson's first year, because they were less than twelve months after the first Tishri 1 of Johnson's presidency. Few people on Earth in 1965 would have said it was Johnson's first year. No American would have called it Johnson's first year. But Jeremiah would have.

Understanding Jeremiah's method of counting years of kingship is crucially important in our appreciation of Daniel's prophecies. For just as no American would consider events in July 1965 to have taken place in Johnson's first year, no Babylonian would consider events in July 584 B.C. to have taken place in Nebuchadnezzar's 19th year. Babylonians would consider July 584 B.C. as his 21st year. This is why many historians think the Jewish Temple was destroyed in July 586 B.C., which Babylonians considered his 19th year. Jeremiah 52:12-16 tells us the Temple was destroyed in Nebuchadnezzar's 19th year. But Babylonians did not write the book of Jeremiah, and this is especially important to our prophetic interpretations if Nebuchadnezzar was made king after the first of Tishri.

Nebuchadnezzar's father Nabopolassar is well documented to have died on the eighth day of the month of Av—August 4, 604 B.C. It took time for word to get from Babylon to the front lines in what is now Syria and Israel, where Nebuchadnezzar was leading the Babylonian army against the Egyptians. The battle of Carchemish took place on what is now the Turkish/Syrian border just a few months earlier, and Nebuchadnezzar was consolidating former Assyrian lands some distance southwest of that when he would have heard of his father's death. In all probability he was near Jerusalem, which is about 520 miles from Babylon "as the crow flies" and almost double that by the meandering route that would be taken on foot. Let's give Nebuchadnezzar the benefit of the doubt and assume he knew a short route with few obstacles and only had to travel 800 miles to Babylon. It is known that Nebuchadnezzar interrupted this military campaign in the month of Elul (late August/ early September) to head back to Babylon to claim the throne.

How fast have similar journeys been? Before modern transportation, "armies covered an average of 16 km (9.9 miles) per day."[7] With new and innovative methods of eliminating anything that would unnecessarily slow them down, "Alexander's army could routinely move at 13 miles a day."[8] Horses could go faster, but only in areas with plenty of water to drink and food to graze on, and even then only for a few days. "Under very favorable (and very rare) circumstances Alexander did manage for a brief period to cover an average of 30 km (18.6 miles) per day... Alexander also rested his army one day out of seven when on the march."[9] Edward Luttwak tells us that Roman troops could march about fifteen miles per day over long distances.[10] Colin Adams tells us that without an army slowing them down, travelers carrying minimal provisions through the desert of ancient Egypt could average 30 kilometers a day.[11]

Let us make some reasonable guesses. If Nebuchadnezzar started his journey after interrupting campaigns in the middle of Elul, (around September 10) and then averaged a relatively fast eighteen miles a day for six days every week, resting every seventh day, he would travel across 800 miles of desert in 51 days (45 days of traveling and just six days of rest) and he would have reached Babylon around October 31. This would be the 7th day of the

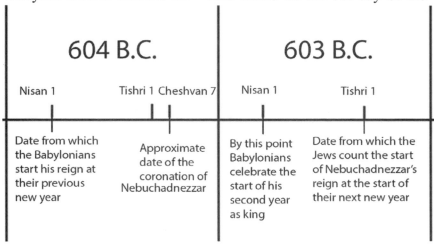

604 B.C.			603 B.C.	
Nisan 1	Tishri 1	Cheshvan 7	Nisan 1	Tishri 1
Date from which the Babylonians start his reign at their previous new year		Approximate date of the coronation of Nebuchadnezzar	By this point Babylonians celebrate the start of his second year as king	Date from which the Jews count the start of Nebuchadnezzar's reign at the start of their next new year

month of Cheshvan. This would be over five weeks after the first of Tishri, and would lead Jews to say his reign began the following first of Tishri in 603 B.C. Then our prophetic interpretation would arrive at 1967.

There is some evidence in favor of this timing. The earliest document of any kind referring to Nebuchadnezzar as king is the tablet of Egibi the "banker," and is dated to the 7th day of Samna, the eighth month. In Hebrew this month is Cheshvan, so this tablet is dated to the exact date we estimate he would have arrived, which in our calendar is October 31, 604 B.C. But that same clay tablet does not clarify that this was the king's day of coronation. Was this mentioned on a missing part of the tablet, or by the absence of such details should we infer that he may have been crowned earlier? Could it have been over five weeks earlier—enough to occur before the first of Tishri and discredit our timetable?

Could the military campaigns interrupted in the month of Elul have allowed him to leave on the first day of the month instead of the fifteenth day? Could he have averaged 24 miles per day through the desert instead of 18 miles? Could he have skipped the days of rest and travelled every day? Could his return route to Babylon have been a mere 700 miles instead of 800 miles? Realistically, the answers to these questions are all "no," but even if they were all correct assumptions, he would still arrive in Babylon after Tishri 1. But it would be more reasonable to assume the trip took even longer, for when Ezra made the reverse trip it took four months: "On the first of the first month he began to go up from Babylon; and on the first of the fifth month he came to Jerusalem, because the good hand of his God was upon him." (Ezra 7:9)

Strangely, many historians say Nebuchadnezzar was coronated on Elul 1—a month before Tishri. They base this on Josephus' account, but that history makes little sense. Josephus wrote that: "his father Nabopollassar fell ill, and ended his life in the city Babylon, when he had reigned twenty-one years; and when he [Nebuchadnezzar] was made aware, as he was in a little time, that his father Nabopollassar was dead, and having settled the affairs of Egypt, and the other countries, as also those that concerned the captive Jews, and Phoenicians, and Syrians, and those of the Egyptian nations; and having committed the conveyance of them to Babylon to certain of his friends, together with the gross of his army, and the rest of their ammunition and provisions, he went himself hastily, accompanied with a few others, over the desert, and came to Babylon... and he received the entire dominions of his father."[12]

It sounds plausible so far; messengers came and made Nebuchadnezzar aware that his father had died, after which he had to settle various affairs regarding the recently subdued Egyptians, Jews, Phoenicians, and Syrians. He had to arrange for captives (like Daniel) to be taken back, and for most of the army to head back. Then he made haste across the desert. But Josephus also wrote that: "For 21 years Nabopolassar had ruled Babylonia. On the eighth of Ab he died; in the month of Elul Nebuchadnezzar returned to Babylon and on the first day of Elul he sat on the royal throne in Babylon."[13]

As we know military campaigns were interrupted in Elul when he heard of his father's death, and we know he started his trip back to Babylon in Elul, Josephus' second mention of Elul makes no sense. How does one return to Babylon in the month of Elul and arrive on the first day of the month in which the trip began? It would make a lot more sense if that second mention of Elul is an ancient "typo" and Josephus put in the wrong month's name. The first of Cheshvan, two months later, would make more sense. For Josephus' "first day of Elul" to be accurate, word of Nabopollassar's death had to come some 800 miles to Nebuchadnezzar, and he had to wrap up his affairs and travel the same distance back to Babylon, where they would make preparations for the ceremonies, then coronate him, all in just 22 days since his father's death on the eighth of Ab. With no time to rest or make preparations, 1600 miles of travel in 22 days means an average rate of just under 73 miles per day, on foot, through the desert, in the August heat. Even half that speed is impossible.

It seems that Josephus made an error which many historians have repeated, but that in reality, Nebuchadnezzar was crowned the first week of Cheshvan, five weeks after the first of Tishri. Babylonians would backdate about seven months from Nebuchadnezzar's actual coronation date, and Jews would post-date about eleven months. This makes for a crucial 18-month difference. More importantly to us, an event in July of 586 B.C. would have been described by a Babylonian as occurring in the 19th year of his reign, but a Jew would have called it the 17th year. For a Jew like Jeremiah to describe an event in July as occurring in the 19th year of his reign, it must have occurred in 584 B.C.

Assuming we have finally determined that the Temple really fell in July of 584 B.C., we have two very interesting outcomes based on Daniel 12:4-13. As with many Bible prophecies, there are two distinct fulfillments. Perhaps the most famous is the arrival of the messiah, and later a second coming. Numbers 24:17 tells us "A star shall come forth from Jacob, A scepter shall rise from Israel." This describes a Messiah that comes twice; once as a star, a source of light and inspiration, then later as a powerful king. Once as a sacrificial lamb, and later as the Lion of Judah. Regarding Daniel's prophecies of 1260 and 1290 days, they have two valid fulfillments: once in days for events at the time of King Antiochus IV and again in years for events ending in 1967. In this case we may be more concerned with the second fulfillment, in which the days are understood as years—but there was an earlier fulfillment with 1260 days and 1290 days:

One of Alexander's four generals started the Seleucid dynasty in Syria, and his descendant King Antiochus IV persecuted the Jews terribly from 171 to 165 B.C. After 1260 days of persecution, in the middle of this week of seven years "he outlawed Judaism and…. Swine were deliberately sacrificed on the altar in order to subject it to the most vile desecration possible."[14] When the Temple was desecrated, Antiochus rededicated it to the Greek god Zeus, "supplying it, very likely, with his own royal face. To the orthodox Jews this was the greatest imaginable blasphemy."[15] 1 Maccabees 1:57 says that in what is 168 B.C. to us "king Antiochus set up the abominable idol of desolation upon the altar of God." (DRA) 2 Maccabees 6:1-5 tells us Antiochus made laws "to force the Jews to abandon the customs of their ancestors and live no longer by the laws of God; also to profane the temple in Jerusalem and dedicate it to Olympian Zeus…. The Gentiles filled the temple with debauchery and revelry; they amused themselves with prostitutes ... even in the sacred court. They also brought into the temple things that were forbidden, so that the altar was covered with abominable offerings prohibited by the laws."

Judas Maccabeus led a revolt and restored Jewish independence, and cleaned and rededicated the Temple 1290 days later, in 165 B.C. This is a prominent event in Jewish history. It is the foundation of the Festival of Lights, the holiday of Hanukkah. And we should not ignore these events. Many people would argue that the events around 168 B.C. were such a clear fulfillment of Daniel's prophecy of the 1260 days and the 1290 days and that we need not look to the future at all for a second fulfillment reckoning these periods with years.

But this would ignore passages like Matthew 24:15 telling us "Therefore when you see the ABOMINATION OF DESOLATION which was spoken of through Daniel the prophet, standing in the holy place (let the reader understand), then those who are in Judea must flee to the mountains." Obviously Matthew and Jesus felt this pertained to future events, and asked us to understand. The 1260 days of the "time, times, and half a time" are interpreted to mean 1260 years without the constant feature of worship at the Temple, starting from the Babylonian destruction of the Temple. 1260 years after 584 B.C. brings us to 677 A.D.

Nothing stands out in the history books from 677 A.D., yet many great events passed by in those 1260 years. Jesus lived and died, but this prophecy about the Temple doesn't mention anything about it. Rome rose and fell, and destroyed the Second Temple in 70 A.D., yet this prophecy about the Temple doesn't mention it. The Seleucid King Antiochus desecrated the Temple in 168 B.C., but the 1260 years of this prophecy passes over those events. The only relevant event in 677 A.D. was the construction of a wooden building.

Muslims who had recently conquered Jerusalem decided to build a great mosque on the Temple Mount, believing the Jewish Temple site to be that of Islam's holy "farthest mosque" mentioned in the Koran. Although the Al-Aqsa Mosque was not completed until the year 691, (and the more prominent Dome of the Rock Mosque came even later) a wooden prototype is believed to have been erected in 677. Christian pilgrims wrote of this mosque in 681.

We need to carefully consider the presence of an Islamic mosque on the Temple Mount beginning in 677. In Daniel 7:25 there is another mention of three and one half times: "He will speak out against the Most High and wear down the saints of the Highest One, and he will intend to make alterations in times and in law; and they will be given into his hand for a time, times, and half a time." Muslims have a new calendar and a new set of laws. Many Christians view this verse as a reference to events in Revelations, regarding the Antichrist, with three and a half times being one half (3.5 years) of the 7 year tribulation. But speaking against the Most High could also refer to the inscriptions on the Dome of the Rock Mosque, and this verse would then associate the mosque with the three and a half times (the 1260 year time frame.)

Around the perimeter of the octagonal mosque surrounding "the rock" is a long Arabic inscription, part of which on the

The Dome of the Rock Mosque in Jerusalem, as seen above the Wailing Wall.

southwest side says: "to God who has not taken a son and who doesn't have any partner." On the south side it also refers to "God, the everlasting, who has not begotten." If that were not enough to rile some Christians, on the east side the inscription very specifically denies what Christianity considers Jesus' special role: "Jesus son of Mary, was only God's messenger." The implication being that he was one prophet among many, but certainly not the son of God or even as special as Mohammed. Inside the building an inscription says "Far be it from his glory that he should have a son." These words can still be read today on the most prominent building in Jerusalem. This forces us to consider 1 John 2:22 "Who is the liar but the one who denies that Jesus is the Christ? This is the antichrist, the one who denies the Father and the Son." Based on these Bible verses, the inscriptions on Jerusalem's Dome of the Rock Mosque, one of Islam's holiest sites, seem to make Islam out to be the antichrist.

But taking 1260 years from 584 B.C. and arriving at the likely founding of Jerusalem's mosque in 677 A.D. does not by itself even get us to 1967, let alone any date in the 21st century. Daniel 12:11-13 sheds additional light on this "From the time that the regular sacrifice is abolished and the abomination of desolation is set up, there will be 1,290 days." This may mean that at some early point the daily sacrifice is stopped, (584 B.C.) but when in addition, the abomination of desolation is set up, (677 A.D.) from that point there are 1290 days until the situation is corrected. These are the 1290 years from 677 to 1967.

Daniel continues: "How blessed is he who keeps waiting and attains to the 1,335 days! But as for you, go your way to the end; then you will enter into rest and rise again for your allotted portion at the end of the age." (Many Bibles, including the King James, read "at the end of the days.") This is the end of the book of Daniel. Standing up for your lot at the end of days may be a reference to the rapture and/or Judgment Day. The people reaching the end of the 1335 days are blessed like those in Revelations 19:9 "Blessed are those who are invited to the marriage supper of the Lamb." These may both be end time events. If we start in 677 and add the 1290 years to reach 1967, when Jerusalem was united under Jewish rule for the first time in over 2000 years, then 1335 years is only 45 years later—2012! As several events that are expected during the tribulation have not yet occurred as of July 2012, this appears to refer to the start of the seven year tribulation in late 2012 or early 2013. This would mean that all prophesized events would be complete by the end of 2019.

It is not just the timing of modern and ancient events which seem to indicate that Daniel's prophecies should lead us to the end times. In Daniel 8:15-17 the prophet expresses confusion over his visions, but the angel Gabriel is sent to help him understand they refer to the last days: "When I, Daniel, had seen the vision, I sought to understand it; and behold, standing before me was one who.... said to me, 'Son of man, understand that the vision pertains to the time of the end.'" Daniel, the wise man so gifted in interpreting visions and dreams, is confused until the angel Gabriel repeatedly explains the end times relevance of the visions to Daniel in verses 17, 19, and 26. It was hard for Daniel to accept this, but Gabriel said it relates to the end times. With such events quite possibly occurring from 2012 to 2019 we may not accept the possibility easily either, but "Daniel is told that the clearest understanding of these prophecies will come only as people approach and enter the end time."[16]

As the year 1967 is the central lynchpin that allows understanding on the timing of Bible prophecy—and one must view the Jewish people and their control over the city of Jerusalem and the Temple Mount as biblically relevant for the events of that year to have meaning—we should clarify the role of the Jews and the Christian Church regarding the Bride of Christ which is so important in the upcoming wedding. From the passage in Hosea 2:19-20 it is clear that the people of Israel are the Bride of God: "I will betroth you to Me forever." But newer scriptures seem to tell us that the "church" is the bride. Is the Lord marrying two brides? Did He divorce one bride, Israel, to marry the church? No—God has told us He hates divorce (Malachi 2:16) and Jeremiah affirms God's everlasting covenant with the Jewish people—Israel (Jeremiah 31:35-37). This too is affirmed by Paul in Romans 9-11. There has always been just one bride—His chosen people. This initially small group began with just the Jewish people of Israel, but it has been enlarged to include those grafted in with Israel, the gentile believers, as Romans 11:17 describes grafting a branch onto an olive tree. Ephesians 3:6 is even more clear that "the Gentiles are fellow heirs and fellow members of the body, and fellow partakers of the promise in Christ Jesus." Everyone on Earth is welcome to accept God.

"Pat" Robertson once said "I believe it is the shared belief of the majority of evangelical Christians in the United States that the possession of all Jerusalem by the Nation of Israel is of utmost significance in the fulfillment of Biblical prophecy."[17] Despite Robertson's assessment of American Christians' beliefs, many Christians will not accept the importance of the year 1967 in prophecy, because they don't believe the Jews are God's chosen people anymore. They believe the Christian Church alone is the new "Israel" because the Jewish people broke their covenants with God too often, and did not accept Jesus as the Messiah. But that would ignore Jeremiah 31:31-37 (and many other passages) which tells us "I will make a new covenant with the house of Israel and with the house of Judah, not like the covenant which I made with their fathers.... I will be their God, and they shall be My people.... for I will forgive their iniquity, and their sin I will remember no more." God clearly offers the Jews complete forgiveness and a new covenant. It does not sound like the Jews are discarded and replaced and that the Christian Church is Israel now. Tim LaHaye comments: "Separating Israel and the Church is one of the major keys to rightly understanding Bible prophecy."[18]

Even if we did not feel the Jewish people remain relevant to Bible prophecy, there are still at least two prophecies bringing us to the year 1967, when the Jews took over Jerusalem. One tells us it happens 2300 Passovers after the Greeks conquer Israel; another tells us it happens 1260 plus 1290 years after Babylonians destroy the Temple. The Temple Mount did revert to Jewish control at the correct time over two thousand years later. And more importantly for those of us living in 2012, Daniel clarified that after the 1290 day period when the Temple Mount is again under control of the Jewish people: "Blessed is he who keeps waiting and attains to the 1,335 days!" Those who witness the events of 1967, after 1260 and 1290 days are told to keep in expectation for something another 45 days (years) later after 1335 days have passed. Forty-five years after 1967 is 2012, when the wondrous signs and events that mark the beginning of the seven year tribulation occur. 2012 followed by a seven year tribulation period means Judgment Day comes in 2019.

Does anything else support this timing? Matthew 24:32 says "Now learn the parable from the fig tree: when its branch has already become tender and puts forth its leaves, you know that summer is near; so, you too, when you see all these things, recognize that He is near, right at the door. Truly I say to you, this generation will not pass away until all these things take place." Is this description of a fig tree spreading out a reference to Israel expanding into newly acquired territory in 1967? How long is the generation, which presumably began before 1967? Many people feel a biblical generation is forty years, as it took forty years for the Jews who fled Egypt with Moses to die off. But God had only cursed the men over twenty, clearly saying that they would not be allowed to enter Canaan, except for Joshua and Caleb, who though over sixty years of age, would be allowed to enter. Thus the normal lifespan of the men wandering the desert must have been over sixty years, and that was under harsh conditions, homeless in a desert. Psalms 90:10 clarifies that "As for the days of our life, they contain seventy years." If seventy years is the correct answer, then a typical 18-year-old soldier fighting the battles of 1967 would have roughly 52 years remaining until "all these things" occur.

Televangelist Jack van Impe has commented repeatedly that he thinks the generation that saw Jerusalem united under Israeli rule in 1967 will see the events of Revelations unfold. He points out that there is some question as to the length of a generation, and notes that in Matthew chapter one, the generations from Abraham to Jesus span 2160 years with 42 generations, almost 52 years per generation. He also references 4000 years from Adam to Jesus over 77 generations, with just under 52 years per generation. Using that figure takes him from 1967 to 2019, and he subtracts seven years for a tribulation beginning in 2012.

Bible prophecies demonstrate that events have continued to come to pass as described in ancient times—right up into our generation. The same prophecies in which Daniel points us to 1967 exhort us to continue on to important and blessed events that begin forty-five years later in 2012. To better understand exactly what is likely to happen in 2012 (and 2019) several additional topics are worth addressing at this point. There is a great deal of evidence from around the world—especially in mythology, astronomy, and other sciences—which will support the ideas we have begun to explore in the Bible. With a broader perspective on how the world has been understood by the Mayans, Egyptians, Indians, astronomers, cartographers, geologists, physicists, and many others, we should have a deeper appreciation for certain scriptures when we circle back to focus on the Bible again.

(Endnotes)

1 Josephus, Flavius. *Antiquities of the Jews,* William Whiston translation. Book 11, chap. 8, sec. 5. Chicago: Unabridged Books, 1981

2 Josephus, Ibid.

3 Clarke, Adam. *Adam Clarke's Commentary on the Bible.* Nashville, TN: Thomas Nelson, 1997

4 Stephenson, Richard F. *Historical Eclipses and the Earth's Rotation.* London: Cambridge University Press, 2008, p. 149

5 Finegan, Jack. *Handbook of Biblical Chronology.* Princeton, NJ: Princeton University Press, 1964, pp. 202-3

6 Malamat, Abraham. "The Twilight of Judah: In the Egyptian-Babylonian Maelstrom" Leiden: Brill, 1975, p. 124

7 http://netsword.com/ubb/Forum4/HTML/000225.html

8 http://www.au.af.mil/au/awc/awcgate/gabrmetz/gabr000a.htm

9 http://netsword.com/ubb/Forum4/HTML/000225.html

10 Luttwack, Edward. *The Grand Strategy of the Roman Empire: From the First Century A.D. to the Third.* Baltimore, MD: Johns Hopkins University Press, 1979, p. 81

11 Adams, Colin. *Land Transport in Roman Egypt: A Study of Economics and Administration in a Roman Province.* Oxford, UK: Oxford University Press, 2007

12 Josephus, Flavius. *Antiquities of the Jews*. Chicago, IL: Unabridged Books, 1981 10.219-27; 1.128-32

13 Josephus, Flavius. Ibid.

14 Asimov, Isaac. *Asimov's Guide to the Bible: The Old Testament.* New York: Avon Books, 1968, pp. 614-615

15 Asimov, Isaac. *Asimov's Guide to the Bible: The New Testament.* New York: Avon Books, 1969, p. 53

16 LaHaye, Tim and Ed Hindson. *Exploring Bible Prophecy from Genesis to Revelation*. Eugene, OR: Harvest House, 2006, p. 266

17 Katz, David and Richard Popkin. *Messianic Revolution: Radical Religious Politics to the End of the Second Millenium*. New York: Hill and Wang, 1998, p. 243

18 LaHaye, Tim. *Revelation Unveiled.* Grand Rapids, MI: Zondervan Press, 1999, p. 110

CHAPTER TWO
THE MAYAN CALENDAR
AND MYTHOLOGY

In the century before Christ, the Roman calendar was an embarrassment to the Empire. Changes and additions had been made for political reasons instead of scientific ones, and the result was gross inaccuracy. Julius Caesar demanded modifications and the Roman calendar was vastly improved with a year of 365.25 days. This was close to being accurate—only eleven minutes and fourteen seconds too slow each year. But over the course of sixteen centuries, the Julian calendar was eventually ten days off from where it had started, and in 1572 Pope Gregory VIII modified the way we handle leap years and added ten days to the date, giving us the Gregorian calendar western civilization uses today.

By comparison, the Mayan calendar has remained extremely accurate over time. Much like our own cycles of seven day weeks interweaving with longer months, years, and centuries, the Maya had an intricate calendar system containing various smaller cycles which allowed them to use a solar year of 365.2422 days. There are 20 kin (days) per Uinal, 18 Uinal per Tun (of 360 days, like a biblical or Babylonian year) then 20 Tuns per Katun (7,200 days) and 20 Katuns per Baktun of 144,000 days, with 13 Baktuns in the Long Count, for a total of 1,872,000 days in a Long Count of over 5,125 years.

It is misleading to refer to the end of the Long Count on December 21, 2012 as "the end of the Mayan calendar." It is the end of the most important cycle within their calendar—the end a Long Count of thirteen baktuns. It is similar to the date they believe marked the end of the previous world (and the beginning of our current world) over 5,000 years ago, which occurred at the end of the last thirteenth baktun. The Maya believed our current world would end at this point in 2012, and that a new world would begin—with a new Long

Count.

The idea of a calendar does not end, and we should not assume that December 21, 2012 corresponds to the end of time any more than the edge of a map indicates the edge of the world. The end of the Long Count is more like our own calendar "ending" at midnight on December 31 or like an odometer turning from all nines to all zeros. On the other hand the 2012 date is not unimportant; it does mark the transition to what the Maya believed would be a "new world."

Some people mistakenly think this Long Count ends on December 24, 2011 or December 23, 2012. The miscalculations leading to those incorrect dates are now well documented. Archeologists and scholars worked on mapping Long Count dates to our Gregorian calendar for centuries before concluding that the beginning date corresponded to August 11, 3114 B.C. This is now known as the GMT correlation after three Maya scholars: Joseph T. Goodman, Juan Martinez Hernandez, and J. Eric S. Thompson. Their correlation yields an end date of 12/21/2012, and their count is the only one synchronized with the calendar in use by surviving descendants of the Maya in Mexico and Guatemala today.[1]

There are additional overlapping periods of time which don't fit into the Long Count but are still meaningful. The haab cycle is 365 days long, comprised of 18 "months" of 20 days, plus a special five day period at the end called the wayeb. Each day has a number and a descriptive word; much like a European might say a certain day is 21 December the Maya had day names like 3 Kankin. But because of the lack of a fractional day or a leap year it does not correspond well to the solar year of 365.242 years; like the Egyptian Sothic cycle it takes about 1500 years to migrate through the seasons and get back to the beginning of the cycle with days at their original time of the year. The main point of this haab cycle may have been to serve as a constant reminder that there are not exactly 365 days in a year, and that precision is needed to keep the calendar right over long periods of time.

The 260 day tzolkin is another overlapping measurement which represents the time from conception to birth, and every day in the cycle has a specific combination of twenty day names and thirteen numbers. The tzolkin number and name combined for 12/21/2012 has the date of 4 Ahau which has meanings of "cross-day-sun" and "four-movement-day."[2] This is very fitting for a day when the sun is at the crossroads of the two celestial lines in the sky—the ecliptic (the lineup of sun, planets, and zodiac signs, always in the same line) and the Milky Way—the bright path of stars along our galactic equator. This tzolkin number and name helps verify that 12/21/2012 is in fact the correct day in our calendar for the end of the Long Count, for when the last Long Count ended in 3114 B.C., the tzolkin cycle name for that last day was also 4 Ahau. In addition, the few Maya communities keeping this count today have the same tzolkin day name for 12/21/2012.

We also know that the tzolkin and haab days for this date (4 Ahau 3 Kankin) were recognized as an important date over a thousand years ago, because they were emphasized by Tortuguero's King Balam Ajaw, who was born on a 7th century incidence of 4 Ahau 3 Kankin. On his birthday, the sun was aligned near the black hole at the center of our galaxy, and the positions of Venus and Jupiter were also in the positions they would be in again over a thousand years later on December 21, 2012. Balam Ajaw used that date to prove to his people that he should be identified with the even greater king they knew would come in association with the very similar date at the end of the thirteenth baktun in 2012.

He chose to ascend to the throne at the end of the thirteenth tun, a lesser calendar unit of 7200 days, as if to reinforce the comparison to this future great king who was expected to come at the end of the thirteenth baktun. As the Maya believed that this greatest of kings would be sacrificed and reborn at the end of the age, and Balam Ajaw wanted to prove himself worthy of comparison to this sun-god-king, he even went so far as to choose the date of his death to be ritually sacrificed and decapitated during an alignment with Jupiter at the black hole on May 19, 679 A.D. His belief is his eventual resurrection with the sun god when the proper alignments recur in our time was that strong. Because of his strong faith in these future events, and to emphasize his direct association with them, King

Balam Ajaw made sure there were elaborate carvings referring to both the 2012 end date and the dates of his birth and death. These are just three of the many alignments with the black hole pointed out on Monument 6 at Tortuguero, but most importantly they include clear references to the Long Count's end date of 13.0.0.0.0.0 (12/21/2012)

These facts are stressed because they prove which day (in our calendar) is truly the correct day matching the end of the Long Count, and knowing the exact day for the end of the Long Count is very important. This date represents the beginning of a transition to a new world in Mayan beliefs. Some people believe the world will end on December 21, 2012. Maya scholars do not; they feel the date is symbolic. I believe there will be world shaking events (political, economic, and geological) from December 2012 to December 2019. The Maya depict the final cataclysm with a clustering of planets that does not occur at the 2012 end date. It does occur seven years later, which is one of many things that indicate the seven year tribulation occurs in between 2012 and 2019. I believe that the Maya are telling us that the world as we know it will end with events in December 2012 that will change our civilization drastically. I believe our current civilization will end seven years later and that many sources, including the Bible and the Mayans, point us to exact dates in 2012 and 2019.

Decades ago the Mayan calendar may have been unknown to all but a few arguing scholars but as we approach its Long Count's end date on December 21, 2012, we can't ignore the growing attention this date receives. Nor should we ignore it. When an ancient calendar over 5,000 years old has been designed to count down to zero in our lifetime we have to wonder why a civilization was so concerned with astronomical cycles and celestial bodies that reach certain positions on that particular end date. We should be even more concerned when we see that the Bible indicates the same time as the start of the tribulation. So let us take a good look into the Mayan culture and their reasons for this thirteen baktun end date.

Until very recently, the 2012 end date had only been found carved in stone with clear references to its meaning just *one time* on

Monument 6 at Tortuguero in Mexico. (A similar date referring to the descent of the creator gods at the current world's creation at the end of the last cycle of 13 baktuns in 3114 B.C. is detailed on Stela C at the ruins in Quirigua, Guatemala.) Many people assume that if the Long Count end date in 2012 was very important to the Maya, we would have more than one carving specifically pointing to that date.

Maya scholar John Major Jenkins responds to these expectations by pointing out that various Mayan cities have pyramids and other structures encoded with information on this date in their arrangements, alignments, and carvings. He focuses on the ballcourt in Izapa, where "monuments depict events in the stories of Seven Macaw, the Hero Twins, and the resurrection of their father, One Hunahpu. These are stone "documents" and "statements" that are as valuable for understanding the Mayan World Age doctrine, and therefore 2012, as any Rosetta stone clearly spelling things out. Perhaps more so, because the site and monuments of Izapa are integrated in a unified paradigm that touches upon mythology, prophecy, religion, and astronomy. In fact, because of this, the Izapan monumental corpus IS a Rosetta stone, since it integrates different representational "languages" into a unified whole; it shows how we can cross-reference symbols and motifs from different representational categories used by the Maya (mythology, prophecy, religion, and astronomy)… In conclusion, once we see that the Popol Vuh Creation Myth (the book and its stone prototype at Izapa) is the playbook for 2012, then we can see that there is not a dearth of 'statements' about 2012."[3]

Recently a second carving has recently been found at Comalcalco explicitly pointing to December 21, 2012. Strangely, the message with the 2012 date was hidden on the inside face of the brick; if the structure had not been dismantled, it would remain undiscovered today. (Were the Maya "veiling" or hiding this information from the uninitiated as the Bible often does?) The carving is sometimes referred to as the "Comalcalco Brick." There is damage on the brick, as it is not made of stone, only sun-baked mud—but the legible part of the text (translated by Mayan epigrapher David Stuart) reads: "At

61

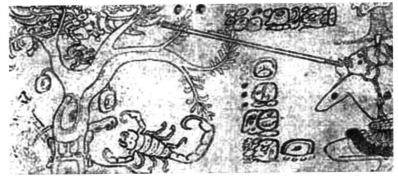

The image above is from a drawing based on a photograph of a Maya ceramic taken by Justin Kerr as can be seen in the book "Maya Ceramic Vases from the Classic Period" or the artwork "The Blowgunner Pot" in the Boston Museum of Fine Arts.

the end of 13 Baktuns, on 4 Ahau 3 Kankin, 13.0.0.0.0 (December 21, 2012); [something] occurs when Bolon Yokte descends." (If only the illegible event written here as "something" were still readable!) Other archeologists interpret the legible parts of the glyphs to mean "it arrives" and "He will descend from the sky." Whatever happens is unlikely to be pleasant... for Maya books tell us of the next day, "5 Ahau... harsh is the face of this day-god and harsh are the things he brings."[4]

Bolon Yokte is a Mayan "Creation Lord" whose name means something like "nine-footed tree," or if we allow a Mayan pun for Balan Yokte (changing the vowel from o to a) "jaguar at the foot of the tree." The jaguar translation makes more sense, because pottery (like the following image from a ceramic piece) and other Mayan art often depicts a world tree with cleft branches and a scorpion right of the tree's base. In front of the scorpion's head there is a single jaguar paw reaching out towards the scorpion from behind the tree. The world tree with the cleft is our Milky Way Galaxy with the dark rift in the center. At the top right of this image is the end of a blowgun, further right (but not shown in our close-up) is a blowgunner who is shooting the false god Seven Macaw out of the tree. The scorpion is the constellation Scorpio, but what is the meaning of the jaguar paw reaching out at the spot representing the galactic center? The spotted jaguar pelt traditionally represents the

Could the jaguar paw reaching out from the galactic center towards Scorpio in the Blowgunner image represent a cosmic dust cloud (like this one in the Eagle Nebula) reaching out from the galactic center?

starry sky, so the jaguar paw may represent a small portion of "sky material" appearing from the middle of the tree/galactic center, just starting to reach out and be visible. (This will make more sense when we discuss dust clouds that emanate from the galactic center.) Bolon Yokte's descent could refer to the tip of something dark which appears to grow after originating at the galactic center.

These events are also described in the "Chilam Balam," a group of documents forming a book of prophecy written in Yucatec Maya with Spanish characters during the 17th and 18th centuries. A principal source of knowledge of ancient Mayan custom, they contain myth, prophecy, medical lore, calendrical information, and historical chronicles. As they were written down long after the Spanish arrived, they are believed to be largely accurate records of ancient Maya beliefs, but with some incorporation of European ideas.

The "Chilam Balam" refers to one of the many destructions by a flood: "When the Great Serpent was stolen, the firmament collapsed and the earth sank. The four gods, the Four Bacab leveled everything. At the moment when the leveling was finished, they were secured in their places... the fire of the sun was revived, his face approached and he burned the Earth..." [when this happens next] "In the Thirteen Ahau Katun, in the late stages of the Katun, the Itza will be swept away... When the men of the Sun, 'Priests-of-the-solar-cult' will come bringing prognostications of the future... [later] the One True Man will come down, in the sacred place, where at one time his redemptive energy will purify us. There he will come on a great cloud."

There are several points made in the "Chilam Balam" which are so reminiscent of Christian thought that the stories may have suffered some cultural cross-contamination before they were written down. Only a few Native American books both survived the flames when Spanish colonists brought the Inquisition to the New World and were old enough to be original Maya ideas. As Friar Diego de Landa said in 1562 "We found great numbers of books [written in the characters of the Indians] but as they contained nothing but superstitions and falsehoods of the devil we burned them all."[5] The most famous of the few purely Mayan books to survive is the "Popol Vuh" or "Book of the Community." It is a narrative about the origins, history, and traditions of the Quiché Maya people as told by an anonymous Guatemalan Indian who produced the book in the 1550s. Around the year 1700 Father Francisco Ximenez copied the manuscript, adding a Spanish translation. Today there are several translations.

It covers a mythology very clearly based on astronomy, and also a genealogy of the rulers of the Quiché Maya kingdom of Guatemala. It describes all facets of Maya culture, starting with Hunahpú -- the civilizing hero of the Quiché-Maya. He is the immaculately-born son of the Supreme Being, and is a redeemer who sacrifices himself for humanity. Hunahpú is identified with the sun, but he transforms himself into human form and has the same substance and life experience that man does, establishing the expected behavior and conduct of the Mayan people. Hunahpú establishes the rules and laws for religion, agriculture, economics, and the astronomical, ritual, and time-reckoning procedures interwoven with those rules. The Popul Vuh can be likened to the Bible in that it covers many similar topics—creation of the world, the relation between man and God, the nature of truth, sin, justice, destiny, and salvation.

The first "Popul Vuh" story covers the failure of the gods to create earthly beings who properly obey them. Disobedient creations were destroyed by the co-creators called Maker or Heart of Heaven, and Kukulkan or Sovereign Plumed Serpent. Neighboring Aztecs called him Quetzalcoatl, the feathered serpent. (There are also very old Christian references to the "heart of heaven," as mentioned in Marsilio Ficino's *The Book of the Sun*, published in 1494 and commenting on traditions going back to Plato.)

The second story describes two mysterious Hero Twins, Hunahpu and Xbalanque, who destroy Seven Macaw, an arrogant celestial being identified with the seven stars of the Big Dipper who boasts and makes himself out to be the top god when he is not. Seven McCaw is a "false ruler" who is "hell-bent on deceiving humanity."[6] The Hero Twins undergo many trials and tests in the underworld, and eventually shoot Seven Macaw off his perch and kill him. A central part of the action involves the twins accepting a challenge to a ritual ballgame, in which a ball (representing the sun) must be hit into a goal ring (a "black hole" representing the galactic center.) Ball courts are generally submerged below ground level to demonstrate that this game takes place in the underworld, understood as equivalent to the night sky, which is below us during daytime. After defeating the Lords of Hell in the ballcourt, and in other trials in the underworld, the Hero Twins give a speech and are lifted into the sky.

By part three of the "Popul Vuh", it is time to create man. Several races of men are created from different inferior materials, considered failures, and destroyed by fires, floods, and the Earth rolling over. There are gods who sacrifice themselves to get the natural order of creation going again. Then the fourth version of man made from corn is good, successful, and intelligent. Perhaps a little too intelligent, having godlike ambitions. "They saw, and could see instantly far, they succeeded in knowing all that there is in the World. When they looked, they instantly saw all around them and they contemplated in turn the arch of the heaven and the round face of the Earth. The things hidden (in the distance) they saw all, without first having to move; at once they saw the World... great was their wisdom."[7] Heart of Heaven (God) blows mist into their eyes so that they could only see what was close, checking their desires to become gods. A different translation claims "they were destroyed by a thick resin that fell day and night and darkened the Earth."[8] Although they previously all spoke the same language, this ability, along with fire, is taken away. It is given back with a price—sacrifices in the form of blood and death.

The book begins much like Genesis in the Bible:

"This is the account of how all was in suspense, all calm, in silence; all motionless, still, and the expanse of the sky was empty. This is the first account, the first narrative. There was neither man, nor animal, birds, fishes, crabs, trees, stones, caves, ravines, grasses, nor forests; there was only the sky. The surface of the earth had not appeared. There was only the calm sea and the great expanse of the sky... Only the Creator, the Maker, Tepeu, Gucumatz, the Forefathers, were in the water surrounded with light."[9]

It may be noteworthy that the word for forefathers is "E Alom" or "e Qaholom" which is literally "those who conceive and give birth" or "those who beget the children." The two terms are translated as the "Forefathers" but they sound a lot like the "Elohim" in the Hebrew Bible, the plural word for God.

The "Popul Vuh" continues: "Thus let it be done! Let the emptiness be filled! Let the water recede and make a void, let the earth appear and become solid; let it be done. Thus they spoke. Let there be light, let there be dawn in the sky and on the earth! There shall be neither glory nor grandeur in our creation and formation until the human being is made, man is formed. So they spoke."

A typical Mayan drawing of Kukulkan as he exists on the crossing point of the four roads, the intersection of the plane of the ecliptic and the axis of our Milky Way galaxy, (the K'an Cross) which in some ways looks very similar to images of Jesus carrying the cross.

The "Popul Vuh" is a long book and this brief introduction hardly does it justice. But even this shows that there are many similarities to the Bible, especially in topics like the creation of the world, and of man. Like God and Jesus, there are two main creators. "Maker" or "Heart of Heaven" is equivalent to God and "Hunapu" (or feathered/plumed serpent, or Kulkulkan/Quetzalcoatl) is equivalent to his son. There is an arrogant Lucifer-like being named Seven Macaw who portrays himself as top god and is cast out of heaven. Early on mankind speaks one language but aims to be too godlike and is punished with natural disasters, the loss of a universal language, and diminished knowledge and wisdom. There is deity-sacrifice to make things right.

One huge difference when comparing the Mayan stories with Christianity is the extremely clear correlation between Mayan hero gods and astronomical bodies. Many famous men have made some similar links in Christianity, especially between Christ and the Sun. Thomas Paine, for example, said "The Christian religion is a parody on the worship of the Sun, in which they put a man whom they call Christ, in the place of the Sun, and pay him the same adoration which was originally paid to the Sun."[10] Some obvious similarities include His corona-like halo, turning water into wine as the sun does through photosynthesis, walking on water as the sun does on the ocean at sunrise and sunset, or worshipping Jesus on Sunday instead of the Sabbath (Saturday) or fixing his "birthday" of Christmas on December 25 when we in the northern hemisphere finally perceive the hours of daylight growing longer, a sign of a new strong sun for a new year. When Jesus says "I am the Light of the world" (John 8:12) many atheists, and a few Christians, suggest that we should not overlook the obvious meaning to search only for figurative ones.

The Bible also makes a few references likening Jesus to Venus (the Morningstar) but most modern comparisons focus on Jesus and the Sun. 2 Peter 1:19 likens Him to both the sun and Venus: "So we have the prophetic word made more sure, to which you do well to pay attention as to a lamp shining in a dark place, until the day dawns and the morning star arises in your hearts." Aside from Gene Roddenberry's Star Trek V movie there is no other modern connection between God and the center of the galaxy.

The Maya clearly have many astronomical bodies as religious figures. All of the major ones require a throne. "The cosmic center is a significant, overarching concept in Mesoamerican cosmology… the cosmic center (also understood as a divine birthplace) was the 'sacred throne.'" The Maya knew of "three possible cosmic centers… they determined one to be false, another to be valid but limited to a specific latitude of observation, and the third to be supreme."[11]

God is "Heart of Heaven," and his throne is at the black hole at the center of our galaxy. He sits on his throne on a holy cross made by two great lines in the sky, the band of the ecliptic in which the sun and planets are always seen, and the Milky Way, the central column of stars in our galaxy. The crossing point is at the dark rift in the central bulge of the Milky Way Galaxy in which clouds of gas and dust block our view of the galactic core. Though not visible to the naked eye, with modern science we know this is the galactic center around which every star in the Milky Way rotates, and it appears that the galactic center is a black hole just like the Mayans described it.

Their false god, similar to our Lucifer, is Seven Macaw, the seven stars of the Big Dipper. This constellation is near Polaris, the pole star in the Little Dipper. The night sky seems to rotate around these polar constellations because Polaris happens to be above the north pole of the Earth's rotational axis. Especially at higher latitudes and in wintertime, these constellations could (wrongly) be viewed as the cosmic center, high in the sky with all the other stars apparently rotating around them. (In reality, this only falsely appears to be a center of rotation due to the way the Earth spins. All the stars in our galaxy rotate around the black hole at the galactic center.) Seven Macaw, in placing his perch at Polaris, can sit on his North Pole Throne high in the sky and imitate the Most High, and sit above the stars of God at the galactic center, the throne of the true God, Heart of Heaven.

The sun or son of God has many names. He was known to the Maya's Aztec neighbors as Quetzalcoatl. In Aztec myth "an ambassador from the Milky Way was sent by God with a message to

El Caracol, the Mayan astronomical observatory at Chichen Itza

the virgin Sochiquetzal to tell her that she would conceive and give birth to Quetzalcoatl, the Son of Heaven."[12]   He is the feathered serpent, known to the Maya as Kukulkan or Hunahpu.

But to say that Kukulkan/Hunaphu is the sun is both accurate and misleading in its simplicity. Like Jesus, his major astronomical identity is solar, but sometimes "Quetzalcoatl was the morning star"[13] (Venus.) Also much like the Eskimo have dozens of different words for snow and ice (because to them there are clearly many distinct types that must be treated differently) the Maya did not view the sun as one unchanging entity. They notice different attributes of the sun at different times and consider it very important whether it is, for example, the sun at its zenith (highest point in the sky) or the sun on the horizon or the winter solstice sun on the shortest day of the year or the summer solstice sun on the longest day. It is also very important if the sun is in conjunction with another astronomical body like Venus, Jupiter, the black hole at the galactic core, or a constellation like the Pleiades.

Distinctions are made, sometimes with numbers. One Hunahpu, ("First Father") for example, is the winter solstice sun. This would apparently be the single most important time for the sun, and when this aligns with the galactic center at the holy crossroads of the ecliptic and the galactic equator (the K'an cross) he reaches his throne.

The moon also has several different heroes named after it, depending on what phase the moon is in. For one example, "Blood Moon" is the waning post-full moon. Various planets and constellations, or conjunctions of two bodies, also have specific names.

The planet Venus was very important to the Maya. In the Dresden Codex (one of very few surviving manuscripts with the "Popul Vuh" story) five pages describe computations on the orbit of Venus. The Maya were most concerned with its average of 584 days, though a range of 581-587 days is observed from Earth.[14] This is probably because Kukulkan's birth is associated with Venus. Just like Jesus, Kukulkan is normally associated with the Sun, but regarding his birth, there are morning star references. This is why so many cultures are interested in "the birth of Venus."

It is important to understand the cosmic affiliations of the heroes and gods of the Maya because their mythology, though told through personified figures, is really about the movement of celestial bodies—events in the sky.

Corresponding events happen on Earth when various astronomical bodies come into position; this is central to Maya ideas of world destruction and renewal. The Maya believe there have been several suns, or worlds, created and destroyed before ours. They believe we are in the fifth sun, or fifth world, which began on August 11, 3114 B.C. The Mayas' Aztec neighbors wrote "Why is the Fifth Sun known as 'The Sun of Movement'? Because, 'the elders say: in it there will be a movement of the earth and from this we shall all perish.'"[15]

For the Maya, December 21, 2012 is, at least symbolically, the last day of our current world. Personally, I suspect that December 22, 2012 will seem like a *somewhat normal* day, with last minute shoppers still crowding the malls. I say somewhat normal because we will be entering a seven year transitional period between worlds, so I also suspect that by December 22 major events will already have initiated a growing sense of impending doom. I think many people may already realize by the end of 2012 that they have seen the last year they will ever consider remotely normal. If future events are like the past, then a new world will be reborn out of this one, with great destruction killing off most of mankind. Whatever the outcome, the Maya were obsessed with recording the movements of the stars and planets and they built huge pyramids and other monuments to track them into 2012.

They reach the era of 2012 three different ways. The most well-known is their calendar, which ends its Long Count on December 21, 2012. A second method involves tracking One Hunahpu—the winter solstice sun—on his approach to the Heart of Heaven, the galactic center. This requires knowledge of the cycle of precession. The Earth spins on its axis like a top floating in space—and like a top, its axis also wobbles. This traces out a circle in the sky over the course of almost 26,000 years. (Some sources say 25,920 years, using 72 times 360, others say 25,800 years, which is probably more accurate.) The sun appears to wander around the ecliptic (the band of stars which appear to circle behind the sun) once a year, but there is another cycle of rotation in the opposite direction which takes almost 26,000 years. For any specific day of the year, the sun seems to move against the background of stars by one degree every 72 years.

Western culture and astrology currently emphasize the position of the spring equinox sun; when this first occurred in Pisces, Greeks and other nearby peoples said we were entering the age of Pisces. The spring equinox sun is now about to enter the age of Aquarius. For another example of precession, we now see the constellation Orion in winter, but in summer the sun is too close and blinds us to Orion. This changes over time. 12,900 years from now (or 12,900 years ago) the summer sun will be opposite Orion and it will best be seen in summer.

This precession cycle allows us to track One Hunahpu's position in the night sky over a great cycle that takes about 25,800 years to complete. As One Hunahpu is the winter solstice sun, he exists every December 21. He appears to be close to the Heart of Heaven (the galactic center) for a short few decades once every 25,800 years, including our era around 2012.

John Major Jenkins says that "the sun itself is one-half of a degree wide, and will in fact be touching the galactic equator on all winter solstices between 1980 and 2016 with 1998 being the year when the center of the sun is in closest alignment with the galactic equator."[16] The galactic equator runs through the middle of the Milky Way Galaxy and of course the black hole at the galactic core is the central feature of the galactic equator, but not quite exactly the point over which the sun and the ecliptic cross. The two never actually line up perfectly from Earth's point of view, but they are extremely close around 2012.

The Mayan Long Count seems to be designed to end when the winter solstice sun is close to the galactic center. Some people seem to think that the near alignment could somehow add together whatever gravitational or electromagnetic pull the sun and the black hole may have on the Earth, and somehow cause devastation on Earth. But in reality the sun appears close to the black hole at some point every year, and has even come close to doing so during "the proper time" at the winter solstice for several decades already. For physical forces to affect the Earth, the galactic center and/or the sun would have to experience a dramatic change. If anything does happen in 2012, it will not merely be because of an alignment. The alignment is just a marker in time.

The third way the Maya alert us to the time frame of 2012 is through the Pyramid of Kulkulkan at Chichen Itza in Mexico. "Kukulkan's pyramid is a precessional clock with its alarm set for the [early] twenty-first century."[17]

Quetzalcoatl is the better known Aztec name for the Mayan Kulkulkan; the co-creator of mankind, the redeemer-god, the feathered serpent, bringer of civilization, and teacher of arts and knowledge, also portrayed as taking the form of a bearded, robed white man who came to Mexico thousands of years ago "from across the sea on a boat without paddles"[18] and would one day return. Some believe he was a survivor of Atlantis, or perhaps a Carthaginian admiral who abandoned the Old World after Rome defeated Carthage. The Aztecs of central Mexico may have believed that Spanish conquistador Hernando Cortez was his reincarnation, and that may have made the Spanish conquest easier. The Spanish came wearing feather-plumed helmets and suits of armor like bright metal scales of serpent skin. In the Aztec calendar, every 52 years, Quetzalcoatl's day of One Reed occurred, and Cortez landed on that day in 1519. Of course he may have merely learned of the story and planned his landing on the right day of the right year to take advantage of it.

Quetzalcoatl may very well be the same figure known in Peru as Viracocha. He was described there as "a bearded man of tall stature clothed in a white robe which came down to his feet and which he wore belted around the waist." This wise teacher was also described

Snake heads at the bottom of the Pyramid of Kukulkan help establish that the tail end of the snake is at the top of the pyramid, where the rattle representing the Sun in conjunction with the Pleiades is directly above at the key moment of return. Could this snake covered pyramid also represent what is known in Maya myth as "Snake Mountain?" In the full image from "The Blowgunner Pot," where the central tree is the Milky Way and the scorpion to its right is Scorpio, the image left of the tree is often labeled "Sagittarius and Snake Mountain."

to have white skin, blue eyes, and gray hair, and to have come to Peru at a time "when society had fallen into disorder" which was "associated with a terrible deluge which had overwhelmed the earth and destroyed the greater part of humanity."[19] His name means "foam of the sea" and after teaching numerous arts and sciences to the ancestors of the Inca he walked into the Pacific and disappeared (like the setting sun) after vowing to return again someday.

Some Mormons believe Quetzalcoatl was the resurrected Jesus coming to his "other sheep" in the new world. Mormon President John Taylor wrote: "The story of the life of the Mexican divinity, Quetzalcoatl, closely resembles that of the Savior; so closely, indeed, that we can come to no other conclusion than that Quetzalcoatl and Christ are the same being." Quetzalcoatl has been called the "Sun of today" after his father Camaxtli the "Sun of yesterday." This would make Quetzalcoatl/Kukulkan the son of the sun or the son of God. He was also born to a virgin, crucified, and resurrected.[20] Lord Kingsborough wrote in *Antiquities of Mexico* that "This great Mexican divinity was essentially the same as the Jehovah Tsebaoth of the Hebrew Scriptures... His portrait is identical, apparently, with the commonly received likeness of Jesus."[21] Especially if that idea has any merit, we should be very interested in the fact that everything pointing to Quetzalcoatl/Kukulkan's coronation as king over the Earth indicates it could happen very soon.

More important for our understanding of precessional alarm clocks is that Kukulkan is symbolized astronomically as the conjunction of the sun with the Pleiades constellation. The pyramid dedicated to Kulkulkan at Chichen Itza is riddled with clues pointing to the Sun and to the Pleiades. Every year around March 20 at the spring equinox the Chichen Itza pyramid experiences shadows that look like a snake moving down the north steps. A snake head carved at the base completes the image.

The pyramid's layers of steps represent a coiled up rattlesnake ready to strike. The Yucatec rattlesnake has a circle with three dots in it on the tail before its rattle—and a circle with three dots is the Mayan glyph for the sun. The Mayan word for the snake's rattle and the Pleiades are also the same. The rattle is like a crown on the tail's solar face, as the Pleiades are for the sun. This conjunction of the sun and the Pleiades points to the sun's coronation as king when the Pleiades rattle is high in the zenith and the cosmic snake is ready to strike us.

Because the sun blinds us to anything near it, Mayan astronomers calculated when such alignments occur by noting when the Pleiades was opposite the sun's future daytime position during the night six months earlier. They knew half a year later it would be in conjunction with the sun at noon, even if they couldn't see it. The Maya were most concerned with this conjunction occurring on certain days of the year around May 23—the first of two dates when the sun appears in the zenith at Chichen Itza—directly overhead in the center of the sky.

Any tropical location has two such zenith days per year, when the sun is directly overhead at noon. Chichen Itza is about 20 degrees 40 minutes north and it first happens on May 23, although the sun begins to touch the zenith, and cast no shadows at noon, on May 20. Every year on these days the sun is directly above the Pyramid of Kukulkan. A 91-step stairway runs up each of the pyramid's four sides. Ninety-one steps on each of four sides add to 364, plus the top in the center as a 365th step, equals the number of days in one orbit around the sun.

But the whole pyramid is more than just a giant cross-marked throne for the sun. It is part of a great combination of crossroads, sun, and Pleiades. Much like a Nativity Cross or a crucifix with Jesus on the cross: "The sacred ruler does not just sit on the throne symbolizing the cosmic center and crossroads; instead, he is the crossroads."[22]

Ideally this solar coronation would occur when the sun is being crowned by the Pleiades directly above the Pyramid Temple with an alignment of the two in the zenith. The sun, by itself, is always in the zenith at Chichen Itza around May 20-25. John Major Jenkins feels that although the most precise day for the zenith at Chichen Itza is May 23, the first day of no shadows at noon is what the Maya would have looked for—and that this occurs on May 20. He uses May 20, 2012 as the "Zero Point" for Pleadies-Zenith alignments.[23]

Zenith passage dates do not change with precession, but alignments of the Pleiades with the sun at zenith do, and this would only occur every May 20-25 over a small range of a few centuries once every precessional cycle. It hasn't happened since approximately 23,400 B.C. but it will again from approximately 2000-2400 A.D. Out of a precessional cycle of almost 26,000 years this is not a large time window, and the beginning of this range in the early 21st century certainly helps confirm that the Maya expected something important around 2012. There was also a solar eclipse on May 20, 2012—further confirming the significance of this year's alignments. The Maya could have built their greatest pyramid at a different latitude to represent other ideas; but they chose to represent what

My wife drew my attention to this monstrance as we looked at displays in the Vatican Library. It is a good example of what looks like a sunburst on a cross. Looking beyond the mere substitution of a sun for Jesus on the cross, the crescent shape at the bottom of the sun-circle may even represent an edge of the sun showing during a near-total eclipse alignment at the cosmic crossroads.

symbolizes their sun god becoming king over the Earth, in or near the year 2012.

Also occurring every year in the early 21st century, but only on December 21 each year, the winter solstice sun is in precessional alignment with the galactic center at the holy K'an cross of the ecliptic and the Milky Way. This alignment at the Heart of Heaven represents the sun god's enthronement as king of Heaven. Mayan mythology, and their ball game involving kicking the sun-ball into the black hole-goal ring, are all about the same celestial enthronements. This sounds somewhat similar to Jesus joining God the Father at the Great White Judgment throne in the book of Revelations, receiving kingship over the Earth and authority to deal with Lucifer.

The Maya also have a false god like our Lucifer. Jenkins describes a stone carving known as Stela 60 which "portrays the final victory over the Lord of the Polar Region... the Hero Twins defeat Seven Macaw by shooting him out of his tree before they begin their attempts to resurrect their father, One Hunahpu... Together, all of these monuments say, 'The gameball is in the goal, the game is over, Seven Macaw is dead, the solstice sun can be reborn.'"[24] The Maya thought Seven Macaw must be shot off his perch by the Hero Twins after they won the ballcourt game, and just before the winter solstice sun god One Hunahpu could be resurrected by the twins. So the twins, which in this case represent the north and south poles, move precessionally to win the game and position the sun-ball into the galactic center / black hole / goal ring of the ballcourt game. Then Seven Macaw is shot off his perch suddenly, just before One Hunahpu, the winter solstice sun, is resurrected. All this astronomical symbolism suggests that the game is over in the early 21st century.

Jenkins also says "If we include the size of the solstice sun (1/2 a degree wide) then, as I pointed out in my book 'Maya Cosmogenesis 2012,' the solstice sun will not have precessed clear of the Galactic equator until roughly A.D. 2018" Perhaps the years around 2012 are a time period which constitutes the victorious ballplayer winning the game, and only after the sun completely passes through its alignment period with the dark rift has the game ball completely passed through the goal ring. Perhaps then Seven Macaw can be shot down, and a coronation can occur, only after 2018, presumably at the next winter solstice in 2019. The "Popul Vuh" tells us "In the episode of the Hero Twin's conception, according to Dennis Tedlock, One Hunahpu's severed head symbolizes the conjunction of Jupiter and Venus... we have an astronomical picture of the conception of the Hero Twins: Jupiter and Venus conjunct in the dark rift... [with] Blood Moon as the waning moon in the east... information in the 'Popul Vuh' encodes the date of the Hero Twin's conception."[25]

The Hero Twins must be born before they can fulfill their destiny to resurrect their father One Hunahpu and for him to claim his throne... This somewhat rare alignment occurs again on 11/23/2019. Jupiter and Venus are in conjunction by the dark rift of the galactic center, while the waning crescent moon is due east.

Mayan ballcourt players, like soccer players, could not use their hands. With a small hole high above the ground, games required many failed shots and often took several days before a single goal allowed a victory. This helped emphasize the long duration of the astronomical processes the game represents: the winter solstice sun passing through the position of the black hole at the galactic center.

A month later, the sun is near the galactic center throne and a solar eclipse occurs. Is this the climactic battle of the ball court games between Captain Sun Disk and Captain Serpent? Is this the scene where One Hunahpu's decapitated head is hung in the cleft of a tree by the road, represented by the eclipsed head of the sun god by the dark cleft of the Milky Way's galactic center?

It could appear as if, at his weakest moment with the shortest days at the start of winter, the light of the sun god is snuffed out. Could there be three days of symbolic death for the sun god? For on 12/28/2019, Jupiter ends its alignment behind the sun, having symbolically touched the sun-king with the scepter Jupiter so often symbolizes. At that moment the sun has been symbolically killed by the eclipse which began on Christmas, has been dead for the three shortest days, and can be resurrected by touching Jupiter as a Hero Twin. The sun can also be crowned as king by touching Jupiter in its role as the scepter.

This happens at the holy cross, the "hol txan" or "hol can be" meaning the "hole in the middle of four roads." One Maya story describes the Hero Twins as "the Kings of Death... you seek [or search] the Silent Day [the night sky], the silent hour so as to transform yourselves, to Hol Txan over mankind, since your waking is like a thief's presence."[26] Destructive activity at the black hole at the galactic center is like a thief in the night. This is similar to the Day of the Lord's wrath coming as a thief in the night as mentioned in Revelations. The Maya call this day "haiyococab," which means "water-over-the-earth"[27] and is drawn on page 74 of the Dresden Codex version of the "Popul Vuh" with an alignment of planets at the cosmic center, from which a giant reptile spits forth a flood.

The Mayan calendar cycle we are in now for the Fifth World ends in 2012, apparently corresponding with the timing of biblical prophecies. But while events described in the Bible are one-time events, the Maya concept of time is like that of India, with repeating events. "The Maya believed that time was cyclical, that the same influence and thus the same consequences would be repeated in history."[28] One recent discovery in Xultun, Guatemala is making the news because dates beyond 2012 were discovered and the press does not understand that 2012 merely marks the end of one important cycle of 5125 years. Later dates will occur in what the Maya would call "the sixth world" that comes after 2012. Without this insight press coverage of the Mayan dates after 2012 seems downright silly. At Discovery.com we are told "The Mayan calendar is going to keep going for billions, trillions, octillions of years into the future," said archaeologist David Stuart of the University of Texas, who worked to decipher the glyphs."[29] Octillions of years? That sounds scientific.

Some coverage, like USA Today's article "Newly discovered Mayan calendar goes way past 2012" portrays this find as if the existence of a later date means we should categorically dismiss the end of the current cycle in 2012 as irrelevant. "'So much for the supposed end of the world,' says archaeologist William Saturno of Boston University."[30] They ignore the basic fact that the Maya believed we are currently in the Fifth World, and that destruction comes in periodic cycles. Dates in the far future do not change the cyclic nature of time. The article emphasizes the ignorance of some writers by ending with the comment: "We can now see astronomy playing a role in ordering their society."[31] Really? Only after this discovery can we see that?

Astronomy dominated Mayan society, both for agriculture and religious beliefs about gods who would bring destruction when they returned to certain positions. Before we dismiss this idea, let us listen to one of the great pioneers in Maya scholarship, Linda Schele. One of the first experts in Maya iconography, she merely wanted to translate their hieroglyphs and art. She did not want to make unnecessary cultural connections to the Old World or our preconceptions about their astronomy, calendar, or end-of-the-world beliefs. But even Schele, kicking and screaming, was dragged into acknowledgement of certain associations. As she describes conversations with David Freidel, with whom she co-authored *Forest of Kings* (1990) and *Maya Cosmos* (1993):

"I had been arguing with Freidel for hours on the phone about where the tree was and where the scorpion is. And he [said]... there was a Maya constellation of the scorpion, and that it had to be

Scorpius... I didn't want to accept it... I got out a star book, opened it up until Scorpius was high in the southern sky and my teeth fell out of my head. I mean, I can remember my chest tightening up, because in the picture there's a perfect picture of the Milky Way going across the sky from south to north as the tree... There are four recreations of the world, and we're living in the fourth... It does us no good to delegate worldviews like the Maya to the realm of superstition and child's stories."[32]

As we contemplate the end of the Fifth World, perhaps we should consider the end of the Fourth World. If the idea of cyclic destruction is correct, then there should be evidence for dramatic events when the Long Count began on August 11, 3114 B.C. Did anything important actually happen at that time? Historical records are almost non-existent that far back—but maybe with good reason?

In 1923 Leonard Wooley led a dig in Iraq below the remains of the tower of Ur. At a level believed to be over 5,000 years old, they hit a layer of clay ten feet thick. Below the sedimentary clay were the potsherds and flint tools of a very primitive society. Wooley telegrammed: "WE HAVE FOUND THE FLOOD."[33]

As Bruce Scofield wrote in "What Really Happened in 3100 B.C.": "There are only a few turning points (or watershed periods) in history that have had significant widespread effects... 3100 B.C. (+/- 100 years) is the most enigmatic... It's possible that this period marks [the] most important and decisive time in the entire history of civilization... This is a generally accepted approximate date for the Early Dynasty period of the Sumerians, the first of several civilizations in Mesopotamia. All the traits of high civilization appeared there almost simultaneously... Ancient Egypt as we know it came into being with the union of Upper and Lower Egypt and the start of the First Dynasty under Menes, king of Upper Egypt. This event is said to have occurred somewhere around 3100 B.C... It was also around 3100 B.C. (+/-100 years) that stone circle building and other types of megalithic structures were being built throughout Britain, Scotland, and Ireland... It was also around this date that pottery appeared along the Pacific coast in Ecuador... In ancient India... the first age, called the Kali Yuga, is said to have begun on February 18, 3,102 B.C."[34] What if all these civilizations "began" simultaneously because something virtually wiped out all their ancestors simultaneously, forcing a global re-start?

The Maya believed in a cycle of destruction that has occurred before and will occur again. They devised a calendar cycle which began at a time when civilization first seems to have appeared in Mesopotamia, Egypt, India, China and Ecuador. They end their cycle in December 2012 and suggest that a cataclysmic event may cause destruction and renewal at that point. Unfortunately there is a great deal of scientific evidence behind the idea that such destructive events occur, in the form of a crustal displacement affecting the entire surface of the Earth—a pole shift.

"Hunab Ku" is a Mayan phrase for "the only God" but both the words and the associated drawing may be relatively modern inventions developed in response to Christianity. Evidence of its use even during colonial times is minimal; and no evidence of use before the arrival of the Spanish can be agreed upon, though many writers suggest there are primitive versions in the "Chilam Balam" and "Popul Vuh." Many attribute the symbol's popularity to twentieth century authors such as Domingo Martínez Parédez, who compared it to the circle and square of masonry, and suggested it could also represent the Grand Architect of the Universe.

(Endnotes)

1 Jenkins, John Major. *Maya Cosmogenesis 2012*. Santa Fe, NM: Bear & Company, 1998, p. 23

2 Jenkins, Ibid, p. 247

3 http://www.alignment2012.com/mayan2012statements.html

4 Von Hagen, Victor W. *World of the Maya*. New York: Mentor Books, 1960, p. 179

5 Hancock, Graham. *Fingerprints of the Gods*. New York: Three Rivers Press, 1995, p. 112

6 Jenkins, John Major. "The Origins of the 2012 Revelation" an essay on pages 35-62 in book *The Mystery of 2012: Predictions, Prophecies, & Possibilities*. Boulder CO: Sounds True, 2007, p. 49

7 Gilbert, Adrian and Maurice Cotterell. *The Mayan Prophecies*. New York: Barnes & Noble, 1996, p. 87

8 LaViolette, Paul. *Earth Under Fire: Humanity's Survival of the Ice Age*. Rochester, VT: Bear & Company, 2005, p. 100

9 Christenson, Allen J., translator. *The Popul Vuh: The Sacred Book of the Maya*. Norman, OK: University of Oklahoma Press, 2007

10 Paine, Thomas. "An Essay on the Origin of Free-Masonry." 1805

11 Jenkins, John Major. *Maya Cosmogenesis 2012*. Santa Fe, NM: Bear & Company, 1998, p. 25

12 Colmer, Michael. *Aztec Astrology*. London: Blandford, 1995, p. 14

13 S, Acharya. *Suns of God: Krishna, Buddha and Christ Unveiled*. Kempton, IL: Adventures Unlimited Press, 2004, p. 13

14 Gilbert, Adrian and Maurice Cotterell. *The Mayan Prophecies*. New York: Barnes & Noble, 1996, pp. 38-39

15 Hancock, Graham. *Fingerprints of the Gods*. New York: Three Rivers Press, 1995, p. 99 originally from Pre-Hispanic Gods of Mexico, p. 24

16 http://alignment2012.com/tonkins-error.html

17 Jenkins, John Major. *Maya Cosmogenesis 2012*. Santa Fe, NM: Bear & Company, 1998, p. 95

18 Hancock, Graham. *Fingerprints of the Gods.* New York: Three Rivers Press, 1995, p. 102

19 Hancock, Graham. Ibid., pp. 46, 47, 52

20 S, Acharya. *Suns of God: Krishna, Buddha and Christ Unveiled.* Kempton, IL: Adventures Unlimited Press, 2004, p. 140

21 S, Acharya. Ibid., p. 13 originally from *Antiquities of Mexico*, 1831

22 Jenkins, John Major. *Maya Cosmogenesis 2012.* Santa Fe, NM: Bear & Company, 1998, p. 77

23 Jenkins, Ibid., p. 349

24 Jenkins, Ibid., p. 290

25 Jenkins, Ibid., p. 59

26 Fought, John G. Chorti (Mayan) *Texts 1*. Philadelphia, PA: University of Pennsylvania Press, 1972, p. 274

27 Von Hagen, Victor W. *World of the Maya.* New York: Mentor Books, 1960, p. 131

28 Von Hagen, Victor W. Ibid., p. 176

29 Pappas, Stephanie. "Nevermind the Apocalypse: Earliest Mayan Calendar Found." Discovery.com 5/11/2012

30 Vergano, Dan. "Newly discovered Mayan calendar goes way past 2012." USA Today 5/10/2012

31 Vergano, Dan. Ibid.

32 Linda Schele, interviewed September 20-22 1997 at her home office in Austin, Texas by Michael Coe and David Lebrun. http://www.nightfirefilms.org/breakingthemayacode/interviews/ScheleTRANSCRIPT.pdf

33 Warshofsky, Fred. *Doomsday: The Science of Catastrophe.* New York: Readers' Digest Press, 1977, pp. 78-79

34 Scofield, Bruce. "What Really Happened in 3100 B.C." http://www.onereed.com/articles/3000bc1.html

CHAPTER THREE
POLE SHIFTS

Imagine that the surface layers of the Earth's crust are only loosely attached to the inner core, and that every so often the surface of the Earth detaches itself and moves in one solid piece over the core. Picture the loosened peel around an orange, or the chocolate around a chocolate covered cherry. The central bulk of the Earth's mass may keep rotating just as it had been underneath us, but the surface we live on would move in a new direction. If it happens quickly, there would be massive earthquakes, volcanos, and tidal waves. The sun, moon, and stars would appear to rise and fall strangely out of place. Polar regions would move toward the equator, and some equatorial regions would move toward the poles. Ice sheets on lands that have moved from the poles towards the equator would start melting rapidly and raise sea levels. Formerly temperate areas moving into polar regions would suddenly enter a new ice age, as Greenland and Antarctica have known for at least the last few thousand years. In some places, the crust would tear apart as it is forced to spread out over the equatorial bulge. Other lands which had been over the bulge would buckle like an accordion and form mountains as they are crammed into a narrower space. Civilization would be destroyed and few people would survive.

If such events do occur regularly there must be some evidence. Things we could hope to find would include:

1—Changing magnetic fields within hardening lava. Volcanic eruptions during such twisting would spew molten lava, with iron and other magnetic minerals in the rock. In liquid lava, these minerals are free to align their molecules with the planet's magnetic field. After cooling, the rock's molecular alignment indicates two things. Most obviously, these molecules point north—or at least, where north had been when the lava hardened. And taking any dip from horizontal into account we can also determine latitude—because magnetic molecules in polar lava will be almost vertical to align with the magnetic field shooting out the pole, while lava that solidified near the equator will have minerals aligned horizontally. Most importantly, if a pole shift were happening very quickly, lava flowing and solidifying over a short time and distance would have changing alignments showing that the pole was moving during the lava's solidification.

2—The alignment of bands of coral. Coral reefs circle the earth, made of skeletons of dead coral. Some species love the hottest tropical waters and others thrive in slightly cooler waters. There are also seasonal variations in growth for corals farther from the equator, while no such variations should occur close to the equator where summer and winter are both hot. If the surface of the planet occasionally realigns to a new polar axis, we should find older bands of coral reefs criss-crossing the Earth.

3—Areas which are now polar and frozen should have well preserved evidence of warmer climates in the recent past. If Antarctica has not always been at the South Pole there should be fossilized or freeze-dried animals and plants. There should be river valleys formed by flowing liquid water, with deltas of sediment, and at least some older evidence of oil deposits, sedimentary rock, or salt flats.

4—Human records. If this has happened before when civilization existed, there could be ancient buildings aligned to the former North Pole, legends of the great cataclysm, records of advanced science, and copies of maps showing lands with strange orientations or areas submerged under oceans or ice caps.

The reverse logic is also true—if such pole shifts never really happen:

1—There should be very good alternative explanations for ice ages, mountain ranges, and any possible alignments of coral reefs or magnetized lava. Most if not all of these explanations should be completely agreed upon, and not rely on controversial theories. This is not the case. For example, one "authority on glaciology" says "concerning the origin of the ice ages: 'one of the greatest riddles in geological history, remains unsolved… the cause still eludes us.'"[1]

2—There should be no evidence of rivers or of temperate or

tropical life thriving in areas like Greenland or Antarctica in what is considered geologically recent history. But remnants of trees and forests have been found in northern Greenland and Antarctica. There are many fossils, oil deposits, and layers of sediment demonstrating the absence of glacial conditions in recent times.

3—There should not be animals maintaining a territorial home and/or breeding ground which they could not possibly have evolved to live in naturally (such as penguins walking hundreds of miles inland into Antarctica to lay their eggs.)

4—There should be no ancient maps of the pre-pole-shift conditions of the Earth. (There are many.) There should not be easily provable historical records of such a cataclysm. (There are.) There should be no arrangements of ancient city foundations aligned to the old North Pole if nothing special is located there today. According to archeoastronomers like Athony Aveni, Robert Bauval, Colin Wilson, and Rand Flem-Ath—The Sphinx Temple, the ziggurat of Ur, the Wailing Wall in Jerusalem, and the entire ancient Mexican capital city of Teotihuacan, Tula, Tenayucan, Copan, and Xochicalco, and many other ancient sites in both hemispheres are all aligned to the former North Pole.

The idea that the Earth could occasionally suffer such catastrophic pole shifts is not new, but it went a long time without discussion before the idea was rediscovered after the dark ages. The British poet John Milton wrote a ten-volume epic poem called "Paradise Lost" in 1667 and this may be one of the earliest "modern" references, as part of his story about man being evicted from Eden mentions: "Some say, he bid his Angels turn askance The poles of earth, twice ten degrees and more, From the sun's axle; they with labour pushed Oblique the centrick globe." Soon after (in 1681) Thomas Burnet wrote "Telluris Theoria Sacra," or "The Sacred Theory of the Earth." He explained: "The Poles of the world did once change their situation, and were at first in another posture from which they are now, till that inclination happen'd… The earth chang'd its posture at the Deluge, and thereby made these seeming changes in the Heavens."

One of the earliest scientific proponents of the theory was a

French zoologist and one of the founders of modern paleontology, Georges Cuvier. In 1813 he published his "Essay on the Theory of the Earth," which detailed his unpopular theories that fossils showed many animal species had gone extinct, and that recurring catastrophic natural events periodically destroyed most of the world. He felt that the last such destruction had come five to six thousand years earlier. As he described his conclusions: "These repeated eruptions and retreats of the sea have neither been slow nor gradual; most of the catastrophes which have occasioned them have been sudden; and this is easily proved, especially with regard to the last of them, the traces of which are the most conspicuous. In the northern regions it has left the carcasses of some large quadrupeds which the ice has arrested, and which are preserved even to the present day with their skin, their hair, and their flesh. If they had not been frozen as soon as killed they must quickly have been decomposed by putrefaction. But this eternal frost could not have taken possession of the regions which these animals inhabited except by the same cause that destroyed them; this cause, therefore, must have been as sudden as its effect. The breaking to pieces and overturnings of the strata, which happened in former catastrophes, show plainly enough that they were sudden and violent like the last; and the heaps of debris and rounded pebbles which are found in various places among the solid strata, demonstrate the vast force of the motions excited in the mass of waters by these overturnings. Life, therefore, has been often disturbed on this earth by terrible events - *calamities which, at their commencement, have perhaps moved and overturned to a great depth the entire outside crust of the globe.*"[2]

Cuvier was far ahead of his contemporaries, who were not able to digest all of his conclusions at once. One of the most extensive book reviews at the time quoted his thoughts on the youth of current surface conditions: "What has taken place on the surface of the globe since it has been laid dry for the last time, and its continents have assumed their present form, at least in such parts as are somewhat elevated above the level of the ocean, it may be clearly seen that this last revolution, and consequently the establishment of our existing societies, could not have been very ancient. This result is one of the best established, and least attended to in rational zoology; and it is so much the more valuable, as it connects natural and civil history together..." but the reviewer dismissed Cuvier's conclusions regarding, as they reworded it, "a great catastrophe and subsequent renewal of the human race." This dismissal seems odd as the reviewer accepts the biblical flood and quotes "antediluvian science." Earlier in the same review, he also accepted and restated Cuvier's most important conclusion well: "the original figure of the earth may have been extremely unlike the present; it may have been vastly irregular; and in the course of the changes which it has undergone, the axis of rotation may have changed its position, and have passed through a series of variations."[3] Confronting deeply held religious views and normalcy bias, coupled with the staggering number of theories and explanations proposed by Cuvier may simply have been too much for most people to handle all at once.

Louis Agassiz, a Swiss student of Cuvier, was invited to the US and became a Harvard professor. He wrote that "All mountains and mountain-chains have been upheaved by great convulsions of the globe, which rent asunder the surface of the earth, destroyed the animals and plants living on it at the time, and were succeeded by long intervals of repose... a time of building up and renewing followed the time of destruction."[4]

Charles Darwin, best known for his theory of evolution, was also aware of the forces that encouraged the process—the occasional destruction of the Earth's surface conditions, leading to a mass die off and the spread of populations of the most adaptable species which survived the events. "To destroy animals, both large and small, in Southern Patagonia, in Brazil, on the Cordillera of Peru, in North America up to Behring's Straits, we must *shake the entire framework of the globe.* No lesser physical event could have brought about this wholesale destruction not only in the Americas but in the entire world."[5] (Many scientists now agree that such disasters may be the primary factor in evolution.)

Another early supporter of the pole shift idea was the French historian and archeologist Charles-Étienne Brasseur de Bourbourg.

He travelled Central America as a Catholic missionary and became the top French expert on Mesoamerican studies. In 1861 he published a French translation of the "Popol Vuh," including sections on Quiche Maya grammar and Central American mythology. His last article in 1872, "Chronologie historique des Mexicains," describes what he believed were several periods of global cataclysms resulting from sudden shifts in the Earth's axis starting around 10,500 B.C.

One of the most famous psychics of all time, perhaps second only to Nostradamus, is the American "Sleeping Prophet" Edgar Cayce. He was not particularly intelligent or well-educated, but after claiming a visit from the Virgin Mary, he suddenly had the ability to go into a trance in which he could understand many languages, make medical diagnoses of faraway patients, and obtain answers about the future from the spirit world. Many books have been written about his medical suggestions and prophecies, and before his death in 1945 he popularized the idea of pole shifts among readers in the United States. He claimed that early evidence of a coming pole shift would start to show no later than 1998. (Between 1900 and 1960, [the north magnetic pole] moved ten feet in the direction of Greenland. That's 2.5 inches, or 60mm, a year. Between 1960 and 1968 the pole also moved another ten feet, this time at a rate of 100mm or four inches per year. Not only is the pole moving, but the rate of motion is increasing."[6] By 1998, our magnetic North Pole was already moving towards Russia at a rate of about forty miles per year.) Some of Cayce's psychic "readings" on previous pole shifts are quoted below:

"Many lands have disappeared, many have appeared and disappeared again and again during these periods, gradually changing as the condition became to the relative position of the earth." Reading 5748-2 (May 28, 1925)

"The Nile entered into the Atlantic Ocean. What is now the Sahara was an inhabited land and very fertile. What is now the central portion of this country, or the Mississippi basin, was then all in the ocean; only the plateau was existent, or the regions that are now portions of Nevada, Utah and Arizona formed the greater part of what we know as the United States. That along the Atlantic board formed the outer portion then, or the lowlands of Atlantis. The Andean, or the Pacific coast of South America, occupied then the extreme western portion of Lemuria. The Urals and the northern regions of same were turned into a tropical land. The desert in the Mongolian land was then the fertile portion. This may enable you to form SOME concept of the status of the earth's representations at that time!" Reading 364-13 (November 17, 1932)

(Q) "Please give a description of the earth's surface as it existed at the time of Atlantis' highest civilization, using the names of continents, oceans and sections of same as we know them today?"

(A) "As to the highest point of civilization, this would first have to be determined according to the standard as to which it would be judged... [It] would depend upon whether we are viewing from a spiritual standpoint or upon that as a purely material or commercial standpoint; for the variations, as we find, extend over a period... there were MANY changes in the surface of what is now called the earth. In the first, or greater portion, we find that NOW known as the southern portions of South America in the Arctic or North Arctic regions, while those in what is NOW as Siberia - or that as of Hudson Bay - was rather in that region of the tropics... changes were brought about in the latter portion of that period, or what would be termed ten thousand seven hundred (10,700) light years, or earth years..." Reading 364-4 (February 21, 1933)

More interesting than his descriptions of previous surface arrangements are Cayce's statements claiming that the final destruction of Atlantis occurred approximately ten to eleven thousand years ago, and that survivors from Atlantis went to four main regions: northeastern North America, the Pyrenees Mountains on the current border between Spain and France, Egypt, and the Gobi Desert in Mongolia. At the time Cayce said such things, that hodge podge of distant locations seemed fanciful and unprovable. Then came advancements in DNA analysis, which helped prove that "oceans are highways, not barriers."[7]

Human migration patterns are now most easily established looking at mitochondrial DNA. The mtDNA is not human; it comes from symbiotic bacteria inside all our cells which help us process sugars. These bacteria are passed on only from mother to child, and they mutate at a fast but predictable rate that allows us to analyze how and when various groups seperated. There are 42 distinct haplogroups of mtDNA worldwide, and only four main groups in North America, all of which can be traced to migrations from Asia. In 1997, a fifth "haplogroup X" was found which is not present in eastern Asia at all.

Analysis of mtDNA from ancient gravesites shows it became prevalent on the coast of northeast North America around 10,000 years ago. It is present today in about 25% of people of Iroquois descent, along with a presence in several other native American tribes—and this "haplogroup X" is also widespread among the Basques of northern Spain and southwest France. It can be found, but is much less prevalent, in people in Egypt and Israel. The only other place with this mtDNA is a small region in the Gobi Desert near Mongolia. The Basque population is especially interesting as they contain the highest levels of Rh- 'O' negative blood on Earth, and also have an extremely low amount of type B blood. Their original language is not related to any other known language. There is also an enigmatic monument in their country which many people believe gives us clues about an upcoming pole shift. Perhaps Edgar Cayce was on to something…

One additional set of questions and answers with Edgar Cayce is worth mentioning. Cayce was asked:

"Q. 1. Are the deductions and conclusions arrived at by D. Davidson and H. Aldersmith in their book on the Great Pyramid correct?

"A. 1. Many of these that have been taken as deductions are correct. Many are overdrawn. Only an initiate may understand."

The most relevant statement from Davidson and Aldersmith's "The Great Pyramid, It's Divine Message" is "The object of the Pyramid's Message was to proclaim Jesus as Deliverer and Saviour of men, to announce the dated circumstances relating to His Coming, and to prepare men… to adapt themselves spiritually to the circumstances of His Coming when the fact of the Message becomes to them a matter of certainty."[8]

The first well-known American scientist who was a proponent of the pole shift theory was the electrical engineer Hugh Auchincloss Brown, who published his hypothesis of deadly and recurring pole shifts in an article titled "Can the Earth Capsize?" in *Time Magazine* in 1948. Brown felt that accumulation of ice at the poles eventually created significant imbalances in centrifugal forces and caused tipping of the axis. He felt this happens approximately every seven thousand years and that we are approximately due for the next one to occur anytime. He expounded upon his theories in his 1967 book *Cataclysms of the Earth*, in which he wrote: "The present ice cap in Antarctica is merely the last of many thousands that have previously existed. Geological records reveal that it is the successor to a long lineage of glistening assassins of former civilizations."[9]

There is modern evidence that such mass imbalances lead to pole shifts on other planets, despite great resistance to accept the idea that the same thing happens on Earth. One example of such evidence involves Tharsis, a giant volcano on the Martian equator which is known to be the largest gravity anomaly in the solar system. "Tharsis could have formed on the equator, but more likely formed elsewhere on the planet and then migrated to the equator via true polar wander because of rotational torques on its excess mass."[10] As Graham Hancock commented on other Martian evidence for the poles' previous locations on what is now the Martian equator: "If crustal displacements can happen on Mars, why not on earth?"[11] Another example is on Europa. "Curved features on Jupiter's moon Europa may indicate that its poles have wandered by almost 90°, a new study reports. Researchers believe the drastic shift in Europa's rotational axis was likely a result of the build-up of thick ice at the poles."[12] While not politically correct to say that ice building up on Earth's poles do the same thing, the same laws of physics on Mars and Europa work here too.

Perhaps the best known writer on pole shifts is Professor Charles Hapgood. His 1958 book *Earth's Shifting Crust* has a forward by Albert Einstein which lends great credibility to an argument many may assume is pseudo-science: "I frequently receive communications from people who wish to consult me concerning their unpublished ideas. It goes without saying that these ideas are very seldom possessed of scientific validity. The very first communication, however, that I received from Mr. Hapgood electrified me. His idea is original, of great simplicity, and - if it continues to prove itself of great importance to everything that is related to the history of the earth's surface... In a polar region there is continual deposition of ice, which is not symmetrically distributed about the pole... The constantly increasing centrifugal momentum produced this way will, when it reaches a certain point, produce a movement of the earth's crust over the rest of the earth's body, and this will displace the polar regions towards the equator."[13]   This forward by Albert Einstein helped readers appreciate that the idea of pole shifts may be radical and unorthodox but it is not some crackpot fantasy devoid of scientific merit. Einstein wrote in a separate letter to Hapgood dated May 8, 1953 "I find your arguments very impressive and have the impression that your hypothesis is correct. *One can hardly doubt that significant shifts of the crust of the earth have taken place repeatedly and within a short time.*"

Just how short a time? Few writers are willing to stick their necks out on this point. Hapgood said "the evidence points to a very rapid transit of the pole from its old to its new home."[14] The Wisconsin ice sheet that dominated North America in the last ice age shows no signs of scoured ground in its center. "It seems that the ice cap did not start in a small area and expand outward, but rather it started all at once over a great area." At the edges, pressure from within the center eventually pushed and scoured the ground. "This suggests a rapid transit of the pole... it was fast enough that the ice did not start growing at the coast and move inland; it started in the Hudson Bay region." Also "very remarkable evidence of the suddenness with which the ice cap was born is the fact that it contained thousands (and perhaps millions) of animals of a temperate climate, many of them frozen entire into the ice... it is evident enough, from the assemblage of species, that *the snow overwhelmed them while they were living in temperate conditions.*"[15]

The analysis of lava flows at Steens Mountain, Oregon is also telling. R.S. Coe brought this topic up in an article titled "New evidence for extraordinarily rapid change of the geomagnetic field during a reversal." The online summary tells us "Palaeomagnetic results from lava flows recording a geomagnetic polarity reversal at Steens Mountain, Oregon suggest the occurrence of brief episodes of *astonishingly rapid field change of six degrees per day*. The evidence is large, systematic variations in the direction of remanent magnetization as a function of the temperature of thermal demagnetization and of vertical position within a single flow, which are most simply explained by the hypothesis that the field was changing direction as the flow cooled."[16] Given Hapgood's assessment that a typical pole shift creates a realignment of about thirty degrees, it is interesting to note that thirty degrees of movement at an average rate of five to six degrees of latitude per day would take less than a week to occur, like the six days in which the world was created (or recreated) in Genesis. Italian naval engineer Flavio Barbiero comments on this "almost instantaneous shift of the poles" when he explains "we can completely and coherently explain what happened at the end of the Pleistocene by admitting the possibility of a shift of the poles of the same magnitude Hapgood hypothesizes, but in a much shorter time: not more than a few days."[17] Hugh A. Brown felt that a pole shift "occurs within a single day" and John White suggests that most pole shift theorists expect the event to take anywhere "from a few days to as little as a few hours."[18]

Hapgood agreed with Brown that the accumulation of ice could be a major factor in setting the Earth's crust in motion over the interior. There are quadrillions of tons of ice in Antarctica which are not centered at the South Pole, but several hundred miles off, along the meridian of 96 degrees east. Hapgood assumed that if the poles relocate again soon, they will probably move roughly thirty degrees along 96 degrees east longitude, with the new North Pole slightly northwest of Lake Baikal, just north of Mongolia.

Hapgood also acknowledged that the Antarctic ice mass of the twentieth century was much more massive than the North American ice cap had been during the North Pole's stay in Hudson Bay, and that the effects of Greenland's ice cap add to this imbalance. Still Hapgood (and Einstein) disagreed with Brown's calculations that ice alone would overcome the friction between layers below ground and set the world in motion. He felt that some other mechanism must be at play, either here in the planet's core, or a distant astronomical cause.

One possible terrestrial cause would be a diminishing magnetic field (as we have been experiencing for centuries.) Changes in the electro-magnetic field can affect the viscosity of a liquid. This means the friction between the liquid magma and the solid crust, which is what keeps the crust attached to the same position, gets weaker with the magnetic field. If it gets weak enough, the imbalance of ice will suddenly overcome friction and the crust will start moving.

For one experimental example, if an object is floating on a pool of liquid mercury and an agitator spins at the bottom, the spin is absorbed by the liquid and the object on top floats without spinning. But if a sufficiently strong electrical field is made around the container, the mercury becomes viscous; the friction between the mercury and the object increases exponentially, and the object will spin.[19] (This is like our crust now, spinning with the core.) Of course if the field is decreased the object disconnects from the surface of the mercury and will stop spinning. Likewise a diminishing terrestrial magnetic field can decrease magma viscosity, and decrease the friction between layers in the crust of the Earth. This may sound like another minor point or crackpot theory, but these ideas (and their underlying magnetohydrodynamics and plasma cosmology) were pioneered by Swedish physicist Hannes Alfven—who won the 1970 Nobel Prize in Physics, the 1971 Franklin Institute Gold Medal, and the 1971 Lomonosov Gold Medal of the USSR Academy of Sciences (among many others) perhaps we should not ignore his unconventional ideas on charged plasmas and electromagnetic fields and how they affect our planet and solar system.

Hapgood and Einstein disagreed with Brown that imbalances in the roughly 19 quadrillion tons of ice at the poles is near the point of overcoming the level of friction between layers in the crust. But contrary to common sense assumptions, global warming means moister air and more snow and ice are being deposited at the poles today—about 293 cubic miles of ice every year, with most of it in

West Antarctica. Eventually this extra weight will weaken a critical layer of rock beneath it. "Every chemical solid has a plastic limit. It will behave like a solid until pressure reaches that limit. Then it will yield suddenly and completely. It does not yield at a rate proportional to the applied force. It is almost like the breaking of the branch of a tree. When the branch breaks, it's strength is suddenly and entirely gone."[20] The compressed rock layers beneath the earth's crust could separate suddenly and entirely during a pole shift.

Sadly, the ice cap does not even have to be increasing for this to occur. Even melting ice caps which are losing mass could overcome this friction if the required friction is decreasing faster than the weight of the ice. Earth's magnetic field has been decreasing, presumably since a strong start at the last pole shift. It is known to have been approximately 300 gauss strong in the distant past. It is now about one half a gauss, and falling at an accelerating rate. If friction is holding layers in place and magnetic fields maintain that friction, it is only a matter of time before mass imbalances overcome friction and one layer slides over another.

The most likely astronomical cause of a pole shift seems to be the pulsation of the galactic center. In the early 1940s Professor Carl Seyfert noticed that roughly one in seven spiral galaxies had an active center. The central black hole in most galaxies quietly draws all nearby stars in to their deaths with an enormous pit of gravity, but about one out of seven spiral galaxies has the central black hole acting as a white hole or quasar—spewing out huge amounts of light, radiation, and matter. Sometimes these active galactic nuclei are so bright that they outshine the rest of their galaxy. Some astrophysicists began to realize these galactic centers may be a source of continuous matter creation, as if perhaps there was not one big bang, but many ongoing bangs. Some theorize that space has more than three dimensions and that once matter exists in our three dimensional reality, it attracts the building blocks of subatomic particles from a fourth spatial dimension. This would mean that the creation of more matter would occur most noticeably where existing matter is already the most dense—at the most massive black holes at galactic centers.

In 1928 British astronomer Sir James Jeans wrote "of 'singular points' at which matter is poured into our universe from some other, and entirely extraneous spatial dimension, so that, to a denizen of our universe, they appear as points at which matter is being continually created."[21] In 1958 Soviet astrophysicist V. Ambartsumian suggested "that galactic nuclei periodically eject large masses of matter" and "that these birth events are quite violent, involving giant cosmic ray-producing explosions." More recently, galactic centers have been referred to as "pockets of creation" and "embryos" of creation by astrophysicists and cosmologists like William McCrea, Fred Hoyle, and J. Narlikar.[22] This would explain many problems in the "big bang" theory; for example, why the universe seems to be expanding everywhere, and not just away from one central point.

Regardless of whether or not matter is brought into existence in galactic cores, a very important realization on Seyfert galaxies came about a generation after Carl Seyfert. Dr. Paul LaViolette realized that it is not that one in seven spiral galaxies is a Seyfert galaxy with an active center, but that one in seven are active right now. These galaxies all have periods of activity at their cores. He found evidence that our own Milky Way has a periodically active galactic nuclei which violently spews out radiation and matter roughly every 10,000 years. (There are also less intense minor outbursts on a more frequent basis.) Dr. LaViolette describes spherical layers of dust and light expanding out from the galactic center, and there is evidence that such highly radioactive dust clouds have passed through our solar system repeatedly with more expanding outwards and on their way towards us all the time. Another author notes "The solar system has only just emerged from a dusty strip a mere 10,000 years ago."[23] There is dust entering our solar system right now from the direction of the center of the galaxy, but our sun's solar wind normally lets very little in.

Dr. LaViolette explains that stars are greatly affected by these periodic phases of galactic core activity. Stars near the threshold of going supernova are often pushed over the edge in groups as they are hit by the gravity waves and other radiation. We can date the last major galactic core explosion because of this effect. Take the year we witness a supernova and subtract the number of years it took the light from that supernova to reach Earth. Subtract again for the number of light-years between the supernova and the galactic center. Repeat the process for several recorded supernova. We now know the year of the galactic core explosion, assuming that our estimates of interstellar distances are accurate and that many supernova give the same result. They do apparently flare into novae in bunches, and the last such event was not that far back.

Most stars are stable and not near the tipping point at which a blast will push them into a supernova—but even stable stars often flare up to a much lesser degree because of the dust cloud that is pushed into them. Our sun has a solar wind, an outward pressure of gas and radiation that keeps our solar system clear of most incoming particles. Other stars do the same thing, and the majority of interstellar dust is kept out of most star systems. But when a blast of energy from a galactic core explosion overwhelms a star's much weaker ability to push dust away, a cloud of dust envelops them. The dust traps heat and other radiation and helps convey electrical discharges.

Stars under these conditions are referred to as T-Tauri stars, which are like our sun, but have lots of dust in their equatorial planes and emit more infrared (heat) radiation. They also flare a lot, with solar flares 100-1000 times as powerful as any solar flares we have ever seen. Such stars would also emit approximately 100,000 times more X-rays, and ten times as much ultraviolet radiation. Commenting on previous occasions during which such cosmic dust clouds would have enveloped our solar system, Dr. LaViolette wrote that "Cosmic dust that was pushed into the solar system by a passing superwave would have activated the Sun and caused it to behave like a T-Tauri star."[24]

T-Tauri stars, with strong flares and energized electromagnetic fields, could wreak havoc on the planets orbiting them. Planets would likely experience relative cold and darkness at first, as dust blocks sunlight, followed by a buildup of heat trapped within the dark dust cloud, and finally a stellar blowout of solar flaring when such conditions finally overwhelm the system's sun. Dust clouds that had

99

accumulated near the inner planets would be pushed outwards by such solar blasts; some dust would become trapped in orbits around the outer planets as rings. Saturn has the most prominent rings and astronomers have been revising the controversial age of that ring system downwards since the 1970s. Some scientists believe the rings around the outer planets have existed not for hundreds of millions of years, but only about ten thousand years, suggesting that some evidence indicates a cosmic event that formed them recently.

A superwave's dust cloud would also be accompanied by radiation and gravity waves. These could cause unusual magnetic reversals and tidal forces, and in conjunction with the imbalance of accumulated ice at the Earth's poles—might lead to a crustal displacement—a pole shift—as described by Dr. Hapgood.

Another astrophysicist who once corresponded with me regularly is Dr. Gary C. Vezzoli. He told me that he (and others) had conducted experiments establishing that gravity has a source in external particles, possibly muon neutrinos, and that momenta transfer from these causes gravitational attraction. "In an external particle model of gravity, astrophysical bodies such as the Sun, moon, and planets then can be expected to interfere with a stream of generally omnidirectional particles and cause local anomalies measurable at Earth."[25] He explains how gravity is not constant, and that graviton particle flux varies with many factors including time of year or orientation "relative to a system of fixed stars."[26] Variations in gravity alter the rate of radioactive decay, the speed of chemical reactions, and other processes.

These claims may strike readers as far-fetched theories but there are arguments between physicists over who proved these effects first. In the April 2008 edition of "Progress in Physics" one scientist (Simon Schnoll) specifically refutes Dr. Vezzoli's claims to have discovered such things, and points out that although his own early publications were primarily in the Soviet Union (and hence largely unknown to the West) he first pointed out these astronomically induced gravitational deviations and their effects on reactions on Earth in the 1980s. We may not be concerned with who discovered the truth first—but we should respect the fact that astronomical alignments affect gravity on Earth enough to have measurable effects. Most interestingly, such variation in gravity affects the rate at which liquid iron molecules solidify on the surface of the planet's solid core, and this affects the overall polarity of the planet, its geodynamo, and potentially the direction of the Earth's rotation.

Like any other group of molecules, iron can structure itself in many different lattices determined by pressure, temperature, and gravity—with very little space between atoms when these variables are high enough. Iron's "d5 transient configuration should be very dominant" at "the earth's outer-core/inner-core boundary... constantly undergoing Fe(solid)->><-Fe(liquid) phase transformation." As the planet slowly cools the solid core slowly grows, bringing more liquid molecules into the polarity of the solid d5 lattice—this will periodically "perturb the earth's dynamo action so as to switch the geomagnetic majority spin orientation, and hence cause a flip in the existing polarity." In summary, Dr. Vezzoli measured iron solidification during an astronomical lineup (in this case, of Earth, the Sun, Jupiter, and Saturn) and "The results indicate that the gravitational effect tends to alter solidification at the core boundary and assists in inducing the polarity reversal."[27]

Dr. Vezzoli never specifically said anything about a crustal displacement of the Earth's surface, only a shift or reversal of the magnetic field. But magnetic flips may help make a crustal displacement possible. As described to us in the "Pancasiddhantika" (written down in India by Varahamihira roughly 1600 years ago) "The round ball of the earth, composed of the five elements, abides in space in the midst of the starry sphere, like a piece of iron suspended between magnets."[28] It is very easy to nudge such an object suspended between magnets, especially a spherical object with no natural preference for one axis over another. Magnetically, it is easy to make a planet realign itself.

Magnetic pole shifts by themselves, could be relatively uneventful, if there were no accompanying crustal displacement. But "studies have found that mass extinctions of land animals... closely correlate with reversals of the earth's magnetic field. Although geomagnetic reversals themselves could not be the cause of these extinctions..."[29]

something else that does cause great destruction often seems to occur at the same time as a magnetic shift or reversal. These also coincide with "episodes of high cosmic ray intensity" and "times of rapid climatic change"[30] which could all be explained by a shifting of the Earth's surface over the interior.

There is less hesitation to acknowledge the possibility of cosmic events causing a pole shift from Dr. Paul LaViolette, who suggests the possibility that galactic core "superwaves periodically jerk the earth's axis" and that "perhaps the Earth's precessional period has become entrained by the heartbeat of the galactic core."[31] If the gravity wave Dr. LaViolette expects from the galactic center passes us soon, the effects could be extreme. (For comparison, the "relatively small" gravity wave from a supernova that hit Earth in December 2004 is believed to be responsible for triggering the Indonesian earthquake and tsunami that killed approximately a quarter million people.)

When considering the terrestrial effects of gravity from distant astronomical objects we should note that the largest measured deviation from normal gravity measured by Dr. Vezzoli came during the 35 seconds in which one particular layer of the sun was directly between Jupiter and Earth—the corona. As Dr. Vezzoli clarified to me in a personal email on 9/5/09:

"Because the Corona is so very hot is why I saw the dip in gravity. I did not measure gravitational effects beyond a few minutes into the syzygy, because my supervisor would not allow me to stay all night at the laboratory to analyze the event continuously. The corona region has a major change in temperature and density -- but I believe that relative to neutrino scattering, the temperature is the important factor. We have shown that G changes as a function of temperature according to $G=G'(1 + aT)$, where "a" is a very small constant of the order of 1×10^{-6}. This is startling information because the equivalence principle has always held that free fall is independent of other parameters such as temperature. The fact is that free fall is quantized, and is NOT continuous, but occurs in quantum levels, and appropriate jitters and jumps. G is also affected by phase, and by shape … i.e. by entropy. Nothing, Dave, is as we thought it was. GCV"

The important point to understand is that during an astronomical alignment, when a heavenly body (such as Jupiter) passes behind the sun's corona as viewed from Earth, the gravitational tug from that heavenly body is suddenly scattered and eliminated. Though tiny in comparison to the total gravitational field of the universe, the difference is sudden, and measurable. Imagine a complicated and three dimensional game of tug-of-war, with a hundred people pulling you in different directions with ropes. One suddenly stops pulling. You would feel a small but sudden jerk in the opposite direction. Such jerking has had noticeable effects on the movement of pendulums during eclipses, as noted by Nobel prizewinner Maurice Allais, Saxl and Allen, and other researchers. But the "Allais Effect" is controversial and has not led to any mainstream reevaluation of gravity. None the less if our planet's ice caps are borderline critical, just at the point where mass imbalances are about ready to initiate a pole shift anyway, gravitational cosmic jerking could be the straw that breaks the camel's back.

On Judgment Day in 2019, Jupiter will appear to be moving in and out from directly behind the sun's corona, and the associated gravitational jerks from such a lineup may be the very reason Jupiter is referred to as the scepter that touches a king as he takes power. It is also possible that when our galactic center becomes active, the same type of celestial on/off switch could jerk our system whenever one of the many billions of stars near the galactic center happens to pass directly in between that black hole and the Earth. And if incoming cosmic dust makes our sun overheat and flare up like a T-Tauri star, then a significantly thicker corona could form, multiplying the likelihood of a gravity-altering alignment through it.

Going back a few topics to Professor Hapgood - his general argument is that there is evidence that the slow and gradual geological processes we are taught—such as continental drift and plate tectonics—are not the correct explanation for ice ages or a great many other things. He explains a pole shift as a long period of stresses in the crust building up, like the bending of a tree branch, followed by the sudden crack and release as the branch, or the Earth's crust finally gives way. Friction is suddenly overcome when motion begins, but unlike a breaking tree branch, the tangential centrifugal force (centripetal force) of ice increases dramatically as the old pole moves towards the equator. Any pole shift should start slowly and then accelerate faster and faster as the imbalance of off-center ice approaches the equator. An imbalance starting just five degrees from the pole has five times the force when it is twenty-five degrees away from the pole.[32] Friction and resistance to slippage between layers in the crust also decreases as temperature in the rock layers increase. The initially slow movement causes friction and heat from layers grinding over each other, then higher temperatures decrease viscosity as momentum increases.[33] For these reasons the process of slippage would get faster and faster after the pole shift starts.

In one meeting between Hapgood, Einstein, and Dr. Campbell, "Dr. Einstein asked Mr. Hapgood what objections geologists had been making to the theory. Mr. Hapgood replied that it was principally a question of the number of such movements; Urry's evidence would imply four such displacements at irregular intervals during the last 50,000 years. Dr. Einstein replied that this seemed to be a large number. However, he said... The gradualistic notions common in geology were, in his opinion, merely a habit of mind, and were not necessarily justified by the empirical data."[34]

Dr. Urry had recently published data on radioactive-dating of organic materials from sediment off the Pacific coast of Antarctica and had concluded that temperate climactic conditions had existed repeatedly, as the red clay sediment identified with cold periods was repeatedly interrupted by layers of highly calcerous ooze full of organic remains. There were also substantial changes in the size of pebbles and gravel indicating a shift from flowing rivers to frozen glaciers scraping the ground. *Dating sediment under the Ross Sea indicates it was ice free just 6,000 years ago.*[35] Research done through the University of Illinois also concludes that "sedimentary core samples show that *rivers were running to the sea in 4,000 B.C.*"[36] "The precise accuracy of the dating is less important than the evidence that, in very recent time, there was deposition of temperate type sediment in the Ross Sea off the Antarctic coast."[37]

Dr. Hapgood continued to work on his theory until 1982, when just before his death, he wrote to Rand Flem-Ath "I have convincing evidence of a whole cycle of civilization in America and Antarctica, suggesting advanced levels of science."[38]   (If only he had not been hit by a car just before publishing more!) Long after Urry and Hapgood passed away, evidence continues to be revealed. In 1988 Hartmut Heinrich made a discovery in ocean sediment cores containing "unusual layers recurring at 5,000 to 10,000 year intervals." Mostly rock grains of continental origin, "deposited so suddenly... as would have occurred if large amounts of sediment were dumped in a matter of hours."[39]

Hapgood's *Maps of the Ancient Sea Kings* focused on an analysis of ancient maps and concluded that most maps in the last thousand years have been copied from far older source maps with remarkable quality and similarity. He wrote of "a worldwide civilization, the mapmakers of which mapped virtually the entire globe with a uniform general level of technology, with similar methods, equal knowledge of mathematics, and probably the same sorts of instruments."[40] Specific maps were analyzed in great detail, such as the Piri Re'is map of 1513 and the Orontus Finneus map of 1532.

One interesting problem with maps of this era is the name of the western continents in the New World. "America" was first written on a map by Martin Waldesseuller in 1507.[41] But why are these continents called the Americas? In high school we are taught that an unimportant cartographer named Amerigo Vespucci had half the world named after him. Wouldn't it have made more sense to name the continents North and South Columbia, or Ferdinand and Isabella? One thing we are not taught is that the Knights Templar already had a tradition about a land to the west called Merica, (L' Merica among the dominant French Templars.) Many believe the Templars found ancient maps of the world in the remains of Solomon's Temple and gained some of their wealth from trade across the Atlantic before the rest of Europe knew "Merica" existed. It is also interesting that the dominant empire in "Merica," at the latitude European ships could drift to even without steering, was

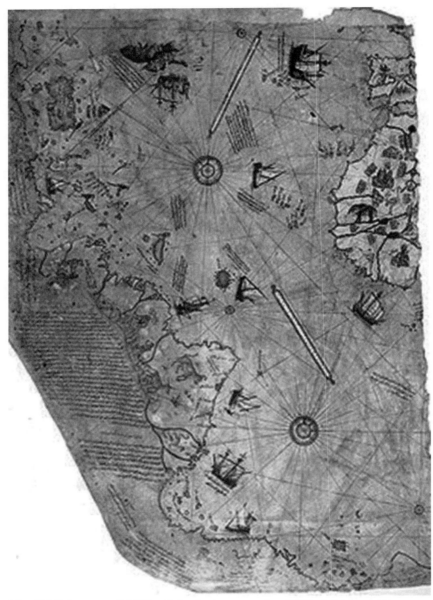

The Piri Reis map of 1513. Cuba looks warped and tilted, because the map projection does not locate "North" above the map as we normally would today. The direction of North depends on what part of the map one looks at.

populated by the "Mexica," (pronounced "meh-hee-cah") who we know today as Aztecs or Mexicans.

Additional evidence of Templar activity in North America abounds. One of the most fascinating pieces of supporting evidence centers on Michigan's Upper Peninsula, where an estimated 500,000 to 1,000,000 tons of copper were mined from approximately 3,000 B.C. to 1,200 B.C. This may have provided the copper used for the Bronze Age in Europe. But equally fascinating is that the mines were restarted about 2,200 years later—and that another 2,000 tons of copper were mined until approximately 1,320 A.D.[42] Given the lack of precision of archeological dating, 1320 is virtually the same as 1307, when the Templars were disbanded.

On the Orontus Finneus world map of 1532, the main problem is that it shows Antarctica with a remarkably accurate shape, and Antarctica was not discovered until the year 1820. The second major problem was the scale—Antarctica looked too big, practically touching South America. Analysis showed that if the map exchanged one circle for another, and replaced Finneus' Antarctic circle with the 80th degree of latitude, the continent's size would be correct. (Finneus must have copied an earlier map of Antarctica he couldn't read correctly, and misinterpreted one circle for another.) A third problem is that West Antarctica's features are drawn much more accurately than East Antarctica's. Since the continent's west was temperate during the previous alignment of the Earth's crust, but the eastern half was still polar—it seems the original map data came from expeditions made prior to the last pole shift when West Antarctica would have been as habitable as Scotland or Sweden. Such expeditions must have taken place more than 5,000 years ago—possibly 10-15,000 years back.

Professor Hapgood contacted Air Force cartographers regarding this map (and the more famous Piri Reis map of 1513) and was told in a reply from Captain Lorenzo Burroughs of the Strategic Air Command in 1961 that "Maps sent to us by you presented a delightful challenge, for it was not readily conceivable that they could be so accurate without being forged... [But] *we have concluded that both of these maps were compiled from accurate source maps... made*

107

before the present Antarctic ice cap... The original source maps (compiled in remote antiquity) were prepared when Antarctica was presumably free of ice... Further, the shape given to the Antarctic continent suggests the possibility, if not the probability, that the original source maps were compiled on a stereographic or gnomonic type of projection (involving the use of spherical trigonometry). We are convinced that the findings made by you and your associates are valid, and that they raise extremely important questions affecting geology and ancient history..."[43]

Some people have brought up the possibility of ancient aliens making these maps; to such suggestions Hapgood once replied that the map is on: "a cartographic projection unsuitable for the polar regions. Aerial photography would have yielded a more accurate

Professor Hapgood made a line drawing of coastlines on the Piri Reis map. As Piri Reis admitted his map was made from copies of many ancient maps, and the lower portion seems to represent Antarctica, we might assume that ancient mapmakers surveyed western Antarctica before it had an ice cap.

map… These are the errors of earth men."[44] What Hapgood did not emphasize was the likelihood that Antarctica was not in a polar region when the original map projection was chosen.

This would also explain the Bauche map of Antarctica from 1737 which showed similar details that were not officially discovered until the twentieth century. And nothing but prehistoric mapmaking with ancient maps being copied into modern times can explain the land bridge between Alaska and Siberia shown on the Hadji Ahmed map of North America from 1559. Not only is the entire North American continent shown fairly accurately, when its coasts had not yet been thoroughly explored by 1559—but the long theorized bridge of land called "Beringia" across which Asiatic peoples are believed to have crossed into North America approximately 12,000 years ago is detailed on the map as a real place. The existence of this connection between Asia and North America merely requires that sea level was several hundred feet lower in that location when the map was drawn, presumably prior to the last shift in the Earth's crust.

Dr. Hapgood also had his students analyze the map of Turkish Admiral Re'is. The class noticed that Piri Re'is map of 1513 had proportional errors between latitude and longitude. (The same type of error was spread evenly across the map.) They concluded that the map used Eratosthenes' ancient estimate for the Earth's circumference, which was about 4.5% off. Eratosthenes' circumference was actually correct, at 252,000 stadia, but later mapmakers may have substituted slightly different measurements such as Egyptian stadia for Attic stadia. Correcting for this, longitudinal errors were almost completely eliminated. Hapgood and his students concluded that Greek cartographers in Alexandria had made the original error when compiling their world map out of much earlier source maps that had been drawn accurately with a correct circumference.[45]

Tradition tells us that Eratosthenes knew of a well at Syene (now Aswan) where the sun was directly overhead at noon on the summer solstice and cast no shadow. Another well in Alexandria allegedly had a shadow of seven degrees twelve minutes of arc at the same time, which is conveniently one fiftieth of a circle. Multiplying the distance of 5040 stades between the two locations by fifty, he allegedly deduced the planet's circumference to be 252,000 stades.

"But Eratosthenes could not possibly have discovered that fact by the methods attributed to him. Syene is not on the tropic of Cancer where the midsummer sun stands overhead at noon. Nor is it on the same meridian as Alexandria which is three degrees of longitude further west, so the distance between the two has no bearing on the problem of measuring round the world. It was also impossible to precisely measure the distance between Syene and Alexandria with a camel-drawn caravan following a meandering path along the Nile River. Since Eratosthenes gave the right answer to that problem, but with the wrong proofs, it must be assumed that his information did not come from scientific research but from some other source. In the Alexandria Library..." he probably found ancient data and invented a faulty method for how he deduced them himself.[46]

Eratosthenes was not a stupid man; he was a mathematician, geographer, astronomer, and the third curator of the Library of Alexandria. He is credited with the invention of geography, latitude and longitude, leap days, and many other ideas. It seems unlikely that his ego goaded him into claiming discoveries that were not his own. Perhaps there was very ancient knowledge he wished to perpetuate, but was limited by the rules of an initiated brotherhood which does not allow anyone to openly explain everything to the masses. Is it more likely that he didn't understand how his ancient predecessors determined the Earth's size, or that he intentionally gave us a faulty explanation, to encourage wise readers to question the explanation?

Did Eratosthenes hope we would eventually notice that 5040 was the key number in Plato's measurements for an ideal city, or that the "5040" stades between the two locations is 1*2*3*4*5*6*7 and is also a number divisible by 8, 9, and 10... which is very convenient for mathematics and easy divisibility—and that stades themselves were a measurement based on the size of our planet? (Feet are as well. Based on an ancient estimate of equatorial circumference, $1/1000^{th}$ of a degree is 365.243 feet, and there are 365.242 days in a year.)[47] Eratosthenes certainly knew that ancient measurements had long and short versions (as his circumference was, as Hapgood noted, off by about 4.5%) and which one to choose. For example, does one choose the Earth's polar circumference, equatorial circumference, or average circumference? And the stade itself, like most other units of ancient measure, has a long and short definition, as navigators determined that a nautical mile equals one minute of latitude, but with one measure at ten degrees north and a shorter version at fifty degrees north. If Eratosthenes didn't understand these facts he would not have been put in charge of the world's greatest library.

He certainly would not have been able to tell us that the distance to the sun is "of stadia myriads 400 and 80,000," as he did in the "Preparatio Evangelica." 400 + 80,000 = 80,400; and a myriad = 10,000, so 804,000,000 stadia... times approximately 184.9 meters per Attic stadia... equals 148,659,600 kilometers—or 92,372,793 miles. NASA's current answer is that our elliptical orbit makes this distance to the sun vary between 147,098,074 and 149,597,888 kilometers.

No known method of calculating the distance between the Earth and the Sun was even thought up until Edmund Halley described a method using parallax calculations and observations of the transit of Venus across the sun. This method required good telescopes, accurate clocks, and careful observation around the world. By 1771 this method had given an estimate of 153 million kilometers, far less accurate than the number from Eratosthenes. By 1874 Simon Newcomb revised this down to 149.59 million kilometers; a great improvement, yet still less accurate than the ancient answer. Our civilization finally bested the ancients in the 20th century with data from radar and satellites. But the fact that someone thousands of years ago could so accurately determine the distance to the sun (and moon: 780,000 stadia) raises many questions about just how advanced ancient technology may have been.

The bottom line is that the ancients had determined the Earth's size accurately and based a system of measurement on it which was used around the world. But something interrupted that ancient civilization's ability to pass the knowledge down intact between the formation of the system and the height of Greek civilization. Eratosthenes apparently wanted to pass this knowledge down to

111

future generations and make sure it wasn't lost for a long time again, but he also wanted to protect the mysteries of the brotherhood, so he gave us accurate measurements without a legitimate explanation of how or when the measurements were obtained.

Going back to the details of the Piri Re'is map, it also shows some (as of 1513) undiscovered areas, such as the west coast of the Americas, and Antarctica. The big problem is the level of detail in West Antarctica—Queen Maud Land in particular. Modern use of radar and sonar shows that the details are not just random jagged lines—the mountains and valleys drawn there accurately represent subglacial features. After being asked for a professional assessment of the Piri Re'is map, Lt. Colonel Harold Ohlmeyer (of the U.S. Air Force 5th Reconnaissance Technical Squadron) wrote to Hapgood on July 6, 1960:

"Your request of evaluation of certain unusual features of the Piri Reis map of 1513 by this organization has been reviewed.

The claim that the lower part of the map portrays the Princess Martha Coast of Queen Maud Land, Antarctica, and the Palmer Peninsular, is reasonable. We find that this is the most logical and in all probability the correct interpretation of the map.

The geographical detail shown in the lower part of the map agrees very remarkably with the results of the seismic profile made across the top of the ice-cap by the Swedish-British Antarctic Expedition of 1949.

This indicates the coastline had been mapped before it was covered by the ice-cap. The ice-cap in this region is now about a mile thick.

We have no idea how the data on this map can be reconciled with the supposed state of geographical knowledge in 1513."[48]

The map was apparently copied from one originally drawn before the formation of the ice cap—before the last shifting of the poles. This means there was an advanced civilization at least equal to 18th century Europe—mapping Antarctica a minimum of 6,000 years ago. Other authors with even more impressive technological evidence make even bolder claims: "The standard of science in remote prehistoric times was at least as high at that which has been achieved in this [twentieth] century."[49] As for problematic maps, they are not limited to Antarctica. The Zeno map of 1380 shows subglacial features of mountains and rivers in Greenland. There are other similar, detailed maps of areas as far away as China. Another interesting finding is the use of spherical trigonometry in the ancient maps.[50] All maps distort the three dimensional shape of the globe to portray it on a two dimensional paper. But the distortions on most ancient maps shows an accurate use of spherical trigonometry. Was this complicated branch of mathematics also in regular use over 6,000 years ago?

Last but not least, consider Christopher Columbus. He was way off estimating latitude; for example, he thought Puerto Gibara was at 42 degrees north, when it is really 21 degrees north. This is a huge error for an experienced navigator, but it is understandable if his analysis of latitudes were heavily influenced by the misinterpretation of a copy of an ancient map in his hands. Assuming he had a map like the one Piri Reis had, using an unfamiliar projection, it could lead someone to think the entire Caribbean was further north.

The US Army used such a projection centered on Cairo in WWII; it shows the Earth as if one were looking down from above Egypt. "North" is almost irrelevant on such a map, as the direction varies from one part of the map to another. Islands like Cuba and Haiti are oriented lengthwise up and down, instead of the usual left to right, and someone unfamiliar with the map orientation, or the Americas, could—as the map had no lines of latitude—easily but mistakenly conclude that such an ancient map had north at the top, and that Cuba is oriented north to south, and that the whole Caribbean is much farther north than it really is.

Columbus may have had an ancient map with a projection like the one above and may have assumed north was above the top of the map, not somewhere closer to the middle. In Columbus' own log for October 4, 1492 (while still approaching the Caribbean) he wrote "In the spheres which I have seen and in the Mappae Mundi (map of the world) it is in this region."[51] The map believed to be Columbus' world map did resurface again centuries later and some believe that astronomical clues on the map indicate that it may have been drawn up originally around 3800 B.C., or even several millennia before that.[52]

It may not be taught in high school history classes, but it is well substantiated that medieval explorers were basing expeditions to unknown lands based on ancient maps from many recently rediscovered sources. Crusaders had made rediscoveries of ancient knowledge in the Middle East, and "the Knights Templar saw themselves as the inheritors of ancient knowledge that went back to Atlantis."[53] Marco Polo brought back a world map from China. The fall of Constantinople led to an exodus of scholars, along with the ancient contents of great libraries. In 1432 the Portuguese Prince Henry the Navigator began sending captains out to claim lands he saw on ancient maps. When he first sent Goncalo Velho to claim the Azores, the captain returned to tell him the islands were not found and must not exist. Prince Henry replied: "There is an island there, go back and find it."[54] The search would have been easier if Europeans could calculate latitude and longitude as well as the original mapmakers, but much knowledge had been lost.

Maps using advanced trigonometry and cartography are not the only evidence of a technologically advanced civilization before our own; entire books have been written describing specific examples. One such book is *The Mysteries of the Great Cross of Hendaye: Alchemy and the End of Time* by Jay Weidner and Vincent Bridges. They describe a strange stone monument in a little French town called Hendaye, in the Basque country on the border between France and Spain. Carving stone is not in itself high technology, but the message on the monument, when decoded as suggested, reveals an ancient understanding of astronomical processes and cycles of destruction.

This monument received almost no attention until a chapter was devoted to it in an occult book by written by one "Fulcanelli," which might just be a pseudonym for a group of initiates who wish to pass down arcane knowledge under a name meaning "sons of Vulcan." (Just as 1778's "The Federalist Papers" include essays written by Hamilton, Madison, and others using the pseudonym "Publius", in honor of a Roman consul.) "Fulcanelli" wrote *Le Mystere des Cathedrales* in 1926, and explained that ancient wisdom was "hidden" openly, built

114

into the stone cathedrals of Europe. If we aren't initiated into ancient wisdom, we are too dumb to appreciate information right in front of us.

Fulcanelli said that the alchemists alleged goal of creating gold is really a thinly veiled cover story for creating a golden age. He explains that there are cosmic disasters which happen in a predictable cycle, and that secret societies have been passing down knowledge of such things for thousands of years. When the next disaster comes, such societies will be ready and able to lead unprepared survivors into a new golden age. Fulcanelli indicated that the most recent physical evidence that these societies still exist and still actively pursue this goal is a stone carving outside a church in Hendaye.

Fulcanelli explains that knowledge of the location of the galactic center is crucial for determining the timing of the next catastrophe, and that this "monument pointed to a specific time period, the intersection point of several celestial cycles," regarding the galactic center, also describing a "double catastrophe" for the world which Weidner and Bridges interpret as Judgment Day.[55] Those authors also indicate there are "politics of secrecy surrounding the knowledge of this oncoming celestial event"[56] and that factions among the secret societies have been fighting over how to handle things for at least a thousand years. (This claim should not be glossed over. If you happen to be familiar with the rumors leaking out from various intelligence agencies in recent years, you already know how the elite plan to handle it.) Weidner and Bridges agree with Fulcanelli that an advanced and ancient wisdom regarding these secrets are encoded on this monument, another leak of secrecy waiting for someone wise enough to understand its message of cataclysm in the early 21st century.

There are countless examples of advanced ancient technology which are far more impressive than the stone monument to the end of the age at Hendaye. It is not within the scope of this book to cover the topic adequately, but merely to review a few of the most glaring examples—just enough to at least acknowledge that civilizations often appear to rise to great technologically advanced heights before they fall. Most of us were taught that ours is the first great human civilization; that our ancestors only recently progressed

Images of aircraft carved in granite at the Osirion Temple at Abydos, Egypt

out of the Stone Age for the first time. But there is evidence that some of our most ancient cultures like India and Sumer and Egypt are legacies—that there was something far greater before them which was destroyed, and that the societies we read about in our schoolbooks were attempts to recreate civilization from the remains of what came before. This is not unexpected to those of us who understand the cycles of destruction, and we should regard evidence of "modern" scientific achievements in the distant past as a warning that our own current civilization could also be obliterated.

We already read about an advanced people who were destroyed in the "Popul Vuh," in which the Maya described some of their abilities: "They saw, and could see instantly far, they succeeded in knowing all that there is in the World. When they looked, they instantly saw all around them and they contemplated in turn the arch of the heaven and the round face of the Earth. The things hidden (in the distance) they saw all, without first having to move; at once they saw the World... great was their wisdom."[57] Could they possibly have used devices like television to achieve this? If our technology were destroyed today, how might our less advanced descendants describe our achievements?

While the ability to perform an abortion is not necessarily "advanced" technology we know our ancestors could do it and how they worded it, describing the ancient ability to perform "the smitings of the embryo in the womb, that it may pass away."[58] The ancient Chinese wrote about a "magic mirror" used to diagnose illnesses. This mirror illuminated the bones and organs of the patient's body—was it an ancient version of an X-ray machine? There are also many stone carvings (sadly, without words to explain them) as on the Osirion Temple at Abydos in Egypt which has carvings that look remarkably like modern military craft. In 1987 Dr. Ruth McKinley-Hover noticed these carvings look like "a helicopter, a rocket, a flying saucer, and a jet plane."[59] Other people see a submarine too... none of which "belong" on an ancient Egyptian temple wall carved into granite.

If the images below represent something other than ancient machines like those we have today, there should be a logical and simple explanation from the Egyptologists someday... But the only relevant quote seems to be: "There is evidence for the existence of a strong tradition of flight in the ancient world with or without the help of airships."[60] There are also many small gold objects from ancient times that seem to be representations of aircraft. There may be many more we don't even recognize if they don't match our own civilization's aircraft... but many such small golden airplanes, only one to two inches long, have been found in northern South America. Although they are often dated to be almost two thousand years old, they appear to have many features of modern jet fighters, including delta shaped wings, landing gear, airfoils, and cockpits.

Most impressive of all are the writings of ancient India, which take about two hundred pages to review the details of vimana (aircraft) covering topics like construction, materials, fuel consumption, speed, altitude, pilot training, control mechanisms, recommendations for food and clothing on long flights, and eavesdropping on the occupants inside enemy vimana. The "Yanta Sarvasva" has a section "Vaimanika Prakarana" with eight chapters on aeronautics, including three types of flying craft: local, long-distance, and interplanetary.[61] There are 113 subdivisions of machines, but all share basic characteristics.

One part tells us "Strong and durable must the body be made, like a great flying bird, of light material. Inside it one must place the Mercury-engine with its iron heating apparatus beneath. By means

Shown above, one of many "airplane" pendants in the Bogota Gold Museum.

of the power latent in the mercury which sets the driving whirlwind in motion, a man sitting inside may travel a great distance in the sky… Four strong mercury containers must be built into the interior structure. When these have been heated by controlled fire from the iron containers, the vimana develops thunder-power through the mercury…"[62]

Interesting rumors state that German efforts towards developing a flying disc during World War II focused on a mercury plasma engine, perhaps of similar design. A more recent rumor claims the American government has "the TR-3B Triangular Anti-Gravity Craft… Built and tested in area S-4 inside Area 51 in Nevada. Supposedly [this] uses a heated mercury vortex to offset gravity."[63]

Despite modern appreciation of the uses of mercury plasma, author V. R. Ramachandra Dikshitar lamented: "There are numerous illustrations in our vast Puranic and epic literature to show how well and wonderfully the ancient Indians conquered the air. To glibly characterize everything found in this literature as imaginary and summarily dismiss it as unreal has been the practice of both Western and Eastern scholars…" Commenting on vimana texts in the "Vimanika Shastra," he says: "In the recently published

118

Samarangana Sutradhara of Bhoja, a whole chapter of about 230 stanzas is devoted to the principles of construction underlying the various flying machines and other engines used for military and other purposes. The various advantages of using machines, especially flying ones, are given elaborately. Special mention is made for their attacking visible as well as invisible objects..." and the author also compares the use of the mohanastra weapon (the "arrow of unconsciousness") to modern gases and weapons.[64]

The ancient Indians also described divisions of time down to a 300,000,000th of a second—a scale only needed for subatomic particle reactions. Which leads us to an interesting description of "the Brahmaastra," what sounds like a nuclear weapon used in the "Mahabharata," written many thousands of years ago:

"Gurkha, flying a swift and powerful vimana, hurled a single projectile charged with the power of the Universe. An incandescent column of smoke and flame, as bright as ten thousand suns, rose with all its splendor... a perpendicular explosion with its billowing smoke clouds... the cloud of smoke rising after its first explosion formed into expanding circles like the opening of giant parasols...

It was an unknown weapon, an iron thunderbolt, a gigantic messenger of death, which reduced to ashes the entire race of the Vrishnis and the Andhakas. The corpses were so burned as to be unrecognizable. Hair and nails fell out; Pottery broke without apparent cause, and the birds turned white... After a few hours all foodstuffs were infected... to escape from this fire the soldiers threw themselves in streams to wash themselves and their equipment...

Clouds roared upward, showering dust and gravel... The earth shook, scorched by the terrible violent heat of this weapon. Elephants burst into flame and ran to and fro in a frenzy... other animals crumpled to the ground and died..."

There are regions in northwest India and southeast Pakistan which even today suffer from high rates of birth defects and cancer, and background radiation levels fifty times the normal rate. Ancient buildings in that area show other evidence of nuclear blasts like stones fused together from intense heat on one side. The ancient city of Mohenjo-Daro has many odd black stones which have been found to be melted pottery at the same street level where irradiated skeletons lie on the ground as if crowds of people were instantaneously killed.

Robert Oppenheimer, father of the United States' atomic bomb program during World War II, was once asked by a student at a college lecture "Was the atomic test at Alamagordo the first nuclear blast?" The student was asking if any secret tests came before the first official one. But Oppenheimer answered: "Yes, in modern times." Did he know something the uninitiated masses don't know?

These examples of advanced ancient technology indicate that civilizations as advanced as ours have been destroyed before. Professor Hapgood was focused on maps and concluded that a prior civilization had mapped the Earth under different conditions than the surface arrangements we know today. He also did research on topics to confirm his theory. The analysis of coastal sediments has already been detailed above. Another topic is soil analysis. Dr. George W. Bain noted that various chemical reactions caused by sunlight in soil vary with latitude. Rocks formed of these distinct land and sea sediments give a permanent rock record of the latitude at which they formed, with polar circles of similar rocks, and temperate and tropical bands around the Earth.

Bain concluded that rocks from hundreds of millions of years ago formed in bands chemically similar to the patterns found today, except that the directions of old climatic zones have no relation to today's equator: "fixity of the axis of the earth relative to the elastic outer shell just is not valid."[65] Bain's soil analysis showed that many lands have soil formed far from their current locations; for example the New Siberian Islands, now in the arctic, had clearly been equatorial. He also decided that "the recurrent change in position of these rings through geologic time can be accounted for now only on the basis of change in the position of the elastic shell of the earth relatively to its axis of rotation."[66] Hapgood added that "frequent changes in climate have had profound effects on the formation of sedimentary rocks... Very seldom can deposits be found that indicate with any certainty the uninterrupted deposition of more than a few thousand years. On the other hand, innumerable cases of conditions interrupted after a few thousand years can be proved."[67] Dr. Bain further speculated that there should be other indications of original latitude in sediments, such as the shells of sea crustaceans and corals. He did not know that a Chinese scientist had already been studying this same issue for decades.

Professor Ting Ying H. Ma was an oceanographer at the University of Fukien, China. After many years spent studying fossil corals, he concluded that several total displacements of the whole outer mantle must have taken place. He of course noticed that corals some distance from the equator experienced seasonal temperature changes and that there were seasonal differences in their rates of growth. Coral cells developed in the slightly cooler winter are small and dense in comparison to the larger and more porous cells of the summer. These two rings make up the year's growth and can be found in any skeletal remains of coral which had lived away from the equator. Likewise total annual coral growth within the range of coral species' mostly tropical habitat was found to increase with proximity to the equator. Corals in cooler waters grew less in total, and seasonal variation in growth rates increased with distance from the equator. As Ma studied the coral data for past eras, it became clear to him that the total width of the coralline seas had not significantly changed in any time period throughout geological history. This of course means that average ocean temperatures have been steady, and that there are no "ice ages" during which the temperature of the entire planet cools down.

Ma also established the positions of ancient coralline seas and realized that the ancient equators were not the same as they are today, rather, that the equatorial band of the tropics clearly changed from one geological age to another. His evidence showed coralline seas ran in all directions with one of his past equators bisecting the Arctic Ocean. (Many others have also found ancient coral in unexpected locations, such as Alaska.[68]) By 1949 Ma concluded that total displacements of the outer shell of the Earth over the liquid core were the logical explanation for his moving equators.[69]

One other interesting fact about coral which Ma did not discuss was the depth of water they can live in—down to about 200 feet. Below that, incoming light is lower, and the single celled algae Zooxanthellae with which corals have a symbiotic relationship cannot photosynthesize. Also pressure is higher and oxygen levels are lower—and coral doesn't form reefs much beyond 200 feet below the ocean surface. Yet there are coral reefs very deep down. For example, around Easter Island, some have been spotted about 1800 feet below the surface. There are coral reefs a mile below the surface off the coast of Scotland. This would seem to indicate a huge change in latitude and altitude since the reefs were formed there. (There are some corals which live in deep and cold waters but they do not form coral reefs.)

Ma realized that the convential wisdom on ice ages—that the whole planet cooled down enough for huge ice caps to grow outwards from the poles—could not be reconciled with the fact that corals—which require warm waters—survived. Similarly, evidence of "ice ages" in Africa, India and other tropical areas are practically proof of pole shifts because tropical plants and animals continued on—the whole planet could not have been covered in ice. Most damning is the fact that the last "ice age" ice sheet—the North American ice sheet—clearly centered on Hudson Bay, and not on our current north pole. It seems more logical to assume that the planet as a whole maintains a relatively stable range of temperatures, but that areas which are temporarily located at the North or South Pole get covered with glaciers and have an "ice age."

Of course if the locations of the continents in regard to the equator change every so many millennia, then we should be able to calculate the approximate duration of current conditions based on the thickness of the ice caps. In a letter from Einstein to Hapgood dated May 8, 1953, Einstein wrote that:

"The thickness of the icecap at the polar regions must, if this is the case, constantly increase, at least where a foundation of rock is present. One should be able to estimate empirically the annual increase of the polar icecaps. If there exists at least in one part of the polar regions a rock foundation for the icecap, one should be able to calculate how much time was needed to deposit the whole of the icecap. The amount of the ice that flowed off should be negligible in this calculation. In this way one could almost prove your hypothesis."[70] Fortunately, the U.S. government has since measured such things for us:

"Each year, about 8 mm of water from the entire surface of the Earth's oceans accumulates as snow on Greenland and Antarctica. The average ice accumulation on Greenland is about 26cm/yr and in [West] Antarctica about 16cm/yr."[71] We must note that the accumulation is given in water, and would be about five times thicker in snowfall. Compression could reduce this 80 cm/year of snow down to perhaps the 16cm/yr mentioned for Antarctica. The heavy snowfall mentioned above is on the thinner ice of West Antarctica, while very little snow falls on the much thicker ice of East Antarctica.

We assume that the deepest ice is in the east not because of current dry conditions, but because even before the last pole shift, the eastern half of Antarctica was already polar, while the western portion was temperate until the last shift. As Rand Flem-Ath tells us: "Greater [East] Antarctica, the 'body' of the continent, holds most of the world's ice, even though now it is a polar desert. The ice sheet is over two miles thick, yet receives hardly any annual snowfall. This disparity between the present amount of annual snowfall of both Lesser and Greater Antarctica and the thickness of the ice sheets demonstrates that Antarctica's climate must have been radically different"[72] in the somewhat recent past. If we merely refer back to the letter from the USAF analysis of Piri Reis' map of West Antarctica, the ice there was said to be "about a mile" thick, and this would lead us to assume a period of roughly 10,000 years would be required for such accumulation. Even these "back of the napkin" level rough estimates suffice to suggest that Antarctica has not been at its current position for tens of millions of years, as continental drift alone would suggest. It does roughly correspond with pole shift evidence, and Bible chronology, indicating about 6,000 years.

Another interesting category of evidence includes animal remains like the frozen mammoths, rhinoceroses, horses, camels, and other animals occasionally found in Siberia. The most famous is the Bereskovka mammoth, which died very suddenly and was flash frozen and well preserved. It had buttercups in its mouth, as if a normal meal had been suddenly interrupted by catastrophe. It had grasses, beans, and mosses in its stomach. Fifty pounds of undigested vegetation including the ripe fruits of these plants indicate the climate of late summer—late July to early August. (The end of the "Fourth World" and the start of the current Mayan Long Count on August 11, 3114 B.C. come to mind.) In 1887 Henry Howorth said "The facts compel us to admit that, when the Mammoth was buried in Siberia, the ground was soft and the climate therefore comparatively mild and genial, and that immediately afterward the same ground became frozen, and the same climate became Arctic, and that they have remained so to this day, and this not gradually in accordance with some slowly continuous astronomical or cosmical changes, but suddenly."[73]

The sudden cooling was not limited to Siberia. "The climatic cooling associated with this event was so sudden that live plants growing in the Peruvian Andes were flash frozen and buried in ice in a matter of hours."[74] Even more evidence comes from underground. The "Usselo horizon" is a ten centimeter thick layer of charcoal, sand, and soot sediments first found in Usselo, Netherlands, but also in the rest of Europe, the US, and around the world - dated to about 10,750 B.C. "This boundary coincides with the terminal Pleistocene mammal extinction, the worst global extinction to occur since the demise of the dinosaurs."[75] North American mammals over one hundred pounds were hit the hardest. 57 species, about 95% of the total, became extinct around 10,750 B.C.[76] All over Alaska, gold mining operations have found silt formations, especially where small creeks join larger ones, rich with gold nuggets and covered over with dozens of species of animals frozen intact above them. This is from a huge wave drowning the area's animals and washing them (and the denser gold that precipitated out first) back downstream.

Many studies show that while these extinctions were international in scope, they did not occur uniformly around the globe. "At the end of the Pleistocene, the Americas, northern Eurasia, and Australia experienced a vast decline in large mammal diversity, while Africa and tropical Asia were hardly affected."[77] First of all, if this were merely the end of a global Ice Age, why would so many animals perish at one time at the end of the Ice Age, when things were warming up, after surviving several thousand years through the harsh glacial conditions? Second, why would the mass die-offs be regional? This makes perfect sense if a pole shift from Hudson Bay to our current North Pole left Middle Eastern regions around a pivot point in the northwestern Indian Ocean with only minor climate changes while areas like Siberia suddenly became polar.

Henri Frankfort elaborates on an ancient Egyptian comment and says "One might like to interpret these texts as expressions of regret..." [or other similes and metaphors for social upheaval] "But the texts are quite explicit in describing the general nature of the catastrophe. Succinctly: 'The country turns round like a potter's wheel.'"[78] Egypt may very well have rotated geographically around a pivot point, but in an effort to be objective, consider that the same reference to Egypt turning around like a potter's wheel can be found in the Ipuwer Papyrus, which could be, but is not clearly, describing a pole shift. The text describes most of the ten plagues from the book of Exodus, along with many other horrible things causing Egypt to suffer. Many of the descriptions in this text are social commentary; but social problems alone do not explain the celestial cloud or pillar of fire or the Nile turning red. And social upheaval would appear in any text describing the death and destruction of a pole shift. If Egypt, near a pivot point, experienced almost no change in latitude but still barely survived, anywhere further away from such a stable pivot must have fared far worse. This could explain why our earliest civilizations from roughly 3100 B.C. are concentrated around the Middle East and northwestern fringes of the Indian Ocean, if those areas maintained a similar latitude and climate because they rotated slightly around a pivot point, instead of suffering a large change in latitude like Siberia, where millions of animals seem to have been flash-frozen and embedded in ice.

Such evidence makes it clear just how devastating a pole shift would be if it happened today. Immanuel Velikovsky described a pole shift in *Earth in Upheaval*: "An earthquake would make the globe shudder. Air and water would continue to move through inertia; hurricanes would sweep the Earth, and the seas would rush over continents... Many species and genera of animals on land and in the sea would be destroyed, and civilizations, if any, would be reduced to ruins... The evidence is overwhelming that the great global catastrophes were either accompanied or caused by shifting of the terrestrial axis... Many world-wide phenomena, for each of which the cause is vainly sought, are explained by a single cause: the sudden changes of climate, transgression of the sea, vast volcanic and seismic activities, formation of ice cover, pluvial crises, emergence of mountains and their dislocation, rising and subsidence of coasts, tilting of lakes, sedimentation, fossilization, the provenience of tropical animals and plants in polar regions, conglomerates of fossil animals of various latitudes and habitats, the extinction of species and genera, the appearance of new species, the reversal of the Earth's magnetic field, and a score of other world-wide phenomena."[79] Velikovsky also pointed out that evolution occurs because of catastrophes. When the population of many

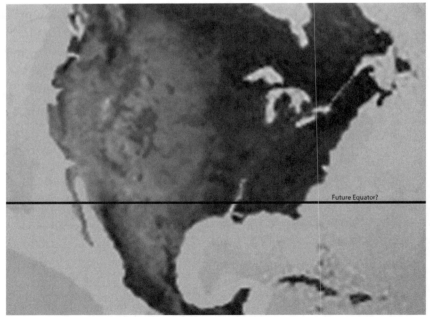

A pole shift could move the Americas south until the new equator is near Atlanta.

species is decimated by the same cosmic catastrophe that irradiates the few survivors, new mutations arise at the precise moment they have the potential to quickly dominate a small remnant population.

Was Seneca writing about an ancient pole shift in "Thyestes" during the lamentation over the sun god Apollo? "You've fled back and plunged the broken day out of the sky… And sent night from the east at a strange time to bury the foul horror in a new darkness… Sun, where have you gone? How could you get lost half way through the sky?... The way things take turns in the world has stopped… I'm stuck with terror in case it's all collapsing… The zodiac's falling… Have we been chosen… to have the world smash up and fall on us?"[80]

Professor Hapgood gave us an idea how some details of the next pole shift might unravel. "We may expect the next displacement to be in the direction of 96 E. Long, from the South Pole. This would involve another southward displacement of the Western Hemisphere, together with another northward displacement of East Asia… we shall have to be satisfied, for the present, with the guess that the next displacement may be of roughly the same magnitude as the last one. If these guesses turn out to be correct, the next North Pole will be in the vicinity of Lake Baikal, in Siberia. North America, moving southward into the tropics, will subside some hundreds of feet relatively to sea level, and the ocean will occupy the river valleys and will divide the continent into several land areas. India will move northward out of the tropics, and since there will be no land to the south to provide a refuge for the fauna and flora, we shall have to expect the extinction of many species of animals and plants now confined to that country. Many other consequences may be unpredictable."[81]

Here is one unfortunate consequence that is very predictable: assuming there are clear signs this is happening, then many more people will eventually know that Mongolia, Kazakhstan, Kyrgyzstan, and a huge majority of China and Russia will become uninhabitable. The new Arctic Circle, starting in Russia, would roughly cross over Archangel, Kazan, and the Aral Sea; the northern borders of Afghanistan, Pakistan, and India, Tibet; Chongqing,

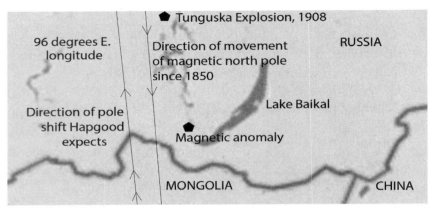

Wuhan, and Nanjing in China, South Korea, the northern tip of Hokkaido Island, Japan; and back into Siberia near the Kamchatka peninsula, and through the Arctic Ocean.

Does anyone assume that China and Russia will go down quietly, allowing their homelands to freeze over without seizing new living space for their populations? Or will they send their armies and populations away from where they expect a new arctic ice age, to claim lands with resources at safer locations? "Such a sudden flip… would set off World War III, as everyone (not just the Europeans) struggled for Lebensraum."[82] [Nazi Germany used this word for 'living space' to justify territorial expansion.] Perhaps this is the reason Revelations 9:13-16 describes Armageddon, an apocalyptic war with an army of two hundred million that will come across the Euphrates River and kill a third of mankind…

If such a pole shift does happen, with the meridian of northward movement along 96 degrees East longitude, (and south along 84 degrees West longitude,) a shift of approximately 30 degrees would put Atlanta near or on the new equator. The hypothetical future map drawn below could prove to be accurate.

Sea level would seem to fall, revealing more land on extending coasts for areas moving a lot closer to the pole. Sea level would seem to rise as coastal areas moving towards the equator submerge under an equatorial bulge comprised largely of seawater. Florida and many other low lying areas would probably disappear under the waves.

And don't just assume that areas with a similar latitude currently will also be moving due south; 180 degrees of longitude away, Chongqing, China will move north to the new Arctic Circle. The new equator would also go through Bermuda; Mauritania in West Africa; Congo; Madagascar; just north of Perth, and just south of Mackay in Australia; south of Hawaii, the middle of Baja California and Hermosillo, Mexico; San Angelo, Texas; Shreveport, Louisiana, and through the middle of Mississippi, Alabama, Georgia, and South Carolina. Atlanta's possible future location near the equator may be relevant to the site of a very modern monument to cycles of destruction: the Georgia Guidestones.

The Georgia Guidestones were paid for by an anonymous man under a fake name that indicates Rosicrucian origins. He contracted a company in Georgia to make a strange granite monument to the post-apocalyptic world. Six granite slabs weighing approximately 240,000 pounds now sit astronomically aligned on a hilltop in Elbert County, Georgia, over 600 feet above sea level. They have ten suggestions for humanity, the first of which is to "Maintain Humanity Under 500,000,000." The population in 2012 is over 14 times that number, topping 7 billion. What kind of depopulation were the people responsible for this monument expecting? The messages are inscribed in English, Spanish, Russian, Chinese, Hindi, Swahili, Hebrew, Arabic, Classical Greek, Sanskrit, Babylonian and Egyptian hieroglyphs. This was not a small prank. This was a major project involving engineers, astronomers, linguistic experts, and master craftsmen. It cost a lot of money. Its presence upsets a lot of people. It was well thought out and the location was certainly chosen for specific reasons, some of which may be altitude, and a future location on the new equator.

A plaque near the guidestones clarifies:

ASTRONOMIC FEATURES:

1. CHANNEL THROUGH STONE INDICATES CELESTIAL POLE.

2. HORIZONTAL SLOT INDICATES ANNUAL TRAVEL OF SUN.

3. SUNBEAM THROUGH CAPSTONE MARKS NOONTIME THROUGHOUT THE YEAR

PHYSICAL DATA:

1. OVERALL HEIGHT - 19 FEET 3 INCHES

2. TOTAL WEIGHT - 237,746 POUNDS

The plaque gives additional details but these will suffice to show the creators of the monument want future readers to be able to analyze the guidestones and understand our units of measure and our current surface arrangement of the earth, which could be rediscovered thousands of years from now through these explanations.

The plaque also gives the

AUTHOR: R.C. CHRISTIAN (A PSEUDONYN)

But the word "pseudonym" is misspelled on the granite; presumably an intentional "mistake" with some significant meaning. Perhaps the name R.C. Christian is an imperfect anagram for a real name of meaning, if only we replace the "N" with an "M." There is no known solution to this potential anagram.

SPONSORS: A SMALL GROUP OF AMERICANS WHO SEEK THE AGE

OF REASON

TIME CAPSULE: PLACED SIX FEET BELOW THIS SPOT

TO BE OPENED ON

There is no date given, the space for a date was left blank.

One guidestone researcher claims there is a single copy of a book in the Elberton library with additional information called: *When Man Awakens Let Him Behold...The Georgia Guidestones.* In it, Robert C. Christian is quoted:

"The group feels by having our identity remain secret it will not distract from the monument and its meaning," said Christian. "The message to be inscribed on the stones is to all mankind and is non-sectarian, nor nationalistic, nor in any sense political. The stones must speak for themselves to all who take note and should be appeal to believers and non-believers, wherever, and at all times...

Stonehenge and other vestiges of human thought arouse our curiosity but carry no message for our guidance. To convey our ideas across time to other human beings we want to erect a monument... a cluster of graven stones... which will silently display our ideas when we have gone. We hope they will merit increasing acceptance and that through their silent persistence they will hasten in a small degree the coming Age of Reason. In 1980, as these stones were being raised, the most pressing world problem was the need to control human numbers. In recent centuries technology and abundant fuels have made possible a multiplication of humanity far beyond what is prudent or long sustainable. Now we can see the impending exhaustion of those energy sources and the depletion of world resources of many vital raw materials. Controlling our reproduction is urgently needed…

We are seriously overtaxing our resources to maintain our present population in the existing state of prosperity. We are destroying our farmland, and we have grown dangerously dependent upon external sources for oil, metals and other non-renewable resources. In these circumstances, reproduction is no longer exclusively a personal matter... Population control is a global problem."[83]

If a pole shift occurs soon, their concerns regarding overpopulation will become irrelevant until mankind rises again. If Hapgood is right that the next North Pole will be near Lake Baikal, then the fact that there is a huge magnetic anomaly near Lake Baikal and that our current magnetic north pole is wandering towards it (almost exactly along the path of 96 degrees East longitude which the off-center Antarctic ice is on) at an accelerating rate of approximately 40 miles per year may not be a coincidence. It may also be noteworthy that perhaps the largest natural explosion ever known occurred in 1908 over Tunguska, Russia.

Estimated to be more powerful than a 10-megaton nuclear bomb, this explosion was slightly northwest of Lake Baikal, not far from 96 degrees east longitude, approximately where the next north pole may soon be located. Whatever caused the Tunguska blast in 1908 may have been attracted to something at that location. Some believe Nikola Tesla attempted to demonstrate that he could send free power anywhere... even the North Pole... but that after the disaster he simply kept quiet, instead of taking credit as he would have if things had succeeded as planned. What if he left out a factor of time, and did transmit to where the North Pole will be? Even if Tesla was not involved, the area beckons our attention with a mysterious impact, a magnetic anomaly, the path our current magnetic North Pole is taking, and the predicted location of the next rotational North Pole.

(Endnotes)

1. Berlitz, Charles. *Mysteries From Forgotten Worlds.* London: Corgi, 1974, p. 204

2 The Cuvier quote is from the internet, but one of the earliest translations from which it may have been taken is by Robert Kerr, Edinburgh: Blackwood & Company, 1813.

3 Anonymous. "Essay on the Theory of the Earth." The Edinburgh Review and London Critical Journal. January 1814.

4 Warshofsky, Fred. *Doomsday: The Science of Catastrophe.* New York: Readers' Digest Press, 1977, p. 98

5 Darwin, Charles. *The Voyage of the Beagle*. London: Cambridge University Press, Diary entry dated January 9, 1834, p. 178

6 "Could Atlantis Still Exist?" at http://www.bbc.co.uk/dna/h2g2/A462403

7 Childress, David Hatcher. *Pirates & The Lost Templar Fleet: The Secret Naval War between the Knights Templar & the Vatican.* Kempton, IL: Adventures Unlimited Press, 2003, p. 109

8 Carter, Mary. *Edgar Cayce on Prophecy*. New York: Paperback Library, 1968, pp. 107-108

9 Brown, Hugh A. *Cataclysms of the Earth*. Boston, MA: Twayne Publishers, 1967, p. 8

10 Kirschvink, Joseph. "Atlas Shrugged," *Engineering and Science Magazine* vol. 3, 1997, p. 6

11 Hancock, Graham. *Fingerprints of the Gods*. New York: Three Rivers Press, 1995, p. 482

12 Atkinson, Nancy. "Pole Shift on Europa," *Universe Today Magazine,* May 14, 2008

13 Hapgood, Charles. *Earth's Shifting Crust: A Key to Some Basic Problems of Earth Science.* New York: Pantheon Books, 1958

14 Hapgood, Charles. T*he Path of the Pole*. Kempton, IL: Adventures Unlimited Press, 1999, p. 149

15 Hapgood, Ibid., p. 164

16 Coe, R. S. "New evidence for extraordinarily rapid change of the geomagnetic field during a reversal." *Nature*, v. 374, 20 April 1994,

pp. 687-692

17 Barbiero, Flavio. "On the Possibility of Instantaneous Shifts of the Poles," pp. 192-209 of *Lost Knowledge of the Ancients: A Graham Hancock Reader.* Glenn Kreisberg, editor. Rochester, VT: Bear & Company, 2010, pp. 209, 200-201

18 White, John. *Pole Shift*. Virginia Beach, VA: A.R.E. Press, 2007, pp. xix, 77, 138

19 White, John. Ibid., p. 150

20 Hapgood, Charles. *The Path of the Pole.* Kempton, IL: Adventures Unlimited Press, 1999, p. 22

21 Jeans, James. *Astronomy and Cosmogeny*, London: Cambridge University Press, 1928, as cited on p. 50 of Paul LaViolette's Earth Under Fire

22 LaViolette, Paul. *Earth Under Fire: Humanity's Survival of the Ice Age*. Rochester, VT: Bear & Company, 2005, p. 50

23 Warshofsky, Fred. *Doomsday: The Science of Catastrophe.* New York: Readers' Digest Press, 1977, p. 181

24 LaViolette, Ibid., pp. 160-162

25 Vezzoli, Gary C. "Gravitational Data During the Syzygy of May 18, 2001 and Related Studies." *Infinite Energy Magazine*, Issue 53, 2004, p. 21

26 Vezzoli, Ibid., p. 25

27 Vezzoli, Gary C. "Note on Indication of nano short range order in liquid iron from analysis of recovered products from molten state: geophysical inferences from the materials science." *Materials Research Innovations Magazine*, May 5, 2002, pp. 223-224

28 de Santillana, Giorgio and Hertha von Dechend. *Hamlet's Mill: An Essay Investigating the Origins of Human Knowledge and its Transmission Through Myth.* Boston, MA: David R. Godine, 1969, p. 66

29 LaViolette, Paul. *Earth Under Fire: Humanity's Survival of the Ice Age*. Rochester, VT: Bear & Company, 2005, p. 317

30 LaViolette, Ibid., p. 91

31 LaViolette, Ibid., pp. 334 and 30

32 Hapgood, Charles. *Earth's Shifting Crust: A Key to Some Basic Problems of Earth Science.* New York: Pantheon Books, 1958, p. 331

33 Hapgood, Ibid., p. 338

34 Hapgood, Ibid., p. 364

35 Hapgood, Charles. *Maps of the Ancient Sea Kings*. Kempton, IL: Adventures Unlimited Press, 1996, p. 98

36 "Could Atlantis Still Exist?" at http://www.bbc.co.uk/dna/h2g2/A462403

37 Hapgood, Charles. *Earth's Shifting Crust: A Key to Some Basic Problems of Earth Science*. New York: Pantheon Books, 1958, p. 56

38 Wilson, Colin and Rand Flem-Ath. *The Atlantis Blueprint: Unlocking the Ancient Mysteries of a Long-Lost Civilization*. New York: Delta Books, 2002, p. 29

39 LaViolette, Paul. *Earth Under Fire: Humanity's Survival of the Ice Age*. Rochester, VT: Bear & Company, 2005, p. 198

40 Hapgood, Charles. *Maps of the Ancient Sea Kings*. Kempton, IL: Adventures Unlimited Press, 1996, p. 145

41 Childress, David Hatcher. *Pirates & The Lost Templar Fleet: The Secret Naval War between the Knights Templar & the Vatican*. Kempton, IL: Adventures Unlimited Press, 2003, p. 126

42 Coppens, Philip. "Copper: a World Trade in 3000 BC?" http://www.philipcoppens.com/copper.html but originally in *Frontier Magazine* 5.5 September-October 1999

43 Hapgood, Charles. *Maps of the Ancient Sea Kings*. Kempton, IL: Adventures Unlimited Press, 1996, pp. 244-245

44 White, John. *Pole Shift*. Virginia Beach, VA: A.R.E. Press, 2007, p. 102, quoting an article in "Info Journal" from November 1974

45 Hapgood, Charles. Ibid, p. 33

46 Michell, John. *The New View Over Atlantis*. San Francisco, CA: Harper & Row, 1986, p. 136

47 Michell, Ibid., p. 134

48 Hapgood, Charles. *Maps of the Ancient Sea Kings*. Kempton, IL: Adventures Unlimited Press, 1996, p. 243

49 Michell, John. *The New View Over Atlantis*. San Francisco, CA: Harper & Row, 1986, p. 126

50 Hapgood, Charles. *Maps of the Ancient Sea Kings*. Kempton, IL: Adventures Unlimited Press, 1996, p. 123

51 Menzies, Gavin. *1434: The Year a Magnificent Chinese Fleet Sailed to Italy and Started the Renaissance*. New York: William

Morrow, NY, 2008, quoting Fernandez-Armesto's Columbus, p. 76

52 Flem-Ath, Rand and Rose. *Atlantis Beneath the Ice*. Rochester, VT: Bear & Company, 2012, pp. 2, 15

53 Childress, David Hatcher. *Pirates & The Lost Templar Fleet: The Secret Naval War between the Knights Templar & the Vatican*. Kempton, IL: Adventures Unlimited Press, 2003, p. 242

54 Flem-Ath, Rand and Rose. *When the Sky Fell: In Search of Atlantis*, New York: St. Martin's Press, 1995, p. 125—but originally from Sanceau's Henry The Navigator, p. 111

55 Weidner, Jay and Vincent Bridges. *The Mysteries of the Great Cross of Hendaye: Alchemy and the End of Time*. Rochester, VT: Destiny Books, 2003, p. 4

56 Weidner, Jay and Vincent Bridges. Ibid., p. 6

57 Gilbert, Adrian and Maurice Cotterell. *The Mayan Prophecies*. New York: Barnes & Noble, 1996, p. 87

58 1 Enoch 69:12

59 Childress, David Hatcher. *Technology of the Gods: The Incredible Sciences of the Ancients*. Kempton, IL: Adventures Unlimited Press, 2000, p. 124

60 Michell, John. *The New View Over Atlantis*. San Francisco, CA: Harper & Row, 1986, p. 204

61 Childress, David Hatcher. *Technology of the Gods: The Incredible Sciences of the Ancients.* Kempton, IL: Adventures Unlimited Press, 2000, p. 166

62 Berlitz, Charles. *Mysteries From Forgotten Worlds*. London: Corgi Press, 1974, p. 32

63 Childress, David Hatcher. *Technology of the Gods: The Incredible Sciences of the Ancients.* Kempton, IL: Adventures Unlimited Press, 2000, p. 177

64 Dikshitar, V. R. Ramachandra. *War in Ancient India*, Madras, India: MacMillan & Company, 1944

65 Hapgood, Charles. *Earth's Shifting Crust: A Key to Some Basic Problems of Earth Science.* New York: Pantheon Books, 1958, pp. 71-76

66 Bain, George W. "Mapping the Climatic Zones of the Geologic Past." *Yale Scientific Magazine*, v. xxvii, No. 5 (Feb., 1953 / 18:46)

67 Hapgood, Charles. *The Path of the Pole.* Kempton, IL:

Adventures Unlimited Press, 1999, p. 186

68 White, John. *Pole Shift*. Virginia Beach, VA: A.R.E. Press, 2007, p. 12

69 Hapgood, Charles. *Earth's Shifting Crust: A Key to Some Basic Problems of Earth Science*. New York: Pantheon Books, 1958, pp. 74-76)

70 Hapgood, Charles. *The Path of the Pole*. Kempton, IL: Adventures Unlimited Press, 1999, p. 328)

71 http://edmall.gsfc.nasa.gov/99invest.Site/science-briefs/ice/ed-ice.html

72 Flem-Ath, Rand and Rose. *When the Sky Fell: In Search of Atlantis,* New York: St. Martin's Press, 1995, p. 75

73 LaViolette, Paul. *Earth Under Fire: Humanity's Survival of the Ice Age*. Rochester, VT: Bear & Company, 2005, p. 225

74 LaViolette, Paul. Ibid., p. 103

75 LaViolette, Paul. Ibid., p. 193

76 LaViolette, Paul. Ibid., p. 203

77 Smith, Norman Owen. *Megafaunal Extinctions: The Conservation Message from 11,000 Years B.P.* Johannesburg, SA: Resource Ecology Group, University of Witwatersand Press, Conservation Biology Vol. 3, No. 4 / Dec., 1989, pp. 405-412

78 Frankfort, Henri. *Ancient Egyptian Religion.* New York: Harper & Row, 1961, p. 85 but originally from Erman, Adolf. The Literature of the Ancient Egyptians. London, A. M. Blackman, 1927, p. 96

79 Velikovsky, Immanuel. Earth in Upheaval. New York: Pocket Books, 1977, pp. 124-5 & 239-40

80 S, Acharya. *Suns of God: Krishna, Buddha and Christ Unveiled.* Kempton, IL: Adventures Unlimited Press, 2004, p. 111

81 Hapgood, Charles. *Earth's Shifting Crust: A Key to Some Basic Problems of Earth Science.* New York: Pantheon Books, 1958, p. 385-386

82 Calvin, William. *How Brains Think.* New York: Basic Books, 1996, p. 162

83 http://www.theoryoflivevolution.com/files/322_Georgia_Guidestones.pdf, referencing a book by the Elberton Granite Finishing Company. *When Man Awakens Let Him Behold...The Georgia Guidestones*. Hartwell, GA: The Sun, 1981, pp. 5-19.

CHAPTER FOUR
GALACTIC SUPERWAVES

Earlier in our discussion of active galactic centers as a potential cause of pole shifts we touched on some of the theories of astrophysicist Dr. Paul LaViolette. He realized that Carl Seyfert's observation that approximately one in seven spiral galaxies has an active center is misleading, because the active minority are not a different type of galaxy, they are merely the ones currently experiencing an active core phase. "Astronomers have come to realize that galactic core explosions occur in all spiral galaxies, even our own, and that the majority of galaxies that have a normal appearance with no sign of core activity are simply galaxies whose cores happen to be in their quiescent phase."[1]

In 1977 astronomer Jan Oort concluded that our Galactic core has been active less than 10,000 years ago. Oort, LaViolette, and others found evidence that our Milky Way galaxy has at its center a periodically active galactic nuclei surrounded by a series of three dimensional rings of dust and light in successive layers around the galactic core. Each event blasts out "an expanding spherical shell that has a thickness of several hundred to several thousand light years. This high-velocity cosmic ray volley [which is ejected with the dust] is termed a galactic superwave."[2] Evidence shows that such highly radioactive dust clouds have passed through our solar system repeatedly, with more expanding outwards and on their way towards us all the time. "Seyfert-like galactic core explosions recur much more frequently than modern astronomers have supposed."[3]

We can look at other galaxies and make some observations that are impossible to see directly in our own galaxy, as we are stuck inside it and cannot look down on our galaxy from above. But what happens in other galaxies is probably a good barometer of what happens in the Milky Way. Andromeda, our closest neighboring galaxy, has several rings around its core. "Centaurus A, the closest galaxy to our own which appears to be currently exploding, contains a similar number of shell structures within 60,000 light-years of its center."[4] In our own galaxy, two or more "superwaves may already have left the Galactic Center and be speeding toward our solar system, but there is no way that we can see them coming," because they approach at light speed.[5]

Dr. LaViolette explains that stars near the threshold of going supernova are often pushed over the edge in groups as they are hit by the gravity waves and other radiation, and we can date the last major galactic core explosion because of this effect. Starting with the year we on Earth witness a supernova, subtract the number of years we estimate it took the light from that particular supernova to reach us. Subtract again for the number of light-years between the supernova and the galactic center. We can then estimate the year of the galactic core explosion, and the last such event was not that far back.

There are two supernovae which, due to size and proximity, appear vastly brighter than others, and are among the easiest for us to analyze. "Cassiopeia A (Cas A) and the Crab Nebula remnants present the best evidence in favor of the superwave theory." Compared to the average of the 3rd radio-brightest to 14th radio-brightest supernova remnants, Cas A is 80 times brighter and Crab Nebula 17 times brighter. Both are just behind the event horizon of the last big superwave that reached Earth around 12,000 B.C.[6] The Cas A supernova is also the most luminous on its west side, where the superwave would have hit, and the energy of the galactic outburst smashes into the star's own explosion.

The Crab Nebula supernova, the Cas A supernova, Vela supernova, and the Tycho supernova are all estimated to have exploded at dates which lead to an estimate of a galactic core explosion affecting our planet from about 12,720 B.C. to about 11,610B.C. Given "the respective uncertainties of these dates, it could be said that all three [four] supernovae were detonated by the same superwave event horizon."[7] If this timing is correct, it may indicate that whatever happened around 3,100 B.C. was by comparison a minor event. So although Bruce Scofield called the 3100 B.C. event the "most important and decisive time in the entire history of civilization" it may have been small compared to events over 10,000 years ago, or to what is headed our way now.

Very few stars are on the brink of going supernova at any given time, but the effects of superwaves may deeply disturb all stars and produce strange, if temporary changes. "Superwaves may also trigger gravitational tides on stars." One theory predicts huge changes in gravitational potential that would change suddenly during a core explosion… "The front of the wave would have a very steep gravitational gradient that would be capable of exerting a very strong inward pull on any planet or star."[8] Most stars are stable—but even stable stars often flare up because of the gravity waves, the radiation pulse, and the dust cloud that is pushed into them.

Our sun has a solar wind, an outward pressure of gas and radiation that keeps our solar system clear of most incoming particles. Other stars do the same thing, and the majority of interstellar dust is kept away. But when a blast of energy from a galactic core explosion overwhelms a star's ability to push dust out, the dust envelops them. The dust traps heat and other radiation and helps convey electrical discharges. As Hannes Alfven said during his acceptance speech for the 1970 Nobel Prize in Physics: "Space is filled with a network of currents that transfer energy and momentum over large or very large distances." Any cloud of radioactive dust pushed into the solar system would have filaments that act like superconductors for transferring electrical charges between planets or between the sun and planets. This could certainly contribute to large and rapid changes in the Earth's magnetic field. (It could even explain references to the gods throwing lightning bolts at each other.)

Commenting on previous occasions during which such cosmic dust clouds would have enveloped our solar system, Dr. LaViolette wrote that "particles of dust could also have energized the Sun. As these large amounts of material fell into the Sun, they would have increased the Sun's energy output and flaring activity."[9] Also "cosmic dust that was pushed into the solar system by a passing superwave would have activated the Sun and caused it to behave like a T-Tauri star."[10] Cosmic dust clouds are crucially important contributors to any terrestrial cataclysm, as superwaves alone should not often push stars or planets over the edge without the side effects initiated by pushing interstellar debris into them. "To account for these catastrophes, a second culprit must have been involved—cosmic dust."[11]

Dust blanketing a star will keep in extra heat, along with much higher levels of X-rays and ultraviolet radiation. Such stars also flare a lot, with solar flares 100-1000 times as powerful as any we have ever seen. These stresses build up until they eventually cause a T-Tauri burst. This would dissipate the dust outwards, which would briefly bake the Earth (and other planets) and melt polar ice.[12]

New evidence for fast solar blowouts of dust clouds has come in as recently as July 5, 2012 when the article "Dust Today, Gone Tomorrow: Astronomers Discover Houdini-Like Vanishing Act in Space" appeared in *Science Daily*. "Astronomers report a baffling discovery never seen before: An extraordinary amount of dust around a nearby star has mysteriously disappeared. 'It's like the classic magician's trick—now you see it, now you don't,' said Carl Melis, a postdoctoral scholar at UC San Diego and lead author of the research. 'Only in this case, we're talking about enough dust to fill an inner solar system, and it really is gone!' The disc around this star, if it were in our solar system, would have extended from the sun halfway out to Earth. 'This disappearance is remarkably fast, even on a human time scale, much less an astronomical scale. The dust disappearance at TYC 8241 2652 was so bizarre and so quick, initially I figured that our observations must simply be wrong in some strange way,'" said co-author Ben-Zuckerman. But this could be explained by a star's T-Tauri reaction to incoming dust, expelling it with a huge coronal mass ejection.

Thomas Gold of Cornell University found evidence in lunar craters of glassy surface rocks which had briefly been exposed to scorching heat. Some craters showed the first small signs of melting, with small droplets beginning to run downwards before resolidifying. Gold felt that his evidence was best explained by a short (on the order of 10 to 100 seconds) burst of sunlight about one hundred times brighter than normal, and he believes this occurred within the last 30,000 years.[13]   There is also evidence of Martian permafrost briefly melting and causing flash flooding before refreezing. And just this spring (March 7, 2012) NASA detected a record-breaking outburst of gamma radiation from our sun which was a thousand times normal strength and lasted approximately twenty hours. Could we get one heck of a sunburn without any increase in the visible light spectrum to warn us? Absolutely. But someday soon we are likely to experience a flare of intense magnitude across the entire spectrum. It may be such a flare that led to the description in Isaiah 30:25-26 "On the day of the great slaughter, when the towers fall. The light of the moon will be as the light of the sun, and the light of the sun will be seven times brighter, like the light of seven days."

T-Tauri stars, with strong flares and energized electromagnetic fields, could wreak havoc on the planets orbiting them. Planets would likely experience relative cold and darkness at first, as dust blocks sunlight, followed by a buildup of heat trapped within the dark dust cloud, and finally a stellar blowout of solar flaring when such conditions finally overwhelm the system's sun. Geologist Robert Schoch has concluded that a massive flare of solar plasma devastated the planet with fire and electrical discharges around 9,700 B.C. Dr. Schoch has recently written a new book titled: *Forgotten Civilization: The Role of Solar Outbursts in Our Past and Future.* Assuming these coronal mass ejections of hot plasma were caused by the same galactic superwave that triggered several supernova at the same time, the accompanying radiation and gravity waves would also cause unusual magnetic reversals and tidal forces, and these might, in

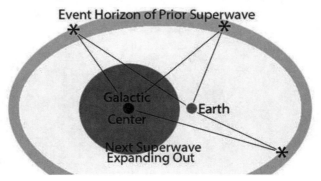

conjunction with the imbalance of accumulated ice at the Earth's poles—lead to a crustal displacement.

Dr. LaViolette suggests that galactic core "superwaves periodically jerk the earth's axis" and that "perhaps the Earth's precessional period has become entrained by the heartbeat of the galactic core."[14] As a galactic superwave passes "through the solar system, it… might generate tidal forces substantially greater than those produced by the Sun or Moon. It could deliver a powerful jolt to the Earth's crust… a sudden crustal displacement."[15] He also describes "the gravity wave, with its ensuing crustal torque, which would have caused earthquakes and volcanic eruptions."[16]

If this has happened many times before, it is possible that our ancestors were civilized enough to understand the cause. Keeping in mind that a bright new source of light would appear in the heavens to coincide with such disasters, it would not have required an advanced level of astrophysics to link the two together. "Seyfert galaxies look blue,"[17] and upon becoming active our galactic core would have looked like a bright new blue star, so bright that it would be visible even in daytime.

Another source comments on this in regard to the Hopi Indian

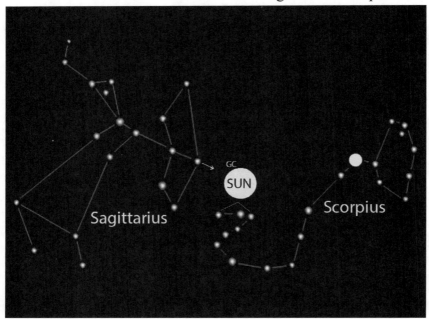

prophecy of a "Blue Star" arriving in the heavens at the time of a pole shift. "Since the cores of distant exploding galaxies are observed to have a bright blue star-like appearance, it is reasonable to expect that the core of our own Galaxy would have a similar appearance during its explosive phase. So the legendary appearance of the Blue Star could be referring to an explosion of our Galaxy's core... [which] would have illuminated the dense gas clouds in the Galaxy's nucleus to create an oval luminous form around the Blue Star... This frightening spectacle may have appeared to ancient inhabitants as a gigantic punishing 'Eye' in the sky, the entire form occupying about a 16 degree field of view, or about 32 solar diameters."[18] It could also be the inspiration for Ezekiel 1:26 "above the expanse that was over their heads there was something resembling a throne, like lapis lazuli in appearance." (The original Hebrew word is "eben-sappir" and is clearly meant to be read not as the NASB's "lapis luzuli" but as "sapphire" like the King James Bible has it. Both stones are blue.)

The initial appearance of the galactic core as a blue star would be immediately followed up with cosmic dust being pushed into our solar system. Ancient ice samples from Greenland "contain much higher concentrations of cosmic dust than do present-day snow and ice... cosmic dust was accumulating on Earth's surface hundreds of times faster than it does today." Many of the dust particles were large, about a quarter millimeter—too big to stay airborne long if blown from ice-free areas far away. They don't resemble volcanic dust in size, shape, or composition. And they are big enough to sting when they hit at very high speed. The Greenland dust findings are also backed up by data from Antarctic glaciologists who found an acidity spike in dust thousands of years ago.[19] "There was a time some ten thousand years ago, and on numerous other occasions prior to that, when the solar system was filled with light-scattering dust particles and when the Sun was in a highly energized, T-Tauri state."[20]

Eventually local dust would be cleared away and we would see the stars again. For centuries we would observe reflected light off the dense clouds in the central bulge of the galaxy. It would take some years for the light to reach stars behind the core, then more years to reach us, slightly behind the roughly 23,000 years it would take for the first light from the core to reach us. Because of the galaxy's central bulge, this would eventually appear like a giant pale blue eye in the sky, with the galactic core itself as the bright pupil.[21]

Dr. LaViolette is convinced that our ancestors did make the connection between the galactic core and catastrophes, and that they encoded a warning about it into the astrological symbols for our zodiac constellations. He notes that only the arrow of Sagittarius and the stinger of Scorpio point at anything, and both point to the galactic center.[22] He also notes a detailed "zodiac cryptogram" and believes this "was devised in an attempt to communicate to future generations that the core of our galaxy underwent a major explosion, comparable to the ones we observe taking place in the nuclei of Seyfert galaxies."[23]

We recently experienced a small version of this effect on 12/26/2004, when a 9.3 magnitude earthquake near Sumatra caused a tsunami that left 240,000 dead. Many earthquakes occur here, because it is at the equator at 96 degrees east longitude—where the imbalanced center of Antarctica's ice cap pushes the crust north over the equatorial bulge. Here the planet's crust is being wedged into a smaller and smaller space the further north we look. The earthquake on 12/26/2004 was ten times more powerful than any other in 25 years. 44.6 hours later we detected the brightest gamma ray burst ever recorded, coming from a star in Sagittarius. It is believed that a gravity wave had preceded the gamma rays and triggered the earthquake. Unfortunately, gravity waves are difficult to detect, and the only two gravity wave telescopes that could have detected it were off for maintenance at the time.[24] Fortunately this was merely a star going supernova; the gravity wave would have been much more intense if it had been from the galactic core.

Very few scientists like to acknowledge such things. "Researchers proposing extraterrestrial causes for terrestrial catastrophes still meet with considerable skepticism from the geological community."[25] When the theory of an asteroid impact killing off dinosaurs came up in 1979, geologists and paleontologists strongly opposed the idea, and that general trend continues today. Evidence of galactic superwaves has been largely ignored for decades, perhaps intentionally.

In the misleadingly titled 2008 article in *Science Daily* "Milky Way's Giant Black Hole 'Awoke From Slumber' 300 Years Ago"— [if it had we wouldn't know for over 20,000 years] Tatsuya Inui of Kyoto University said: "We have wondered why the Milky Way's black hole appears to be a slumbering giant. But now we realize that the black hole was far more active in the past." In another article scientists analyzing data from the Chandra X-ray Observatory noticed signs of an event at the galactic center and instead of concluding that our galaxy is a Seyfert galaxy, they decided that "Ten thousand years ago a supernova exploded very close to Sagittarius A*."[26] In an article from November 11, 2010 called "NASA Scientists Discover Huge Bubbles of Energy in Galaxy" Astronomer Doug Finkbeiner comments "One theory being explored is that the supermassive black hole at the centre of the Milky Way may have had some kind of outburst."[27] It seems hard to believe that 67 years after Carl Seyfert, and about 30 years after Paul LaViolette, leading astrophysicists still act like they don't know these concepts.

Rogue geologist Dr. Robert Schoch generally agrees with Dr. LaViolette, stating in his most recent book that: "the last galactic superwave hit Earth around 12,900 years ago." Schoch also emphasizes that "our sun is not as stable as most people generally believe," and that "Astrophysicist Thomas Gold, in an offhand way, guessed that major plasma events might impact the Earth approximately every ten thousand years. It has been 11,700 years since the last one." Not one to hold back on the controversial topic of cosmic events wiping out human civilization, Schoch clarifies: "The catastrophes that occurred over ten thousand years ago, eradicating this early, forgotten civilization, appear to be on the verge of happening once again." Near the end of his recent book, Schoch again clarifies his thesis that major solar events help cause the end of world ages: "Geological data indicate that the last ice age ended extremely suddenly, catastrophically, around 9700 B.C.E." [which he continues to categorize as] "the date of a major solar outburst."[28]

Galactic superwaves may not be widely accepted as a cause of pole shifts anytime soon, as pole shifts themselves are largely discounted as fairy tales. Perhaps instead of waiting for mainstream science to universally accept the causes of the next pole shift, we should look to ancient cultures for descriptions of the last one.

(Endnotes)

1 LaViolette, Paul. *Earth Under Fire: Humanity's Survival of the Ice Age*. Rochester, VT: Bear & Company, 2005, p. 51

2 LaViolette, Paul. Ibid., p. 68

3 LaViolette, Paul. Ibid., p. 67

4 LaViolette, Paul. Ibid., p. 312

5 LaViolette, Paul. Ibid., p. 292

6 LaViolette, Paul. Ibid., p. 299-300

7 LaViolette, Paul. Ibid., p. 306

8 LaViolette, Paul. Ibid., p. 308

9 LaViolette, Paul. Ibid., p. 94

10 LaViolette, Paul. Ibid., pp. 160-162

11 LaViolette, Paul. Ibid., p. 94

12 LaViolette, Paul. Ibid., p. 194

13 Gold, Thomas. "Apollo II observations of a remarkable glazing phenomenon on the lunar surface," *Science* v. 165, 1969, pp. 1345-49

14 LaViolette, Paul. *Earth Under Fire: Humanity's Survival of the Ice Age*. Rochester, VT: Bear & Company, 2005, pp. 334, 30

15 LaViolette, Paul. Ibid., p. 333

16 LaViolette, Paul. Ibid., p. 72

17 LaViolette, Paul. Ibid., p. 71

18 http://www.goldenmean.info/superwave/

19 LaViolette, Paul. *Earth Under Fire: Humanity's Survival of the Ice Age*. Rochester, VT: Bear & Company, 2005, pp. 114-121

20 LaViolette, Paul. Ibid., p. 165

21 LaViolette, Paul. Ibid., p. 73

22 LaViolette, Paul. Ibid., p. 32

23 LaViolette, Paul. Ibid., p. 54

24 LaViolette, Paul. Ibid., pp. 354-356

25 LaViolette, Paul. Ibid., p. 370

26 "A Mystery in the Galactic Center." at http://science.nasa.gov/science-news/science-at-nasa/2002/21feb_mwbh/ Feb. 21, 2002

27 Finkbeiner, Doug. "NASA Scientists Discover Huge Bubbles

of Energy in Galaxy." http://thetechjournal.com/science/nasa-scientist-discover-huge-bubbles-of-energy-in-galaxy.xhtml
28 Schoch, Robert. *Forgotten Civilization: The Role of Solar Outbursts in Our Past and Future*. Rochester, VT: Inner Traditions, 2012, pp. 138, 90, 102-103, 8, 253

CHAPTER FIVE
WORLD MYTHOLOGY

Two of the most comprehensive books on comparative mythology are Joseph Campbell's "The Hero of a Thousand Faces" and Giorgio de Santillana and Hertha von Dechend's *Hamlet's Mill: An Essay Investigating the Origins of Human Knowledge and its Transmission Through Myth*. Campbell explained that heroes of almost every myth experience the same transformative journey. Hamlet's Mill covers myths with descriptions of "catastrophes and the periodic rebuilding of the world."[1] Myths are a fantastic way to convey specific details about such events to future generations: "the great strength of myths as vehicles for specific technical information is that they are capable of transmitting that information independently of the knowledge of individual story-tellers. In other words as long as a myth continues to be told true, it will also continue to transmit any higher message that may be concealed within its structure— even if neither the teller nor the hearer understands that message."[2]

For a modern example, let us assume that a person has read or watched "The DaVinci Code" and is aware of the theory that Jesus married Mary Magdalene at Cana and had offspring. Dan Brown and others allege that Jesus had at least one child with Mary, who brought the holy bloodline to southern France. The Knights Templar allegedly discovered evidence of this in Jerusalem during the Crusades and blackmailed the Vatican, keeping the heresy a thinly veiled secret in exchange for wealth and power. "SAN GRAEL" or "Holy Grail" sounds the same as "SANG REAL" or "Blood Royal," and Templars may have known they not only sound the same, but are the same.

Stories of Knights protecting the Holy Grail, allegedly a cup from the last supper used by Joseph of Arimathea to catch the dripping blood of Christ at the crucifixion, are (again, allegedly) really about Knights protecting Jesus' bloodline. Either way, the contents of the grail (Jesus' blood) were the important part, and the stories tell us his blood was brought from Israel to Western Europe. European royalty, initially through France's Merovingian dynasty, allegedly holds this bloodline. As most of the original Templars were French nobles like their founder, Godfroi de Bouillon, and many princes and princesses found spouses among the nobility, the Templars also were the Holy Grail, descendants of the same bloodline.

But how many people, even after familiarizing themselves with this idea, ever make the connection to the nursery rhyme: "MARY had a LITTLE LAMB, (bore Jesus a child) whose fleece (genetic heritage) was white as snow (of divine purity.) And everywhere that Mary went, (France) the lamb (Jesus' bloodline) was sure to go." Have you recited that countless times? Have you ever done so consciously realizing what veiled information you might be passing on to future generations, or that someone may have intentionally written it so that you would pass the hidden message on to your children?

There are a lot of first century churches devoted to biblical Maries in southern France. Tradition holds that she emigrated there with other Jews we know from the Bible. The last Sinclair Earl of Orkney, believed to be a descendant of the Knights Templar, held the odd title "Knight of the Cockle and the Golden Fleece" and was reputed to have knowledge of "the Holy Grail, the Holy Blood of the Merovingian kings, and the destiny of the new continent across the Atlantic."[3] If nothing else, it can be interesting to question the original meanings of nursery rhymes and other stories, which can easily convey messages through many generations without the listener or the storyteller understanding until one day, more information is revealed, which makes the original encoded meaning clear to the wise.

In cultures around the world, myths often begin with a "theory about 'how the world began' [which] seems to involve the breaking asunder of a harmony, a kind of cosmogonic 'original sin' whereby the circle of the ecliptic [with the zodiac] was tilted up at an angle with respect to the equator, and the cycles of change came into being."[4] How often does this occur? Possibly every one-fifth of a precessional cycle. "When one finds numbers like 108, or 9 * 13, reappearing under several multiples in the Veda, in the temples of Angkor, in Babylon, in Heraclitus' dark utterances, and also in the Norse Valhalla, it is not an accident."[5] 108 degrees span the inside angles of a pentagon, and frequent use of the numbers 108 ("a fifth" of a pentagon's 540 degrees) and 72, (one fifth of the 360 degrees in a circle) seems to indicate that ancient writers wanted us to be aware of a division of something in five.

A less obvious but very significant number is 43,200. There are 43,200 stanzas in ancient India's epic "Rig Veda." The ratio between the height of the Great Pyramid at Giza to the radius of the Earth is 1 to 43,200. In Norse mythology, Odin leads 43,200 noble warriors to fight with him at the end of the world. Night (or day) lasts 12 hours, 720 minutes, or 43,200 seconds. These and many other examples cannot be coincidences; for many cultures to use this number so often there must be some reason it is considered sacred and important.

When so many ancient civilizations record the same unusual numbers for posterity in their myths and monuments, perhaps we should consider the famous modern astronomer Carl Sagan and his comments on how alien extraterrestrials would, hypothetically, attempt to communicate with us. "Extraterrestrials would, of course, wish to make a message sent to us as comprehensible as possible. But how could they? Is there in any sense an interstellar Rosetta Stone? We believe there is a common language that all technical civilizations, no matter how different, must have. That common language is science and mathematics."[6]

And if we were going to build something to display our knowledge of math and science, of the dimensions of the Earth and its periodic cataclysms, might we not put it at the center of the world's land masses, in Egypt? "If one is to send a message the prime requirement is of course that people will read it, it is no good putting it in a bottle, throwing it in the ocean and then hoping that it will be found. One must place the message somewhere where it simply cannot be missed, a place so significant that its very location makes a notable statement in itself."[7] As another student of Egyptology said: "That monument stands in a more important physical situation than any other building erected by man."[8]

The three main pyramids in Egypt are aligned with the Nile River as Orion's belt stars are aligned with the Milky Way. Angkor Watt and its temple complex in Burma are similarly aligned to match the stars of the constellation Draco. Angkor has five gates, with 108 statues lining the road to each gate. There are 540 statues in all, the number of degrees in the inside angles of a pentagram; this is all clearly indicating a division in five. Pole shifts occurring every fifth of a precessional cycle may be why the pentagram is considered an evil symbol. Less obvious than the pentagram's five sides are the pyramid's five sides (when considering the bottom) and five corners. The architect of the Great Pyramid encoded many ratios into its structure, but "there is one arithmetical number that is prominent in the Pyramid, and that number is 5. The number 5, and its multiples, powers and geometrical proportions of it runs through the Great Pyramid and its measure references."[9] It may be significant that the apple so central to one early record of a pole shift—mankind's being kicked out of the Garden of Eden—has five divisions inside it.

72 degrees make one fifth of a circle, and Angkor is 72 degrees east of the Great Pyramid. "Angkor" could even be derived from the Egyptian "Ankh-Hor" which would mean "Horus (the sun) lives." It takes 72 years to notice a one degree change in precession. In Egyptian mythology, Seth killed his brother Osiris, the sun-god and Lord of the Dead, (sometimes called "the King of Kings" and "Lord of Lords") with 72 co-conspirators. There were 72 Sanhedrin (Jewish rabbis/elders/judges) who led the cause against Jesus. There were 72 master masons who helped Zoroaster build the Tower of Babel. Noah had 72 grandsons. Muslims expect 72 virgins in heaven. The Mayan Hieroglyphic Stairway of the Pyramid at Copan has 72 steps. The wall of the New Jerusalem is measured to be 72 yards in Revelations 21:17. Our attention is repeatedly drawn to the number 72 and a 72 degree measurement, to divide a circle of 360 degrees in five parts and to associate it with death, the flood, the end of civilization, and the death of the sun-god. The masonic Washington Monument, like the middle of a giant sundial

to measure time, also draws us to measurement in fives, for it is 555 feet 5 inches high, with a 55-foot base and windows 500 feet high. We should thank modern Freemasonry for carrying some of these ancient traditions forward as a New World reminder.

Apparently the ancients must have understood precession, and five ages within that great cycle. But how could they possibly have measured something that happens slowly over approximately 25,800 years? It would take 72 years of observation to record even one degree of change in celestial positions. But it would be easy to notice that monuments aligned to stars at the time they were built were far out of alignment centuries later. This was clearly understood in Egypt and many other societies, and the length of this cycle, or "great year" was understood to correspond to recorded cycles of destruction. Precession "was conceived as causing the rise and the cataclysmic fall of ages of the world."[10]

Dr. LaViolette might argue for interpreting the zodiac to mean that only four events of unequal magnitude occur throughout a precessional cycle, and possibly only two really big events. It may be worth noting that "the ice core beryllium-10 record indicates that galactic superwaves pass us about once every 26,000 +-3,000 years, approximating the period of one polar precession cycle, with the possibility of a 13,000 year recurrence interval [halfway through each cycle.] This periodicity may originate in the mechanism that generates superwaves at the Galactic core."[11] The idea of a pole shift every 12-13,000 years may remind readers of Psalm 90:4 "For a thousand years in Your sight Are like yesterday when it passes by, Or as a watch in the night." Twelve "hours" or twelve watches in the night could be like 12,000 years between suns.

By a zodiac interpretation, the greatest destruction may come every 25,800 years, with a slightly less drastic version of the events 12,900 years later at the middle of the cycle, (almost 13,000 years ago) and even more mild (but still civilization-ending) catastrophes at points one-quarter and three-quarters through the cycle (about 6,000 years ago.) Other clues like the Mayan Long Count suggest dividing a precessional cycle in five. Some evidence indicates both divisions are relevant; that the sun has five major electromagnetic events every precessional cycle, and that the galactic center has four outbursts per cycle. Either way, the ends of both the final fifth and the final quarter coincide in our immediate future.

Our scientists cannot even agree on the cause of precession, let alone if destruction comes a certain number of times per cycle. Many scientists assume a luni-solar cause for precession, explaining that the sun and moon pull our equatorial bulge and cause the wobble. But the timing of the equinoxes should also precess if this were the cause, and they have remained at the same point in our year. Other planets also have precession, ruling out a lunar cause. Others point out that measurements for precession seem to be increasing slightly; meaning that the rate of precession is accelerating—and that this is best explained by the theory that our sun is one of two stars in a binary system, with both rotating in a slightly elliptical path around the center of mass. An accelerating precession rate would seem to indicate that our solar system is approaching the closest point in its orbit to this binary center of mass. This theory could also explain the recently discovered sheer edge to our solar system. Instead of matter gradually becoming less and less dense with distance from the sun, there is a clear edge beyond the orbit of Pluto, as if that is approximately midway between our sun and another massive object which sweeps matter away beyond a certain point.

Regardless of the cause, be it luni-solar, an undiscovered binary companion, or the heartbeat of the galactic core—the precessional cycle does seem to be linked to cycles of destruction here on Earth. Most dates given for the extinction of Neanderthal man estimate it happened between 24-28,000 years ago—just one precessional cycle back—and perhaps the geomagnetic changes and high cosmic dust levels that are known to have accompanied their demise[12] were also accompanied by an extinction-level-event—a shifting of the planet's crust over the interior.

Newer evidence also indicates that Neanderthals nearly died out two precessional cycles back: "Some event - possibly changes in the climate - caused Neanderthal populations in the West to crash around 50,000 years ago… The amount of genetic variation in geologically older Neanderthals as well as in Asian Neanderthals [prior to the event around 50,000 B.C.] was just as great as in modern humans... The variation among later European Neanderthals was not even as high as that of modern humans in Iceland."[13] What these scientists are telling us is that Neanderthals had a huge and genetically diverse population, comparable to ours, prior to the end of the precessional cycle around 50,000 B.C. Then the population was almost wiped out, and a small group of survivors repopulated Neanderthal Europe until one precession cycle back, when they went completely extinct. What does that tell us about the imminent end of this precessional cycle?

The authors of "Hamlet's Mill" note a significant difference in myth and religion between societies with known records of many world ages versus cultures who remember only the last destruction. Comparing the stories of old societies like India and European cultures of newer formation with this point in mind: "it is Vishnu's function to return as avenger at fixed intervals of time... But in the West, where the continuity of cosmic processes as told by myth has been forgotten... it is an unrepeated event accomplished by one figure."[14]

The cyclical nature of cosmic processes seems to have been institutionally "forgotten" by the early fourth century Church. Gnostic Christians were proud of ancient knowledge and felt "that the numerical science of the pagan philosophers could be adapted to prove the truth of Christianity. The Church, on the other hand, taught that the coming of Christ was a unique event that had raised human understanding above its previous level, rendering all earlier religions obsolete."[15] It is pleasant to think of one's future as a straight line, moving forward in linear progress, and to ignore the fact that the universe is based on circles and cycles. The future can seem less meaningful, if everything merely repeats... One major result of this paradigm shift in thought to linear time, and not honoring the idea of cyclic time or ancient wisdom is that Christianity does not emphasize cyclic destruction, but explains the need to remake the world only one more time (and only a few times altogether between Genesis and Revelations.)

This is not to say that the Christian Bible does not describe such events, but it does so differently than many eastern myths, which are more clear in their descriptions. Hebrew stories are influenced by the Egyptian idea that celestial wisdom is to be a secret understanding between the initiated priesthood "who were able to read the astronomical allegories in which deeper secrets, not granted to the common herd, lay concealed. We presume that these people were once called the 'Followers of Horus.'"[16] In ancient Egyptian initiation rites of Crata Repoa, a high priest would say to an initiate: "To you who come hither to acquire the right of listening I address myself: the doors of this Temple are firmly closed to the profane, they cannot enter hither, but you, Menes Musee, Child of Celestial works and research, listen to my voice, for I am about to disclose to you great truths." The initiate would then learn that various phrases and names "had a higher signification than was known to the people."[17]

The Jews were influenced greatly by this Egyptian way of thinking. They lived in Egypt for centuries, and we know that when they left their great leader "Moses was educated in all the learning of the Egyptians." (Acts 7:22) Joseph and Mary also took Jesus to Egypt for many years, so it is not surprising that "Christ addressed himself to 'those who have ears to hear'"—only those initiated into the knowledge of astronomical mysteries would understand.[18] As the great Egyptologist P. Le Page Renouf said of Egyptian religious texts: "The difficulty is not in literally translating the text, but in understanding the meaning which lies concealed beneath familiar words. A great part of Egyptian literature is cryptic; its true significance was probably unknown in the Ptolemaic period even to the Egyptians themselves."[19] There is a Hermetic tradition stating that the Egyptian wisdom god Thoth "succeeded in understanding the mysteries of the heavens [and to have] revealed them by inscribing them in sacred books which he then hid here on earth, intending that they should be searched for by future generations but found only by the fully worthy."[20] Perhaps it is not that the books themselves are hidden, but that the wisdom is hidden in books which are widely available.

This may be similar to a mention of secret books in the non-canonical writings of Esdras. The following activities were omitted in the Latin translation (and the English ones based on it) but in some old versions God appears to Ezra and commands him to write down and restore the laws. Ezra gathers five other scribes and recites the words while they write them. Forty days later they have completed ninety-four books; twenty-four books we know in the Old Testament and seventy secret books. These details help us better understand: "Make public the twenty-four books that you wrote first, and let the worthy and the unworthy read them; but keep the seventy that were written last, in order to give them to the wise among your people." (2 Esdras 14:45–46 RSV; 4 Ezra 12:45–46) Could there really be missing books three times the size of the Old Testament that are hidden from us? Or could there be "books worth" of messages in the Bible right now, hidden from the masses, which only the wise will recognize when they read it?

The Bible often uses "Initiatic language, intended to be misunderstood alike by suspicious authorities and the ignorant crowd."[21] Archaic language has wording carefully chosen to show relationships between words—as many as possible—while modern wording is more abstract and self-contained. For example, if reading, "there is a box" today we keep that thought of an undefined box out of context and think little of it. No additional details are assumed unless and until more clarification is given. We may hope the author tells us more, we may expect more, but we do not strive to fill in mental blanks with known relationships. The archaic reader would have been more likely to immediately wonder if the author was hinting at a coffin, a treasure chest, or Pandora's box.

Ancient writing was crafted with the assumption that educated readers would be looking for relationships and secondary meanings of phrases. These are often lost over time and with translation into new languages. India's "Rig Veda" and "Mahabharata," Homer's "Iliad" and "Odyssey," the Mayan "Popul Vuh" and "Chilam Balam," the Old and New Testaments of the Bible, Egypt's "Book of the Dead," "Book of Gates," "Book of What is in the Duat," the "Coffin Texts," and the "Pyramid Texts"… these "have been studied by scholars—the majority of whom would not dispute that they incorporate a complex network of astronomical references, symbols, allegories and allusions. Only a handful of researchers, however, have considered the possibility that these astronomical characteristics could constitute the essence of the texts." (the author [Hancock] is referring mostly to the Egyptian books.)[22] Specifically commenting on the "Book of the Dead," Santillana and von Dechend complain that most historians and interpreters feel the numbers and symbols are just "'mystical' talk, and must be treated as holy mumbo jumbo… even 370 specific astronomical terms would not" deter them from their focus on mystical interpretations.[23]

Another form of information encoded into most ancient stories made use of gematria, a lost art very few people use or recognize today. But "the founders of Christianity… are known to have framed their sacred writings in a number code, and thus it comes about that many passages and whole books in the New Testament are susceptible to numerical interpretation."[24] Gematria is based on the idea that letters have specific numerical values, and that words, phrases, and names of the same numerical values were understood to have similar or related meanings. For one example, we can consider words with the total letter value 729 as being related. The relationships in the following examples (which are almost entirely from "Jesus Christ, Sun of God" by David R. Fideler) may seem merely like interesting coincidences to us, but to ancient readers these were extremely meaningful facts that bound and reinforced central ideas.

Remember Plutarch said: "the mystic symbols are well known to us who belong to the brotherhood."[25] Worship of the sun and other astronomical bodies was universal and ancient, and it was understood that symbolism, myths, stories, and allegedly historical people and events were often just personifications of the sun. Was there really a "Jason" who sought to recover a real Golden Fleece; or is the golden fleece a phrase for the sun in Aires (the fleece-covered ram) and a reference to that zodiac age which ended so many thousands of years ago, during the Golden Age just before the dawn of the civilizations we know from 3100 B.C.? "Astrotheology has been the principal religious concept globally since the dawn of human history"[26] and our ancestors based many symbols, numbers, myths, and religions around the sun.

Consider the number 729. Plutarch, a priest of Apollo at Delphi, said 729 is a number of the sun. Socrates said 729 "is closely concerned with human life, if human life is concerned with days and weeks and months and years." (Socrates also "called the Sun not God himself but the son of God.")[27] This indicates a solar/calendar link to the number, maybe even an eschatological link between 729's gematria and the end of the world. The number of Cephas, the Aramaic name for Peter, is 729, which is both 9*9*9 and 27*27 — a square number and a cube number. As 6 is a number of man, and 8 is a number of the Lord, then a cube, having six sides and eight corners, unites the two. So 729, the number of Cephas/Peter, (the rock) unites man and God as Christ (the sun) is mediator between heaven (the cube of 3D space) and earth.

Peter's position as the rock and Heaven's gatekeeper should not be overlooked if we should, through the gematria of 729, assume that the sun is decisive at this gate of heaven. A cube of 729 cubic units has sides 9 units long, forming 6 squares of 81 square units area per side - total surface of 486 square units. 486 is the number of Peter (Petra) "the rock" in Greek. If Cephas/Peter is the rock the church is built on, and his name was chosen to indicate the sun, (and squares and cubes) then the sun is central to Christianity. A magic square of 729 (a square of numbers where all columns and rows add up to the same total) has 365 in the middle box, the number of days in a year.[28] The sun-god Mithras, who was prominent immediately prior to Christianity, has a name value of 365 in gematria.[29] These cannot all be coincidences.

Another interesting number from the Bible is 153. "Archimedes, in his treatise 'On the Measurement of the Circle' uses the whole number ratio 153:265 to accurately approximate the irrational ratio" the square root of three. (Technically the author quoting Archimedes should have this ratio inversed, 265/153 is 1.732.) As for the vesica piscis he mentions later, (an eye shaped cross section between overlapping circles that cross each other's centers) it does have a top to bottom measure of 153 relative to a left point to right

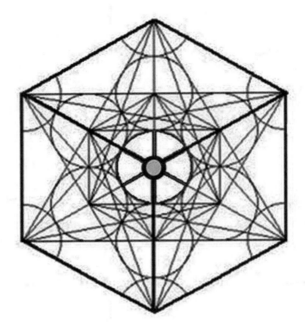

point measure of 265. "Moreover, Archimedes uses this value (153) in such a manner as to suggest that this approximation was well known to his contemporaries, it required no word explanation at all."[30]

Much like 3.14 is instantly recognizable to any educated person today as the value of Pi, the ratio between a circle's diameter and circumference, ancient readers (only the elite were literate) were expected to understand that a mention of the uncommon number 153 was a reference to the square root of three, and that this indicates the length of the diagonal across opposite corners of a cube. Mere mention of 153 could tell an ancient reader to consider the diagonal axis of the cube of space, which if viewed head on from a corner, reducing this diagonal to a point, shows a pattern much like the Kabbalah's "Tree of Life" with six of the cube's eight corners forming a six pointed star on the outside, and the front and back corners overlapping each other in the center over the diagonal axis.

The Kabbalah is the Jewish mystical tradition which expounds on the books of the Old Testament. Its first book is the "Sephir

Yetzirah," which translates as the "book of creation" and "describes constructing the cube of infinite space."[31] Leonora Leet comments on this and tells us that many mythical meanings must be grasped through numeric and geometric associations.

Some believe the mere mention of 153 is a request to consider "the sun behind the sun," the alignment of the galactic center great sun behind the sun, or an even more distinct astronomical arrangement where every point on the cube corners is represented by a heavenly body. Two Hebrew names of God "Jahweh" = 26 and "Jah" =15 have a ratio of 1.733, again like the square root of three (which can be approximated even more accurately using 265 and 153) and Jahweh and Jah may refer to that same alignment of sun and galactic center. The biblical reference to catching 153 fish in John 21:11 would have made educated Greeks of that era recall the cube of space, the sun behind the sun, and the vesica piscis and know that the net holding the fish would geometrically be made up of rhombuses with a short 153 axis and a long 265 axis.[32] They would also know the gematria of Apollo (1061) Zeus (612) and Hermes (353) and know that 1061/612 is about the same (1.7337) as is 612/353 (1.7337) Educated readers in ancient times would also know that "fishes"= 1224 and "the net"= 1224, both of which are 8 times 153, as if to draw attention to the Lordly number 8 and possibly to point out the eight cube corners, including the sun, and the one behind it.[33] It would also help illustrate that the (winter solstice) sun in the galactic center is like the fishes in the net; that the time when this alignment occurs is important to Jesus as the fisher of men.

"The god Apollo" has a value of 1415 in gematria, like the square root of two, 1.415. "The god Apollo" therefore draws attention to the square, and the cross shaped letter X. The Roman value of X is 1000, which multiplied by the square root of 2 (1.415) equals 1415 for "the god Apollo." This hints at putting the sun-god on the cross of the ecliptic and Milky Way, as depicted on the Glory Cross or Nativity Cross. The square root of 2 times the square root of 3 equals 2.448, just as 2448 is the sum of the two 1224s from "fishes" plus "the net."

In John 21:3-11 Simon Peter decides to go fishing on the Sea of Galilee. Other disciples join him, but they catch nothing that night. In the morning, Jesus spoke to them from the nearby shore, but they didn't know it was him. He told them to cast the net to the right of the boat, and they then caught 153 fish. He didn't help them catch "hundreds of fish," they caught exactly 153, and we should not overlook the significance of the number just because we today are not used to thinking in terms of gematria and related meanings. This reference to the boat may be to the sun boat, the Egyptian "Boat of Millions of Years," the sun as it travels across the zodiac in the cycle of precession. At the end of the cycle, in the 21st century, the sun-boat is just left of the galactic center. Casting a net from the sun-boat to the right would net the galactic center, the central sun behind the sun in the cube of space. Are all these gematria values coincidences? Or are there real and important relationships between these names, numbers, words, and phrases?

On the internet we can also find Daniel Gleason's thoughts on gematria. On one web site he appears to be writing a book which may eventually be published under the title "The Gospels seen as Sacred Geometry Plays: A Gematria Based Commentary on Mark" or "Jesus 8880: The Sacred Geometry Mysteries of Christianity." He says "The purpose of this book is to demonstrate that the entire gospel of Mark is a gematria play filled with exquisite geometry riddles, a geometric cartoon book from the first verse to the last. Every single verse is geometrically true. The same goes for the Book of Revelation."[34] He also has a site at Jesus8880.com at which he clarifies: "Each gospel verse is a drawing instruction based on very clever puns and word play that occur in virtually every verse... The word 'gematria' comes from the Greek word geometria having the dual meaning 'earth-measure' and 'geometry.' Gematria is Sacred Geometry. The definition of gematria goes way beyond adding up the numerical values of the letters in a word... Gematria is the union of the number value of Greek words with the dimensions of geometric objects such as the perimeters of circles and squares or the lengths of symmetrical groups of lines that converge on circles and squares. The power and mystery of gematria is only unleashed when it is used in conjunction with geometry, graphs, and/or diagrams."[35]

Perhaps it is best applied to geometry in the sky, as Acharya S tells us that for many word-plays "the key to their decoding was essentially astrotheology."[36] Gleason draws an analogy between raising a number one row on an abacus, which effectively multiplies it by ten, and raising Jesus, at least numerically: The "1st 3 words of Revelation (Apocalypse Jesus Christ) have a value of 3880, which is a "RAISED" number (multiplied by ten, as raising a level on an abacus would do) of 388, (the sun) just like 8880 is Jesus/888 raised."[37] Is raising Jesus to heaven the same as raising the sun to the galactic center?

Is this all related to the main symbol of Freemasonry, the square and compass with the mysterious "G" in the middle? The square and compass are definitely used to measure and draw squares and circles, and many believe the "G" stands for God, and Geometry… and Gematria. Freemasons may be the one society left still initiating higher level members into the mysteries of the magi and the Followers of Horus, and their rituals are loaded with astronomical symbolism. But after a few years as a mason and not being able to make any progress learning about masonic astrology or related hidden concepts, Albert Pike's comments on keeping such knowledge from lower level members feels accurate to me: "The initiate… is intentionally misled by false interpretations. It is not intended that he shall understand them; but it is intended that he shall imagine he understands them."[38] Statements such as these are maddening to someone who hoped to learn a lot more on such topics in a reasonable number of years, but perhaps as some allege there is a fraternity within the fraternity. As the organization's highest members are very tight-lipped about their deepest secrets and I dropped out of masonry I will never know firsthand.

It is also unfortunate that every interesting old book on masonic astrology which may have shed light on this subject is rare and hard to obtain. The only place which should by law have a copy of every book, the Library of Congress, has somehow allowed every interesting title on a "wanted" list of masonic astrology books to be "stolen." Gleason hints at an interesting book which one society will show you—but only after fifteen probationary years of membership in their organization. They must believe it holds important secrets.

There are countless other related tangents (Enoch, Metatron's Cube, etc.) which we must avoid getting into if we are ever to get back to "Hamlet's Mill" and a more direct emphasis on mythical wordplay hinting at pole shifts. As one author tells us, "initiates into one or more mystery schools and secret societies... relate esoteric information, such as deliberately created plays-on-words, based not necessarily on those words' primary meanings."[39] The fifth century writer Macrobius said "Those who have learned the mysteries should hide the unsearchable secrets." This can be very misleading if one doesn't understand the need to look for secondary hidden meanings; fortunately we do.

De Santillana and von Dechend called their book *Hamlet's Mill* because *Hamlet* is the best-known English version of a common story in which a golden age under a good king ends, followed by worse times and the quest of the hero—the son of the first good king—and his attempt to reclaim the throne and restore a golden age. The reason for the word "Mill" in the title is that these stories usually involve a rotating millstone, often with a tree as an axis, which breaks and is relocated. Mayan "accounts of the Flood and the erection of world trees" take place repeatedly, in all three books of the "Chilam Balam."[40] "The mill tree is also the world axis" and "the unhinging of the Mill is caused by the shifting of the world axis."[41] With hundreds of similar references from around the world, "The Mill is thus not only very great and ancient, but it must also be central to the original Hamlet story."[42]

"The sphere of heaven was imagined as a turning millstone, and the North Pole as the axle bearing in which the mill-iron turns."[43] After comparing many similar stories from around the world, the authors point out: "The identity of the Mill, in its many versions, with heaven is thus universally understood and accepted. But... why does it always happen that this Mill, the peg of which is Polaris, had to be wrecked or unhinged? Once the archaic mind grasped the forever-enduring rotation, what caused it to think that the axle jumps out of the hole? What memory of catastrophic events has created this story of destruction? Why should Vainamoinen (and he is not the only one) state explicitly that another Mill has to be constructed? Why had Dhruva to be appointed to play Pole star—and for a given cycle? For the story refers in no way to the creation of the world... What actually comes to an end is a world" but not the world.[44] One positioning, one set of climactic conditions and ocean currents, one distribution of empires and races of people—is destroyed and replaced with survivors under the new conditions.

There are many Bible references along these lines as well. For one example, Isaiah 22:25 says "'In that day,' declares the LORD of hosts, 'the peg driven in a firm place will give way; it will even break off and fall, and the load hanging on it will be cut off, for the LORD has spoken.'" This is probably referring to earth's axis of rotation and to pole stars like Kochab whose name means "mill peg" in Arabic. We will inspect more such Bible passages that describe a pole shift and a change in the Earth's axis later.

There are countless myths and stories of a catastrophic flood from around the world. Most Westerners are familiar with the description of Noah's flood. But this story confuses readers by emphasizing forty days of rain, and not emphasizing waters rising up from the deep. The cause of the flood was not rainfall, that was a side effect of the pole shift. Even if the atmosphere could hold the required amount of water for such rain, and even if it could have rained enough for sea level to rise approximately 17,000 feet to the top of Mt. Aararat on which many believe the ark came to rest—that would require an average of 425 feet of rainfall per day—almost four inches of rain per minute over the entire surface of the planet for forty days straight. A more likely explanation is the shifting of the crust, which would make the oceans slosh out of their basins in massive tsunamis. A tsunami coming up the Tigris-Euphrates River Valley would also explain why Noah's ark would travel uphill to Turkey instead of being washed out to sea. Undersea volcanism along countless new faults would boil millions of tons of seawater which would fall back as rain—just not enough for 425 feet of rain per day.

The Sibylline Oracles are attributed to the Greek prophetess

167

Sibyll and were allegedly based on her frenzied utterances while in a trancelike state. She lived several centuries before Christ but the written oracles may have been edited and rewritten as late as the fifth century A.D. The 1918 translation by H.N. Bate includes the following line from Book V: "And then in his anger the immortal God who dwells on high shall hurl from the sky a fiery bolt on the head of the unholy: and SUMMER SHALL CHANGE TO WINTER IN THAT DAY." Bate himself feels the original words may have been changed, and offers a similar line from Book VIII for comparison: "And then the imperishable God who dwells in the sky in anger will cast a lightning bolt from heaven against the power of the impious. INSTEAD OF WINTER THERE WILL BE SUMMER ON THAT DAY." Modified or not, the Greek stories definitely tell a tale of God casting down a bolt from heaven and reversing the seasons, which could only occur along with a major change in the position or rotation of the Earth's crust.

A pole shift would also explain records of a wayward sun. Consider the originally oral tradition of Phaethon, put into the form of a written story by Ovid, Nonnos, and other ancient Greek writers. The sun god Helios took an oath by the river Styx that he would grant any wish made by his half-mortal son Phaethon, who was visiting his father for the first time. Phaethon had only one wish—to drive his father's sun-chariot for a day. Helios knew this would be a problem, and gave his son a poetic introduction to astronomy, warning him of many possible problems. As feared, Phaethon could not handle the reins, and with the solar horses out of control, Ovid wrote that Phaethon draws back in fear as he approaches the stinger of Scorpius, and lets go of the reins. The sun wanders the sky, scorches the earth, and Atlas "fails to balance the world's hot axis on his shoulders." Nonnos wrote that "the very axle bent which runs through the middle of the revolving heavens."

It is worth noting that the stinger of the Scorpius constellation is close to and pointing at the galactic center. So when Helios (the sun—probably the winter solstice sun) took an oath by the river Styx (the sun was at the edge of the Milky Way) Phaethon drove the sun to the stinger of the scorpion (reached the galactic center near Scorpio's tail) and the world was almost completely destroyed. Zeus eventually came to the rescue, zapping Phaethon with a bolt of lightning to end his wild ride. Another Greek story tells us "Zeus tilted a 'table'... And in tilting the 'table' caused the Flood of Deukalion, the 'table,' of course, being the earth-plane through the ecliptic."[45]

Such a story could easily be a description of pole shift events, which were better understood in ancient times. For example, in his famous "Laws," Plato wrote over 2500 years ago of a conversation on such cycles of destruction between Clinias and an unnamed Athenian:

Athenian: Do you consider that there is any truth in the ancient tales?

Clinias: What tales?

Athenian: That the world of men has often been destroyed by floods, plagues, and many other things, in such a way that only a small portion of the human race has survived?

Clinias: Everyone would regard such accounts as perfectly credible.

Athenian: Come now, let us picture to ourselves one of the many catastrophes—namely, that which occurred once upon a time through the Deluge.

Clinias: And what are we to imagine about it?

Athenian: That the men who then escaped destruction must have been mostly herdsmen of the hill, scanty embers of the human race preserved somewhere on the mountaintops.

Clinias: Evidently...

Athenian: Shall we assume that the cities situated in the plains and near the sea were totally destroyed at the time?

Clinias: Let us assume it...

Plato added further to the mystery when he wrote in his dialogue "The Statesman": "At periods the universe has its present circular motion, and at other periods it revolves in the reverse direction...Of all the changes which take place in the heavens this reversal is the greatest and most complete." Plato warns this period of reversal is far from orderly: "There is at that time great destruction of animals in general, and only a small part of the human race survives." In 1889 Marshall Wheeler wrote "The whole world should be informed of the fact and means taken to forever perpetuate the knowledge so that when the dread event transpires, mankind should not lapse again into prehistoric barbarism."[46] Of course our ancestors have taken means to forever perpetuate this knowledge. (But if an elite exists today with member families looking out for their own survival and power, and these rich and powerful elites look forward to the mass depopulation of "useless eaters" then it is not in their interests to let everyone know ahead of time...) Many other pole shift researchers, (even the conservative Charles Hapgood) convinced by the evidence most people know little about, suggest that governments should make plans to quickly relocate populations in peril.[47] One group in Illinois has taken this upon themselves. As Tom Valentine wrote of the Stelle Group in "The Life & Death of Planet Earth": "We intend to survive, not only with our skins, but with technology, so that mankind need not revert again to a stone age existence. We intend to implement the great plan of the Brotherhoods as best as we can."[48]

Plato also wrote in "Timeaus" of an Egyptian high priest named Sonchis initiating the Greek Solon into their mystery schools of wisdom and teaching him about their long historical records of cycles of destruction:

"There have been, and will be again, many destructions of mankind arising out of many causes; the greatest have been brought about by the agencies of fire and water, and other lesser ones by innumerable other causes. There is a story, which even you have preserved, that once upon a time Phaeton ... having yoked the steeds in his father's chariot, because he was not able to drive them in the path of his father, burnt up all that was upon the earth, and was himself destroyed by a thunderbolt. Now this has the form of a myth, but really signifies a declination of the bodies moving in the heavens around the earth, and a great conflagration of things upon the earth, which recurs after long intervals; at such times those who live upon the mountains and in dry and lofty places are more liable to destruction than those who dwell by rivers or on the seashore.

170

When, on the other hand, the gods purge the earth with a deluge of water, the survivors in your country are herdsmen and shepherds who dwell on the mountains, but those who, like you, live in cities are carried by the rivers into the sea. Whereas in this land, neither then nor at any other time, does the water come down from above on the fields, having always a tendency to come up from below; for which reason the traditions preserved here are the most ancient. The fact is, that wherever the extremity of winter frost or of summer does not prevent, mankind exists, sometimes in greater, sometimes in lesser numbers. And whatever happened either in your country or in ours, or in any other region of which we are informed — if there were any actions noble or great or in any other way remarkable, they have all been written down by us of old, and are preserved in our temples.

Whereas just when you and other nations are beginning to be provided with letters and the other requisites of civilized life, *after the usual interval*, the stream from heaven, like a pestilence, comes pouring down, and leaves only those of you who are destitute of letters and education; and so you have to begin all over again like children, and know nothing of what happened in ancient times, either among us or among yourselves."

If this distinction between the educated and uneducated was appreciated by the uneducated survivors, it may be relevant that God's first instructions to man included a warning not to eat from the tree of knowledge. Survivors of a pole shift may have noticed that all the sophisticated people with books and universities were washed away, perhaps because they knew too much and God didn't want them to. Instead of trying to recover as much knowledge as possible from the remains of civilization, many cultures might develop a fear of books, wisdom, and other artifacts as things that bring down the wrath of God. What little evidence that might remain after a pole shift may be intentionally destroyed by many cultures, who often wrote that the last people before the destruction had great knowledge and abilities and tried to be too godlike.

Fortunately for us this was not the case in Egypt, where astronomy and other sciences were viewed as divine truths to be maintained and

171

revered by kings and priests. To give an idea of just how far back Egyptian recordkeeping may go, the "Turin Papyrus" (currently in a museum in Turin, Italy) has a list of kings before King Menes, who united Upper and Lower Egypt around 3,100 B.C. The list says that the Shemsu Hor, the Followers of Horus, ruled for a total of 13,420 years, and that others before them reigned a total of 23,200 years. The papyrus even adds up these reigns (plus a few other mortal kings) so there is no misunderstanding when it reads "Total 36,620 years." As that is the total before Menes, this list, if accurate, contains records going back over 40,000 years. Ancient Indian records also claim a history spanning tens of thousands of years.

The conversation describing reversals of rotation was comparatively recent, having taken place approximately 560 B.C., when Sonchis told Salon that approximately 9,000 years earlier, a great empire called Atlantis had been destroyed. Rand and Rose Flem-Ath, authors of "When the Sky Fell: In Search of Atlantis," believe that Atlantis existed in West Antarctica prior to a pole shift that occurred around 9,600 B.C. and removed Antarctica from a more temperate position. Geologist Robert Schoch cites evidence for a major rise in the temperature of North Atlantic seawater (14 degrees Fahrenheit) within 15 years around 9645 B.C.[49] Animal remains buried in the silt clay of the Gulf of Mexico's Soto Canyon can be carbon dated to approximately 11-12,000 years ago. This coincides with a huge influx of fresh water (melting glaciers) which geology professor Dr. Cesare Emiliani dates to 9,600 B.C.[50]

Most Egyptian temples, however, including the Great Pyramid and the Sphinx, are astronomically aligned to the position stars had been located at even further back, in 10,500 B.C. The Egyptians referred to this era as "Zep Tepi"—"The First Time." Perhaps they had a high civilization at that point, and commemorated an important event then by showing us how our skies would have looked at a date far back in time. This date before the shift may have been very important to them even if their nation was later devastated at a date of more importance to us around 9,600 B.C. If America's destruction came today, would future archeologists find anything

built to commemorate 2012 or 2019, or just 1776?

Egypt was not always a desert; conditions were once much more suitable to civilization. Schwaller de Lubicz analyzed the Temple of Amun-Mut-Khonsu at Luxor (Temple of Man) in Egypt for twelve years. After studying its measures and proportions, its axes and orientations, the symbolism of its bas-reliefs, and additional related medical and mathematical papyri, de Lubicz wrote "The Temple of Man" to demonstrate how advanced the civilization of Ancient Egypt was, for he felt the Egyptians had built an architectural encyclopedia in stone to record everything they knew about humanity and the universe. Many authors feel the same way about the pyramids at Giza. The base perimeter to height ratio is Pi, demonstrating the ancient understanding of circles, and that the pyramid perimeter represents a circle. The ratio of Earth's polar radius to pyramid height is 43,200, which shows they knew the size of the Earth, and that the pyramid perimeter represents the equator, with the whole pyramid representing the northern hemisphere. The angle from a corner to the King's Chamber above the base is 23.5 degrees, the angle of Earth's axial inclination. The base length of the Great Pyramid is 365.242 cubits—the same number of days per year as it takes our planet to orbit the sun.

The Sphinx has also been analyzed by geologists such as Dr.

173

Robert Schoch. Schoch isn't trying to make grand claims about Egyptian civilization but he does conclusively demonstrate massive erosion of the Sphinx' surface by rainfall—to a degree not possible under current climactic conditions. In his efforts to be conservative he only goes on record pushing the envelope back slightly—saying the erosion by rainfall on the Sphinx had to take place at least 7,000-9,000 years ago. But such rainy conditions in North Africa are known to have occurred approximately ten to fifteen thousand years ago. His collaborator John Anthony West writes "I remain convinced that the Sphinx must predate the breakup of the last Ice Age."[51]

Of course we were all taught in school that the pyramids and the Sphinx are a mere 4500 years old. We were taught that the face on the Sphinx represents the Pharaoh Khafre, all because the single syllable "Khaf" was found inscribed on a stela near the Sphinx. But royal names were always and without exception carved with an oval surrounding their entire name; these are called cartouches.[52] Even if this example is the only exception in all of Egyptian civilization, and that one syllable really refers to Khafre, it doesn't necessarily mean he built anything—he may have simply organized a restoration (if he did anything there at all.) But if Khafre, or any known Pharaoh,

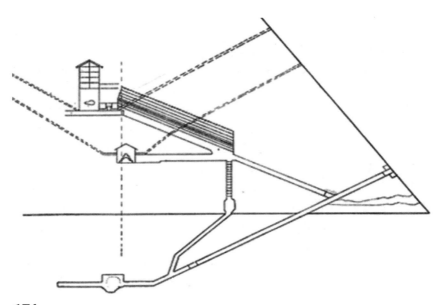

really built the Sphinx or the Great Pyramids of Giza within the last 5,000 years, then the Egyptians (who documented fine details on many things) have a strange absence of documentation on their most impressive construction projects. The Cambridge Archeological Journal quotes Mark Lehner anyway and stubbornly supports the mainstream claim: "Although we are certain that the Sphinx dates to the Fourth Dynasty, we are confronted by a complete absence of Old Kingdom Texts which mention it."[53]

Mark Lehner, interestingly, had a large portion of his education (to become an Egyptologist) paid for by the Edgar Cayce Association for Research and Enlightenment—but Lehner later renounced any beliefs he may have once shared with them regarding psychic abilities or the Atlantean origins of Egyptian civilization. Some people believe he caved in to pressure from Zawi Hawass and 'sold out' to be accepted and have a career in mainstream Egyptology. Zawi Hawass used his position as the powerful, long-reigning, but thankfully (as of 2011) former Chief Inspector of the Giza Pyramid Plateau and Minister of State for Antiquities Affairs to restrict exploration and reject evidence of anything extremely ancient. For example, when presented with certain evidence of very ancient artifacts which had been verified by carbon dating he said: "Carbon-dating is useless. This science will never develop. In archeology we consider carbon dating results imaginary."[54] On DNA testing he said: "It is not always accurate and it cannot always be done with complete success when dealing with mummies. Until we know for sure that it is accurate, we will not use it in our research."[55] As John Anthony West once said (to Graham Hancock) "Egyptologists are the last people in the world to address any anomaly."[56] Many researchers suspect that Hawass has excavated secret digs and knows with certainty that Egypt had a civilization over 10,000 years ago. If he is hiding and suppressing interesting artifacts and information, we may never know.

Assuming that mainstream Egyptologists are not just completely lying and withholding the truth, perhaps the majority of the site at Giza is very ancient but some major additions were made around 2,500 B.C.—for there is no recorded description of anyone building the pyramids or the sphinx; only a few mentions of digging away the surrounding sand and restoring them. It is possible that the bases of the pyramids were built as observatories long before additional layers were added to reach a point closer to the top; especially if ancient builders viewed their "unfinished" pyramids as symbolic representations of man's striving towards divine perfection without ever being able to reach it.

This idea received fresh support in the spring of 2012 when a video went viral on Youtube showing dozens of stars etched into the ceiling of the "air shaft" just before "Gantenbrink's Door" in the Great Pyramid. Twenty years ago a German team sent a robot with cameras up the tunnel in the pyramid until it reached a door blocking the way. At the time everyone was fascinated by the existence of the door and no one noticed that pock marks on the ceiling corresponded to stars and constellations—as they were aligned around 9,200 B.C. As the long shaft is only eight inches wide; it had to be carved when the pyramid was built.

When authors like Schoch and West and Hancock first set out to show that the Sphinx and pyramids were far more than 5,000 years old they were met with great criticism and the consensus was that there simply wasn't any civilization much before 3,100 B.C. But more evidence has come to light since 1990, like the ruins of Gobekli Tepe in eastern Turkey. The German Archeological Institute has been excavating there since 1994 under Klaus Schmidt, and they have proven that the monoliths and other carvings there date to 9,000—10,000 B.C. Dr. Schoch comments on this: "When I first presented my findings on the age of the Great Sphinx, I was told over and over again by mainstream archaeologists and historians that my dating was simply impossible because it was well known that nothing so elaborate and sophisticated, requiring an advanced level of social organisation, could occur so early. Göbekli Tepe proves these assertions false and helps place the Great Sphinx in a larger context."[57] Other geologists like Colin Reader and David Coxill now back Schoch's opinion on the weathering and dating of the Sphinx. Unfortunately for mankind something seems to have destroyed whatever early civilizations existed around 12,000 years ago, and we mostly find the remains of newer civilizations after about 3,100 B.C.

Egyptian civilization at this time was at its height as it began; a leftover relic of something earlier that declined after it first appeared. "Egyptian science, medicine, mathematics and astronomy were all of an exceptionally higher order of refinement and sophistication than modern scholars will acknowledge... [and] many of the achievements of the earlier dynasties were never surpassed or even equaled later on."[58] "The great riddle in the quest for the origin of human culture is that civilizations appear suddenly, at their peak, as if ready made."[59] If there were civilizations 6,000 years ago, they barely left a trace, unless we consider that the civilizations which appeared so suddenly about 5,000 years ago were already fully developed.

But even at its peak, the Egyptian civilization we know was not capable of building the Great Pyramid. Many of the stones over 200 tons—and they are cut so smoothly and placed so closely that a sheet of paper cannot go between them. They have many mathematical numbers encoded in the measurements—the height is 1/43,200th of the Earth's radius. The circumference to height ratio is Pi—3.14. The unit of measure is the Royal Egyptian Cubit—0.5236 meters. This measure may not seem relevant at first, until we analyze the modern metric system. The French decided to make a "new" unit of measure—the "metre" equal to 1/10,000,000th the distance from the equator to the pole. But the French Freemasons were really making a unit very similar to that of their forefathers in Egypt, for the cubit was also based on that 1/10,000,000th the distance from the equator to the pole—for a circle with that diameter (one meter) divided by six is exactly one cubit. And that cubit was the unit of measure (or a fraction of it) in many places in the ancient world— from Egypt to Stonehenge to Mexico. "The Standard Teotihuacan Unit... is equivalent to the 'Jewish rod' of 3.4757485 ft., the same unit which represents the width of the Stonehenge lintels, a six-millionth part of the earth's polar radius and one part in 37,800,000 of its mean circumference."[60]

If the capstone were in place on top of the Great Pyramid it would be about 4 inches over 481 feet high. As this height is analogous to the Earth's polar radius, multiply by two for a diameter of about 962 feet 8 inches, multiply by Pi (3.14) and get just under 3023 feet— the circumference of a circle matched by the base of the four sides. This accurately demonstrates the builders understood the value of Pi. Multiply the 481 feet four inches by 12 inches for 5780 inches in height. In the Hebrew calendar it is the year 5772 right now— mid 2012 A.D. In December 2019 the Hebrew year will be 5780, the height of the completed pyramid in inches. Some researchers believe that measurements of the pyramid's internal passageways in inches represent prophecies in years, and that changes in the passageways indicated major events for 1453 B.C. (the Exodus) in 33 A.D. (the crucifixion) and 2012 A.D.—but aside from pyramid height pointing to 2019 I don't see much other conclusive evidence in the pyramids pointing to future events, despite other author's beliefs that the pyramid points out a second coming somewhere near the year 2000.

More credible to this author are the conclusions of Scott Creighton and Gary Osborn. They have analyzed numerous angles in and around the pyramids and determined that the ancients knew more than we thought they did, including not only the 23.5 degree tilt in the Earth's axis but a 6.5 degree shift in the latitude of Giza. They believe the "air shafts" in the pyramid really aim at the post-pole shift position of Osiris' star, Al-Nitak (in Orion's belt) and that the sealed shafts represent the pre-pole shift position of the same star.[61] They also believe that angles between key points on a circle drawn around all the pyramids and the Sphinx lead them to a "Giza-Orion time line" with past and future dates indicating potential cosmic destruction. The two future dates are approximately 8980 A.D., which is too far ahead for our immediate concern, and right now, approximately 2012 A.D.[62] Like the Mayan Pyramid of Kukulkan, they conclude "the Giza pyramids... served as an astronomical clock or calendar that would allow their descendants to know the precise timetable of this deadly Earth calamity and perhaps also the next date of the cycle."[63]

Graham Hancock notes that William Petrie and Charles Piazzi Smith viewed the Great Pyramid as "an advance-warning mechanism" for the Second Coming and suggests the Egyptian measurements could be "vehicles to carry an elaborate and ingenious 'message' from a past epoch otherwise long forgotten to a specific epoch in the future—from the 'First Time' to an astronomically defined 'Last Time.' …We think the evidence suggests a continuous transmission of advanced scientific and engineering knowledge… for the previous 8000 years"[64] [from 10,500 B.C. to 2,500 B.C.]

Of course, once modern investigators started finding interesting links to what may have been a pre-Egyptian source of culture, Muslim authorities lost interest in allowing their research to continue. Anything going against the official history in the Koran is religious heresy; it simply isn't allowed, and that goes for very ancient weathering by rain, very ancient advanced mathematics or technology, finding South American nicotine and cocaine in almost every mummy, and a great many other things which are easily hidden by not allowing any foreign researcher near the Great Pyramid since 1995 or to the Sphinx since 1993.

A similar wall of political correctness prohibits anyone with a PhD in ancient American history from claiming transatlantic contact. The entire concept is institutionally viewed as racist, as if such contact claims Mediterranean societies are superior and American civilizations could not have developed independently.[65] But new discoveries and new understanding of what the pyramids measure (on both sides of the ocean) and represent will come eventually no matter how much authorities try to hide it. Truth is hard to suppress, especially in an age of easily distributed information. And Isaiah 19:19-20 tells us that in the future our perception of the pyramids will change: "In that day there will be an altar to the LORD in the midst of the land of Egypt, and a pillar to the LORD near its border. It will become a sign and a witness to the LORD." The odds of a newly built altar seem slim—perhaps the proof is what will be newly understood, proof regarding a very old altar already in Egypt.

Going back to the era of French and Turkish and British rule in Egypt, there were investigations then where researchers could publish any results and conclusions they came to, without fear of being shut out of Egyptian archeology afterwards. Nineteenth century British archeologists were not constrained by the political correctness of current Egyptology or by the religious concerns of the Koran. C. Piazzi Smyth's *New Measures of the Great Pyramid by a New Measurer,* published in 1884, has a very interesting title for part two, chapter four: "Change in the Position of the World's Axis of Rotation Since the Great Pyramid was Founded." Smyth comments more on gradual precession than pole shifts, but he also mentions "the John Taylor time passage theory"[66] that measurements of the Great Pyramid's internal passageways correspond to prophetic years, and that abrupt changes in the passageways correspond to major events. He had earlier predicted something for 1882 based on this, and perhaps the British conquest of Egypt in that year fulfilled that expectation.

The Egyptian view on the changes in the heavens which lead to catastrophes are even more intriguing. The historian Herodotus writing in 446 B.C. recalls that Egyptian priests told him that over the course of their history "four times within this period the sun changed his usual position, twice rising where he normally sets, and twice setting where he normally rises." (If this happens every half precessional cycle of roughly 13,000 years, then Egypt's records covered a minimum of over 40,000 years of history at the time this was mentioned—as their king's list indicates.) The Egyptian "Book of the Dead" also gives us interesting clues about this. It may help readers to know that Ra is an ancient name for the Egyptian sun-god (at one point in history) but there are many other later names, including Osiris, and Horus. In some myths Ra was replaced by Osiris, who later dies and is replaced by his son Horus, who then becomes Osiris, and the cycle of the sun dying and being reborn continues. In this ancient "Book of the Dead," which is at least five thousand years old, the sun-god Ra, riding in the Boat of Millions of Years, "entered at the head of his holy mariners and established himself on the throne of the two horizons. The holy one had grown old, he dribbled at the mouth, his spittle fell upon the earth... and the sacred serpent bit him. The flame of life departed from him."

It sounds like the Egyptians and the Mayans may have had

similar views on the throne of heaven. The Maya revered the holy crossroads of the two great paths in the sky, the Milky Way and the ecliptic, making that point at the galactic center the "Heart of Heaven." Some believe the Greeks felt that "Zeus signifies the Galactic core."[67] The same can be said for Christianity; as author Tim LaHaye says: "the central object of heaven is the throne of God."[68] It is "the gate of the LORD" of Psalms 118:20, and as Jacob described it in Gen 28:17 "This is none other than the house of God, and this is the gate of heaven."

The Egyptians describe the "throne of the two horizons" and "the tabernacle of the gods in the great double house." The Maya were concerned with the sun-god's death at the time when One Hunahpu, the winter solstice sun, was in alignment with the galactic center, which occurs for many years around 2012. The Egyptians tell us that the sun god Ra is just past his throne on the two horizons when he is dying, and that he says "I had come forth from my tabernacle." Phaethon crashes Apollo's sun-chariot when stung by Scorpius at the galactic center, Ra is bitten by a serpent, quite possibly indicating the same location near the galactic center. The Maya say Heart of Heaven blows mist into people's eyes when he destroys them; Egyptians tell us Ra's spittle and slobber fall to earth.

Osiris became king of the gods "on that day of the union of the two earths... in the double horizon." The "Book of the Dead" continues to clarify that on that day "of the union of the two earths, the gathering of the two earths it is at the sarcophagus of Osiris, the soul living in Suten-henen, the giver of food, the annihilator of sins, he guideth along the road of eternity." So the sun-god Osiris who removes sins dies and is reborn as the sun-god Horus, and he dies at the meeting place of the two horizons. The sun goes dark after suffering from the poison of the serpent's bite, and while the goddess Isis tries to heal Ra, "the divine one hid himself from the gods, and the throne in the Boat of Millions of Years was empty." In Genesis 3:15 God tells the serpent that a great descendant of Eve will kill him, whereas the serpent will only be able to "bruise him in the heel." In a different version of what seems to be the same story, Horus is stung in the foot by a scorpion, and Isis gets the Boat of Millions of Years to stop moving, until the poison is precipitated down to earth. The sun remains stationary in the sky, near Scorpio.[69] In Norse mythology, during Ragnarok—the battle at the end of the world—the sea serpent that encircles the world, Jormungandr (possibly the Milky Way) will arise from the ocean, poisoning the land and sea with his venom and causing the sea to rear up and lash against the land.

There are many similarities to other world myths when during a great catstrophe or even a fight between pantheons of gods, power is transferred from one sun-god to another, possibly during a pole shift. Greeks described a "great year" of about 26,000 years, with a great summer of fire (ekpyrauses) and a great winter of ice (kataclysmos) separated by about 13,000 years.[70] In Greek myth the god Uranus was the first universal ruler. There was a battle in which he cast the Cyclopes and the Hecatoncheires down to Tartarus, like stars falling below the horizon. Their grieving mother Gaia encourages Uranus' son, the Titan Chronos, to lead a rebellion. Chronos castrates Uranus with a sickle and frees the banished gods when he takes power, but later he again banishes the Cyclopes and the Hecatoncheires down to Tartarus. Chronos was prophetically warned that his own son would eventually take power from him, so Chronos ate all his children, except for Zeus, who escaped. Zeus later led his fellow Olympians in a war against Chronos and the other Titans. This war was known as the Titanomachy and was described in many classical Greek poems. The Olympians defeat the Titans and force Atlas to bear the world on his shoulders—as his homeland Atlantis does today, if Atlantis is in fact Antarctica. Our planet is generally viewed as being suspended in space with Antarctica on the bottom, sometimes depicted as resting on Atlas' shoulders.

In Egypt, power passes from Ra to Osiris to Horus, but at various times they are all the sun god, and they all have allied siblings while they fight Set or Seth, often depicted as a scorpion, and his 72 conspirators. Christians have an ancient heavenly dispute in which Lucifer and his angels are cast out of heaven, and a future battle in heaven between good and evil in which Jesus will eventually move towards the right hand of God and take the throne with Him, where he will be given power and kingdom to make a new heaven and a new Earth. Could it be that all these stories are talking about the sun moving to the position of the galactic center, and being empowered by it?

In Norse mythology there was an earlier war in heaven between the gods of the Aesir and the Vanir and Jotuns, but the final battle of Ragnarok takes place in the future and is much more widely known. At the "Fimbelvetr" (terrible winter) the gods will once again fight each other to the death and the Sun and the Earth will barely survive. Odin's eye was long ago placed at Mimir's well of wisdom (the sun at the galactic center) and we are told of "Odin's eye appearing as a visible object in the sky during times of calamity… the sudden appearance of Odin's eye was a presage to a world-encompassing disaster."[71] The story tells us that Heimdall's horn is sounded like a trumpet to announce the world's fate. The dragon Nidhug gnaws through the roots of Yggdrasil, the world tree from which Odin once hung himself as a sacrifice. Jormungandr, the Midgard serpent, rises from the depths and thrashes violently in an attempt to find dry land; this causes the seas to boil over and flood the world.

Thor kills Jormungandr, but before it dies it spatters the sea and sky with so much poison that Thor drowns in its venom. Odin leads the immortals of Asgard and the 43,200 reincarnated noble warriors from Valhalla's 540 doors onto the final battlefield. Odin is killed by the wolf Fenris/Fenrir, but Odin's son Vidar kills the wolf. Stars fall, and darkness covers the world. Surt flings fire over the Earth, and the great tree Yggdrasil burns. The seas flow over the earth, and the sun and moon are dead and gone.

In Snorri's "Gylfaginning," King Gylfi asks "What happens when the whole world has burned up, the gods are dead, and all mankind is gone?" An Aesir answers "The earth rises up from the sea again… children of men will be found safe… and strange to say, the sun, before being devoured by Fenrir, will have borne a daughter."[72] Many other Norse gods pair off and kill each other. In summary, there is a central world tree, hell, middle earth, and heaven, and a final battle involving a venomous dragon, boiling seas, flooded lands, and the death of almost everything—the sun and moon and stars, and the world tree axis, and most of the gods and mankind.

In ancient India Hinduism tells of four exterminated worlds, and describes the galactic center as "a grand center, the seat of Brahma,"[73] or even as the high god himself: "the galactic center is called 'Brahma,' the creative force, or 'Vishnunabhi,' the navel of Vishnu."[74] In the story of Dhruva, he contemplated this cosmic center as Vishnu's seat, and the mere act of focusing on the idea of Vishnu's seat at the galactic center made the Earth bend and shake and sink down, until eventually Vishnu transformed Dhruva into the pole star, Polaris. Why do so many cultures associate this point in the sky with their highest gods, and with a pole shift? Ancient Indian stories hint at this; the "Rig Veda" itself testifies that it has a hidden meaning in verse 4.3.16.

In Egypt "we can deduce from the texts that Ra, i.e. the sun's disc, was seen somehow to merge or to unite—or 'coalesce'—with Horakti." (Horus of the Horizon) With the astronomical alignment of the sun and the galactic center "the composite deity Ra-Horakti" comes into being. Nothing dramatic happens when they are not united together, but at the alignment when Horus and Osiris are both at the throne—or Atum-Ra—or Ra-Horakti—then new powers are manifested and devastation follows. "Osiris remained 'inert, asleep or listless, and completely passive' until the Horus-King was able to undertake a 'journey' to the Duat [a region of underworld/sky] and

'visit his father' and 'open his mouth' i.e. bring him back to life."[75] The winter solstice sun over 25,800 years of precession cycles back to the galactic center (visits his father) and there is a Seyfert core explosive phase which "opens his mouth" and makes him active.

In this active and brought back to life form, Ra/Osiris the father / galactic center becomes a giant oval of light which we know as the "eye of Ra," the activated galactic core in its Seyfert phase, spewing massive amounts of light, radiation, and dust. The galactic center could be like a pupil in the eye, with an oval of dimmer light around it, light reflected off clouds of gas and dust blown out from the center. The goddess Hathor, whose name means "house of Horus" is both the mother and daughter of Ra. She is also known as his agent of destruction, associated with the eye of Ra under her bloodthirsty avatar Sekhmet. The eye of Ra sent Sekhmet to punish mankind, but when she came too close to exterminating all of humanity, Ra tricked her into a drunken stupor and humanity was spared. Our concern with her is as the house of Horus—for the sun is located in her (the eye of Ra) when she descends to kill humanity. She is also associated with the Milky Way and the Great Flood.

In Egypt's "The Papyrus of Ani" Horus (the sun) says "I have made the way to the place in which Ra and Hathor are there. If be known chapter this he becometh as an intelligence provided in the netherworld, not is he shut out at any door in Amenta in entering and coming out of the sky." This translation of the hieroglyphics seems to describe our favorite astronomical alignment of the winter solstice sun arriving at the galactic center, and comments further that anyone wise enough to understand this concept will not be shut out of the door of heaven, which may be most relevant when Ra dispatches Hathor as an agent of his destruction. There is a temple dedicated to Hathor at Dendera in Egypt, and the temple's most notable feature is an intricate zodiac on the ceiling (a replica now, as the original was considered too important by some very wise men... and moved to Paris in 1821. It has been in the Louvre since 1964.) On this zodiac, Michael Evans believes the scepter of Osiris, the uas scepter which symbolizes the restoration of order from chaos, is a clue left for us today, a cipher to show the positions of the last North

Pole and the current one.

There are similar (though less detailed) myths to substantiate these stories around the world, in Iceland, Finland, Iran, China, India, Japan, and Iraq. They usually end with an event like a pole shift. The Persian sacred text Bundahis tells us that "the evil spirit [Ahriman], with the confederate demons, went toward the luminaries... He stood upon one-third of the inside of the sky... he injured the whole world and made it dark at midday as though it were dark night... Blight was diffused by him over the vegetation, and it withered away immediately... the celestial sphere was in revolution... The planets, with many demons, clashed against the celestial sphere, and they mixed the constellations; and the whole

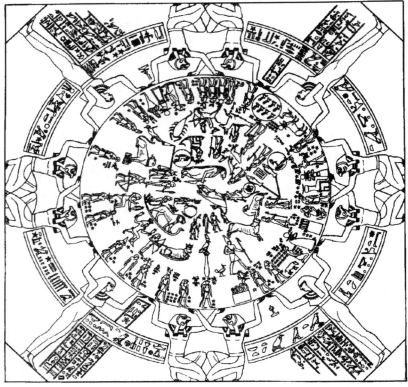

The engraving above is a depiction of the Dendera Zodiac from the ceiling of the Temple of Hathor at Dendera, Egypt, as published by Denon in 1802 in his book *Voyage dans la Basse et la Haute Egypte.*

creation was disfigured as though fire disfigured every place."[76]

Babylonia's god Era said "Open the way, I will take the road, the days are ended, the fixed time has past." The high god Marduk then says "When I stood up from my seat and let the flood break in, then the judgment of Earth and Heaven went out of joint... The gods, which trembled, the stars of heaven—their positions changed, and I did not bring them back."[77]

Islamic prophecies also describe a series of natural disasters (following an apocalyptic war against Christianity, which may very well happen during the second half of the seven year tribulation.) These are some of "The Final Signs of Qiyaamah." They include:

The ground will cave in in the east, in the west, and in the Hejaz section of

Saudi Arabia.

Smoke will cover the sky for forty days.

A night three nights long will follow the days of smoke-clouded skies.

After the night which is three nights long, the next day the sun will rise in the

west.

The holy Ka'aba shrine in Mecca will be destroyed.

The pilgrimages to Mecca and Medina will end.

The Koran also tells us "Know that God revives the earth after its death... We have indeed made clear the signs and Revelations (to enable such revival and) that you may reason and understand" (Surah 57, verse 17) and God also "revives the earth after its death" in another reference in Surah 30 verse 19.

In Chinese myth a monster or an evil king wreaked havoc, tearing down the Heavenly Bamboo (world axis) flattening mountains, tilting the Earth and tearing a hole in the sky. Fires raged out of control, the waters overran the world, and the cardinal points became misaligned. Nu Kua restored order, fixed the directions and the pillars of heaven, controlled the water and put out the fires, and repaired the sky. There is (on page 273 of "Hamlet's Mill") a Chinese drawing from about 2,000 years ago showing Nu Kua and her male counterpart, Fu Hsi, measuring the squareness of the Earth and the roundness of heaven with a square and compass like the symbols of modern masonry. This may seem strange, to consider the Earth square, but ancient cultures defined the Earth-plane by the position of the four cardinal zodiac constellations—by our angle of incline compared to the heavens. As a pole shift changes this, measuring and mapping out the newly re-formed world is a recurring part of such myths.

In the Hawaiian myth Kumulipo we are told a new world comes out of chaos, but "it is a chaos which is simply the wreck and ruin of an earlier world."[78] "Now turns the swinging of time over on the burnt-out world, Back goes the great turning of things upward again, As yet sunless the time of shrouded light; Unsteady, as in dim moon-shimmer, From out of Makalii's night-dark veil of cloud, Thrills, shadow-like, the prefiguration of the world to be."[79] Makalii is believed to be the Pleiades and often is described as casting a net from a hidden location in which he remains in the dark.

In Finland the Lapps say that when the archer Arcturus "shoots down the North Nail with his arrow on the last day, the heaven will fall, crushing the earth and setting fire to everything."[80]

The Americas are also full of similar myths and concerns for such events happening again. The Kutenai of British Columbia "look for Polaris every night. Should it not be in place, the end of the world is imminent" as they would know a pole shift was happening.[81] Pawnee legends warn that "the command for the ending of all things will be given by the North Star."[82] The Pawnee also tell us that during the last pole shift the moon was dark, the sun was dim at first then "darker than in an eclipse" and "the South Star was given permission to move through the heavens to look for the North Star."[83] The Araucanians of Chile believed that the great flood was the result of a violent earthquake and volcanic eruption, and they rush away from the sea and into the mountains whenever there were earthquakes. The Inca of Peru had similar fears of eclipses.[84]

The Aztecs and the Maya believed their ancestors came from a white island (Could the white island be the icy continent of Antarctica?) in the eastern sea called Aztlan, which was destroyed

188

by a flood. The name is strikingly similar to Plato's Atlantis, which was destroyed by a flood. Heinrich Schliemann, who discovered Troy and proved it was a real historical place, believed that Atlantis was real and the cradle of our civilization. The Egyptians said their ancestors came from an island known as the Homeland of the Primeval Ones, before it was destroyed by a flood. The Sumerian mythical homeland of Dilmun was south across the sea. Ancient India's Mahabaratha describes an ancient homeland of the gods where "The day and night together are equal to a year." In the Surya Siddhantha they clarify that many days elapse between the first light of dawn and the eventual appearance of the sunrise. Antarctica fits these descriptions well.

What would Santa Claus think about our focus on the South Pole? Would he tell us we should not forget the north pole, or the possibility that an initiated brotherhood still exists in modern times and still hides astronomical details in modern mythology? Santa would probably point out that he shares an obvious calendric association with Jesus—what with Santa bringing children presents on December 25, on Jesus Christ's alleged birthday… But there is a darker side to Santa. Who receives a million letters from anxious children every December? Not Jesus. Who do more parents encourage their children to believe in—and behave well for? Who promises rewards every year in this life—without waiting for the next? And when children finally "grow up" and realize they were tricked into believing in Santa, who doesn't really exist—might their distrust of beings without physical evidence carry over to ruin their faith in Jesus, or God?

Like Seven Macaw and Satan, Santa is like a false god associated with theNorth Pole and north star.

Santa is a fairly omnipotent deity—"he knows when you've been bad or good"—and he levels judgment.

Santa drives a sky-chariot like the sun god Apollo.

Santa's sun chariot is tied to eight reindeer, like the sun has eight planets.

These reindeer have names that make it clear the planets they represent move violently—they dash and dance and prance (Dasher,

Dancer, Prancer)—they are like bad celestial omens with events like thunder and lightning and comets and war (Donner and Blitzen and Comet.) Even Cupid shoots arrows into hearts, like his celestial counterpart Sagittarius, who aims his arrows at the "heart of heaven" at the galactic center. By comparison Vixen is almost a nice reindeer name, it is merely a reference to being ill-tempered or malicious. Why don't they have nicer names? Why not something like: "On Music, on Laughter, on Bounty and Plenty, on Healthfulness, Happiness, Friendship and Family!" Perhaps because, at the level of myth, Santa does not represent these things.

Santa, on his sun-chariot, leaves his position at the North Pole at the winter solstice holiday—indicating an eventual pole shift at this time of year. Santa's holiday is often symbolized by the axis with pole star above it—the world tree with a star on top. Often "the center is conceived as an axis… represented as a mountain, a stairway or ladder, a pole, or very commonly, a tree. It is symbolized in our Christmas tree, with the pivotal star at its summit."[85]

Santa will not enter a house through the door, only through the chimney. This is important. In John 10:9 Jesus says "I am the door; if anyone enters through Me, he will be saved." Santa is the opposite of salvation, he represents the materialism of this world and he comes with fire and ash and soot along the vertical axis. In many cultures Santa comes with a sinister companion with a name like Knecht Rupprecht; Pelznickle; Swarthy; Krampus; Dark One; Dark Helper; or Black Peter. Such helpers, depending on the culture, scare children, whip them for punishment, or even "drag them off to hell." In other cultures, Santa is the dark helper. John 10:1 says "truly, I say to you, he who does not enter by the door into the fold of the sheep, but climbs up some other way, he is a thief." A thief of children's beliefs, misdirected at Christmastime.

In the classic 1947 film *A Miracle on 34th Street* there is no focus on God or Jesus. But Susan's mother (played by Maureen O'Hara) tells young Susan (Natalie Wood) "You must believe in Mr. Kringle—and keep right on believing. You must have faith in him." Little Susie is soon repeating over and over, "I believe, I believe." This author doesn't hate Santa Claus, but Santa is a thief when it comes to stealing the spotlight from God and Jesus, and we should understand that the details of his story were created by wise men in modern times... to convey the idea that around December 25 we should expect both judgment and the north pole and sun-chariot leaving their normal positions.

Santa's myth focuses on the North Pole, but many myths have twins stationed at both poles. A well-known legend of the Hopi Indians talks of the axial poles as twins that hold the Earth in place. At the end of each age these twins are instructed to leave their posts and let the world plunge into chaos on Nuutungk Talonguaqa—the last day. After this last occurred a new world was born, there was a great shudder and a splintering of ice, and the Earth began revolving again. In another version Sotuknang came to destroy the Earth. But he spared a few good people, warning them to go underground with the Ant-people. Then he told the pole guards to leave their positions. "The twins had hardly abandoned their stations when the world, with no one to control it, teetered off balance, spun around crazily, then rolled over twice. Mountains plunged into the sea with a great splash, seas and lakes sloshed over the land... Waves higher than mountains rolled in upon the land. Continents broke asunder and sank beneath the seas. And still the rains fell, the waves rolled in."[86] Survivors crossed small islands to a great continent as their original lands sank.

Innuit myth tells us a strange high tide caused a worldwide flood, leaving evidence like seashells in the mountains. Orowignarak Eskimo in Alaska say that a great flood combined with an earthquake, flushed the land of its people and only a few escaped in canoes to the mountaintops. The Dogrib and Slavey Indians of Alberta tell a myth of Black Bear hiding the sun, moon and stars in a bag. (LaViolette's cosmic dust cloud could appear as a giant black bag growing and enveloping the sky.) When other characters release them, snow melts quickly, floods rise, animals relocate, and mankind's universal language is lost.[87]

The Chaco of western Paraguay describe "cataclysms [that] generally result in the total or near total destruction of humanity... In place of creation myths Chaco narrators tell stories about the

191

re-establishment of the world after one of the cataclysms."[88] Lake Titicaca in Bolivia seems to have risen over two miles in altitude from sea level to its present location. The ancient shoreline of the lake, now twelve miles from the current shore, had huge stone wharfs at Tiahuanaco weighing as much as 440 tons per block. Many construction stones are fitted together with H-shaped metal clamps. Its pottery and sculptures shows many extinct animals like toxodons (like a cross between a large hippopotamus and rhinoceros.) The city's main entrance at the Gateway of the Sun has 46 carvings of toxodon heads, and they have been extinct for at least 11,000 years. Despite being approximately two miles high today, Lake Titicaca is home to seahorses and other oceanic life indicating an uplifting from the seafloor. Even more interestingly, the ancient lakeshore is tilted compared to ground level. The north end was once 295 feet higher; the south end was 274 feet lower.

The city of Tiahuanaco has been determined by astro-archeology and other evidence to be older than any other city in the world. Dr. Arthur Posnansky of the University of La Paz analyzed directional and astronomical alignments in buildings there and after considering changes in both precession and the slow variation of the angle of the obliquity of the Earth's axis (currently 23 degrees 27 minutes off from vertical) he concluded that Tiahuanaco is approximately 15,000 years old.[89] Dr. Rolf Muller of the Astrophysical Institute of Potsdam supports this prehistoric dating. Some think Atlantis was here in Bolivia.

"The Barasana Indians preserve one of the most sophisticated and complex of all the South American cataclysm folklore." They begin their zodiac with "The Star Thing" (Pleiades) the same way many use the surrounding constellation Taurus in the Middle East. The Barasana names for star groupings near the Galactic center are deadly: the closest is Headless One, followed by, in order of proximity to the core: Caterpillar Jaguar (a poisonous caterpillar), Poisonous Snake, Scorpion, Vulture, Corpse Bundle, and Poisonous Spider. Opposite the galactic center, 180 degrees away, are the constellations Old Star Thing, Otters, Ant, Fish Rack, Adze, Star Thing, and Jacunda Fish—none of which are poisonous or deadly.

The stars near the galactic core are considered bad stars and Caterpillar Jaguar (Scorpio) is the worst, the leader of this "Old Star Path."[90]

The Yurok tribe of California say: "The sky fell and hit the water, causing high breakers that flooded all the land. That is why one can find shells and redwood logs on the highest ridges. Two women and two men… were the only people saved. Sky-Owner gave them a song, and many days later the water fell when they sang it. Sky-Owner sent a rainbow to tell them the water would never cover the world again."[91]

(Endnotes)

1 de Santillana, Giorgio and Hertha von Dechend. *Hamlet's Mill: An Essay Investigating the Origins of Human Knowledge and its Transmission Through Myth*. Boston, MA: David R. Godine, 1969, p. 3

2 Hancock, Graham. (paraphrasing Santillana and von Dechend's ideas in Hamlet's Mill, in) *Message of the Sphinx: A Quest for the Hidden Legacy of Mankind*. New York: Random House, 1996, p. 241

3 Childress, David Hatcher. *Pirates & The Lost Templar Fleet: The Secret Naval War between the Knights Templar & the Vatican*. Kempton, IL: Adventures Unlimited Press, 2003, p. 242

4 de Santillana, Giorgio and Hertha von Dechend. *Hamlet's Mill: An Essay Investigating the Origins of Human Knowledge and its Transmission Through Myth*. Boston, MA: David R. Godine, 1969, p. 5

5 de Santillana, Giorgio and Hertha von Dechend. Ibid., p. 7

6 Sagan, Carl. *Cosmos*. New York: Ballantine Books, 1980, p. 245

7 Tatler, John. "The Great Pyramid: Reflections in Time" as quoted by Scott Creighton and Gary Osborn. *The Giza Prophecy: The Orion Code and the Secret Teachings of the Pyramids*. Rochester, VT: Bear & Company, 2012, p. 178

8 Mitchell, Henry. Chief Hydrographer of the United States Coast Survey, 1868

9 Capt, E. Raymond. *The Great Pyramid Decoded*. Muskogee, OK: Artisan Publishers, 1999, p. 58

10 de Santillana, Giorgio and Hertha von Dechend. *Hamlet's Mill: An Essay Investigating the Origins of Human Knowledge and its Transmission Through Myth*. Boston, MA: David R. Godine, 1969, p. 59

11 LaViolette, Paul. *Earth Under Fire: Humanity's Survival of the Ice Age*. Rochester, VT: Bear & Company, 2005, p. 322

12 LaViolette, Paul. Ibid., p. 322

13 Rincon, Paul. "DNA reveals Neanderthal extinction clues."

BBC News, 2/27/2012 http://www.bbc.co.uk/news/science-environment-17179608

14 de Santillana, Giorgio and Hertha von Dechend. *Hamlet's Mill: An Essay Investigating the Origins of Human Knowledge and its Transmission Through Myth.* Boston, MA: David R. Godine, 1969, p. 82

15 Michell, John. *The Dimensions of Paradise.* Rochester, VT: Inner Traditions, 2008, p. 63

16 Hancock, Graham and Robert Bauval. *The Message of the Sphinx: A Quest for the Hidden Legacy of Mankind.* New York: Random House, 1996, p. 241

17 Hall, Manly P. *Freemasonry of the Ancient Egyptians.* Los Angeles, CA: Philosophical Research Society, 1937, pp. 84-85

18 de Santillana, Giorgio and Hertha von Dechend. *Hamlet's Mill: An Essay Investigating the Origins of Human Knowledge and its Transmission Through Myth.* Boston, MA: David R. Godine, 1969, p. 330

19 Hall, Manly P. *Freemasonry of the Ancient Egyptians.* Los Angeles, CA: Philosophical Research Society, 1937, p. 14

20 Fowden, Garth. *The Egyptian Hermes.* London: Cambridge University Press, 1987, p. 33

21 de Santillana, Giorgio and Hertha von Dechend. *Hamlet's Mill: An Essay Investigating the Origins of Human Knowledge and its Transmission Through Myth.* Boston, MA: David R. Godine, 1969, p. 347

22 Hancock, Graham and Robert Bauval. *The Message of the Sphinx: A Quest for the Hidden Legacy of Mankind.* New York: Random House, 1996, p. 133

23 de Santillana, Giorgio and Hertha von Dechend. *Hamlet's Mill: An Essay Investigating the Origins of Human Knowledge and its Transmission Through Myth.* Boston, MA: David R. Godine, 1969, p. 373

24 Michell, John. *The New View Over Atlantis.* San Francisco, CA: Harper & Row, 1986, pp. 154-155

25 Hall, Manly P. *Freemasonry of the Ancient Egyptians.* Los Angeles, CA: Philosophical Research Society, 1937, p. 48

26 S, Acharya. *Suns of God: Krishna, Buddha and Christ Unveiled.* Kempton, IL: Adventures Unlimited Press, 2004, p. 53

27 S, Acharya. Ibid., p. 75, originally from Marsilio Ficino's 1494 work *The Book of the Sun.*

28 Fideler, David R. *Jesus Christ, Sun of God: Ancient Cosmology and Early Christian Symbolism.* Wheaton, IL: Quest Books, 1993, pp. 276-277

29 Michell, John. *The Dimensions of Paradise.* Rochester, VT: Inner Traditions, 2008, p. 66

30 Fideler, David R. *Jesus Christ, Sun of God: Ancient Cosmology and Early Christian Symbolism.* Wheaton, IL: Quest Books, 1993, p. 307

31 Leet, Leonora. *The Universal Kabbalah: Deciphering the Cosmic Code in the Sacred Geometry.* Rochester, VT: Inner Traditions, 2004, p. 5, p. 3

32 Fideler, David R. *Jesus Christ, Sun of God: Ancient Cosmology and Early Christian Symbolism.* Wheaton, IL: Quest Books, 1993, p. 284

33 Fideler, Ibid., p. 284

34 Gleason, Daniel. Work in progress found at http://www.jesus8880.com/chapters/download.htm Work may someday be published under "The Gospels seen as Sacred Geometry Plays: A Gematria Based Commentary on Mark" or "Jesus 8880: The Sacred Geometry Mysteries of Christianity."

35 Gleason, Daniel. Work in progress found at jesus8880.com

36 S, Acharya. *Suns of God: Krishna, Buddha and Christ Unveiled.* Kempton, IL: Adventures Unlimited Press, 2004, p. 66

37 Gleason, Daniel. Work in progress found at http://www.jesus8880.com/chapters/gematria/risen-sun-3880.htm

38 Pike, Albert. *Morals and Dogma.* As quoted by Horn, Thomas. Apollyon Rising 2012. Crane, MO: Defender Books, 2009, p. 242

39 S, Acharya. *Suns of God: Krishna, Buddha and Christ Unveiled.* Kempton, IL: Adventures Unlimited Press, 2004, pp. 64-65

40 Karl Taube, quoted by Adrian Gilbert & Maurice Cotterell in *The Mayan Prophecies.* New York: Barnes & Noble, 1996, p. 135

41 de Santillana, Giorgio and Hertha von Dechend. *Hamlet's Mill:*

An Essay Investigating the Origins of Human Knowledge and its Transmission Through Myth. Boston, MA: David R. Godine, 1969, pp. 111, 146

42 de Santillana, Giorgio and Hertha von Dechend, Ibid., p. 87

43 de Santillana, Giorgio and Hertha von Dechend. *Hamlet's Mill: An Essay Investigating the Origins of Human Knowledge and its Transmission Through Myth.* Boston, MA: David R. Godine, 1969, p. 138, but originally from Ludwig Ideler *Untersuchung uber den Ursprung und die Bedeutung der Sternamen* (1809, p. 17)

44 de Santillana, Giorgio and Hertha von Dechend, Ibid., pp. 140-141

45 de Santillana, Giorgio and Hertha von Dechend, Ibid., pp. 278-279

46 Wheeler, Marshall. The Earth—Its Third Motion. 1889, p. 10, cited in John White's *Pole Shift: Predictions and Prophecies of the Ultimate Disaster.* New York: Doubleday, 1980, p. 56

47 White, John. *Pole Shift.* Virginia Beach, VA: A.R.E. Press, 2007, p. 106

48 White, John. Ibid., p. 316

49 Hancock, Graham. *Underworld: The Mysterious Origins of Civilization.* New York: Crown Publishing, 2002, p. 74

50 Warshofsky, Fred. *Doomsday: The Science of Catastrophe.* New York: Readers' Digest Press, 1977, p. 80

51 West, John Anthony. *Serpent in the Sky: The High Wisdom of Ancient Egypt.* Wheaton, IL: Quest Books, 1993, p. 229

52 Hancock, Graham and Robert Bauval. *Message of the Sphinx: A Quest for the Hidden Legacy of Mankind.* New York: Random House, 1996, p. 12

53 Hancock, Graham and Robert Bauval. Ibid., p. 10

54 Creighton, Scott and Gary Osborn. *The Giza Prophecy: The Orion Code and the Secret Teachings of the Pyramids.* Rochester, VT: Bear & Company, 2012, p. 153

55 "Unravelling the Mummy Mystery—Using DNA (citing Interview with *al-Ahram* issue 512.)" Egyptology Online. Retrieved April 10, 2009

56 Hancock, Graham. *Fingerprints of the Gods.* New York: Three

Rivers Press, 1995, p. 417

57 Schoch, Robert. "Searching for the Dawn and Demise of Ancient Civilization." *New Dawn Magazine*, Special Volume #8, p. 23

58 West, John Anthony. *Serpent in the Sky: The High Wisdom of Ancient Egypt.* Wheaton, IL: Quest Books, 1993, p. 1

59 Michell, John. *The New View Over Atlantis.* San Francisco, CA: Harper & Row, 1986, p. 162

60 Michell, John. Ibid., p. 131

61 Creighton, Scott and Gary Osborn. *The Giza Prophecy: The Orion Code and the Secret Teachings of the Pyramids.* Rochester, VT: Bear & Company, 2012, pp. 228-231

62 Creighton, Scott and Gary Osborn. Ibid., pp. 275, 281, and 286

63 Creighton, Scott and Gary Osborn. Ibid., p. 263

64 Hancock, Graham and Robert Bauval. *Message of the Sphinx: A Quest for the Hidden Legacy of Mankind.* New York: Random House, 1996, pp. 110, 224, 248

65 Childress, David Hatcher. *Pirates & The Lost Templar Fleet: The Secret Naval War between the Knights Templar & the Vatican.* Kempton, IL: Adventures Unlimited Press, 2003, p. 24

66 Smyth, C. Piazzi. *New Measures of the Great Pyramid by a New Measurer.* London: Robert Banks, 1884, p. 74

67 LaViolette, Paul. *Earth Under Fire: Humanity's Survival of the Ice Age*. Rochester, VT: Bear & Company, 2005, p. 248

68 LaHaye, Tim. *Revelation Unveiled*. Grand Rapids, MI: Zondervan Press, 1999, p. 113

69 LaViolette, Paul. *Earth Under Fire: Humanity's Survival of the Ice Age*. Rochester, VT: Bear & Company, 2005, pp. 109-110

70 LaViolette, Ibid., p. 322

71 http://www.luthielssong.com/blog/2007/06/01/2012-mayan-astrology-norse-mythology-the-end-of-the-world-and-luthiels-song/

72 de Santillana, Giorgio and Hertha von Dechend. *Hamlet's Mill: An Essay Investigating the Origins of Human Knowledge and its Transmission Through Myth.* Boston, MA: David R. Godine, 1969, pp. 160-161

73 Yukteswar, Sri. *The Holy Science.* Los Angeles, CA: Self-

Realization Fellowship Press, 1990, p. 7

74 Frawley, David. *Astrology of the Seers.* Salt Lake City, UT: Passage Press, 1990, p. 48

75 Hancock, Graham and Robert Bauval. *Message of the Sphinx: A Quest for the Hidden Legacy of Mankind.* New York: Random House, 1996, pp. 166, 159

76 LaViolette, Paul. *Earth Under Fire: Humanity's Survival of the Ice Age.* Rochester, VT: Bear & Company, 2005, p. 99

77 de Santillana, Giorgio and Hertha von Dechend. *Hamlet's Mill: An Essay Investigating the Origins of Human Knowledge and its Transmission Through Myth.* Boston, MA: David R. Godine, 1969, p. 325

78 Dixon, Roland B. Oceanic Mythology. Boston, MA: Marshall Jones, 1916, p. 15

79 Bastian, A. *Die Heilige Sage der Polynesier.* Leipzig, Germany: F.A. Brockhaus, 1881, pp. 69-121

80 de Santillana, Giorgio and Hertha von Dechend. *Hamlet's Mill: An Essay Investigating the Origins of Human Knowledge and its Transmission Through Myth.* Boston, MA: David R. Godine, 1969, p. 383 Originally in U. Holmberg's F*inno-Ugaric and Siberian Mythology.* 1964, p. 221

81 Turney-High, Harry. *Ethnology of the Kutenai.* Mildwood, NY: Draus Reprint, 1974, p. 96

82 de Santillana, Giorgio and Hertha von Dechend. *Hamlet's Mill: An Essay Investigating the Origins of Human Knowledge and its Transmission Through Myth.* Boston, MA: David R. Godine, 1969, p. 309

83 Burland, Cottie. *North American Indian Mythology.* New York: Peter Bedrick Books, 1985, p. 88

84 Flem-Ath, Rand and Rose. *When the Sky Fell: In Search of Atlantis.* New York: St. Martin's Press, 1995, p. 27

85 Campbell, Joseph. *The Mythic Image.* Princeton, NJ: Princeton University Press, 1981, p. 190

86 Waters, Frank. *Book of the Hopi.* New York: Penguin Books, 1963, pp. 12-22

87 LaViolette, Paul. *Earth Under Fire: Humanity's Survival of the*

Ice Age. Rochester, VT: Bear & Company, 2005, pp. 182-183

88 Bierhorst, John. *Mythology of South America.* New York: William Morrow, 1988, p. 145

89 Hancock, Graham. *Fingerprints of the Gods.* New York: Three Rivers Press, 1995, pp. 65-66

90 LaViolette, Paul. *Earth Under Fire: Humanity's Survival of the Ice Age.* Rochester, VT: Bear & Company, 2005, pp. 277-281

91 Bell, Rosemary. *Yurok Tales.* Etna, CA: Bell Books, 1992. p. 68

CHAPTER SIX
BACK TO CHRISTIANITY
AND THE BIBLE

Sky-Owner sending a rainbow to tell the Indians water would not cover the world again sounds similar to the Rainbow Covenant in the Bible. After Noah's flood, people were scared that God would send more floods. God told them the natural catastrophes by global flooding were done (for a very long time at least) and clarified in Genesis 9:11-16 "I establish My covenant with you; and all flesh shall never again be cut off by the water of the flood, neither shall there again be a flood to destroy the earth… I set My bow in the cloud, and it shall be for a sign of a covenant between Me and the earth. It shall come about, when I bring a cloud over the earth, that the bow will be seen in the cloud… When the bow is in the cloud, then I will look upon it, to remember the everlasting covenant between God and every living creature of all flesh that is on the earth."

Unfortunately floods have destroyed the planet repeatedly and will likely do so again. Some would say that God has promised not to flood the world again, so it cannot ever happen again. But God does not always keep his promises *as we would expect*; they are sometimes later proven to be conditional. For a few examples, in Genesis 17:8 God promises to give Abraham the land of Canaan, but he dies with the promise unfulfilled. In Numbers 14:30, God says "Surely you shall not come into the land in which I swore to settle you." In Jeremiah 24:6 God says "I will build them up and not overthrow them, and I will plant them and not pluck them up." Yet in Jeremiah 45:4 he says "what I have built I am about to tear down, and what I have planted I am about to uproot."

In Isaiah 24:1-6 we are told of the earth's future destruction: "the LORD lays the earth waste, devastates it, distorts its surface and scatters its inhabitants. The earth will be completely laid waste and completely despoiled, for the LORD has spoken this word. The earth mourns and withers, the world fades and withers, the exalted of the people of the earth fade away. The earth is also polluted by its inhabitants, for they transgressed laws, violated statutes, broke the everlasting covenant. Therefore, a curse devours the earth, and those who live in it are held guilty. Therefore, the inhabitants of the earth are burned, and few men are left." Man's disobedience can ruin divine agreements like the rainbow covenant, and we could experience catastrophes like Noah's flood again.

Have such floods been foretold for our near future? One of the few modern miracles acknowledged by the Catholic Church took place in 1917 in Fatima, Portugal—where three shepherd girls reported several visitations by the Virgin Mary, who gave them warnings of horrible future events. The girls claimed that Mary came to them every thirteenth of the month, starting in May 1917. On July 13, 1917, Mary is said to have given the children three secrets. At first no one took the girls seriously. Their parents beat them for making things up. But their visions eventually received great attention, and approximately seventy thousand witnesses were present for the sixth (and final) appearance expected on October 17. Lúcia had claimed for months that the Virgin Mary would perform a miracle in October "so that all may believe." Witnesses up to 25 miles away reported that the sun seemed to change colors and rotate, lighting the land up like a multi-colored wheel of dancing fire. The sun appeared to plunge towards the Earth, and many witnesses feared it was the end of the world. The popular expression, according to the local newspaper, was that the sun "danced," and this event became known as the Miracle of the Sun. It was widely reported in Portuguese newspapers, and even generated a small article in the New York Times on October 17, 1917.

Two of the three secrets, believed to relate to WWI and WWII, were revealed in 1941 in a document written by Lúcia, at the request of the Bishop of Leiria. The third was considered too horrible to relate. But in 1943 Lucia fell ill with influenza - which had killed her two cousins with whom she shared the secret visions, and for a time Lucia believed she was dying. The bishop of Leiria then ordered her to write down the third secret, which she did, sealing it in an envelope to be opened by the Pope either in 1960, or when she died, whichever came first. But throughout the twentieth century, various newly elected popes have cried when they first read the details and it was decided to not divulge any secrets.

In 1967, on the 50th anniversary of the events at Fatima, Pope Paul VI said: "What terrible damage could be provoked by arbitrary interpretations, not authorized by the teaching of the Church, disrupting its traditional and constitutional structure, replacing the theology of the true and great Fathers of the Church with new and peculiar ideologies..."[1] Could the pope be referring to a message about cyclic destruction, a message which would undermine the basic concept of Christianity's linear timeline of events? Let's cut to the chase—the idea that mankind suffers periodic cycles of destruction—and that the next one will just be one of many that came before and will presumably continue to come after—is not what most Christians think the Bible says.

There are many hints of this, however. Christianity's climax event—the holy wedding of Christ—is to a woman who is never referred to as a fiancé; she is always called a bride or a wife. The NASB usually translates the Greek word "γυνὴ" as bride but Young's Literal Translation, among others, correctly translates it as wife, as in "his wife did make herself ready." Why is she already the wife—before the wedding makes it official? Many commentaries tell us Christ is so sure of the situation that he already views his fiancé as his wife... but perhaps it is because this event is cyclical, and the wedding ceremony has already occurred many times.

Consider Ecclesiastes 1:9-11 "That which has been is that which will be, And that which has been done is that which will be done. So there is nothing new under the sun. Is there anything of which one might say, "See this, it is new"? Already it has existed for ages which were before us. There is no remembrance of earlier things; And also of the later things which will occur, There will be for them no remembrance Among those who will come later still." This passage certainly fits the idea that civilizations are destroyed by pole shifts, and leaves itself open to very broad interpretations.

If there will be no remembrance of people who will come to be later, what of even older people like Moses and Jesus—are there times ahead when Jews and Christians and their religions have long since been forgotten? 2 Peter 3:5-6 is also fascinating: "it escapes their notice that by the word of God the heavens existed long ago and the earth was formed out of water and by water, through which the world at that time was destroyed, being flooded with water."

The Bible clearly describes (at most) three occasions on which the world has been devastated and re-formed, (the re-creation of the world in Genesis 1:1-2, mankind being kicked out of the Garden of Eden, and Noah's Flood) and portrays the fourth (next) time as the final judgment. The suggestion that there could be a fifth or sixth or hundredth devastation of the Earth far in the future does not easily conform to the central message of Christianity—eternal salvation. To help avoid this dilemma at least temporarily, let us assume that our souls do not go through cycles like the Earth does. Let us also assume that God wants the cycles of planetary destruction to end and that He wants the next time to be the last one humanity suffers through. Perhaps we will be given the technology to prevent future disasters. Perhaps in the new heavens and new Earth these events don't happen. Perhaps it will be irrelevant to us if we are no longer on the Earth, but are in heaven. For the moment, let us assume that God is more than capable of making next time the final time.

Fourteen years after Pope Paul VI made comments about unconventional ideologies that might be spawned from explaining the contents of the third Fatima secret to the public, Pope John Paul II mentioned them in an interview in Fulda, Germany. He said "Given the seriousness of the contents, my predecessors on the throne of Peter diplomatically preferred to postpone publication so as not to encourage the world power of Communism to make certain moves. It should be sufficient for all Christians to know this much: If there is a message in which *it is said that the oceans will flood entire sections of the earth that from one moment to the other millions of people will perish*… there is no longer really any point in wanting to publish this secret message. Many want to know merely out of curiosity, or because of their taste for sensationalism, but they forget that 'to know' implies for them a responsibility. It is dangerous to want to satisfy one's curiosity only, if one is convinced that we can do nothing against a catastrophe that has been predicted... it is possible to alleviate this tribulation, but it is only in this way that the Church can be effectively renewed."[2]

There are many interesting pieces of information given here. Pope John Paul II clearly told us the secrets describe a coming cataclysm in which "the oceans will flood entire sections of the earth" and that "millions of people will perish" in moments. He tells us there will be a tribulation, but that it could be minimized or alleviated (perhaps if people cooperated and made efforts for some portion of the population to survive) but it is not all bad because the Church will be renewed through these events. And he also felt that communist nations would take this seriously and act on the information.

Perhaps the Vatican sees Catholicism losing ground to modern science, and with attendance and birthrates of Catholics falling, Europe is expected to be a Muslim continent in just one more generation (by 2040-2050.) Perhaps the Vatican is expecting to see a cataclysmic pole shift with tidal waves wiping out millions, if not billions, of people—and they look at this as the only way the Church can be renewed—with the fear of God and the absence of scientific civilization. Only then can the ignorant descendants of our few survivors in the mountains be brought back to a renewed Church. If a pole shift occurs and puts the North Pole near Lake Baikal in Siberia, and if leaders in Moscow and Beijing were convinced this would occur, then the West's major communist rivals in China and the Soviet Union may have started WWIII in the twentieth century to secure more secure living space for their people.

Officially, the Vatican released some information in the year 2000, stating that the third secret of Fatima was about the assassination attempt on Pope John Paul II in 1981. This failed attempt hardly seems worse than the events of the last two world wars, and many people do not believe this really has anything to do with the terrible third secret. It certainly does not seem like it could overturn ideology or drown millions of people in tidal waves.

Vittorio Messori also quotes then Cardinal Ratzinger (now Pope Benedict VI) in his book *The Ratzinger Report* stating that Fatima secrets include "perils that threaten humanity."[3]   Unfortunately, Pope Benedict is notoriously tight-lipped on the subject of Fatima. I had an opportunity to meet him in 2007 through a Jesuit friend at the Vatican, but it was obvious no new light would be shed on this topic, so I decided to let my friend remain in good standing and not waste his limited ability to orchestrate papal audiences.

The revelations given at Fatima do seem to back up the idea that a huge death toll caused by floods and other side effects of a pole shift could be in our near future. But some question whether these miracles at Fatima happened at all, let alone whether they detail a cataclysmic flood during a pole shift. So let's return directly to the Bible and review a great many relevant passages now that we understand the perspective that perhaps there are recurring pole shifts at specific points in the precessional cycle.

For the purpose of focusing on the Bible's somewhat hidden messages on this topic, let us temporarily ignore the Bible's main purpose—its spiritual messages of faith and grace and salvation— to focus on passages with astronomical meaning symbolizing the sun, the galactic center, pole shifts, and their cosmic causes and timing. As the great 12th century rabbi Maimonides wrote almost a thousand years ago: "Study astronomy and physics if you desire to comprehend the relation between the world and God's management of it."[4]

When reading the Bible, remember that there is a black hole at the galactic center, and that it occasionally becomes active and spews radiation and light and pushes out vast clouds of dust. Recognize that many cultures describe a catastrophe when the winter solstice sun reaches the galactic center, and that previous catastrophes probably wiped out earlier civilizations. Bear in mind that if a pole shift does occur there will be massive earthquakes and floods, and that the stars in the night sky will appear to move, with some falling to or below the horizon. Most important, remember that Christianity has deep roots in stories describing solar events as if the sun were a human protagonist.

Even at the height of the Inquisition, when heretical views were fought to the death, Catholic writers still wrote that "the virtue and divinity of God—can be seen through the Sun" and that ancient (pagan) religious tradition from before Alexander the Great to well after the establishment of the Roman Church "freely embraces a similar comparison of the Sun to God" or His Son.[5] With all these ideas in mind, many of the facts about Abraham, Moses, Jacob, Elijah, Samson, Jonah, and Jesus suddenly make more sense. There are many hundreds of relevant Bible passages to consider; hopefully some of the most interesting ones discussed below are sufficient to make the point that these topics are central to understanding the Bible's end times message.

Genesis 1:1-2 "In the beginning God created the heavens and the earth. The earth was formless and void, and darkness was over the surface of the deep, and the Spirit of God was moving over the surface of the waters." Contrast this with the more accurate version from Young's Literal Translation: "In the beginning of God's preparing the heavens and the earth—the earth hath existed waste and void, and darkness [is] on the face of the deep, and the Spirit of God fluttering on the face of the waters." Why would God create the Earth formless, void, and waste? The word waste implies a former state of higher organization. Consider another translation: "In the beginning ... [when] the earth became formless and void." It is argued that the word "was" can be more correctly translated as "became." "Properly speaking, this verb hayah never has the meaning of static being like the copular verb 'to be.' Its basic notion is that of becoming or emerging as such and such, or of coming into being."[6]

This implies that the Earth already existed, but had passed into decay, and was now being shaped anew. This view is more consistent with mainstream science with respect to the age of the Earth, as we know science says the planet is about 4.5 billion years old whereas biblical timelines tell us this version of Earth was formed about 6,000 years ago. "The biblical chronology is about a million times shorter than the evolutionary chronology... This is not a peripheral issue that can be dismissed with some exegetical twist, but is central to the very integrity of scriptural theology."[7] If we accept that Genesis is merely describing the remaking of the surface of the globe from one arrangement to another, the planet can be billions of years old while "this earth"—this alignment—is only thousands of years old. As Maimonides said, "Conflicts between science and religion result from misinterpretations of the Bible."[8]

The actual Hebrew phrase "tohu va bohu" means "became." It is important to note the phrase for "became" is only used two times in the entire Bible, once in the old testament, and once in the new testament: Genesis 1:2, and Jeremiah 4:23. The passage in Jeremiah also refers to the land becoming a desolate wasteland. Most readers see the word "was" as translated in the King James Bible translation of Genesis 1:2 "the earth was without form" and think this describes a passive situation... but Hebrew verbs at the beginning of Genesis are generally causative, with God actively doing something. "This causative form (eie) appears more than twenty times in chapter one of Genesis alone, and everywhere denotes a change, and not mere existence."[9]

The earliest known Aramaic language version of Genesis 1:2 was translated by Custance to mean "the earth was laid waste." He elaborates: "after studying the problem for some thirty years and after reading everything I could lay my hands on pro and con and after accumulating in my own library some 300 commentaries on Genesis, the earliest being dated 1670, I am persuaded that there is, on the basis of the evidence, far more reason to translate Gen 1:2 as 'But the earth had become a ruin and a desolation, etc.' than there is for any of the conventional translations in our modern versions."[10]

There is also the issue of the Hebrew word Bereshith, conveniently translated here as "in the beginning" yet the same word elsewhere in the Bible is not translated as "in the beginning." There is a Hebrew word for the phrase, "merosh," which is used to mean beginning, as used in Proverbs 8:23: "From the beginning, from the earliest times of the earth." Even the word "bara" which is often translated as "created" would be better understood as "perfected" or "finished." These lines could easily be translated to refer to an extended early period at which a different state (chaos) was converted into

Crouching like Leo the Lion, the Sphinx asks us a riddle. Like Samson, it challenges us to think and investigate it.

something else (order.) So perhaps we should really read the opening of Genesis as "At a time when the earth became formless and waste, God re-created and perfected the earth, and God's active force moved over the surface of the waters."

The importance of this more accurate translation cannot be overstated. It means that God was actively re-forming an older world which had been laid waste. It means the six-day creation described afterwards is not the first creation of the world, but is at least the second time around. As William Buckland commented almost two centuries ago: "The word beginning, as applied by Moses, expressed an undefined period of time, which was antecedent to the last great change that affected the surface of the earth… 'Tohu wa bohu' often 'chaos' in Greek may be geologically considered as designating the wreck and ruins of a former world."[11]

Genesis 3:3 "from the fruit of the tree which is in the middle of the garden, God has said, 'You shall not eat from it or touch it, or you will die.'" In Gen 3:5 the serpent tells Eve she should eat from the tree of knowledge for "For God knows that in the day you eat from it your eyes will be opened, and you will be like God, knowing good and evil." We have all seen drawings depicting Satan the serpent up in the apple tree above Eve. This middle tree is like the world tree in mythology and represents the Earth's central axis of rotation. The serpent above coiled around the tree represents the polar constellation Draco, who tries to deceive us away from the true God. (This is much more clear in Mayan stories of Seven Macaw, as the Maya understood that the pole star is a false center around which the heavens appear to rotate, although they really rotate around Heart of Heaven, the galactic center.) The Bible has mankind kicked out of Eden, which probably described a bountiful homeland where the climate was ruined by a pole shift that altered its latitude. We were not allowed to eat from Eden's trees of Life and Knowledge. Perhaps with enough knowledge and technology we would be able to achieve the New World Order's dream of "Novus Ordo Seclorum"—a new order of the ages—in which we don't have to suffer through the civilizational destructions of pole shifts any more.

Genesis 6:7 "The LORD said: 'I will blot out man whom I have created from the face of the land.'"

Genesis 6:17 "I am bringing the flood of water upon the earth, to destroy all flesh in which is the breath of life, from under heaven; everything that is on the earth shall perish."

Genesis 11:6-8 could refer to advanced Atlanteans fleeing their homeland: "The LORD said, "Behold, they are one people, and they all have the same language. And this is what they began to do, and now nothing which they purpose to do will be impossible for them. Come, let Us go down and there confuse their language, so that they will not understand one another's speech." So the LORD scattered them abroad from there over the face of the whole earth."

Genesis 6:1-4 may also be describing such survivors when they mention the Nephilim: "Now it came about, when men began to multiply on the face of the land, and daughters were born to them, that the sons of God saw that the daughters of men were beautiful; and they took wives for themselves, whomever they chose... The Nephilim were on the earth in those days, and also afterward, when the sons of God came in to the daughters of men, and they bore children to them. Those were the mighty men who were of old, men of renown." Many people believe these Nephilim are giants or fallen angels; but perhaps a simpler explanation is that refugees from an advanced but destroyed homeland, who had grown taller than the locals due to better health and nutrition (as we today are significantly larger than our shorter ancestors of even 200 years ago.) These tall and wise newcomers arrived with sophisticated tools in what we now know as Egypt and Israel (which is backed up by mtDNA analysis.) As is still true on the ships of any fleet today, the overseas survivors arriving from a devastated civilization were undoubtedly mostly male. They were big, wise, mighty men who easily attracted local "daughters of men" as wives. Is it more reasonable to assume Nephilim were aliens, fallen angels, giants, or humans?

Genesis 28:10-12 Jacob "came to a certain place and spent the night there, because the sun had set; and he took one of the stones of the place and put it under his head, and lay down in that place. He had a dream, and behold, a ladder was set on the earth with its top reaching to heaven; and behold, the angels of God were ascending and descending on it. And behold, the LORD stood above it." As stones do not make good pillows, we must assume our attention is being drawn to using this stone (probably the Earth) as a base for Jacob's ladder, which is quite probably the Milky Way. The Milky Way would have stars in a nearly vertical column, and stars have been likened to angels many times. This pathway of ascending/descending stars is crossed by the plane of the ecliptic, with the galactic center at the crossing point. It is the galactic center Jacob is referring to when he wakes up from the dream and in Genesis 28:16-17 says "Surely the LORD is in this place, and I did not know it… How awesome is this place! This is none other than the house of God, and this is the gate of heaven."

This is certainly what the Maya believed about their holy crossroads, and what the Egyptians believed about the "Ladder of Horus" which led to a "sun-door."[12] If this is a correct interpretation, then the gate of the heavens, the center of the galaxy at the galactic crossroads of the Milky Way and the ecliptic—is also the heavenly

211

location of the ancient Hebrew's "house of God"—which of course in Hebrew, is "Beth-El," from which names like Bethlehem are derived. This heavenly location may prove important when Christ returns, for he was born in Bethlehem, and the winter solstice sun is reborn at the galactic center.

As we continue to read Genesis and Exodus, we encounter some interesting facts that may raise questions about the roots of Judaism. In Genesis 12:5 Abram leaves Haran at age 75 with his wife Sarah. In 12:13 Abram asks Sarah to pretend she is his sister, because she is beautiful and the Egyptians may kill Abram to take her knowing he is her husband. What 75 year old has a sister so beautiful (young too, can we assume?) that a man would fear being killed so others could steal the woman away? Perhaps this possible inconsistency is to draw our attention to the pair, and realize the connection to the very similarly named Brahma and Sarai, Brahma being the supreme Hindu deity and Sarai his sister/wife.

In Genesis 20:12 Abram admits to Pharaoh that Sarah is his sister (through the father only) and his wife. But the similarities don't end there. Abram later has two prominent sons, Isaac and Ishmael. The Hebrew Isaac (Ishaak) may be from the Sanskrit Ishakhu ("Friend of Shiva") and Ishmael from the Sanskrit Ish-Mahal ("Great Shiva")—in which case we have the father/offspring relationship quite possibly derived from the Hindu pantheon as well. If these names are not coincidental, but are demonstrating a link to Hinduism and ancient Indian beliefs, then perhaps these names were used to encourage educated readers to consider cyclical time, with Brahma as creator, and Shiva as destroyer, at the very foundations of Judaism and Christianity.

Many facts in the book of Exodus, and elsewhere, have led to the theory that Moses may have been the Egyptian Pharaoh Akhenaten. That pharaoh attempted to overthrow the Egyptian priesthood and install a monotheistic religion in Egypt. The priesthood was too powerful, and his efforts to have Egypt worship one god were ruined. What if the priests offered him a chance to go away, taking his religious beliefs and a horde of foreigners with him?

In Exodus 3:13 "Moses said to God, 'Behold, I am going to the sons of Israel, and I will say to them, 'The God of your fathers has sent me to you.' Now they may say to me, 'What is His name?' What shall I say to them?'" This does not indicate that the Israelites had worshipped a single god; if they had, wouldn't they know his name? But if Akhenaten had tried and failed to create monotheism in Egypt, and if as Moses he was making up early Jewish history as he went - that could also explain why the Jews would not be familiar with God. Hosea 13:4-5 tells us "Yet I have been the LORD your God Since the land of Egypt; And you were not to know any god except Me, For there is no savior besides Me." So the Jews did not know one God before their time in Egypt?

They certainly would have recognized the ten commandments before Moses brought them down from Mt. Sinai. The Egyptian "Book of the Dead" is much older but its Spell 125 has every "commandment" written in slightly different form: "I have not stolen, I have not killed, I have not told lies…" etc. Even the story of Moses himself seems lifted from Egypt's religion, as Osiris had also been floated down the Nile River. "This special procedure [of a baby being placed in a basket in the Nile and saved by a princess] could only be related to royalty and was an international tradition for royal children as heirs to the throne. This implies that Moses must also have been a royal child when in the first place thus able to partake in this rite."[13] In fact there were very similar figures named Manou in India, Minos in Crete, and Mises in Egypt.

Moses really being a Pharaoh would also explain some of the haughty references he wrote about himself. Numbers 12:6-8 says "If there is a prophet among you, I, the LORD, shall make Myself known to him in a vision. I shall speak with him in a dream. Not so, with My servant Moses, He is faithful in all My household; With him I speak mouth to mouth, Even openly, and not in dark sayings, And he beholds the form of the LORD." A king raised to view himself as one of the gods would expect no less. In Exodus 4:16 God tells Moses that Aaron "shall speak for you to the people; and he will be as a mouth for you and you will be as God to him." Moses would be a god only because he was pharaoh. And apparently he needed help to speak to the Jews. We are also told that "Moses was educated in all the learning of the Egyptians." (Acts 7:22) Of course Moses would have known such things, for if he had been the pharaoh he would automatically be trained as a high priest.

In other myths like Oedipus, the child of the king is secretly raised by peasants, and learns his royal identity late in life. Moses was raised in Pharaoh's court, bucking the trend of more typical stories about kings switched at birth. Exodus 4:20 says "Moses taketh the rod of God in his hand." Is this Pharaoh's scepter? If not, what rod is it? Exodus 12:35-36 tells us the Israelites were allowed to leave Egypt with a lot of silver and gold. Slaves don't get to do that. A Pharaoh being compensated to abandon his claim to the throne might.

Another even more unusual theory claims that the cosmic dust clouds from galactic superwaves have high concentrations of monatomic gold. While we all have this inside us in tiny quantities, huge amounts may have fallen to earth as a white powder during previous superwave events. This could be the manna that fell from heaven. Some believe the Pharaohs hoarded this "mfkzt" for its alleged abilities to promote health and longevity, help DNA to repair itself, enhance our brains' perception, and generally energize us. Supporters of this idea believe that this powdered monatomic gold is what Moses/Akhenaten "stole" to give to all his followers. When the Egyptian priesthood discovered that Moses had stolen the elite's hoard of monatomic metals and planned to waste them on the common people, they decided to undo this heresy, and send the army to chase after the exodus and retrieve their special metals.

The Bible tells us God parted the Red Sea for the Israelites and sent it crashing back to drown the pursuing Egyptian army. There is a temple dedicated to Hathor in the Sinai desert, possibly established or expanded by Moses, and this temple contained a vast supply of traffic cone-shaped "stones" of this white, powdered gold which have been tested to exhibit many unusual properties. Some writers believe Revelations 2:17 refers to this material: "To him who overcomes, to him I will give some of the hidden manna, and I will give him a white stone." If stories about monatomic gold are legitimate, then it has been hoarded by those in the know who keep it a secret, and its superconductivity will have very noticeable effects when it returns in a cosmic dust cloud.

With or without monatomic gold, there is a strong case for Akhenaten leaving Egypt as Moses. Perhaps even this theory is wrong. But if it is right, as Sigmund Freud and several other intelligent people believe—then the roots of the Old Testament and the Jewish people are in question. The role of Egypt as a source of ancient wisdom becomes much more important to us, as do the mystery schools Jesus may have been introduced to between the ages of twelve and thirty, of which so little is known. Matthew 2:13 tells us he fled to Egypt. Luke 2:52 tells us "Jesus kept increasing in wisdom."

We could easily have a whole chapter devoted to the oddities of the Hebrew judge Samson. He is impulsive and violent, yet he reigns as a judge for about twenty years. "The story of Samson stands out in the Bible as a grand tissue of absurdities."[14] In Judges 15:15 he slayed a thousand men with the jawbone of an ass, then threw it, then declared his thirst to God, who made water come out of the hollow of the jaw. These details seem quite odd, unless we realize that in ancient Babylon, the god Marduk uses the same celestial jaw as a boomerang to kill monsters.

When the Bible tells us something happened, and the literal interpretation of events is not physically possible, we are probably dealing with a clue to look for an astronomical solution. In Judges 14:5-6 Samson (whose name means "belonging to the sun,") encounters a young lion, and tears it in two with his bare hands. Could this be a way of telling us the events described through Samson at this point occurred halfway through the Age of Leo? If so, these ancient stories depict events from over 12,000 years ago. As de Santillana and von Dechend would describe Samson (and many other "historical" figures: "mythical figures have invaded history under counterfeit presentments."[15]

In Judges 14:11-13 Samson asks a riddle and offers 30 undergarments and 30 outfits to the 30 groomsmen if they can guess it right. There are 30 degrees in a zodiac sign, like Leo, or Aquarius... His wife Delilah, by the way, has a name meaning "hers" and "water pitcher," which loosely translates as "she of Aquarius." We have noted that in Judges 15:15 Samson kills a thousand men with the jawbone of an ass. This is a very odd choice of weapons, and not one that could realistically be used to kill a thousand men. Few people would recognize that this is a reference to the Hyades star cluster, the "watery" jaw of Taurus. The only two star clusters bright enough to be seen with the naked eye, the Hyades and the Pleiades, are both in Taurus, and both are mentioned in various pole-shift stories. The jawbone reference may be a way of dating a deadly event, hinting that it occurred when the sun was in the Hyades. This seems even more likely if we consider the events in Judges 14 more thoroughly.

In Judges 14:5-6 Samson is walking towards his parents' house when "a young lion came roaring toward him. The Spirit of the LORD came upon him mightily, so that he tore him as one tears a young goat though he had nothing in his hand." This could mean that God's active force, possibly emanating from the galactic center and invigorating and empowering the sun, led to a world-shaking event during the young lion: the beginning of the age of Leo. The great and very real stone monuments of Egypt—the lion-like Sphinx, and the Great pyramids—are aligned to stars as they were at the age of Leo, approximately 10,500 B.C.

Soon after Samson finds a woman he likes, he decides to take her home and to hold a banquet, and he gathers 30 groomsmen. (We must assume this is for a marriage.) In Judges 14:12-13 he asks them a strange riddle, as the sphinx was known to do: "Let me now propound a riddle to you; if you will indeed tell it to me within the seven days of the feast, and find it out, then I will give you thirty linen wraps and thirty changes of clothes. But if you are unable to tell me, then you shall give me thirty linen wraps and thirty changes of clothes." Is the riddle meant for the groomsmen, or readers like us—to make us consider the sun and pole shifts? The seven day feast matches the week of a Jewish wedding, but the references to thirty are not part of weddings. If these events are about pole shifts, it may be relevant that a typical pole shift is about 30 degrees of movement. The last one took our North Pole from Hudson Bay

[83 degrees West and 60 degrees North] to its current location [90 degrees North]. If the guests are wise enough to understand the riddle, they are wise enough to prepare for the pole shift. If they prepare supplies at a sensible location, the sun-god gives them a new world; if they can't solve the riddle they don't understand and will be unprepared and will have all their possessions removed, including their clothing (the body that clothes the soul.)

Judges 14:14 "So he said to them, 'Out of the eater came something to eat, And out of the strong came something sweet.' But they could not tell the riddle in three days." We know the sweet food is a reference to the lion he killed earlier, where a swarm of bees had made honey in the lion's carcass. But his thirty groomsmen proved unable to answer the riddle for three days (like Jonah in the dark belly of the whale for three days, or Jesus in the tomb for parts of three days.) The groomsmen soon threaten Samson's bride, telling her she must fool him into revealing the secret solution to his riddle. "Then it came about on the fourth day that they said to Samson's wife, 'Entice your husband, so that he will tell us the riddle, or we will burn you and your father's house with fire.'" (Judges 14:15) On the seventh day her weeping finally pressures Samson to tell her, and she passes on the information. The groomsmen present the solution to his riddle, but he responds in Judges 14:18-19: "If you had not plowed with my heifer, You would not have found out my riddle. Then the Spirit of the LORD came upon him mightily, and he went down to Ashkelon and killed thirty of them and took their spoil and gave the changes of clothes to those who told the riddle. And his anger burned, and he went up to his father's house." Burning fire is mentioned, Samson refers to the source of their answers as a cow, (Taurus) and then goes off to cause destruction measured by thirty. The last part about going to his father's house is reminiscent of Jesus going to his father's house.

So far in Samson we have what may be a veiled description of a pole shift at the beginning of the age of Leo. Our solar hero has God's force activate him, and he tears the lion in two. Afterwards a golden age starts anew, flowing with honey. Our solar hero has God's force activate him again, this time referencing a young cow.

Perhaps there was another pole shift early in the age of Taurus? We already know he uses "the jawbone of an ass" (which is part of the Taurus constellation) to kill a great many people; perhaps the sun was located there at the time of a pole shift. These two constellations—Leo and Taurus—are two of the four cardinal ones—the important ones every three zodiac signs.

The next cardinal age is the age we are entering now, Aquarius. And our solar hero's wife has a name (Delilah) which refers to Aquarius. There are repeated references to the marriage of our solar hero and to destruction at the beginning of cardinal zodiac ages, resulting in transfers of 30, perhaps 30 degrees? Christianity has a new name for the current solar hero/savior/god now, but Jesus was also sold out for a transfer of 30—in pieces of silver. When Jesus comes back it will be to marry his bride, when he has prepared a place for us at His father's house. It would not be out of place for another marriage story (for Jesus) to take place along with another pole shift at the beginning of the next cardinal zodiac age, which we are currently entering—the age of Aquarius.

In Judges 16:3 Samson is expected to rise at dawn, (like the sun) but "Samson lay until midnight, and at midnight he arose and took hold of the doors of the city gate and the two posts and pulled them up along with the bars; then he put them on his shoulders and carried them up to the top of the mountain." This could refer to the sun not rising on time, and moving our axis of rotation. This may seem a stretch but in the NWT translation the axis is mentioned a few sentences later, when in Judges 16:5 five Philistine "axis lords" come to Delilah and offer her 5500 pieces of silver to trick Samson into allowing them to take his powers away and enslave him. Could the 5500 represent the years between two pole shifts?

Like Adam in Eden, Samson is betrayed by his wife. Delilah eventually discovers her husband's secret source of strength, and shaves off his seven braids of hair for the five Philistine princes / axis lords, who put out Samson's eyes and enslave him to grind in prison. Perhaps the eyes represent the sun and moon, whose light fails, when Samson's hair (the sun's magnetic field?) is temporarily removed. Grinding at the prison mill represents the

218

circular precessional motion of the cosmic mill. Eventually God grants Samson's request to restore his power, so that in Judges 16:29-30, while standing at the center of the Philistines' temple in Gaza, "Samson grasped the two *middle pillars* on which the house rested, and braced himself against them, the one with his right hand and the other with his left. And Samson said, 'Let me die with the Philistines!' And he bent with all his might so that the house fell on the lords and all the people who were in it." Samson destroying two pillars at Gaza is very similar to Hercules' destruction of two pillars at Gadiz—which the Egyptian priests at Thebes dated to 18,500 B.C. "St. Augustine believed that Samson and the sun god Hercules were one."[16]

Just possibly, we have Samson representing the Sun, who suffers a loss of strength/magnetic field, and goes dark, and then later regains strength and destroys the Earth's axis (middle pillars) while "dying" himself. If the story of Samson does in fact tell the story of actual solar events thousands of years ago, it could explain why his character is described very similarly around the world. The Japanese version of Samson mentioned in the "Nihongi" is named Susanowo. When his hair is tied to the palace rafters, he pulls the palace down. Susanowo also throws the back half of his stallion at his sun-goddess half-sister Amaterasu, (like Enkidu threw the hind quarter of the Bull of Heaven in Ishtar's face, or how Samson throws the jawbone of an ass.) Amaterasu (the sun) withdrew in anger into a cave, the world went dark, and other gods had to trick her back out. In New Zealand the Maori hero Whakatau pulled ropes tied to the posts of the house, taking it down and killing the whole tribe, then setting the house on fire. In Mexico, the Mayan "Popul Vuh" tells us Zipacna carries a huge log 400 youths could barely drag, makes it a ridgepole for a house, then when they try to kill him, he brings down the house and kills them, and they become the Pleiades.[17]

1 Samuel 2:8 "For *the pillars of the earth are the Lord's, And He set the world on them.*" God sets the Earth's axis.

1 Kings 18:46 "Then the hand of the LORD was on Elijah, and he girded up his loins." Other versions of the Bible translate this as

"tucking his cloak into his belt." (NIV) The belt is mentioned even more clearly in 2 Kings 1:7-8, when men are asking for a description of a man who had prophesied. When they were told this man had a belt, they knew immediately it was Elijah. "'What kind of man was he who came up to meet you and spoke these words to you?' They answered him, 'He was a hairy man with a leather girdle bound about his loins.' And he said, 'It is Elijah the Tishbite.'" Certainly a belt was not such an uncommon article of clothing that it could really identify someone. But there is a celestial figure immediately recognized by his belt. The Egyptians called him Osiris, Lord of the Dead, but we know him as Orion the Hunter, one of the only constellations repeatedly mentioned in the Bible, whose belt stars are positioned near the Milky Way exactly as the three main pyramids in Egypt are positioned alongside the Nile.

This belt of stars was extremely important in the ancient near east, and if it tells us that Orion represents Elijah, this will be important to us later on. For Elijah comes ahead of the messiah to anoint him; and as our messianic signs are astronomical we know Orion will appear first. Orion is a "winter" constellation that is most prominent in the northern hemisphere's skies from November to February, and depending on one's latitude, may first become visible as early as September. If Orion is Elijah and comes before the messiah, the messiah comes after September. Orion is probably referenced in the song celebrating the king's marriage in Psalms 45:3 "Gird Your sword on Your thigh, O Mighty One." In Greek myth, Orion was a mighty hunter who boasted too much about his skills. The Greek gods sent Scorpius to kill him. After being stung, and knowing he would be placed in the sky, his dying wish was to be put far from this deadly scorpion. Orion is opposite the galactic center and Scorpio, but he has a "reflection" in the very similar constellation Ophiuchus, which also represents a man 180 degrees away, with Scorpio at his heel. The relationship between these constellations may be similar to that between John the Baptist and Jesus.

2 Kings 2:11 Elijah and Elisha were walking when "As they were going along and talking, behold, there appeared a chariot of fire and horses of fire which separated the two of them. And Elijah went

220

up by a whirlwind to heaven." So Elijah disappears when a fiery chariot appears. In ancient times sun gods like Apollo were depicted riding a fiery sky chariot drawn by horses. Could 2 Kings 2:11 be describing the stars of Orion fading away with the overpowering light of the rising sun dominating the sky? It is very interesting that Orion's celestial position is opposite that of the galactic core, and of course on 12/21/2012 the galactic core shares that position in conjunction with the sun. So on that day Orion sets in the west as the sun rises in the east.

What happens six months earlier? In June the sun is not in conjunction with the galactic core, it is half a year away—and out of alignment by half a rotation through the sky. Six months earlier, the sun is opposite the galactic core, at Orion. At that time Orion is standing on the eastern horizon when the rays of the rising sun obliterate our view of him, and he is absorbed into the light of that fiery sky chariot we know as the sun. So this disappearance of the belted man into the fiery sky chariot happens to Orion six months before 12/21/2012 and 12/21/2019 (as it happens six months before every winter solstice at our point in the precessional cycle.) It may be relevant that the Egyptian concept of the Duat, a portion of the underworld/sky through which the sun travels and where the gods judge the dead, "was considered by the ancient Egyptians to be active only at the time of the summer solstice when Orion and Sirius rose (with the sun) heliacally."[18]

Have we come too far from the story of our belted Elijah for this to seem relevant? Let us not forget that Elijah could raise the dead, and Osiris/Orion was Lord of the Dead. Let us not forget that Elijah is supposed to return before the coming of the messiah to anoint him. Remember that Jesus is clearly the sun, and that Jesus himself tells us that John the Baptist, who wore the same camel hair cloak and leather belt that Elijah wore (Mark 1:6) and who was born six months before Jesus, is the prophetic fulfillment of Elijah's return. We are being told that Orion is six months off from the winter solstice sun at the time of the second coming. Because of precession, Orion is not always six months off from the winter solstice sun—but it is right now in the early 21st century. This is one of many ways the Bible indicates our times are the end times.

Job 9:5-9 "it is God who removes the mountains, they know not how, When He overturns them in His anger; *Who shakes the earth out of its place, And its pillars tremble*; Who commands the sun not to shine, And sets a seal upon the stars; Who alone stretches out the heavens And tramples down the waves of the sea; Who makes the Bear, Orion and the Pleiades, And the chambers of the south." (Arcturus/Bear/Ursa Major/Big Dipper, Orion, Pleiades)

Job named the most northern constellation by the false pole god, the hunter Orion in opposition to God (the Galactic Center) and the Pleiades—which have long been associated with prophecy, death, endings, new birth, and beginnings. The Pleiades now rise in mid-November, but before 1582, when our western calendar jumped ten days from the Julian to the Gregorian count, the Pleiades rose around Halloween. The Pleiades are linked to the living and the dead, a gate between worlds, and perhaps to world ages.

There are references in the Talmud (an ancient book of Jewish commentaries interpreting the Bible) to the Pleiades and Noah's Flood. There are legends about this connection and the Pleiades' "missing" star(s); perhaps a change was observed at the time of a worldwide cataclysm. Accounts of it are found in several cultures from Native Americans to Australians. The time of the biblical flood is given as the 17th day of the second month, which is around the end of October. The date for Noah's entrance into the ark is the same date on which the dead Osiris was put into a coffin and floated down the Nile. The occurrence of a festival of the dead, or recognition of the Pleiades at this time of year, also goes back into ancient times and may be the original source of Halloween.

The small size and dimness of this little cluster of stars, (which is actually part of the constellation of Taurus the Bull) makes it an odd choice for so many ancient references. One would expect more prominent stars to be chosen, if writers were making a choice. But perhaps its faintness is the reason for its mention—because if interstellar dust pours into our solar system from the galactic core to help cause events in the Sun and the Earth which contribute to a pole shift, then the faintest stars might "disappear" from view for a long time, even after most things stabilize. This may explain why the Talmud tells us the Pleiades are believed to be a possible location of God's sign in a future end times judgment. Some Jewish sages tell of the change being two missing stars at the time of the flood rather than just one. Perhaps this is because Estrope, which is generally not visible at all without perfect weather conditions, has recently been found to be a double star. This could also explain why the constellation had been known as the seven sisters—if the ancients also knew Estrope was a double star. This could explain why the Torah sages wrote that God "took two stars away from KIMAH and brought the flood!"[19]

Job 28:20-21 "Where then does wisdom come from? And where is the place of understanding? Thus it is hidden from the eyes of all living And concealed from the birds of the sky. Abaddon and Death say, 'With our ears we have heard a report of it.' God understands its way, And He knows its place. For He looks to the ends of the earth." Perhaps the hint of "the ends of the earth" refers to Antarctica, where many believe Atlantis was located, or to both poles at the northern and southern ends of the world, as one can hardly be wise regarding pole shifts without understanding the planet rotates on an axis and has two poles of rotation.

Job 38:13-14 "That it might take hold of the ends of the earth, And the wicked be shaken out of it? It is changed like clay under the seal." To the extent that a round object has ends, the poles are the north and south ends of the Earth.

Job 38:22-23 "Have you entered the storehouses of the snow, Or have you seen *the storehouses of the hail, Which I have reserved for the time of distress*?" That certainly sounds like God is reserving polar ice for the time of distress—a Judgment Day pole shift.

Job 38:37-38 *"the water jars of heaven—who can tip them over, When the dust pours out* as into a molten mass"? (NWT) The NASB reads "Who can count the clouds by wisdom, Or tip the water jars of the heavens, When the dust hardens into a mass"? Is this hinting at cosmic dust clouds at the age of Aquarius, the water-bearer?

Psalms 2:6 "I have installed My King Upon Zion, My holy mountain." (Jesus/the sun is enthroned at the galactic center.)

Psalms 18:9-11 "He bowed the heavens also, and came down With thick darkness under His feet... He made darkness His hiding place... Darkness of waters, thick clouds of the skies."

Psalms 19:4-5 "He has placed a tent for *the sun, Which is as a bridegroom* coming out of his chamber." The sun is the groom because Jesus is the sun. This describes part of the wedding events on Judgment Day, 12/28/19.

Psalms 29:10 "The LORD sat as King at the flood." Does this mean there is a flood during enthronement? The RSV reads "The Lord sits enthroned over the flood."

Psalms 46:2 "Therefore we will not fear, *though the earth should change And though the mountains slip into the heart of the sea.*"

Psalms 84:11 "the LORD God is a sun and shield." This likens him to the sun and the eye of Ra, a huge blue oval with the bright galactic core in the center.

Psalms 89:36 "*his throne as the sun before Me.*" We could not ask for a clearer description of Jesus becoming king as the sun is in front of the galactic center.

Psalms 104:2 "Covering Yourself with light as with a cloak" sounds like the Eye of Ra around the galactic center.

Psalms 110:1 "The LORD says to my Lord: 'Sit at My right hand Until I make Your enemies a footstool for Your feet.'" The sun is at the galactic center's right until the time of action, when Draco and Scorpio fall.

Psalms 114:3-7 "The sea looked and fled; The Jordan turned back. The mountains skipped like rams, The hills, like lambs. What ails you, O sea, that you flee? O Jordan, that you turn back? O mountains, that you skip like rams? O hills, like lambs? Tremble, O earth, before the Lord."

Ecclesiastes 1:9-11 "That which has been is that which will be, And that which has been done is that which will be done. So there is nothing new under the sun. Is there anything of which one might say, "See this, it is new"? Already it has existed for ages Which were before us. There is no remembrance of earlier things; And also of the later things which will occur, There will be for them no remembrance Among those who will come later still."

Ecclesiastes 3:15 "That which is has been already and that which will be has already been."

Isaiah 2:19 "Men will go into caves of the rocks And into holes of the ground Before the terror of the LORD And the splendor of His majesty, When He arises to make the earth tremble."

Isaiah 4:2-5 "In that day the Branch of the LORD will be beautiful and glorious, and the fruit of the earth will be the pride and the adornment of the survivors of Israel. It will come about that he who is left in Zion and remains in Jerusalem will be called holy— everyone who is recorded for life in Jerusalem. When the Lord has washed away the filth of the daughters of Zion and purged the bloodshed of Jerusalem from her midst, by the spirit of judgment and the spirit of burning, then the LORD will create over the whole area of Mount Zion and over her assemblies a cloud by day, even smoke, and the brightness of a flaming fire by night."

Isaiah 6:11-13 "Until cities are devastated and without inhabitant, Houses are without people And the land is utterly desolate, The LORD has removed men far away, And the forsaken places are many in the midst of the land. Yet there will be a tenth portion in it, And it will again be subject to burning."

Isaiah 13:10 "For the stars of heaven and their constellations Will not flash forth their light; The sun will be dark when it rises And the moon will not shed its light."

Is 13:12-13 "I will make mortal man scarcer than pure gold And mankind than the gold of Ophir. Therefore I will make the heavens tremble, And *the earth will be shaken from its place* At the fury of the LORD of hosts In the day of His burning anger."

Isaiah 14:13 God says to Satan, "you said in your heart, 'I will ascend to heaven; I will raise my throne above the stars of God, And I will sit on the mount of assembly In the recesses of the north. 'I will ascend above the heights of the clouds; I will make myself like the Most High.' "Nevertheless you will be thrust down to Sheol, To the recesses of the pit." This indicates God's place is with certain stars, which Satan can appear to be above when he is polar.

Isaiah 22:25 *"In that day,"* declares the LORD of hosts, *"the peg driven in a firm place will give way; it will even break off and fall, and the load hanging on it will be cut off.*" This sounds like a change in the axis of rotation.

Isaiah 24:1-6 "*the LORD is going to lay waste the earth and devastate it; he will ruin its face and scatter its inhabitants... The earth will be completely laid waste...* The earth is defiled by its people; they have disobeyed the laws, violated the statutes and broken the everlasting covenant. Therefore a curse consumes the earth; its people must bear their guilt. Therefore earth's inhabitants are burned up, and very few are left." Man apparently ruins the rainbow covenant.

Isaiah 24:18-20 "the windows above are opened, and *the foundations of the earth shake. The earth is broken asunder, The earth is split through, The earth is shaken violently. The earth reels to and fro like a drunkard And it totters like a shack,* For its transgression is heavy upon it, And it will fall, never to rise again."

Isaiah 30:25-26 "on the day of the great slaughter, when the towers fall. The light of the moon will be as the light of the sun, and the light of the sun will be seven times brighter, like the light of seven days."

Isaiah 34:4 "And *the sky will be rolled up like a scroll.*" There is a reason the Chicken Little story is thousands of years old, and that people were concerned about the sky falling. Stars have "fallen out of the sky" and gone below the horizon before, and they will again.

Isaiah 65:17 "*I create new heavens and a new earth*; And the former things will not be remembered or come to mind."

Jeremiah 4:23-28 "I looked on the earth, and behold, it was formless and void; And to the heavens, and they had no light. I looked on the mountains, and behold, they were quaking, And all the hills moved to and fro. I looked, and behold, there was no man, And all the birds of the heavens had fled. I looked, and behold, the fruitful land was a wilderness, And all its cities were pulled down Before the LORD, before His fierce anger. For thus says the LORD, "The whole land shall be a desolation, Yet I will not execute a complete destruction. For this the earth shall mourn And the heavens above be dark."

Jeremiah 25:33 "Those slain by the LORD on that day will be

from one end of the earth to the other. They will not be lamented, gathered or buried; they will be like dung on the face of the ground." (There will be not be enough survivors left to wail or bury them all.)

Ezekiel 1:26 "above the expanse that was *over their heads there was something resembling a throne, like lapis lazuli (sapphire) in appearance.*" This sounds like the blue star of the Hopi, an active Seyfert galactic center.

Ezekiel 32:7 "*When I extinguish you, I will cover the heavens and darken their stars; I will cover the sun with a cloud* And the moon will not give its light."

Ezekiel 38:20-22 "All the men who are on the face of the earth will shake at My presence; the mountains also will be thrown down, the steep pathways will collapse and every wall will fall to the ground."

Daniel 4:10-11 "*There was a tree in the midst of the earth* and its height was great. The tree grew large and became strong And its height reached to the sky, And it was visible to the end of the whole earth."

Daniel 4:23 "In that the king saw an angelic watcher, a holy one, descending from heaven…" This should remind us of the archangel Metatron, famous for transmitting secret Kaballistic knowledge to man, like many other messengers or wisdom gods such as Hermes or Thoth or Prometheus. Metatron's name has many meanings in Hebrew and Greek including "keeper of the watch," "co-occupant of the divine throne" and "one who serves behind the throne" or "one who occupies the throne next to the throne of glory."[20] Many of these meanings seem relevant to the idea of watching for an alignment of the winter solstice sun and the galactic center to predict a pole shift.

Going back to Daniel 4:23 "…an angelic watcher, a holy one, descending from heaven and saying, "*Chop down the tree and destroy it*; yet leave the stump with its roots in the ground, but with a band of iron and bronze around it in the new grass of the field, and let him be drenched with the dew of heaven, and let him share with the beasts of the field *until seven periods of time pass* over him." Could this mean the axis is moved in the crust, while the rootstock of the rotational axis deep in the iron core stays intact, and that any world age lasts into a seventh millennium (between six and seven thousand years)?

Daniel 7:9-10 "I kept looking Until thrones were set up, And the Ancient of Days took His seat; His vesture was like white snow And the hair of His head like pure wool. His throne was ablaze with flames, Its wheels were a burning fire. A river of fire was flowing And coming out from before Him; Thousands upon thousands were attending Him, And myriads upon myriads were standing before Him; The court sat, And the books were opened." Judgment comes when thrones are in place among the stars of the Milky Way.

Daniel 7:13-14 "Behold, with the clouds of heaven One like a Son of Man was coming, And He came up to the Ancient of Days And was presented before Him. And to Him was given dominion, Glory and a kingdom." Christ gets the kingdom when he accesses the throne of God. See Revelations 3:21 in which Jesus says he "sat down with My Father on His throne." Also consider Revelations 22:3 which mentions "the throne of God and of the Lamb"—they share the throne in a conjunction / alignment in the Bible's final passages.

Joel 2:1-2 "The day of the LORD is coming; Surely it is near, A day of darkness and gloom, A day of clouds and thick darkness." Cosmic dust blocks sunlight.

Joel 2:30-31 "I will display wonders in the sky and on the earth, Blood, fire and columns of smoke. The sun will be turned into darkness And the moon into blood Before the great and awesome day of the LORD."

Joel 3:14-17 "For the day of the LORD is near in the valley of decision. The sun and moon grow dark And the stars lose their brightness. The LORD roars from Zion And utters His voice from Jerusalem, And the heavens and the earth tremble. But the LORD is a refuge for His people And a stronghold to the sons of Israel. Then you will know that I am the LORD your God, Dwelling in Zion, My holy mountain." As Tim LaHaye says, "This is not the earthly Mount Zion but the heavenly."[21] The heavenly Mt. Zion is the galactic center throne, the Jerusalem from which God utters His voice.

Amos 5:8 "Who calls for the waters of the sea and pours them out on the surface of the earth, The LORD is His name."

Amos 8:8-9 "will not the land quake And everyone who dwells in it mourn? Indeed, all of it will rise up like the Nile, And it will be tossed about And subside like the Nile of Egypt. 'It will come about in that day,' declares the Lord GOD, 'That I will make the sun go down at noon And make the earth dark in broad daylight.'"

Amos 9:1 *"I saw the Lord standing beside the altar, and He said, 'Smite the capitals so that the thresholds will shake,* And break them on the heads of them all!'" The King James Bible reads "Smite the lintel of the door, that the posts may shake." The NIV says "I saw the Lord standing by the altar, and he said: 'Strike the tops of the pillars.'" When Jesus is stationed near the altar, the earth is rocked through its pillars—a pole shift when the sun is in the right position.

Jonah 1:17 "And the Lord appointed a great fish to swallow Jonah, and Jonah was in the stomach of the fish three days and three nights." *When the Bible tells us something happened, and the most literal interpretation of events is not physically possible, we should probably consider the event as a clue to look for an astronomical solution.* In this case, Jonah comes from the Hebrew "Yona," which means dove, associated with peace. The Prince of Peace is Jesus, the sun—and in all probability the three days Jonah spent in the belly of the whale or "great fish" is really a reference to three days of darkness in which the sun is in the "cosmic leviathan," the dark rift of the Milky Way's central bulge.

Nahum 1:3 "the LORD will by no means leave the guilty unpunished. In whirlwind and storm is His way, And clouds are the dust beneath His feet."

Habakkuk 3:10-11 "The mountains saw You and quaked; The downpour of waters swept by. The deep uttered forth its voice, It lifted high its hands. Sun and moon stood in their places; They went away at the light of Your arrows, At the radiance of Your gleaming spear."

Zephaniah 1:2-3 "'I will completely remove all things From the face of the earth,' declares the LORD. 'I will remove man and

229

beast; I will remove the birds of the sky And the fish of the sea, And the ruins along with the wicked; And I will cut off man from the face of the earth.'"

Zephaniah 1:18 "On the day of the LORD'S wrath; And all the earth will be devoured In the fire of His jealousy, For He will make a complete end."

Zephaniah 2:3-5 "Perhaps you will be hidden In the day of the LORD'S anger... *Woe to the inhabitants of the seacoast... I will destroy you So that there will be no inhabitant.*"

Zechariah 2:13 "Be silent, all flesh, before the LORD; for He is aroused from His holy habitation." The galactic core becomes active.

Zechariah 14:6-9 "In that day there will be no light; the luminaries will dwindle. For it will be a unique day which is known to the LORD, neither day nor night, but it will come about that at evening time there will be light. And in that day living waters will flow out of Jerusalem, half of them toward the eastern sea and the other half toward the western sea; it will be in summer as well as in winter. God Will Be King over All And the LORD will be king over all the earth; in that day." This affects both hemispheres. Day on one side, night on the other; winter in the north, summer in the south.

Malachi 3:1 "Behold, I am going to send My messenger, and he will clear the way before Me. And the Lord, whom you seek, will suddenly come to His temple." Elijah, probably Orion, comes first; then the winter solstice sun is the astronomical version of the true Lord, and He arrives at the galactic center.

Malachi 4:1-2 "Behold, the day is coming, burning like a furnace; and... the day that is coming will set them ablaze... the sun of righteousness will rise."

Malachi 4:5 "Behold, I am going to send you Elijah the prophet before the coming of the great and terrible day of the LORD. He will restore the hearts of the fathers to their children and the hearts of the children to their fathers, so that I will not come and smite the land with a curse." These are the final words of the Old Testament, and they tell us that [unless mankind suddenly changes] God will strike the Earth to destroy it, through a special sun, a burning like a

230

furnace, with God himself "producing a special property." (Malachi 3:17, NWT) Before this happens, we have a warning in the form of Elijah's return. The Bible is clear that Elijah shares a belt like Orion, and that Orion comes ahead of the messiah. The Bible is less clear that Orion disappears into the fiery whirlwind of the rising sun precisely six months ahead of the sun's alignment with the galactic center, but this author believes the point is made and is very relevant in timing the Second Coming to approximately the 21st century.

This is no small matter to gloss over. This is the closing paragraph of the Old Testament. Understanding what represents Elijah is crucial to understanding the coming of the messiah. This is probably the main reason the Jews did not believe Jesus was the Messiah. Jewish religious leaders knew that Elijah's return must happen before Christ would come, therefore anyone who seemed like a possible Messiah without Elijah returning from heaven first must not be a true Messiah. In Matthew 17:12 Jesus responds to the disciples mentioning this expectation of the Rabbis, and said "I say to you that Elijah already came, and they did not recognize him…" and in Matthew 17:13 "Then the disciples understood that He had spoken to them about John the Baptist." John was born six months before Jesus, as Orion/Elijah disappears into the sun six months before the winter solstice.

Now John the Baptist didn't descend in a chariot of fire. He even denied being Elijah when asked in John 1:21. We are asked to assume that John is Elijah, and that Elijah is not returning in his former body. Elijah is not even reincarnated with his knowledge and personality into John's body. We are told that the prophecy is satisfied merely by John having the same great qualities Elijah had, the same holy nature. This is understandably unsatisfying for those expecting the clouds to open up and reveal a fiery chariot on which Elijah would clearly and visibly descend from heaven—but it is similar to the non-dramatic "return" Orion makes to its position six months off from the winter solstice sun.

One early conversation on this topic between a Christian and Jew in was detailed approximately seventy years after Jesus died, in a book by Justin Martyr called "The Dialogue with Trypho the

Jew." The Rabbi Trypho responds to Justin's acceptance of Jesus as Messiah by saying "But Christ- if he has indeed been born, and exists anywhere... has no power until Elijah comes to anoint him." Trypho, and the Jews in general, certainly did not understand the celestial clues.

Matthew 13:11 "To you it has been granted to know the mysteries of the kingdom of heaven, but to them it has not been granted."

Matthew 13:13 "Therefore I speak to them in parables; because while seeing they do not see, and while hearing they do not hear, nor do they understand." Centuries earlier Plato advised his students to consider "a pattern set in the heavens, where those who want to see it can do so."

Matthew 13:16-17 "But blessed are your eyes, because they see; and your ears, because they hear. For truly I say to you that many prophets and righteous men desired to see what you see, and did not see it, and to hear what you hear, and did not hear it."

Matthew 13:34 "All these things Jesus spoke to the crowds in parables, and He did not speak to them without a parable."

Matthew 19:28 "In the regeneration when the Son of Man will sit on His glorious throne, you also shall sit upon twelve thrones." As the Earth is recreated anew, we continue to follow the sun through the twelve zodiac signs.

Matthew 21:1-7 "When they had approached Jerusalem and had come to Bethphage, at the Mount of Olives, then Jesus sent two disciples, saying to them, 'Go into the village opposite you, and immediately you will find a donkey tied there and a colt with her; untie them and bring them to Me. If anyone says anything to you, you shall say, 'The Lord has need of them,' and immediately he will send them.' This took place to fulfill what was spoken through the prophet:

'Say to the daughter of Zion,

'Behold your King is coming to you,

Gentle, and mounted on a donkey,

Even on a colt, the foal of a beast of burden.'

The disciples went and did just as Jesus had instructed them, and brought the donkey and the colt, and laid their coats on them; and

He sat on the coats."

Some skeptics who like to find fault with the Bible point out the difficulty of Jesus riding both the ass and the foal which is the colt of the ass. Some people try to explain that the second mention is merely clarification of the first, and there is only one ass ridden, but they are mistaken. Matthew 21:4 mentions "the prophet" and refers to Zechariah 9:9 "Rejoice greatly, O daughter of Zion! Shout in triumph, O daughter of Jerusalem! Behold, your king is coming to you; He is just and endowed with salvation, Humble, and mounted on a donkey, Even on a colt, the foal of a donkey." Both passages are also related to 2 Samuel 16:1 which mentions two donkeys with Christ's predecessor, King David: "Now when David had passed a little beyond the summit, behold, Ziba the servant of Mephibosheth met him with a couple of saddled donkeys." In every reference there are two asses.

Should we gloss over this strange reference as a curiosity and take the easy road of mental darkness? Or should we *assume that when the most literal interpretation of Biblical events is not physically possible, we are being handed a clue to look for an astronomical solution*? In ancient Greek mythology, Dionysus rode two asses into battle against the Titans, and their loud braying helped Dionysus and his father Zeus to defeat the Titans. (The son of the highest god rode two asses.) As a reward the donkeys were transferred to the sky at the head of the constellation Cancer, the Crab. Babylonians and Hebrews also associated this constellation with two asses; instead of "Cancer" they called it "The Ass and Foal" and even today we refer to two of the stars in Cancer as the asses, North Aselli and South Aselli.

The sun (Jesus) was just passed its highest point (the summer solstice around June 22) on top of the two asses at the beginning of July. This is very similar to "David had passed a little beyond the summit" as mentioned in 2 Samuel 16:1 when he had two donkeys. The passage in Matthew is telling us that the sun just past its highest point in the sky is analogous to Jesus just past the Mount of Olives. It tells us that when Jesus comes to Jerusalem he comes as the sun. As the galactic center is the heavenly Jerusalem and Mount Zion, this reference leads us to associate the alignment of the sun and the galactic center with the return of Jesus—if we are initiated into wisdom and do not gloss over details.

Matthew 21:42-43 "Jesus said to them, 'Did you never read in the Scriptures, THE STONE WHICH THE BUILDERS REJECTED, THIS BECAME THE CHIEF CORNER stone... Therefore I say to you, the kingdom of God will be taken away from you and given to a people, producing the fruit of it." Christianity interprets the rejected stone as Jesus. Muslims interpret it as Ishmael. What if the rejected stone is simply the forgotten idea that the dense galactic core "stone" is the source of all energy, matter, and transformation in our galaxy? That any understanding of the destructive ends of world ages must acknowledge the central role of galactic core explosions? What if Jesus understood that any religion foretelling and hoping for a new heaven and a new Earth should have this knowledge as its foundation?

Matthew 16:3 "Do you know how to discern the appearance of the sky, but cannot discern the signs of the times?" The leaders of the Jewish religion still watched the skies for some astronomical events but had forgotten the most important details of what signs they were looking for. They had come to focus on the zodiac constellations as being inherently important, and no longer correctly viewed them as mere indicators or marker posts along the path the sun travels to reach the galactic center. Isaiah 1:3 is also relevant: "An ox knows its owner, And a donkey its master's anger, But Israel does not know, My people do not understand." The Jewish priests forgot this wisdom, probably between 500 B.C. and 100 B.C. The astronomers in Persia did not forget. Their wise men still knew what Daniel had taught the Babylonians, so they were able to come to Jerusalem at the right time to find Jesus.

The Persian astronomers knew what to watch for and correctly realized when Jesus was born. The Jewish rabbis in Jerusalem didn't know what the magi were talking about until they explained everything, as the Jewish leaders hadn't remembered enough of their traditions to correctly anticipate the coming of the messiah. Is there anyone left today who has been taught these mysteries, in an unbroken line of priestly initiates, who will still know the signs and correctly anticipate when the messiah returns? Or will Hosea 4:6 prove accurate for most Jews and Christians: "My people are destroyed for lack of knowledge. Because you have rejected knowledge, I also will reject you from being My priest. Since you have forgotten the law of your God, I also will forget your children."

Matthew 24:41-44 "Two women will be *grinding at the mill*; one will be taken and one will be left. Therefore be on the alert, for you do not know which day your Lord is coming. But be sure of this, that if the head of the house had known at what time of the night the thief was coming, he would have been on the alert and would not have allowed his house to be broken into. For this reason you also must be ready; for the Son of Man is coming at an hour when you do not think He will." Grinding at a mill is symbolic of the rotating axis of the Earth. Anything that alters or damages the mill, or removes those working it or guarding it, is usually meant to indicate a shifting of the axis. We are encouraged to keep watching and measuring the heavens to detect such changes starting, especially if we have lost the prior civilization's ancient knowledge and don't know in what watch (in what age, or zodiac sign) these things will occur. But Matthew 24:43 indicates that the knowing watchman would not allow the thief to rob his house, implying that we can save ourselves if we keep awake (maintain the traditions of astronomical knowledge) and are prepared at the proper time.

Matt 27:44 "The robbers who had been crucified with Him..." Jesus dying on the cross may symbolize the sun having a rare field change, a death and rebirth event, when aligned in conjunction with the galactic core at the crossing of the ecliptic and Milky Way—and this grand cross in the sky has other small crosses near it, like the Thieves' Cross.

Matt 27:45 "*From the sixth hour darkness fell upon all the land until the ninth hour.*" This is commonly thought of as an eclipse during the crucifixion; another example likening Jesus to the sun. And again, the duration is for three units of time, though hours in this case, as opposed to the usual three days. This is clarified again in Mark 15:33 "*When the sixth hour came, darkness fell over the whole land until the ninth hour*." But no eclipse can last even eight minutes.

Matthew 28:1-2 "Now after the Sabbath, as it began to dawn toward the first day of the week, Mary Magdalene and the other Mary came to look at the grave. And behold, a severe earthquake had occurred, for an angel of the Lord descended from heaven and came and rolled away the stone." Mary went to the tomb at *sun*rise on *Sun*day to find that Jesus had arisen. Perhaps we should look for a future event in which there is an eclipse, when the moon moves away from the sun, such that the dead/hidden sun is replaced by the glowing sunrise. Such an eclipse occurs December 26, 2019, ending at sunrise in Israel. At this time the great earthquake of a pole shift should be underway.

Mark 4:11-12 "To you has been given the mystery of the kingdom of God, but those who are outside get everything in parables, so that WHILE SEEING, THEY MAY SEE AND NOT PERCEIVE, AND WHILE HEARING, THEY MAY HEAR AND NOT UNDERSTAND." As astronomer-priests in ancient times guarded their heavenly secret wisdom, so is the case with Christianity. The uninitiated may memorize the Bible and pass it on to the next generation, but only the initiated will understand the deeper astronomical messages.

Mark 4:22-23 "For nothing is hidden, except to be revealed; nor has anything been secret, but that it would come to light. If anyone has ears to hear, let him hear." Whoever is wise and initiated has ears to hear; read on and truly understand the hidden message. No doubt one from this wise minority wrote Isaiah 50:4 "He awakens My ear to listen." Another initiated brother named Plato later wrote in "Laws" that analyzing astronomy's mathematical relationships "wakes up the individual who is by nature sleepy."[22]

Mark 13:18-19 "*Pray that it may not happen in the winter. For those days will be a time of tribulation such as has not occurred since the beginning of the creation.*" Such events have not occurred since the last time the poles shifted and the world was re-created.

Mark 13:24-26 "But in those days, after that tribulation, THE SUN WILL BE DARKENED AND THE MOON WILL NOT

GIVE ITS LIGHT. AND THE STARS WILL BE FALLING from heaven, and the powers that are in the heavens will be shaken. Then they will see THE SON OF MAN COMING IN CLOUDS." This occurs after the tribulation.

Luke 11:29-30 "This generation is a wicked generation; it seeks for a sign, and yet *no sign will be given to it but the sign of Jonah. For just as Jonah became a sign to the Ninevites, so will the Son of Man be to this generation.*" Three days in the belly of Leviathan could mean three days of darkness for the sun by the dark rift of the Milky Way. This may be the only sign available to the uneducated masses. Even a jungle tribesman with no contact with the outside world and no knowledge of astronomy or religion or current events will see the sun go dark for three days right before Judgment Day.

Luke 17:28-30 "It was the same as happened in the days of Lot: they were eating, they were drinking, they were buying, they were selling, they were planting, they were building; but on the day that Lot went out from Sodom it rained fire and brimstone from heaven and destroyed them all. It will be just the same on the day that the Son of Man is revealed." As in Noah's day and Lot's day, the coming destruction is known only to a select few, destruction through cosmic fire and flood comes suddenly upon the ignorant masses. The following quote is non-canonical, from the rejected Book of Noah. Parts of the Book of Noah have been found in the Dead Sea Scrolls and even more of it in Jubilees and The Book of Enoch. Despite not being in our Bibles one quote seems very relevant here. Noah 65:1 "And in those days, *Noah saw the Earth had tilted and that its destruction was near.*" The moment Noah describes would be analogous to what I expect in late December, 2019—after the pole shift has started, but before the worst events on Judgment Day.

Luke 17:35 "There will be two women grinding at the same place; one will be taken and the other will be left." Imagery of grinding grain at a mill when end times events occur probably refers to a shifting axis.

Luke 21:10 "Nation will rise against nation and kingdom against kingdom, and there will be great earthquakes, and in various places plagues and famines; and there will be terrors and great signs from heaven." WWIII is likely during the tribulation as our civilization's fraudulent debt-based financial system / casino finally collapses into economic chaos. During depression, famine, and war, Russia and China will probably attempt to seize lands that will not be an arctic waste. But as likely as WWIII is, and although it is possible that China (even by itself but certainly with allies) could raise an army of 200 million as described in Revelations 9:16, that reference just may be astronomical:

Revelations 9:14-16 reads "Then the sixth angel sounded, and I heard a voice from the four horns of the golden altar which is before God, one saying to the sixth angel who had the trumpet, 'Release the four angels who are bound at the great river Euphrates.' And the four angels, who had been prepared for the hour and day and month and year, were released, so that they would kill a third of mankind. The number of the armies of the horsemen was two hundred million; I heard the number of them." If the sun/Jesus is the golden altar, and the galactic center is God, then maybe the great river is the Milky Way, the two hundred million is an estimate of its stars, and the four angels are the bright stars of the cardinal zodiac constellations. The ancients defined "an earth" by its reference to the ecliptic plane between Regulus in Leo, Antares in Scorpio, Aldebaran in Taurus, and Fomalhaut (which although sticking out in Pisces, is far brighter than nearby Sadalmelik, which the brightest (but not noticeably bright) star in Aquarius. These four angels/stars being released to kill a third of mankind could refer to their apparent movement during a pole shift.

Luke 21:21-22 "Then those who are in Judea must flee to the mountains, and those who are in the midst of the city must leave, and those who are in the country must not enter the city; because these are days of vengeance."

Luke 21:25-27 "There will be signs in sun and moon and stars, and on the earth dismay among nations, in perplexity at the roaring of the sea and the waves, men fainting from fear and the expectation of the things which are coming upon the world; for the powers of the heavens will be shaken. Then they will see THE SON OF MAN

COMING IN A CLOUD."

Luke 21:34-36 *"Be on guard... and that day will not come on you suddenly* like a trap; for it will come upon all those who dwell on the face of all the earth. But keep on the alert at all times, praying that you may have strength *to escape* all these things that are about to take place, and to stand before the Son of Man." If we are on guard and awake and alert we can escape the destruction that otherwise falls on all mankind. But we must understand what is going to happen, when it will happen, and what we need to do both when it happens and in preparation beforehand. As told in Luke 21:21-22, we should get away from lowlands and cities and into the mountains.

Luke 22:10 "When you have entered the city, a man will meet you carrying a pitcher of water; follow him into the house that he enters." Aquarius, the water bearer, is a man carrying such a jug of water. We are being told to follow the winter solstice sun to the heavenly Jerusalem, the galactic center, as the vernal equinox sun enters into the age of Aquarius. This is the zodiac age we are entering now; the only one that inherently describes pouring out water in a flood. As John the Baptist is both identified as the heavenly water-man and is considered by many to be the last prophet of the Old Testament (instead of ending it at Malachi) these associations also tell us to link the end of the old world (the one we have known) to the age of Aquarius and Jesus' Second Coming just as we view John as the immediate precursor to Jesus' first visit. Matthew 11:14-15 "John himself is Elijah who was to come. He who has ears to hear, let him hear." Jews leave a glass of wine out on their Passover table for Elijah (Elijah/John the Baptist) near the spring equinox but how many Jews will recognize his arrival if what it really symbolizes is the dawning of the age of Aquarius? About as many as recognized John the Baptist.

Luke 24:45 "Then He opened their minds to understand the Scriptures, and He said to them, 'Thus it is written, that the Christ would suffer and rise again from the dead the third day.'" Could this mean that He revealed a deeper layer of hidden astronomical meaning about a reborn sun when He opened their minds?

John 20:17 "I have not ascended to the Father... I ascend to

My Father." It is not yet time for all these things to start happening until the winter solstice sun reaches the galactic center. (This first occurred in 1998.)

John 21:11 "Peter went up and drew the net to land, full of large fish, a hundred and fifty-three." 153 refers to the ratio with 265, equal to the square root of three, the length of the cube's diagonal, hinting that we should view opposite corners of a cube head on, with one (sun) in front of another (galactic core.)

Romans 1:20-23 "They became futile in their speculations, and their foolish heart was darkened. Professing to be wise, they became fools, and exchanged the glory of the incorruptible God for an image in the form of corruptible man and of birds and four-footed animals and crawling creatures." The four fixed signs of the zodiac are Aquarius, (a man) Leo, (a lion, a four-footed creature) Taurus, (a bull, four-footed creature) and Scorpio (usually a scorpion, a crawling thing, but less often as an eagle, a bird.) This correlation to zodiac signs is even more apparent in Revelation 4:7 "The first creature was like a lion, and the second creature like a calf, and the third creature had a face like that of a man, and the fourth creature was like a flying eagle."

Romans 1:20-23 is basically saying that the rabbis (and of course the common people) had forgotten the importance of the galactic core; they had lost the old understanding of God as the incorruptible (but now invisible) galactic core causing destruction, and had substituted knowledge of the very visible zodiac signs, which the sun merely travels through. These signs are rightly used as markers in time to track the timing of galactic core explosions... but they are not the cause. After too many generations had passed, the Jewish priests "exchanged the truth of God for a lie, and worshiped and served the creature rather than the Creator." (Romans 1:25) When Jews and other ancient peoples sacrificed bulls or rams to God, it was an acknowledgement that a zodiac age like Taurus (the bull) or Aires (the ram), though it would last for thousands of years, was fleeting and insignificant compared to the power and permanence of God at the galactic center.

But eventually this understanding was lost, and the people began to worship the images of the animal representing the zodiac age they lived in; as with the golden calf. This lost appreciation for God as the occasionally active galactic center also refers to the stone which the builders rejected; from the center of the galaxy God is capable of sending out light and radiation and gravity waves (Holy Spirit?) and recreating a new Earth and a golden age. The philosopher's stone that allows alchemists to make gold at the right time under the right astronomical conditions is a thinly veiled reference to the incomprehensibly dense "stone" matter of the galactic core black hole and the alignment with the winter solstice sun. Failing to remember the original astronomical teachings, the Jewish leaders in Jerusalem were surprised by the arrival of the magi. "They are shepherds who have no understanding." (Isaiah 56:11) They were embarrassed and upset that foreign astronomers had come looking for the already born Jewish Messiah when they themselves had forgotten how to anticipate His birth. Regarding all these lost understandings, consider Hebrews 2:1 "For this reason we must pay much closer attention to what we have heard, so that we do not drift away from it."

Romans 8:22 "The whole creation groans and suffers the pains of childbirth."

Romans 13:11 "Knowing the time, that it is already the hour for you to awaken from sleep." Even in 33 A.D. they were already in the final "hour"—the last twelfth of the night, the last twelfth of the precession cycle, the last zodiac age before the grand alignment.

1 Corinthians 2:7 "but we speak God's wisdom in a mystery, the hidden wisdom which God predestined before the ages."

1 Corinthians 14:22 "Prophecy is for a sign, not to unbelievers but to those who believe." And for those who understand.

1 Corinthians 15:24-26 "then comes the end, when He hands over the kingdom to the God and Father, when He has abolished all rule and all authority and power. For He must reign until He has put all His enemies under His feet. The last enemy that will be abolished is death." Death is associated with Scorpio, the last zodiac constellation through which the sun will pass before it reaches the galactic center. Empowered by a galactic superwave, the sun will

be active during the pole shift tribulation through Judgment Day. But the sun will hand over the kingdom back to God the Father because the sun will go back to normal while the galactic center will be entering an active blue Seyfert phase.

1 Corinthians 15:55 "O DEATH, WHERE IS YOUR VICTORY? O DEATH, WHERE IS YOUR STING?" Scorpio has a stinger. We are familiar with Psalm 23:4 "Even though I walk through the valley of the shadow of death, I fear no evil, for You are with me…" Rabbi Joel Dobin, author of "Kabbalistic Astrology," says that "the shadow of death" is strangely mistranslated and should really be understood as Scorpio. This prompted me to go to the original Hebrew of Amos 5:8, for which Dobin says specifically that this refers to death and Scorpio, even though the English version in the NASB translates this as "the Pleiades and Orion." The Westminster Leningrad Codex version of the Bible in Hebrew reads:

"וַיְהִי שַׁחֲרַה הֵלַיָל סוֹיִּו תֹּלֶוָמֶל צַרֹרְקֵב-לֹ." in Amos 5:8 and translate.google.com clearly yields "the shadow of death" when this phrase is translated from Hebrew to English, not "the Pleiades and Orion." This major discrepancy in translation should make us take Dobin seriously when he claims "it would be better to suppose that the word means 'Scorpio' and that the valley takes its name from this meaning."[23] Assuming this is correct, then the Biblical references to "the valley of the shadow of death" really refers to the "valley" of Scorpio, between Scorpio and Sagittarius, where the sun aligns with the galactic center and "dies" for a few days, where the Son of Man is bruised in his heel (Scorpio's sting, a major event during the alignment in 2019) just as Ra and Horus, as sun-gods, survived being bitten at that location, where Phaethon lost control of the sun-chariot. We can understand now that 1 Corinthians is really mocking the ineffective sting of Scorpio, as the sun/Jesus has victory over Death in just three days. Isaiah 25:8 says "He will swallow up death" and this may mean that the reborn sun (Jesus) and/or the new second sun of the galactic center (God) hide Scorpio (Death) in their intense light.

Ephesians 3:18 "Comprehend with all the saints what is the breadth and length and height and depth." Many numbers and ratios revealed through gematria point to how we should look at a cube of space—like the New Jerusalem. The New Jerusalem is 1500 miles on a side, or *"7920* thousand feet" and the Earth's diameter is *7920* miles.[24] The New Jerusalem's unwieldy size (if it were really a city) would require changes in the laws of physics; otherwise the Earth simply could not gravitationally maintain its shape or rotation with anything so massive attached to its side. But if the "7920 thousand foot" measurement is viewed as a thinly veiled proportional reference to the Earth's 7920 mile diameter, then the New Jerusalem is really meant to be understood as a New Earth.

"According to His promise we are looking for new heavens and a new earth." (2 Peter 3:13) And if a new Earth formed through a pole shift has been happening every one-fifth of a precessional cycle, every 72 degrees we move through that great circle of 360 degrees, then is it any wonder that the boundaries of this new planet in space and time are compared to 72 degrees? "He measured its wall, seventy-two yards, according to human measurements, [yards] which are also angelic measurements [degrees]." (Revelations 21:17) *Comprehend that with the saints: the new earth has a heavenly measurement of one fifth of a precession cycle.*

1 Thessalonians 5:1-4 "Now as to the times and the epochs, brethren, you have no need of anything to be written to you. For you yourselves know full well that the day of the Lord will come just like a thief in the night. While they are saying, "Peace and safety!" then destruction will come upon them suddenly like labor pains upon a woman with child, and they will not escape. *But you, brethren, are not in darkness, that the day would overtake you like a thief.*" A huge distinction is made here between "they" and "them" (the unknowing) and "you, brethren" who know better. You are wise and initiated, you know the timing, you will not be surprised. And why should the wise be surprised? They know the general season of the wedding must be after the groom has gone to his father's house, which the winter solstice sun has done in the early 21st century. The wise also know it was customary for one of the groom's friends to go to the bride's house ahead of the groom, to shout and announce that the bridegroom comes, to make absolutely sure the bridal party

is ready. So the wise know that there will be signs to confirm these long-anticipated events!

Hebrews 1:1-3 "God, after He spoke long ago to the fathers in the prophets… in these last days has spoken to us in His Son, whom He appointed heir of all things, through whom also He made the world. And He is the radiance of His glory and the exact representation of His nature, and… when He had made purification of sins, He sat down at the right hand of the Majesty on high." The galactic core, an enormous round and dense astronomical radiation spewing object with other bodies trapped in its gravitational well, is in those aspects similar to our sun, which sustains all life on the Earth. The Earth would not have formed without the sun. This sun approaches the galactic core from stage right.

Hebrews 1:8 "YOUR THRONE, O GOD, IS FOREVER AND EVER, AND THE RIGHTEOUS SCEPTER IS THE SCEPTER OF HIS KINGDOM." The galactic core throne is always in the same spot in the sky, where the sun, through a heavenly scepter, is enthroned as king over a new earthly kingdom—because these galactic core explosion events cause the harmonic cycles which regulate orbits and rotation and precession.

Hebrews 1:10-12 "THE HEAVENS ARE THE WORKS OF YOUR HANDS; THEY WILL PERISH, BUT YOU REMAIN; AND THEY ALL WILL BECOME OLD LIKE A GARMENT, AND LIKE A MANTLE YOU WILL ROLL THEM UP; LIKE A GARMENT THEY WILL ALSO BE CHANGED." The skies will appear to fall like a scroll being rolled up, or clothing being removed.

Hebrews 2:9 "Jesus, who was made a little lower than the angels…" (KJB) In the old view of the cosmos, with Earth at the center, and seven or more heavens each one bigger, further, and higher up, of course the stars (angels) are farthest away (highest) while the sun (Jesus) is relatively close and low.

Hebrews 4:4-5 "concerning the seventh day: 'AND GOD RESTED ON THE SEVENTH DAY FROM ALL HIS WORKS' and again in this passage, 'THEY SHALL NOT ENTER MY REST.'" If a day is as a thousand years (as in 2 Peter 3:8 "with the Lord one day is like a thousand years, and a thousand years like one day") then mankind has about six thousand stable years per age, but we are not allowed very far into the seventh millennium. Interestingly, in the gravity well of a supermassive black hole like our galactic center, Einstein's theories tell us time dilation would be extreme; little time would seem to pass by there while ages would pass by here. In the simple terms of ancient times it would be accurate to say that a thousand years here on Earth would be like a day for God. If these lines were not describing the time frames of cosmic processes, but were merely describing the work of an all-powerful God—why would He ever need to rest?

Hebrews 4:14 "We have a great high priest who has passed through the heavens, Jesus the Son of God." The sun appears to pass through the zodiac.

Hebrews 5:6 God says to Jesus "YOU ARE A PRIEST FOREVER ACCORDING TO THE ORDER OF MELCHIZEDEK." And Hebrews 5:10 "…being designated by God as a high priest according to the order of Melchizedek."

Hebrews 6:1 "Therefore leaving the elementary teaching about the Christ, let us press on to maturity." Spirituality and religion are important, but there is a lot of hidden wisdom in the Bible for those who know what to look for. That maturity was hinted at in the prior sentence in Hebrews 5:14 "But solid food is for the mature, who because of practice have their senses trained" or as the NWT reads "perceptive powers." So if we are wise and mature enough to see it, there is clearly more than the basic religious message at hand, there is a deeper message for those capable of perceiving it.

Hebrews 8:1 "Now the main point in what has been said is this: we have such a high priest, who has taken His seat at the right hand of the throne of the Majesty in the heavens."

Hebrews 9:13 talks about animal sacrifice: "For if the blood of goats and bulls and the ashes of a heifer sprinkling those who have been defiled sanctify for the cleansing of the flesh, how much more will the blood of Christ"? This tells us that if astronomical sacrifices help purify us for heaven, the sacrifice of the sun is the supreme sacrifice.

245

Hebrews 10:4 "For it is impossible for the blood of bulls and goats to take away sins." These represent the passage (death) of the ages of Taurus and Aires, showing that though the sun has passed through these constellations; that they are not the greater powers.

Hebrews 9:23 comments further "Therefore it was necessary for the copies of the things in the heavens to be cleansed with these, but the heavenly things themselves with better sacrifices than these." This portrays zodiac constellations as in need of cleaning through superior sacrifice. Perhaps this is because of their role in cyclic destruction? As Jesus is clearly the sacrifice, and has been likened repeatedly to the sun, perhaps the sun itself appears to be sacrificed and reborn on the galactic cross?

Hebrews 10:13 "UNTIL HIS ENEMIES BE MADE A FOOTSTOOL FOR HIS FEET." When the winter solstice sun reaches the galactic center, Death/Scorpio will be below the sun, at His feet. And if the poles reverse, Draco would appear "on the bottom" at the South Pole.

Hebrews 12:26-27 "'YET ONCE MORE I WILL SHAKE NOT ONLY THE EARTH, BUT ALSO THE HEAVEN.' This expression, 'Yet once more,' denotes the removing of those things." This is interesting, to draw our attention to something then deny the obvious meaning of it. Wouldn't "Yet once more" imply that the world has been shaken like this on previous occasions?

2 Peter 2:5 God "did not spare the ancient world... He brought a flood."

2 Peter 3:5-8 "It escapes their notice that by the word of God the heavens existed long ago and the earth was formed out of water and by water, through which the world at that time was destroyed, being flooded with water. But by His word the present heavens and earth are being reserved for fire, kept for the day of judgment and destruction of ungodly men. But do not let this one fact escape your notice, beloved, that with the Lord one day is like a thousand years, and a thousand years like one day." Here we are clearly told that God has destroyed the earth and will do so again. This is in line with a theory of recurring cycles of destruction roughly every six thousand years. Is this an indication that the seventh millennium,

starting approximately now, is that special day?

Jude 1:6 "And angels who did not keep their own domain, but abandoned their proper abode, He has kept in eternal bonds under darkness for the judgment of the great day." Are these angels stars that fell below the horizon during the last pole shift?

Revelations 1:4 "the seven Spirits who are before His throne" (Planets)

Revelations 1:12-13 "I saw seven golden lampstands; and in the middle of the lampstands I saw one like a son of man." Seven lampstands could be seven shining planets, with the sun in the middle of them.

Revelations 1:15-16 "His feet were like burnished bronze, when it has been made to glow in a furnace, and His voice was like the sound of many waters. In His right hand He held seven stars, and out of His mouth came a sharp two-edged sword; and His face was like the sun."

Revelations 1:20 "As for the mystery of the seven stars which you saw in My right hand, and the seven golden lampstands…" Officially these are angels and churches, but as we look for secondary astronomical meanings, the seven planets are lampstands.

Revelations 2:5 "Therefore remember from where you have fallen… or else *I am coming to you and will remove your lampstand out of its place*." If planets are lampstands, God will move our lampstand, the Earth.

Revelations 3:3 "*If you do not wake up, I will come like a thief*, and you will not know at what hour I will come to you." Which implies that those awake will know the hour.

Revelations 3:8 "I have put before you an open door which no one can shut." This is reminiscent of the Mayan view of the dark cleft at the center of the Milky Way. Viewed "as a portal or doorway, this astronomical feature was symbolized by a door."[25] The sudden appearance of God in the Milky Way's dark cleft is also hinted at in the Song of Solomon 2:14 "in the clefts of the rock, in the secret place of the steep pathway, let me see your form."

Revelations 3:14 "The Amen, the faithful and true Witness, the Beginning of the creation of God." Amen is a name for the Egyptian sun god, suns are the first things a galactic center creates.

Revelations 3:21 "Sit down with Me on My throne, as I also overcame and sat down with My Father on His throne." This is very reminiscent of Egypt's god Osiris, and his son Horus, who becomes Osiris. This also invites us to be present at the conjunction of the winter solstice sun and the galactic center, as we are invited guests at the wedding.

Revelations 4:2-3 "Behold, a throne was standing in heaven, and One sitting on the throne. And He who was sitting was like a jasper stone and a sardius in appearance; and there was a rainbow around the throne, like an emerald in appearance." The NIV says "jasper and ruby" so we can assume the sun looks red and is surrounded by green light, perhaps a result of dust.

Revelations 4:6-7 "Before the throne there was something like a sea of glass, like crystal; and in the center and around the throne, four living creatures full of eyes in front and behind. The first creature was like a lion, and the second creature like a calf, and the third creature had a face like that of a man, and the fourth creature was like a flying eagle." This is the Milky Way, with the four cardinal zodiac signs, Leo, Taurus, Aquarius, Scorpio.

Revelations 5:6 "I saw between the throne (with the four living creatures) and the elders a Lamb standing, as if slain, having seven horns and seven eyes, which are the seven Spirits of God." Near the galactic center, in the zodiac, there will be a dead-looking sun and seven planets.

Revelations 6:1-2 "Then I saw when the Lamb broke one of the seven seals, and I heard one of the four living creatures saying as with a voice of thunder, 'Come.' I looked, and behold, a white horse, and he who sat on it had a bow; and a crown was given to him." Sagittarius is a combination of horse and archer, crowned with the sun at the time of the end.

Revelations 6:3-4 "When He broke the second seal, I heard the second living creature saying, 'Come.' And another, a red horse, went out; and to him who sat on it, it was granted to take peace from the earth, and that men would slay one another; and a great sword was given to him." The rider on the red horse brings war, probably

WWIII and Armageddon.

Revelations 6:5-6 is a warning about terrible inflation and the importance of conserving of basic supplies. A denarius was typical pay for a day of work for an unskilled laborer. Imagine how hungry most people would be if a quart of wheat were a day's income, or perhaps in other words, if a loaf of bread were a hundred dollars? Are you ready for that level of inflation and scarcity? "When He broke the third seal, I heard the third living creature saying, 'Come.' I looked, and behold, a black horse; and he who sat on it had a pair of scales in his hand. And I heard something like a voice in the center of the four living creatures saying, 'A quart of wheat for a denarius, and three quarts of barley for a denarius; and do not damage the oil and the wine.'"

Revelations 6:7-8 "When the Lamb broke the fourth seal, I heard the voice of the fourth living creature saying, 'Come.' I looked, and behold, an ashen horse; and he who sat on it had the name Death; and Hades was following with him. Authority was given to them over a fourth of the earth, to kill with sword and with famine and with pestilence and by the wild beasts of the earth." A quarter of the remaining population is killed by starvation and disease.

Revelations 6:9 "When the Lamb broke the fifth seal, I saw underneath the altar the souls of those who had been slain." If the altar is the sun, something very strange must happen if we can see under it, as the sun is normally too bright to allow us to see anything else near it. Perhaps the sun goes out for three days.

Revelations 6:12-13 "I looked when He broke the sixth seal, and there was a great earthquake; and the sun became black as sackcloth made of hair, and the whole moon became like blood; and the stars of the sky fell to the earth, as a fig tree casts its unripe figs when shaken by a great wind."

Revelations 6:15-17 "Every slave and free man hid themselves in the caves and among the rocks of the mountains; and they said to the mountains and to the rocks, 'Fall on us and hide us from the presence of Him who sits on the throne, and from the wrath of the Lamb; for the great day of their wrath has come, and who is able to stand?'"

Revelations 7:10 "Salvation to our God who sits on the throne, and to the Lamb." The Lamb still does not yet share the throne. The sun may have just reached the point where we would have thought it is almost as close to a conjunction with the galactic center as it ever gets, yet enthronement has not happened yet.

Revelations 7:15 "He who sits on the throne will spread His tabernacle over them." A dust cloud spreads through the galaxy from this point.

Revelations 8:3 "the golden altar which was before the throne." The golden sun is the altar.

Revelations 8:5 mentions "the fire of the altar." The altar is in heaven, by the throne, is golden, and has fire. It's the sun.

Revelations 8:5 (in full) "Then *the angel took the censer and filled it with the fire of the altar, and threw it to the earth*; and there followed peals of thunder and sounds and flashes of lightning and an earthquake." This sounds like a coronal mass ejection (a really bad solar flare) hitting the earth.

Revelations 8:8 "The second angel sounded, and something like a great mountain burning with fire was thrown into the sea."

Revelations 8:10-11 "The third angel sounded, and a great star fell from heaven, burning like a torch, and it fell on a third of the

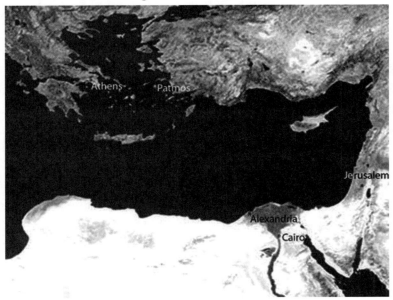

rivers and on the springs of waters. The name of the star is called Wormwood; and a third of the waters became wormwood, and many men died from the waters, because they were made bitter." Radiation comes with the coronal mass ejection.

Revelations 9:1-2 "Then the fifth angel sounded, and I saw a star from heaven which had fallen to the earth; and the key of the bottomless pit was given to him. *He opened the bottomless pit, and smoke went up out of the pit*, like the smoke of a great furnace; and the sun and the air were darkened by the smoke of the pit." A black hole is effectively a bottomless pit. From this black hole at our galactic center a vast cosmic dust cloud may enter the solar system. There is evidence that when such dust clouds come towards us, micrometeorites, no larger than grains of sand, swarm down to ground level at extremely high speed. There are many rocks and bones, from specific periods which bear the marks of these tiny projectiles on one side (which was facing up) but not on the other side. Imagine the constant stings of these incoming particles.

Revelations 9:3-11 "Then out of the smoke came locusts upon the earth, and power was given them, as the scorpions of the earth have power. They were told not to hurt the grass of the earth, nor any green thing, nor any tree, but only the men who do not have the seal of God on their foreheads. And they were not permitted to kill anyone, but to torment for five months; and their torment was like the torment of a scorpion when it stings a man. And in those days men will seek death and will not find it; they will long to die, and death flees from them. The appearance of the locusts was like horses prepared for battle; and on their heads appeared to be crowns like gold, and their faces were like the faces of men. They had hair like the hair of women, and their teeth were like the teeth of lions. They had breastplates like breastplates of iron; and the sound of their wings was like the sound of chariots, of many horses rushing to battle. They have tails like scorpions, and stings; and in their tails is their power to hurt men for five months. They have as king over them, the angel of the abyss; his name in Hebrew is Abaddon, and in the Greek he has the name Apollyon."

Revelations 10:6-7 "There will be delay no longer, but in the days of the voice of the seventh angel, when he is about to sound, then the mystery of God is finished." In Greek, the word translated here as delay is kronos, which literally means time, not delay. Could this mean the end of time, or the end of a calendar or of an age?

Revelations 16:8 *"The fourth angel poured out his bowl upon the sun,* and it was given to it to scorch men with fire." This could be the cosmic dust cloud pushed into our solar system, initiating a flaring T-Tauri phase. Even Tim LaHaye tells us "the plague poured out of the fourth bowl seems to cause what would be called today a solar flare."[26]

Revelations 16:15 "Behold, I am coming like a thief. Blessed is the one who stays awake and keeps his clothes." Many other translations say "remains clothed" or "keeps his outer garments." If God comes as a thief in the night, and the one that stays awake is happy about it, then the one who stays awake must not be robbed. Our outer garment could be the body around our soul, in which case keeping awake—knowing when He is coming—will allow us to live, and not be robbed of our lives.

Revelations 16:18-20 "And there were flashes of lightning and sounds and peals of thunder; and there was a great earthquake, such as there had not been since man came to be upon the earth, so great an earthquake was it, and so mighty… And the cities of the nations fell… And every island fled away, and the mountains were not found."

Revelations 18:21 "Then *a strong angel took up a stone like a great millstone and threw it into the sea."* A millstone spins around an axis, and throwing it traditionally represents a pole shift.

Revelations 21:1 "Then I saw a new heaven and a new earth; for the first heaven and the first earth passed away." A pole shift would explain new surface conditions for the earth, and a new field of view with many different stars and constellations in the night skies after the repositioning.

Revelations 21:2 "And I saw the holy city, new Jerusalem, coming down out of heaven from God, made ready as a bride adorned for her husband." The cubical city (Revelations 21:16 "its length and width and height are equal") represents the cube of space and Earth's new orientation in three-dimensional material reality, in addition to its 7920 thousand foot width representing Earth's 7920 mile diameter. *The New Jerusalem is the Earth and the Earth is the bride*, ready for the Sun/groom when the galactic core father says so.

Revelations 22:1-5 "Then he showed me a river of the water of life, clear as crystal, coming from the throne of God and of the Lamb…" (The Lamb finally shares the throne with God! Perhaps the sun, energized by dust to a T-Tauri phase, has an expanded corona. Perhaps the galactic core is now a large bright spot illuminating cosmic dust clouds like the ancient eye in the sky. Either way, the sun now overlaps the galactic center throne, as they finally share a throne.) "…in the middle of its street. On either side of the river was the tree of life, bearing twelve kinds of fruit, yielding its fruit every month; and the leaves of the tree were for the healing of the nations. There will no longer be any curse; and the throne of God and of the Lamb will be in it, and His bond-servants will serve Him; they will see His face, and His name will be on their foreheads. And there will no longer be any night; and they will not have need of the

Mosaic of St. John writing the Book of Revelations, above a church door on the Greek island of Patmos off the southwest coast of Turkey.

light of a lamp nor the light of the sun, because the Lord God will illumine them."

The Milky Way flows outward from the galactic center, which is now a throne for both, as the winter solstice sun has finally joined the galactic center throne in an alignment. The Milky Way is the river, and there are several planets visible nearby on both sides of the river which, in a certain configuration we will discuss later— represent the tree of life. As in the last Garden of Eden, the world has been newly recreated, there is a tree in the middle of the garden, and there is no sin. As the galactic center now appears as a giant oval of light for the next few centuries, it will light our planet like a second sun.

Revelations 22:13 "I am the Alpha and the Omega, the first and the last, the beginning and the end." The active phase of the galactic core, symbolizing God because of its great light and devastating power, dominates the beginning and end of every cycle of ages.

There are even more relevant passages but the ones quoted above

Another church on Patmos was built to protect the entrance to the cave where St. John experienced the visions he wrote about in the Book of Revelations.

should be sufficient to demonstrate that God's plans for the end times seem to take the form of a galactic core explosion and pole shift when the winter solstice sun has reached the galactic center. As Gerald Massey wrote over a century ago: "The fulfillment of scripture was the completion of astronomical cycles."[27] It is not pleasant to think that we are so close to a devastating pole shift that will kill most of humanity. That this bitter message of cosmological destruction is hidden in plain sight amongst the Bible's more numerous references to love and grace and salvation, makes me wonder how John felt on the island of Patmos as he came to understand the Apocalypse. He knew full well how this age will end, contrasted with how wonderful Christianitys basic message sounds as we preach only the sweet hope of salvation. As an angel said to John of this mixed message: "Take it and eat it; it will make your stomach bitter, but in your mouth it will be sweet as honey." (Revelations 10:9)

(Endnotes)

1 Petrisko, Thomas W. *Fatima's Third Secret Explained.* McKees Rocks, PA: St. Andrew's Productions, 2001, p.44

2 Interview of Pope John Paul II for the 10/13/1981 issue of *Stimme des Glaubens,* as quoted in Petrisko, Thomas W. *Fatima's Third Secret Explained.* McKees Rocks, PA: St. Andrew's Productions, 2001, p.45

3 Petrisko, Ibid., p. 46

4 written by Maimonaides in *The Guide for the Perplexed* in 1190, as quoted by Schroeder, Gerald L. *Genesis and the Big Bang: The Discovery of Harmony Between Modern Science and the Bible.* New York: Bantam, 1990, p. 16

5 S, Acharya. *Suns of God: Krishna, Buddha and Christ Unveiled.* Kempton, IL: Adventures Unlimited Press, 2004, p. 71, originally from Marsilio Ficino's 1494 work *The Book of the Sun.*

6 Archer, Gleason. *A Survey of Old Testament Introduction.* Chicago, IL: Moody Publishers, 1974, p. 184 footnote

7 Morris, Henry. *The Biblical Basis for Modern Science.* Grand Rapids, MI: Baker Books, 1984, p. 115

8 Schroeder, Gerald L. *Genesis and the Big Bang: The Discovery of Harmony Between Modern Science and the Bible.* New York: Bantam, 1990, p. 27

9 Johnson, Robert Bowie, Jr. *The Parthenon Code: Mankind's History in Marble.* Annapolis, MD: Solving Light Books, 2004, p. 205

10 Custance, Arthur. *Without Form and Void: A Study of the Meaning of Genesis 1:2.* Ancaster, Ontario: Classic Reprint Press, 1970, p.7

11 Buckland, William. "Geology and Mineralogy Considered with Reference to Natural Theology," in *Bridgewater Treatises,* vol. 1, Pickering, London: 1836

12 S, Acharya. *Suns of God: Krishna, Buddha and Christ Unveiled.* Kempton, IL: Adventures Unlimited Press, 2004, p. 505

13 http://www.moses-egypt.net/book1/moses1-cap2_en.asp is unclear. This may have been written by Ove von Spaeth in *The*

Supressed Record: New Data Reveal Moses' Unknown Egyptian Background. Copenhagen: C.A. Reitzel, 2004

14 de Santillana, Giorgio and Hertha von Dechend. *Hamlet's Mill: An Essay Investigating the Origins of Human Knowledge and its Transmission Through Myth*. Boston, MA: David R. Godine, 1969, p. 165

15 de Santillana, Giorgio and Hertha von Dechend. Ibid., p. 48

16 S, Acharya. *Suns of God: Krishna, Buddha and Christ Unveiled*. Kempton, IL: Adventures Unlimited Press, 2004, p. 105 and 109

17 de Santillana, Giorgio and Hertha von Dechend. *Hamlet's Mill: An Essay Investigating the Origins of Human Knowledge and its Transmission Through Myth*. Boston, MA: David R. Godine, 1969, pp. 169-175

18 Hancock, Graham and Robert Bauval. *Message of the Sphinx: A Quest for the Hidden Legacy of Mankind*. New York: Random House, 1996, p. 138

19 *Talmud Rosh HaShana*, 11b and *Talmud Baba M'tzia*, 106b, and *Ta'anith* I bottom of 64a; and *B'midbar Rabbah* 10

20 www.marquette.edu/maqom/metatronname.html

21 LaHaye, Tim and Ed Hindson. *Exploring Bible Prophecy from Genesis to Revelation*. Eugene, OR: Harvest House, 2006, p. 526

22 Michell, John. *The Dimensions of Paradise*. Rochester, VT: Inner Traditions, 2008, p. 124

23 Dobin, Joel. *Kabbalistic Astrology: The Sacred Tradition of the Hebrew Sages*. Rochester, VT: Inner Traditions International, 1999, p. 136

24 Michell, John. *The New View Over Atlantis*. San Francisco, CA: Harper & Row, 1986, p. 178

25 http://www.mayaexploration.org/pdf/MEC_Facebook_Discussion_2010_Jenkins.pdf, p. 4, John Major Jenkins, 4/15/2010

26 LaHaye, Tim and Ed Hindson. *Exploring Bible Prophecy from Genesis to Revelation*. Eugene, OR: Harvest House, 2006, p. 540

27 Massey, Gerald. *The Historical Jesus and the Mythical Christ*. New York: Cosimo, 2006, p.108-109

CHAPTER SEVEN
PRACTICE EXERCISE—
WHEN WAS JESUS BORN?

After learning how to look for hidden meanings in the Bible, we can now see hundreds of references to pole shifts and astronomical alignments. We should also be able to do something useful with the wisdom and insight we have acquired. Assuming that the insights described so far really do allow Judgment Day and the day of Jesus Christ's Second Coming to be calculated then with similar amounts of reasoning we should be able to use the astronomical approach to deduce the day Jesus was born the first time around.

It may be hard for some readers to take this chapter seriously if they are fascinated with the end of the world without necessarily taking organized religion seriously. Such readers may accept that astronomy can be used to time the pole shifts which occasionally devastate the world, while not believing that God ever sent down His Son, or even that He exists at all. For such readers, even if they accept that the Bible was written to encode an astronomical warning, it may seem comical to analyze "facts" and deduce the birth date of a fictional character.

I suggest such readers focus on the astronomy and the encoded information of the Bible. For the purpose of understanding why 2019 is the crucial year for our survival, it is not necessary to have faith in Jesus or God. Long ago, Docetists developed the idea that Jesus Christ was never born at all; that He never existed as a flesh and blood person. Docetism suggests that when John 1:14 tells us "And the Word became flesh" that what is really meant is people made up details to personify the concept of a messiah. Docetists assume the gospels took solar details and mythologized them into a story, allegedly of a real historical human being—who never really existed.

Students of sun-god mythology may note that religions were

often re-created at the start of every zodiac age; that Egypt was focused on duality in the age of Gemini, sacrificing bulls in Taurus, and sacrificing rams and lambs in Aires. Some suggest that as we progressed into the age of Pisces around 2,100 years ago, the elite of Alexandria or an international brotherhood of initiates or a united front of Judean and Samaritan priests simply decided it was time to create an updated version of the sun-god in the Fisher-King form of Jesus Christ.[1] Docetists would suggest we reconsider Paul's words in 1 Corinthians 4:1 "Let a man regard us in this manner, as servants of Christ and stewards of the mysteries of God." They would allege, like Voltaire: "If God did not exist, it would be necessary to invent him."

Either way, the link between Jesus and the sun is indisputable, and we will rely on these comparisons to time his date of birth. In doing so we must also reject the common idea of His birth at Christmas. The timing of Christmas was chosen centuries after Jesus, to compete with other holidays celebrating the resurgence of the winter solstice sun through other gods. The shortest days of the year are those from about December 21 to December 24, so many ancient religions celebrated festivals on December 25, the first day of obviously lengthening daylight. Long before Jesus, there were holidays for Horus and Apollo on December 25. A newer Roman development was Saturnalia, a weeklong festival ending December 24. In 274 A.D. the Emperor Aurelian declared a civil holiday on December 25 (the Festival of the birth of the Unconquered Sun, or Sol Invictus) to celebrate the birth of Mithras, the Persian Sun-God whose cult was becoming popular among the Roman military. Mithras was called the "Son of God" and "The Good Shepherd." He had a last supper with bread and wine for twelve followers, and was killed by crucifixion and reborn just after the spring equinox.[2]

Horus also had dozens of similarities to Jesus, so there was little reason to avoid creating one more through the timing of Christmas. In some versions of his story, Horus was born to a woman who was a virgin, after an angel announced the birth. He was the only son of the highest god. His birth was heralded by a star rising in the east. His birth was witnessed by shepherds, later Herut tried to kill him.

He was baptized by Anup in a river, then Anup was later beheaded. As an adult, he was taken into the desert by his rival, his uncle Set, where Horus avoided temptation. He raised Osiris from the dead, and was later resurrected himself at Bethanu. Of course Jesus was born to a virgin, and the birth was announced by an angel. He is the son of God. A star heralded his birth, seen from the east. His birth was witnessed by shepherds, later Herod tried to kill him. He was baptized by John in a river, then John was later beheaded. As an adult, he was in the desert with Satan, where Jesus avoided temptation. He raised Lazarus from the dead, and was later resurrected himself at Bethany. There are many more comparisons but it is not worth making them all here. "Adonis, Dionysos, Herakles, Mithra, Osiris, and other deities, were all savior-gods whose deaths were regarded as sacrifices made on behalf of mankind."[3]

Christianity had to compete with these pre-existing and popular pagan religions with holidays for the dying and reborn sun-god at this time of year, and the best way to displace the worship of Mithras, Sol Invictus, Horus, Apollo, and countless other solar deities was to claim the holiday as Jesus' own birthday. We know this was a late development because all other important Christian holidays, such as Easter, were determined far earlier when the Greek culture in the Middle East used a lunar calendar—this is why Easter and all the other initial holidays vary on our modern solar calendar. Easter can be anywhere from March 22 to April 25. But Christmas is always December 25—because it was a solar holiday celebrating the sun, and it was created centuries after the other lunar Christian holidays when the basis of our solar calendar was already established. In addition, Luke 2:8 tells us that at the time of Jesus' birth, "In the same region there were some shepherds staying out in the fields and keeping watch over their flock by night." By December 25, the mountainous region of Jerusalem and Bethlehem has usually seen two nights with snow, having a low temperature of about 43-46 degrees Fahrenheit, with many nights far colder. The average nightly low temperature around three months before Christmas is 61-63 degrees—much more pleasant for sleeping outside with the flocks.

As Adam Clarke wrote in his Bible commentaries: "It was an ancient custom among the Jews of those days to send their sheep to the fields and deserts about Passover (early spring) and bring them home at commencement of the first rain... as these shepherds had not yet brought home their flocks, it is a presumptive argument that October had not yet commenced, and consequently, our Lord was not born on the 25th of December."[4]

Other commentaries support the same facts: "As is well known, the shepherds in Palestine do not abide in the fields during the winter season because of the extreme, cold temperatures. The shepherds always bring their flocks in from the mountain slopes and fields no later than October 15th!"[5] There would have been a lack of vegetation for pasturage; with few grasses or other plants to eat shepherds would have had no reason to expose their flocks to the cold.

We also know from Luke 2:1-7 that Joseph's family came to Bethlehem for a census: "Now in those days a decree went out from Caesar Augustus, that a census be taken... the first census taken while Quirinius was governor of Syria. And everyone was on his way to register for the census, each to his own city. Joseph also went up from Galilee, from the city of Nazareth, to Judea, to the city of David which is called Bethlehem, because he was of the house and family of David, in order to register along with Mary, who was engaged to him, and was with child. While they were there, the days were completed for her to give birth. And she gave birth to her firstborn son; and she wrapped Him in cloths, and laid Him in a manger, because there was no room for them in the inn."

God would not have let Jesus stay in an cold manger in wintertime. The Romans knew that for an accurate census it had to be held when weather was agreeable to travel. And if it had been a cold December night, what kind of husband and father would take his pregnant wife out as she approached her due date, to climb mountains for a census? Census-taking was at the end of the harvests in early autumn, around the Jewish new year in late September. (Much like any census in the United States today would be concerned with where we live on January first.) There was no room at the inn because many people born in Bethlehem had to revisit their home town for the census at the start of the year.

So we know Jesus was not born on December 25; it seems he was born a few months earlier. What more do we know about the timing of his birthday?

Luke 1:5 tells us that "In the days of Herod, king of Judea, there was a priest named Zacharias, of the division of Abijah; and he had a wife from the daughters of Aaron, and her name was Elizabeth." These are the parents of John the Baptist. Luke 1:13 says "the angel said to him: 'Do not be afraid, Zacharias, for your petition has been heard, and your wife Elizabeth will bear you a son, and you will give him the name John.'"

Temple priests at that time were divided into 24 groups, and as mentioned above, Zechariah was in the division of Abijah. There are 51 weeks per year in the lunar calendar used in ancient Israel, and there were three weeks of holidays during which all the priests were required to officiate at the Temple in Jerusalem. Deuteronomy 16:16 clarifies this: "Three times in a year all your males shall appear before the LORD your God in the place which He chooses, at..." (Passover, Shavuot, and Sukkot) That leaves 48 other less important weeks for the 24 divisions of priests to handle, and each group took over for one week at a time, twice a year, before the cycle repeated itself.

1 Chronicles 24:7-19 gives us the sequence in which the priestly divisions officiated, and 24:10 clarifies "the eighth for Abijah" meaning the eighth week of the 24 regular weeks is their responsibility. But because Passover and Shavuot occur early in the year (before the eighth regular priestly week in the series) it is the tenth week of the year when Zechariah performs this eighth non-holiday week of duties at the Temple. This starts with the second Sabbath of the third month of Sivan, usually corresponding to early June in our calendar.

Luke 1:23-24 tells us "When the days of his priestly service were ended, he went back home. After these days Elizabeth his wife became pregnant." This means John the Baptist was conceived no earlier than the fourth Sabbath in Sivan; in our calendar, probably around June 8-29, 7 B.C. We should not ignore the sun's northern location at the summer solstice in June, especially since the Feast Day, the Nativity of St. John the Baptist, is June 24. Let's assume John was conceived on that day. Then Elizabeth "kept herself in seclusion for five months, saying, 'This is the way the Lord has dealt with me in the days when He looked with favor upon me, to take away my disgrace among men.' Now in the sixth month the angel Gabriel was sent from God to a city in Galilee called Nazareth, to a virgin engaged to a man whose name was Joseph, of the descendants of David; and the virgin's name was Mary." (Luke 1:24-27) Gabriel tells Mary in Luke 1:31 "You will conceive in your womb and bear a son, and you shall name Him Jesus."

Mary is disturbed by the idea of baring a child for God and questions Gabriel, saying "How can this be, since I am a virgin?" (Luke 1:34) Luke 1:35-36 explains "The angel answered and said to her, 'The Holy Spirit will come upon you, and the power of the Most High will overshadow you; and for that reason the holy Child shall be called the Son of God. And behold, even your relative Elizabeth has also conceived a son in her old age; and she who was called barren is now in her sixth month.'"

This is very important, for it establishes the six month difference between the births of John the Baptist, and Jesus. Elizabeth is in her sixth month, meaning more than five months but less than six months pregnant, when Mary is told "You will conceive." We must assume Gabriel announced this shortly before the conception and that Mary's next ovulation came soon after and was immediately fruitful. So it would have been in the ninth month of Kislev when Gabriel tells Mary she will conceive and by the end of the month she had probably conceived. It is no coincidence that the 25th day of the ninth month is the first night of Hanukkah, the Festival of Lights, when Jews celebrate a miracle. Adding to the original miracle when only one day's worth of oil in the Temple failed to burn out in a day, but remained lighted for eight days, now "the Light of the World" (John 8:12) has been conceived on that December day.

Another relevant reference is found in Matthew 17:10, when the disciples had questions concerning how Jesus could be the messiah if Elijah had not returned first. Jesus' "disciples asked Him, 'Why then do the scribes say that Elijah must come first?'" Of course they knew very well that the last paragraph of the Old Testament says: "Behold, I am going to send you Elijah the prophet before the coming of the great and terrible day of the LORD." (Malachi 4:5) Christ's disciples were confused because the Messiah was with them, yet apparently Elijah had not been sent first as they expected. Jesus replied: "Elijah is coming and will restore all things; but I say to you that Elijah already came, and they did not recognize him… Then the disciples understood that He had spoken to them about John the Baptist." (Matthew 17:11-13)

Religious Jews still set out an extra place for Elijah with a glass of wine at the dinner table at Passover, as they expect Elijah to eventually return at Passover (which starts at sunset near the spring equinox.) John the Baptist, whom Jesus told us is Elijah, would most likely have been born in the middle of the month of Nisan, right at the time of Passover. Since Jesus was conceived about six months after John, he was probably born six months after him, in the middle of the month of Tishri—right at Sukkot, the Feast of Tabernacles, which occurs around late September in our calendar. This is not a surprising time for the Messiah to be born, as we would expect him to arrive on a major holiday, when all the priests and men of Israel would come to worship at the Temple. This particular Jewish holiday is about gathering the harvest and building booths (tabernacles) in the fields of crops as shelter during the harvest. Of course Jesus came to dwell or tabernacle with us, and shelter us during the great harvest, for he is eventually coming back for the harvest of souls. And the ideas that God's son is the Sun and that He had "placed his tabernacle in the Sun"[6] are very ancient, as discussed by Plato centuries before Christ.

Assuming that the scriptures are correct and the deductions based on them are sensible, we have arrived at a very likely birthday for Jesus, the fifteenth day of the Hebrew month of Tishri. What about the year?

We know Herod was king of the Jews when Jesus was born, and that almost two years passed after his birth before the wise men from the east told Herod that they had seen his star and that he had been born some time earlier. Matthew 2:1-4 "Now after Jesus was born in Bethlehem of Judea in the days of Herod the king, magi from the east arrived in Jerusalem, saying, 'Where is He who has been born King of the Jews? For we saw His star in the east and have come to worship Him.' When Herod the king heard this, he was troubled, and all Jerusalem with him. Gathering together all the chief priests and scribes of the people, he inquired of them where the Messiah was to be born."

It seems the astrologers from the east had maintained some traditions of wisdom and knowledge which had been not been maintained by the Jews in Israel. The magi knew exactly what to look for in the heavens, so they recognized the signs and came to Jerusalem assuming everyone there had monitored the same things and already knew all about the messiah amongst them. Instead they surprised and embarrassed King Herod and the local priests. "His watchmen are blind, All of them know nothing... They are shepherds who have no understanding." (Isaiah 56:10-11) Of course Jesus does later point out to Jerusalem's rabbis and priests in Hebrews 5:12 that of "this time you ought to be teachers, you have need again for someone to teach you the elementary principles of the oracles of God." Regarding Jesus' birth it was the magi who had to re-educate the Jewish priesthood about the timing of important events.

King Herod wanted help from the astronomers from the east so he could find and kill this rival king, (the infant Jesus) but the magi left without giving him more information. Matthew 2:16 tells us "Then when Herod saw that he had been tricked by the magi, he became very enraged, and sent and slew all the male children who were in Bethlehem and all its vicinity, from two years old and under, according to the time which he had determined from the magi."

Since Herod died a well-documented death on November 27 in 4 B.C., and he would not have cared about threats to the throne from a baby while he near death, any orders to kill the male babies near Bethlehem must have occurred well before his death. This would indicate that Jesus was probably born no later than around January or February at the beginning of 5 B.C. Since we know with reasonable certainty that Jesus was born around late September, the autumn of 6 B.C. or 7 B.C. seem more likely. We also know that Augustus Caesar had ordered a census to be taken, for Joseph was on his way to Bethlehem for the census when Jesus was born. Augustus had a long reign and ordered three censuses to be taken, in 28 B.C., 8 B.C., and 14 A.D. The only census anywhere near the right time frame is the one decreed in 8 B.C., which in an era of slow communications, could easily take one or two years to finish. We also know from Luke 2:2 that Quirinius was governor of Syria but he ruled from 12-2 B.C. and this does not help narrow our already brief window in time any further. For the moment it seems likely that Jesus was born on Tishri 15 in either 7 B.C. or 6 B.C.

Luke 3:23 tells us "When He began His ministry, Jesus Himself was about thirty years of age." In John 2:19 Jesus tells Jews who are arguing with him "Destroy this temple, and in three days I will raise it up." Now Jesus was of course talking about his own body ascending to heaven after three days of death, but the Jews thought he meant the stone building they worshipped at, and replied that "It took forty-six years to build this temple, and will You raise it up in three days?" (John 2:20) Some say the Temple was still unfinished, and that this was the 46th year of construction so far. Others argue it had been finished in 46 years. Either way, since construction of Herod's Temple is documented to have begun late in 19 B.C., their conversation could not have been underway any earlier than around late 28 A.D.

Even if this was about three years into Jesus' ministry, then his ministry could not have begun much before 25 A.D.—but it could have begun several years later, if the Jews merely meant that the Temple had been completed in 46 years. Luke tells us Jesus was approximately 30 years old when he started his ministry, but the Son of God may have had "good genes" and looked exceptionally young and healthy. Let us assume He was probably no older than about 35 when he started, and that this occurred no earlier than about 22 A.D. Based on this—Jesus was probably born sometime around 13 B.C. to 2 B.C.—but almost definitely no earlier than that. Unfortunately this does not specifically confirm that Jesus was born around 6 or

7 B.C. But assuming the two points above—that no one would have said anything about 46 years of Temple construction prior to 28 A.D., and that if Jesus was older than 35 when he started his ministry, Luke would not have said he was "about 30"—then it does seem like our target years are in the appropriate range.

Jesus' ministry spanned at least three separately mentioned Passovers, so it lasted at least a little over two years, and many scholars assume it lasted about three years, making him at least (approximately) 33 years old when he died. Of course his ministry may have lasted longer than three years, and he could have been significantly older than 33 when he died. We know Pontius Pilate was in charge when Jesus was crucified and he was only in Jerusalem from 26-36 A.D. We know from John 19:42 that Jesus was buried on the eve of the Sabbath (Friday afternoon) and the eve of Passover (the fourteenth day of the month of Nisan.) Any good Hebrew calendar converter on the internet shows that during the 11 years Pilate was in Jerusalem, three years had a Friday Nisan 14. They are the Hebrew years 3786, 3793, and 3796—or 26, 33, and 36 A.D.

Not far from where I waded into the Jordan River is the site believed to be the exact location of that most famous of baptisms. The photo is taken in Israel, but you could easily throw a rock and hit Jordan on the opposite bank.

We can rule out the earliest date in 26 A.D. because we know John the Baptist was beheaded, and we know why, and we know it happened while Jesus was still alive. John had denounced the marriage of King Herod Antipas to his niece Herodias in 28 A.D., after which he was later imprisoned and eventually executed. Matthew 14:12 does not clarify what year this happened, but it does tell us "His disciples came and took away the body and buried it; and they went and reported to Jesus." This was probably years after Herod's incestuous marriage in 28 A.D., but certainly not two years earlier. Most historians think John was killed somewhere from 32 to 36 A.D.

(Some would argue that John's beheading is symbolic and astronomical; that we celebrate "The Beheading of the Forerunner" on August 29 because around 30 A.D. in Israel this was the day of the year when Aquarius, the water-man, is "beheaded" by the king (Leo.)[7] Checking my astronomical programs, indeed in that era in Israel at sunrise, the Kingly star Regulus in Leo is rising in the east just ahead of the Sun at the same time that the two shoulder stars of Aquarius, Sadalmelik or "Lucky One of the King" and Sadalsuud or "Luckiest of the Lucky" are falling below the horizon in the west.)

Luke 3:1 also clarifies that John was called to preach and baptize "in the fifteenth year of the reign of Tiberius Caesar," and fortunately history clearly records his reign began September 18, 14 A.D. Therefore John the Baptist began preaching between late 28 A.D. and September of 29 A.D. with Jesus starting shortly afterwards, quite probably six months afterwards, most likely in late 29 or early 30 A.D.

If Jesus died in the spring of 36 A.D. he would have been at least 40 years old if born in 6 B.C., and 41 if born in 7 B.C. If he started his ministry three years earlier, he would have been at least 37 and a half years old, even assuming the later year of birth in 6 B.C. This is not especially supportive of Luke's claim that Jesus was about 30 years old when his ministry started. Of course if Jesus died in 33 A.D. he would have only been about 34 and a half years old when he began his ministry—again assuming he was born in 6 B.C. and that his ministry was about three years long. It is possible his

269

ministry was over three years long, and that he was not yet 34 years old when he started. Friday April 3, 33 A.D. seems the most likely time for his death.

Unfortunately, determining Jesus' likely date of crucifixion still does not help us determine with certainty whether he was born in 7 B.C. or 6 B.C. Perhaps we should again consider an astronomical solution, as there is that pesky and unsolved "Star of Bethlehem" problem. Astronomers from the east saw a star in the sky which they interpreted as the birth of the Messiah. They probably had traditions foretelling such an event, knowing there would be astronomical signs, because they knew the prophecies of the Old Testament. Daniel 2:48 tells us that the king of Babylon, centuries earlier, had put Daniel in charge "over all the wise men of Babylon." Daniel would have taught Jewish traditions and prophecies to the Babylonian astronomers, and the Persians would have learned of such things after they conquered Babylon. We are told that these eastern magi traveled west to Bethlehem knowing that was where the savior would be born, and that the star they were watching hovered over Bethlehem.

If anything unusual occurred in the sky at that time, why is there no agreement whatsoever on what this "star" was? Various theories suggest it was an eclipse, a supernova, an alignment of planets, a comet, or even a pair of meteors. But there is no agreement on the date such an event occurred, nor is there a notation amongst any of the civilizations in the region that anything astronomically extraordinary occurred during the years around Jesus' birth. Surely at least one set of astronomical records in Babylon, Egypt, Persia, Rome, China, or Mexico would have recorded something that clearly stood out.

Another problem is that nothing in the sky maintains its apparent position. As our planet rotates beneath the skies: "Anything celestial—whether supernova or planet—rises and arcs and sets below the horizon as the evening wears on. No heavenly body could remain motionless in the sky over Bethlehem."[8] *When the Bible tells us something happened, and the most literal interpretation of events is not physically possible, we are dealing with a clue to look for an astronomical solution.* Do not allow yourself to gloss over such points and assume they are just miraculous mysteries of God beyond our abilities to understand. Do not ignore such oddities and sleep in mental darkness when you have the means to be awake in the light of understanding—from the same perspective as the initiated brotherhoods of old. Consider that *many stories allegedly taking place on the ground are really meant to be understood as taking place in the sky.* In this case, we are already dealing with following a star in the sky, so the clue to look for a solution in the sky is obvious. We know the earth rotates, and that any observation of a star from the ground would show it passing over a city like Bethlehem—not stopping to set there. We also know that there is a real city of Jerusalem on the ground, and another Jerusalem in the heavens—as mentioned in Revelations.

What if there is another Bethlehem in the sky? What if these wise men who followed a star were members of the same traditional ancient brotherhood of astronomer-priests as the Shemsu Hor— The Followers of Horus—in Egypt? The Bible tells us they are astronomers and magi, so we can safely assume that many traditions from Egypt and Israel were continued in Babylon and Persia. Making this very likely assumption, then the magi followed Horus, the brightest and closest star—the sun—as it circles the zodiac over the almost 26,000 year cycle of precession. When Jesus himself asked us to follow him, he said "I am the Light of the world; he who follows Me will not walk in the darkness, but will have the Light of life." (John 8:12) Jesus was asking us to follow the sun through its cycle of precession. All ancient astronomers followed the sun on this journey through the sky, and magi from Babylon or Persia would be no exception. If there is a Bethlehem in the sky, and if that location is within the band of the zodiac through which the sun appears to travel, then observers would be able to watch the sun— our star—hover over Bethlehem for years.

The word Bethlehem, in Hebrew, means "house of bread." This alone leads many people to interpret a cosmological association with the star Spica, the stalk of wheat in Virgo's hand. Bethel, or "Beth-el" means house of God, and "lehem" means bread—so Bethlehem is often interpreted as either "house of God" or "house of bread." If we interpret Bethlehem as "House of God" (and we have already established that God's throne is at the galactic center) then perhaps the magi were interested in the same type of alignment as the Maya. Any astronomers keeping track of the sun's precessional progress through the sky could easily follow the sun to the galactic center, just as the Maya did with their ball game, their Pyramid of Kukulkan, and their calendar. Unlike the more popular "Star of Bethlehem" candidates which would fall out of sync with any point of view showing them over the Judean city of Bethlehem in a few minutes, astronomers watching the winter solstice sun over the galactic core would have a conjunction that lasts for years. The magi would have known that when this happens, right around now, in the early 21st century—that this would be the time frame for the Messiah to come. But if this interpretation is right, what would make them think there would be a prior birth of Jesus around 6 B.C.?

The magi were wise men well versed in astronomy and religion. As Daniel had been placed over all the wise men of Babylon centuries earlier, subsequent generations of wise men would be well versed in all things Daniel found important—including Jewish prophecies. And that category of knowledge includes the prophecy of the seventy weeks described in Daniel 9:22-27. "You are to know and discern that from the issuing of a decree to restore and rebuild Jerusalem until Messiah the Prince there will be seven weeks and sixty-two weeks; it will be built again, with plaza and moat, even in times of distress. Then after the sixty-two weeks the Messiah will be cut off." (Dan 9:25-26) This is interpreted to mean weeks of years, so 7+62=69 weeks (years), times seven days per week = 483 biblical years of 360 days. This comes to just over 476 solar years of 365.252 days.

Since Nehemiah tells us the order to rebuild Jerusalem came from the Persian King Artaxerxes in the 20th year of his reign, and as the beginning of his reign is well established historically, we can determine quite a bit. We know the Persians dated his reign from 465 B.C. and that Nehemiah started a little later from the Jewish reckoning in the fall of 464 B.C. The spring of 444 B.C. would, to

Nehemiah, have been in his 20th year. Educated wise men (magi) paying attention to such things would have anticipated the Messiah being "cut off" 476 solar years later—in the spring of 33 A.D. They would have anticipated such a man beginning his ministry at approximately the age of fullness and adulthood—30 years old. This would not be enough to tell them exactly when the Messiah would be born, but it would narrow it down to a small range of likely years, probably around 10 B.C. to 2 A.D.

The magi would have anticipated a birth near Bethlehem, for this is where Micah 5:2 tells us the Messiah would be born. "You, Bethlehem Ephrathah, Too little to be among the clans of Judah, From you One will go forth for Me to be ruler in Israel. His goings forth are from long ago, From the days of eternity." The name "Bethlehem Ephrathah" clarifies which Bethlehem is meant, as there is more than one town by that name, and this tells us the one in Judah is meant. But what about the idea that Bethlehem represents a location in the sky? The early 21st century has the winter solstice sun near the "house of God" at the galactic core for the Second Coming when Jesus returns as the Lion of Judah, but the first time around when he is the sacrificial lamb, should we consider the main definition of "Beth-lehem"—the house of bread? Could this be another case where a Bible prophecy has two valid realizations or fulfillments in different eras? Of course it could. So if we ask, why would the magi expect the birth of the savior around 6 B.C., another perfectly valid answer is, of course, the position of the sun at the house of bread.

The star Spica is the brightest star in the constellation Virgo, the Virgin. In any drawing of Virgo she is holding a sheaf of wheat over the position of Spica, which is associated with the wheat, the harvest, and the branch—in this case, the branch of David, the genetic line of descent through which the Messiah is prophesied to be born. In Hebrew, Spica is called Tsemech; in Arabic, Al Zimach—which means the branch. There are several references to the Messiah as a branch, including Jeremiah 23:5-6: "I will raise up for David a righteous Branch; And He will reign as king." The Messiah also compared himself to a kernel of wheat in John 12:23-24. "The hour

273

has come for the Son of Man to be glorified. Truly, truly, I say to you, unless a grain of wheat falls into the earth and dies, it remains alone; but if it dies, it bears much fruit." This sounds like the rebirth of Egypt's sun-god Osiris symbolized through growing grain: "The death of the grain and the death of the god were one and the same: the cereal was identified with the god who came from heaven; he was the bread by which man lives."[9]

We know the Messiah will come at the harvest, as mentioned in Matthew 13:39 "the harvest is the end of the age." Most importantly, in John 6:35 and 6:48 Jesus says "I am the bread of life." These references connecting Christ to the branch, the harvest, wheat, and bread could all point to a birth with the sun near Spica, the wheat in the hand of the constellation Virgo the Virgin.

This idea gets even more interesting when we consider that in Hebrew, the name of the constellation Virgo is Bethulah, the Hebrew word for virgin. Now if lehem means bread and Bethulah means virgin, then Bethulah-lehem is the bread of the virgin, and astronomically could only be the wheat in the Virgin's hand, the star Spica. Is this "Bethulah-lehem" ("the bread of the virgin") what the magi were really talking about? Astronomically speaking it looks like Jesus as the sun was born at Spica, at Bethulah-Lehem or Bethlehem. Any Hebrew dictionary or concordance (like Strong's) will also point out that the secondary meaning of "Bethulah" is a city, lending further credence to this interpretation. Even "Ephrathah" has a relevant meaning here. Micah 5:2 tells us Jesus would be born in "Bethlehem-Ephrathah" to clarify which Bethlehem would see His birth. Ephrath is a Hebrew word meaning fertility and could easily refer to the womb or midsection of Virgo in an astronomical sense. So of two possible Bethlehems in Israel, Ephrathah clarifies that we should look at the one near Jerusalem. Of the two possible Bethlehems in the sky, it clarifies we should look for the one associated with fertility—the one in the middle of Virgo, the virgin.

At sunset on that most likely date for Jesus' birth on the 15th of Tishri (September 27) 6 B.C., the sun is practically on top of Spica, the wheat/bread of the virgin. If the magi had been looking for signs of heavenly activity over the earthly city of Bethlehem, and the entire sky appears to slowly rotate east to west, anything seen in the sky would rotate out of position from being above the earthly city of Bethlehem within minutes. But because the sun and Spica are both in the sky, apparently moving at the same pace due to the Earth's rotation, the alignment of the setting sun hovering just above Spica lasts for a long time. The sun would blind observers to Spica or anything else nearby, but astronomers would know Spica was near the sun all day. They would know this alignment at the autumnal equinox lasts for decades, occurring in late September every year from approximately 50 B.C. to 40 A.D. On any particular day of observation Spica and the sun would move together in an arc through the sky. At sunrise, Spica would be above the sun; in midday they would be next to each other, but at sunset, the sun would be above Spica, as Spica falls below the horizon. This may be yet another fulfillment of the phrase: "This is the bread which comes down out of heaven." (John 6:50) This event could be described as "our star" (the sun) hovering over Bethulah-Lehem (Spica) as it sets and the new day begins.

As the sun must set in the west when the proper position over Spica exists, any magi watching this must see it from the east—where we are told the magi come from. We should also consider that with the sun in Virgo, the Messianic birth is occurring in the celestial virgin. In Revelations 22:16 Jesus also says: "I, Jesus, have sent My angel to testify to you these things for the churches. I am the root and the descendant of David, the bright morning star." Venus may represent the angelic witness. Venus as an angel also makes sense regarding Exodus 23:20 "Behold, I am going to send an angel before you to guard you along the way and to bring you into the place which I have prepared." Venus passes Spica several days ahead of the sun in 6 B.C., leading the sun down the road of the ecliptic and preceding the Messiah as Elijah does. Venus is also known as the morning star. And with Venus in the sky below Virgo's knees, the Morningstar—Jesus—is being "born" to the virgin. Although Jesus is primarily identified with the sun, there is a secondary association with the sun's close companion Venus for the purposes of foretelling his birth.

This brings to mind Isaiah 7:14 "Therefore the Lord Himself will give you a sign: Behold, a virgin will be with child and bear a son, and she will call His name Immanuel." This is clearly a reference to the future birth of the messiah—but why use the Hebrew word "almah" instead of "bethulah" for virgin? Bethulah is the only Hebrew word for virgin. Almah means a young woman hidden from sight. In context of some Middle Eastern women who, even today, are not permitted outside without male relatives as chaperones, we understand "almah" to mean a protected, sheltered, young woman hidden from sight (and therefore probably still a virgin, despite the lack of specific comment on her virginity.) This is especially interesting in regard to Spica and Virgo on 9/27/6 B.C., when the sun is about as close as possible to Spica, and one could say that the woman (Virgo) is clothed with the sun. The sun hides Virgo from our view, for it is right next to the sun, and we are blinded to anything else in the heavens by the brilliant sunlight.

We know the wise men would be looking for signs of the coming Messiah. We know they would understand the meaning of Bethlehem and Bethulah-lehem and expect the setting sun above Spica, and that this would happen for many years on either side of about 5 B.C. We know they would expect the Messiah to be "cut off" or sacrificed around the spring of 33 A.D., and subtracting time for a ministry and about thirty years for reaching full adulthood, would be pointed to the decade before our year one for the time of his birth. They would probably have been looking for interesting astronomical alignments on Jewish holidays near the autumn equinox (around late September) in the appropriate range of years, and would have calculated well in advance when meaningful positions would exist. They would have known that the astronomical association of the son of God would generally be our sun, but that Venus, the Morningstar, would also represent Jesus at his birth. They would have expected that at his virgin birth Venus must be located near the lower legs of the constellation Virgo, the Virgin. They would have calculated the future positions of Venus, and the sun, and Spica, and noted that in the most likely years from about 10 B.C. to 1 A.D. only once does everything line up right—in 6 B.C.

The Feast of Tabernacles on the 15th of Tishri is not always so close the fall equinox; in the old lunar calendar of the Jews it can move several weeks away from our September 22. And Venus could be in a variety of constellations at that time of year—Scorpio, Leo, not necessarily in Virgo at all. But on the feast of Tabernacles in 6 B.C., the date in our calendar is September 27. The date is close to the fall equinox and the sun (the star they follow) is still over the wheat (or bread) in Virgo's hand. Venus is near Virgo's feet "being born." The magi would also have calculated the partial solar eclipse occurring two weeks earlier at sunset on Rosh Hashanah, the first of Tishri and the beginning of the year. With no other remotely interesting astronomical lineups in their time frame of interest, they could have known, even centuries ahead of time, to expect the birth of the Messiah on September 27, 6 B.C. For this priestly brotherhood of astrologers, this date would have been looked forward to for generations, even centuries. How happy those magi alive in 6 B.C. must have been to see their long-anticipated alignment take place in the sky, and know that they could travel west to the earthly city of Bethlehem and see Jesus in the flesh!

(Endnotes)

1 S, Acharya. *Suns of God: Krishna, Buddha and Christ Unveiled*. Kempton, IL: Adventures Unlimited Press, 2004, pp. 490-493, 504

2 S, Acharya. Ibid., pp. 128-134

3 S, Acharya. Ibid., p. 86

4 Clarke, Adam. *Adam Clarke's Commentary on the Bible*. Nashville, TN: Thomas Nelson, 1997, p. 547

5 Mede, Joseph. *Mede's Works*. London: 1679, Discourse xlvii

6 S, Acharya. *Suns of God: Krishna, Buddha and Christ Unveiled*. Kempton, IL: Adventures Unlimited Press, 2004, p. 74, originally from Marsilio Ficino's 1494 work *The Book of the Sun*.

7 S, Acharya. *The Christ Conspiracy:The Greatest Story Ever Sold*. Kempton, IL: Adventures Unlimited Press, 1999, p. 177 also in Acharya S. *Suns of God: Krishna, Buddha and Christ Unveiled*. Kempton, IL: Adventures Unlimited Press, 2004, p. 460

8 *Discover Magazine*, December 1991, pp. 78-79

9 Larson, M. A. *The Story of Christian Origins*. Cited by Scott Creighton and Gary Osborn, *The Giza Prophecy: The Orion Code and the Secret Teachings of the Pyramids*. Rochester, VT: Bear & Company, 2012, p. 265

CHAPTER EIGHT
THE RAPTURE, THE SECOND
COMING AND JUDGMENT DAY

At the beginning of this book's introduction I mentioned having a moment of revelation, an insight that allowed me to look at the Bible from a new perspective and understand the timing of the end. We have discussed this as the realization that many Bible passages, and especially its end times prophecies, describe a future series of astronomical events through the details of an ancient Jewish wedding ceremony. The correlations are no accident; the sensible conclusion is that ancient priests viewed the astronomical signs of cosmic destruction as a divine wedding and modeled the mortal wedding ceremony after it.

We also reached a specific time frame for the events of the wedding in the early 21st century through the prophecies of Daniel. We got most of the way there using two completely different prophecies to reach the year 1967, when the Israelis reclaimed the ground where the Jewish Temple had stood. 1967 was 2300 years after the first victories of Alexander the Great against the Persians, and 1967 is also 1260 plus 1290 years after the destruction of the Temple by the Babylonians in 584 B.C. Encouraging us to keep waiting beyond the last 1290 "days" that led us to 1967, Daniel continues: "Happy is the one who is keeping in expectation and arrives at the one thousand three hundred and thirty-five days!" The extra 45 "days" between "day" 1290 and "day" 1335 are meant to be understood as years for this fulfillment of prophecy—so we should add 45 more years after 1967 for the difference between the 1290 and the 1335— and this leads us to 2012. Coupled with the Mayan Long Count ending on December 21, 2012 we have a very specific time frame for that start of world-changing events.

Through the 1990s, and perhaps as late as 2004 or 2005, we might even have assumed that Daniel and the Maya were telling us 2012 would be the conclusion of all prophesized events. But the Bible describes a seven year tribulation that comes before the end, and as of July 2012, signs that should occur at the beginning and middle of the tribulation have not occurred. We did not have to accept the mark of the beast to buy or sell; there is no rebuilt Jewish Temple in Jerusalem and no antichrist has proclaimed himself to be God in it. World events, while disappointing, are hardly evidence of an ongoing tribulation nearing its end. Therefore the only logical prophetic possibility left for 2012 is that it could mark the beginning of the seven-year tribulation. Astronomical software has also become available to verify dates in 2019. We now know that Judgment Day is in 2019, seven years of tribulation after 2012.

December 2012 may be the point at which we realize the world as we knew it is falling apart and rapidly transforming into something we fear. But it is not the end of everything. Astronomically, very little of note occurs in 2012, contrasted with numerous astronomical matches to the details of an ancient Jewish wedding ceremony in late December 2019.

We were led to 2012 through the prophecies of Daniel, who mentions several time frames including one of "1335 days" which has two fulfillments for the end times. We have already reviewed how 1260 and 1290 days (years) get us from 584 B.C. to 1967, and that 45 "days" (years) more bring us to 1335 days and the year 2012. The second half of the tribulation may involve these numbers again, for the final time, in days. Near the end of the second half of the seven year tribulation is October 14, 2019: the Second Coming. If that is counted as day 1260, then we add thirty days for judgment to get to day 1290 and forty-five more days for wrath to get to day 1335—on Judgment Day, December 28, 2019.

If we are fortunate enough to be amongst the (saved) invited guests at both expressions of 1335; at the beginning of the tribulation in in 2012 (when Daniel tells us "blessed is he who keeps waiting and attains to the 1,335 days!" and we will know we are only seven

280

years from salvation) and at the Judgment Day wedding dinner on December 28, 2019 ("Blessed are those who are invited to the wedding supper of the Lamb") we should indeed be happy to have survived and have a chance to participate in tikkun olam: the rebuilding of the world.

Many pages back we briefly discussed a very important Egyptian drawing of the zodiac—the Dendera Zodiac—which was removed from the ceiling of the Temple of Hathor in Dendera, Egypt and taken to Paris. We mentioned Michael Evans' interpretation that one of the items drawn on the zodiac—Osiris' uas scepter—symbolizes a restoration of order, and was drawn in a way that indicates the positions of the last North Pole and our current one. We mentioned that the goddess Hathor, and her Temple at Dendera, are associated with the eye of Ra, and the destruction of mankind by flood. The Dendera zodiac was built into the ceiling in an orientation opposite to today's skies, which commemorates devastation half a precessional cycle ago. The entire zodiac describes the 25,800 year precessional wobbling of the planet's axis of rotation, and the regular occurrence of devastating pole shifts at regular points in the cycle.

In his work *Skies of Memory*, John Lash summarizes his evidence that the Dendera zodiac shows more than just precession of the Earth's axis. Lash feels the four obvious axes across the zodiac are important, but that a fifth through the star Spica is most important. "We should recognize Virgo's wheat stalk as her brightest star, known today as Spica, but in the Hebrew as Al Zemach meaning the branch which is one of the prominent titles of the Promised Seed, or offspring of God, in the Old Testament [Jer 23:5-6]. What is unique about this as it relates to Dendera's zodiac is that Spica/Al Zemach is only one of two individual stars marked on this entire star map, the other being Sirius."[1]

Sirius is the brightest star in the entire sky, and its appearance above the horizon every summer coincided with the annual flooding of the Nile River in Egypt. So it is no surprise that Sirius is shown on an Egyptian representation of the zodiac. The question is, what makes Spica so special that it is the only other star depicted on their zodiac? Spica is not the second brightest star; it is only the sixteenth brightest star in the sky. Lash further elaborates on his theory that we should view the Dendera Zodiac as if it were bisected by a line drawn through the star Spica: "Sirius is placed between the horns of the sacred cow on axis B, and Spica, the star traditionally identified with Virgo's sheaf of wheat. This led me to wonder what an axis inscribed from Spica through the Jackal pole would look like… First, the axis culminates by bisecting the altar mounted by 4 ram's heads… Second, Axis E [Spica axis] crosses Pisces at the tail of the lower or foremost fish exactly where the spring equinox occurs today. Third, Axis E, extended to Virgo's feet marks the tail of Leo at a point that corresponds by precession to 10,500 BC. All in all, axis E marks the moment of precession when one full cycle ends and a new one begins."[2]

The first observation Lash points out is that the line of the Spica axis bisects the Ram altar on the periphery of the zodiac. This shows the correlation between the sun's position at the Feast of Tabernacles

The zodiac from the Beth Alpha Synagogue in Israel

near Spica with the altar of sacrifice that the Promised Seed would endure to pay the price for forgiveness of sins, the sacrifice that only Christ could pay for all mankind. It brings to mind Psalm 118:27: "The LORD is God, and He has given us light; Bind the festival sacrifice with cords to the horns of the altar." Lash elaborates on his second observation as follows: "As the total pattern came into focus, I recognized that axis E signals this moment of epochal transition in a vivid intentional way. Whoever designed Dendera was looking ahead in time to our age, when the spring equinox occurs under the tail of the western fish, because this is the time that the entire cycle culminates. With the spring equinox just at that position in Pisces, the axial cross locks into unique alignment with the Galaxy."[3] We should also note that Spica's wheat is associated with the great harvest of souls in Matthew 3:12 "He will thoroughly clear His threshing floor; and He will gather His wheat into the barn, but He will burn up the chaff with unquenchable fire." (KJB) Lash is basically saying that Spica is central to the Dendera Zodiac, which overall is pointing out the end of a great cycle in the early 21st century, one associated with Hebrew details on the coming of the Messiah.

This makes another zodiac in the Middle East even more interesting for its apparent lack of messianic symbolism. The zodiac built in the floor of the Beth Alpha Synagogue near Galilee was built in the sixth century A.D., when Israel was no stranger to the Christian idea of a messiah. But the zodiac built there does not orient the sky properly for the time it was built; it positions the marker for the spring equinox with the Virgo-Leo boundary, which would have been accurate in 10,700 B.C. Were the Hebrew builders of this zodiac, like those who made the Dendera Zodiac, pointing back to the last epoch of cataclysm?

Mythologist and historian Joseph Campbell noted the Hebrew zodiac signs are way off from how they would normally be oriented, but assumed the builders simply lacked astronomical knowledge or disregarded it as unrelated to Jewish religion.[4] But if people took the time to create a map of the sky in stone they did understand. Paul LaViolette writes "these ancient masons knew what they were doing and purposely set their zodiacal chronometer to this particular celestial position in remembrance of this all important 12,700-years-B.P. date... Campbell was also perplexed by the religious significance of the icon at the zodiac's center, which displays the sun god Helios."[5] As Campbell wrote: "The problem of the religious significance of Helios, the zodiac, and the seasons to a Jewish community of that time is not easy to resolve."[6]

Perhaps we don't recognize something those Jewish builders took for granted—that the Messiah is the sun-god, and that the cycle of his precession through the zodiac determines when he returns. Today, our culture has "forgotten" that the sun represents Jesus or that Jesus represents the sun. 2 Kings 23:5 tells us the kings and people of Judah had worshipped "the sun and the moon" and other astronomical bodies. "These facts were deliberately suppressed so that the astrotheological nature of Christianity would be lost."[7] But 1500 years ago Jews knew the sun-god as the messiah. They knew that he returns right about now, at the beginning of the Age of Aquarius.

The age of Aquarius, defined by the position of the sun at the vernal equinox, is the age we are entering now; the last zodiac age in the cycle. In Daniel 8:17 the prophet expresses confusion over his visions of our times, but the angel Gabriel is sent to help him understand that they do refer to the last days: "Son of man, understand that the vision pertains to the time of the end." Of the 2300 Passovers that bring us to 1967, Gabriel clarifies in Daniel 8:26 "The vision of the evenings and mornings Which has been told is true; But keep the vision secret, For it pertains to many days in the future." After reaching 1967 we add Daniel's final 45 years to reach 2012. If our interpretation of Daniel's prophecy is correct, and the seven year tribulation begins in 2012, then it seems unlikely that the end date of the Mayan calendar is an unimportant coincidence. We should pay special attention to their last day on December 21, 2012. Shortly after this date, probably in early 2013, there should come a day when huge signs are witnessed including the start of a seven year peace treaty with Israel brokered by the antichrist. The Jewish Temple should be rebuilt, and three and a half years later, the antichrist should break the peace treaty, and proclaim himself to be God while standing in the Temple. Another three and a half years later, after a complete seven year tribulation, Judgment Day should come in December 2019.

Before getting into more detail on the astronomical alignments in December 2012 and 2019, let us briefly consider the middle of the tribulation in June 2016, when the antichrist will stand in the Temple. In the NASB Isaiah 14:12 reads "How you have fallen from heaven, O star of the morning, son of the dawn!" The King James Bible reads "O Lucifer, son of the morning" and this is the only mention of Lucifer by name in the Bible. He is clearly described as Venus, the morning star. Where is Venus (in this case, Lucifer) on June 6, 2016, 1260 days after the tribulation began? *Directly behind the middle of the Sun.* As the Sun is Christ and Venus is on the opposite (anti-) side we have our astronomical anti-Christ. One could say he stands at the altar in the Temple. Two witnesses speak out against this and die before being brought back to life three days later. Witnesses and angels are generally planets, and Saturn and Mars are both near the claws of Scorpio, the constellation of Death. After three and a half days the temporarily "dead" witnesses have moved on and are resurrected (away from Death's claws.) This

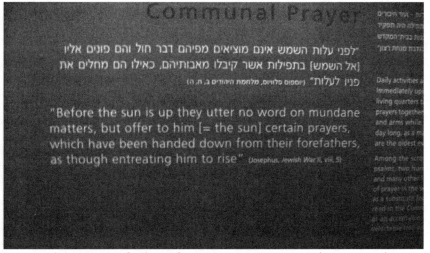

Even today you can find a reference to ancient Jewish sun-worship on the wall of a museum in Jerusalem.

gets us to June 9, 2016, and then exactly 1290 days later, as written in Daniel 12:11, we reach the end of the seven year tribulation on December 21, 2019.

It seems noteworthy that the alignment of the winter solstice sun with the galactic center, which is associated with the end of the Mayan calendar on December 21, 2012, is really spread out over a range of dates. The most knowledgeable scholar on the Maya, John Major Jenkins, clarifies that "the sun itself is one-half of a degree wide, and will in fact be touching the galactic equator on all winter solstices between 1980 and 2016" with "1998 being the year when the center of the sun is in closest alignment with the galactic equator."[8] The United States Nautical Observatory and other astronomers agree. Jenkins tells us "that December 22 of 1998 might be called day one of the next 26,000-year precessional cycle."[9]

Obviously there is no special gravitational kick from these alignments between the Earth, Sun, and galactic center which would cause terrible destruction on its own, or we would have already experienced it. Anticipating doom while watching these alignments year after year without catastrophes, one could feel like the impatient servant in Luke 12:45 who says: "My master will be a long time in coming."

But if we consider Revelations 8:1 it may shed new light on this for us: "When the Lamb broke the seventh seal, there was silence in heaven for about half an hour." If the Lamb is the winter solstice sun and the seventh seal is reaching an alignment near the galactic center... Then if a day is as a thousand years, and a half hour is one forty-eighth of a day, about twenty years and ten months of silence occur. Could this mean that, after the best conjunction of the winter solstice sun and the galactic equator on 12/22/1998—approximately 21 years and 10 months pass without incident? That would lead us to October 2019.

It may be worth mentioning some predictions from the great French psychic Nostradamus, who wrote approximately a thousand prophecies of future events back in the 16th century. Although most of his prophecies seem vague, one of his most impressive direct hits is a description of what seems to be the Soviet Union. This was given in paragraph 25 of his letter to King Henri II of France, in which he said (of what sounds like the Soviet Union) "it will only last for seventy-three years and seven months." The Bolsheviks seized power in the Russian Duma on January 18, 1918—and then over the next few months gained control over the entire nation. On August 18, 1991, there was a coup against Mikhail Gorbachev, and by the end of the year every republic had declared independence and the Soviet Union had ceased to exist.[10] The timing of events Nostradamus described in paragraph 25 of the letter to King Henri seems accurate to the day.

So perhaps we should pay attention to his description of events in paragraph 24 of that letter as well, for he said there will be "a solar eclipse more gloomy than any since the creation of the world, except that after the death and passion of Jesus Christ. And it will be in the month of October that the great translation will be made and it will be such that one will think the gravity of the earth has lost its natural movement and that it is to be plunged into the abyss of perpetual darkness."[11] This could be a reference to a pole shift.

A few things stand out here. For starters, Nostradamus was a very wise and educated man. He was a doctor, an astronomer, and a master of languages, religions, and the occult. He knew very well that there could not have been a solar eclipse when Jesus died, no matter what was written in Luke 23:44-45: "It was now about the sixth hour, and darkness fell over the whole land until the ninth hour, because the sun was obscured." The King James Bible says "the sun was darkened" and this is universally discussed as a solar eclipse of three hours duration (despite the fact that the gospels do not specifically call it an eclipse.)

But Nostradamus knew that no total solar eclipse, ever, can last even eight minutes. The moon moves by too quickly. He also knew one could never happen on the fourteenth day of the month of Nisan, when Jesus died—because Jewish months, by definition—always start at the new moon, when the moon appears to be near the sun, and every month would always have the moon appear far away from the sun in the middle of the month. No good Christian wants to say that the writers of the gospels may have added such details for dramatic effect—and Nostradamus certainly would not have wanted to point out such an inconsistency during the heyday of the Inquisition. But the moon did not eclipse the sun when Jesus died on Nisan 14, so we have to wonder what made Matthew, Mark, and Luke describe the darkness of failed sunlight at Jesus' death. Were they just trying to link the end of sunlight to his death, to tell us Jesus is the sun? Or is there something besides the moon that can make the sun go dark—something they are telling us will happen in

A woodcut of Nostradamus

2019?

Nostradamus certainly knew the impossibility of a three hour eclipse at the crucifixion, but chose to make an unnecessary reference to it anyway. This is odd and curious, and this reference to the eclipse at the crucifixion should make us pay attention. Was Nostradamus trying to point out that Jesus is the sun, or that something else can make the sun go dark? Was he emphasizing that something very dark and gloomy happened at the creation of the world, and drawing a parallel to these upcoming events as another act of world-creation? He is certainly drawing our attention to an eclipse that has to do with messianic events, and linking it to a great translation in October, which may be related to a pole shift.

Could he have possibly meant that the "great translation" in October is the Second Coming, when Jesus relocates from heaven to earth, and that this is linked to a pole shift and solar eclipse two and a half months later, when the sun is dark for three days and then eclipsed by the moon? If nothing else Nostradamus certainly links the pole shift—"the earth has lost its natural movement"— with the moment when the light of the sun goes out and Earth "is plunged into the abyss of perpetual darkness." Both of which are somehow connected to the death and resurrection of Jesus Christ. If only Nostradamus had mentioned the month of December these events would seem to make even more sense, for both our pole shift and our eclipse of the dead and reborn sun take place in December. The "dec" root of the word December means "ten" and October is now our tenth month, but this is not a convincing link between the two. The timing still seems off, as it was for a biblical eclipse on the 14th of Nisan. Of course, in paragraph 39, Nostradamus admits "I present these predictions almost with confusion, especially as to when they will take place."[12] (He did not want to risk a high degree of clarity and be burned at the stake by the Inquisition, after all.) Perhaps we need to back up even further and consider what Nostradamus was saying in paragraph 23 of his letter.

In that paragraph he describes what might be World War III, with the Holy Ghost eventually coming to chase out the Antichrist, "whose reign will be for a time and to the end of time." That is the end of paragraph 23. Continuing into paragraph 24, "...the end of time. This will be preceded by a solar eclipse more dark and gloomy than any since the creation of the world..."[13] Maybe Nostradamus is saying that the end of time is preceded by the especially dark and gloomy solar eclipse. This is also in line with the only other prophecy in which Nostradamus seems to indicate a pole shift. Most of his prophecies are organized in four line poems called quatrains, and in quatrain 2:46 he says "After great trouble for humanity, a greater one is prepared, The Great Mover renews the ages."[14] This could easily mean that after the great trouble of the seven year tribulation, a greater trouble occurs when God starts a new world age, with a pole shift at the beginning of the age of Aquarius—"the end of time"—which we are entering now in the 21st century.

In quatrain 2:41 Nostradamus tells us: "The great star will burn for seven days; The cloud will cause two suns to appear: The big mastiff will howl all night; When the great pontiff will change country."[15] While this is too vague to be attributed to 2019 with certainty, the description does include many end times ingredients: a great cloud which appears with a second sunlike object in the sky, a period of seven days, and presumably devastation intense enough to require the papacy to abandon Rome and relocate to a new country.

Nostradamus' prophecies seem to agree with our astronomical analysis of the Bible, for we have a pole shift beginning at the end of the tribulation on December 21, a temporarily extinguished sun for a few days before Christmas, followed by a total solar eclipse ending December 26, and Judgment Day on December 28. On that day the week-long recreation by pole-shift ends, Draco has fallen from the sky, and Jupiter finally coronates the Jesus-sun as King of the Earth.

Let us look at what will be going on in the sky in late 2019. The Jewish new year 5780 starts on the first day of Tishri—the Feast of Trumpets, corresponding to our September 30, 2019. Venus, the brightest planet, the morning star, can be a confusing astronomical indicator because it has (on rare occasion) represented Lucifer in addition to representing Jesus during birth events, although Jesus is generally identified with the sun (whenever His birth is not referenced.) At the time of the Second Coming Venus represents Jesus, and on 9/30/2019 Venus is "in the womb of the Virgin" near Virgo's pelvis, near the star Spica. The sun is at the height of Virgo's chest and upper arms. The moon is at Virgo's feet. As Virgo (and the sun) rise in the east in the morning, Virgo is preceded by the stars of the royal constellation Leo above her head. This is probably the astronomical arrangement described in Revelations 12:1-2 "A great sign appeared in heaven: a woman clothed with the sun, and the moon under her feet, and on her head a crown of twelve stars; and she was with child; and she cried out, being in labor and in pain to give birth." Let us not underestimate the importance of this astronomical arrangement to the return of Jesus. There are many other signs in Revelations; this one is the "great sign" of the highest importance.

Revelations 12:3 tells us "Then another sign appeared in heaven: and behold, a great red dragon having seven heads and ten horns, and on his heads were seven diadems. And his tail swept away a third of the stars of heaven and threw them to the earth." Assuming that Satan and the dragon are associated with the polar constellation Draco, it is very interesting to note that there is a meteor shower coming from Draco in early October. The Draconid meteor shower is most visible every October 8-9, and it comes from the part of the sky that the constellation Draco the dragon could (if it could move) sweep with its tail.

The intensity of the Draconid meteor shower depends on where its parent comet (21P/Giacobini-Zinner) is in its orbit and where our planet crosses the debris trail in a given year. A peak of 500 meteors per minute were seen in 1998. A record was set on October 9, 1933 when approximately 100 meteors were seen in just five seconds, and one astronomer "observed over 22,500 meteors in just a few hours and estimated the peak rate hit 480 per minute."[16] We should assume there will be an even more spectacular display in 2019 if it looks like a third of the stars are falling from the sky.

We know Jesus is associated with the harvest and that his first birth was on Tishri 15, the Harvest Holiday of Sukkot, the Feast of

Tabernacles. In 2019 this holiday is on Monday October 14. When Jesus was born in 6 B.C. the sun was near Spica, Virgo's wheat— which could also be known as Bethulah-lehem, the bread of the Virgin, or as the house of bread, a celestial Bethlehem. After 2,000 years of precession, and as the Hebrew calendar is primarily lunar and the timing of Sukkot varies on our solar calendar, the sun sets near Spica again on October 14, 2019, in the right hand of Virgo, as if she is giving us the sun. Venus has dropped from the level of Virgo's womb to Virgo's feet over the preceding two weeks. At least astronomically—the Morningstar, Jesus—has once again been born to the Virgin. (We may assume that he does not return as a newborn baby this time, but that the position of the morning star in Virgo once again determines, or is a sign of, his arrival. "The Morning Star is the brightest and most visible planet. It is not a star, but it is always referred to as the Morning or Evening Star. It represents the Lord Jesus Christ in His Second Advent when He returns to establish the Millennial Kingdom."[17]

In Revelations 22:16-17, Jesus refers to Venus as an angelic witness when he says: "I, Jesus, have sent My angel to testify to you these things for the churches. I am the root and the descendant of David, the bright morning star. The Spirit and the bride say, 'Come.'" This certainly verifies that Jesus is the morning star, and that his marriage to us, the bride, is imminent at this point.

Many Christians view the church as the bride, and a pre-tribulation rapture as the moment when Jesus comes for his bride. But the bride must do a few things to prepare herself before she is taken. According to ancient Jewish wedding traditions the bride must go through a ritual immersion in water, a baptism-like cleansing, to symbolize washing away any ties to former things before starting a new life with her husband. The bride is also expected to prepare new garments to clothe herself with in preparation for the wedding. And let's not forget that the final act of the bride-to-be in a Jewish wedding is the "Hakafot" ("the circling of the groom") in which she circles the groom seven times after arriving at the (altar) "huppah" where the groom is waiting for her.

These bridal activities sound a lot like what the Earth will be doing in the end times! On December 21, 2012, the sun/Jesus/groom has reached its winter solstice alignment with the altar position of the galactic center and the seven year tribulation begins. Earth orbits the sun once a year and circles the sun seven times in seven years just as the Jewish bride circles her groom at the altar seven times before the wedding commences. After exactly seven years of tribulation the pole shift begins on December 21, 2019, with oceans sloshing out of their basins and continents repositioning themselves. The bride, the Earth, will be washed with water and will establish new outer garments.

We find Earth depicted as a bride in ancient sources as far away and as far back in time as Egypt's Osirian legends, of which Macrobius tells us "Osiris is none other than the sun and Isis, as we have said, is none other than the earth."[18] The same pairing of sun and earth as husband and bride is also found in the puranas of ancient India. These Hindu myths are alleged to have taken place at the creation of the current world, "when Brahma the Creator, seated on the [blue] lotus of Vishnu…" (sun and galactic center aligned

Christians believe that Jesus will return and enter Jerusalem through its eastern gate [as would the sunrise] so funeral plots just east of this gate have been very expensive for those who want to be among the first to rise from death at the Second Coming, and the hill near where I took this photo was taken is densely packed with graves. Notice also that the Muslims, who denounce Jesus as not being God's son on the Dome of the Rock Mosque, (barely visible to the left) bricked up the eastern gate to the city to seal it, just in case the Christians are right—as if that would prevent His entrance.

during active Seyfert phase) upon recognizing that the Earth was lost and submerged, created a giant boar "like a powerful lion" which "was radiant as the sun." This strange sun-god "plunged into the cosmic sea. Whereupon the goddess Earth" beheld this form of Vishnu as her rescuer and announced "Hence, in this world I am known as 'Vishnu's bride.'"[19] The Earth goddess declares herself to be the great god's bride in Hindu myth… and we already know that Judeo-Christianity's earliest roots may go back to Hinduism.

Abram and Sarah may be derived from the very similarly named Brahma and Sarai, and Abram's two sons, Isaac (from the Sanskrit Ishakhu—"Friend of Shiva") and Ishmael (from the Sanskrit Ish-Mahal "Great Shiva") probably are as well. Therefore Hindu ideas, including cyclic destruction, with Brahma as creator, Vishnu as rescuer, Shiva as destroyer, and the Earth as the bride, may be at the very foundations of Judaism and Christianity. The westward spread of Indian religious concepts, initially through Persia, is well documented. "As the Persian fire-worship and the main part of the Persian religion were derived from India, the sacrifice, death, and Resurrection of Mithra become but counterparts of Vishnu's incarnation, sacrifice, etc. in Krishna."[20] Even the "Catholic Encyclopedia" admits there are "tales of Krishna that are almost identical with the stories of Christ"[21] in the gospels, that Krishna dates to the fourth century B.C., and that he is an avatar of Vishnu. Of course Vishnu and Shiva are opposite halves of a dual combination (V-I-SH is just SH-I-V backwards) or as Joseph Campbell summarized "the grace that pours into the universe through the sun door is the same as the energy of the bolt that annihilates."[22]

No discussion of the Earth as the bride would be complete without mentioning the New Jerusalem. It has 72 yard walls which are also "angelic measures" of 72 degrees: a fifth of a precessional cycle between pole shifts. And we already covered Ephesians 3:18 "Comprehend with all the saints what is the breadth and length and height and depth." This refers to how we should look at a cube like the New Jerusalem, which is 1500 miles on a side, or "7920 thousand feet" like the Earth's 7920 mile diameter.[23] The New Jerusalem dimensions share the same 7920 number of units

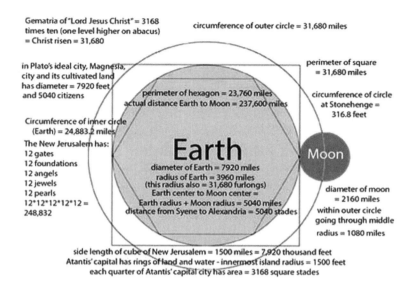

Gematria of "Lord Jesus Christ" = 3168
times ten (one level higher on abacus)
= Christ risen = 31,680

circumference of outer circle = 31,680 miles

in Plato's ideal city, Magnesia,
city and its cultivated land
has diameter = 7920 feet
and 5040 citizens

perimeter of square
= 31,680 miles

circumference of circle
at Stonehenge =
316.8 feet

Circumference of inner circle
(Earth) = 24,883.2 miles

The New Jerusalem has:
12 gates
12 foundations
12 angels
12 jewels
12 pearls
12*12*12*12*12 =
248,832

perimeter of hexagon = 23,760 miles
actual distance Earth to Moon = 237,600 miles

Earth

diameter of Earth = 7920 miles
radius of Earth = 3960 miles
(this radius also = 31,680 furlongs)
Earth center to Moon center =
Earth radius + Moon radius = 5040 miles
distance from Syene to Alexandria = 5040 stades

Moon

diameter of moon
= 2160 miles
within outer circle
going through middle
radius = 1080 miles

side length of cube of New Jerusalem = 1500 miles = 7,920 thousand feet
Atantis' capital has rings of land and water - innermost island radius = 1500 feet
each quarter of Atantis' capital city has area = 3168 square stades

with the Earth's size because the New Jerusalem is not a golden city but a renewed golden age, a thinly veiled description of the New Earth. As Revelations 21:2 says: "And I saw the holy city, new Jerusalem, coming down out of heaven from God, made ready as a bride adorned for her husband." The New Jerusalem is the Earth and the Earth is the bride.

The preceding diagram is based on what John Michell calls "the New Jerusalem diagram" in *The Dimensions of Paradise*. Michell explains that the ratios of the Earth and Moon measurements have established the proportions for many systems of measurement, from before ancient Egypt on up to English units of measure—and that these divine measures are all related and used in the blueprints for many ancient temples like Plato's imaginary ideal city of Magnesia, Atlantis, Stonehenge, Glastonbury, and the New Jerusalem.

To clarify and emphasize an important point: past civilizations were extremely advanced, allowing our ancient ancestors to know precise measurements of the Earth, the Moon, and the Sun. They derived units of measure based on these heavenly bodies; not merely making measurements in units they already had, but redefining their scale of measure, creating a new (though ancient to us) measurement system based on astronomical and terrestrial distances. These measures are still meaningful in English units today because there are strict ratios (like 25/24ths) between Egyptian, Roman, Greek, and English systems. This is also true for measurements in ancient Mexico, Israel, Stonehenge, and quite possibly Atlantis. The same cannot be said for the metric system.

So it is by design, not coincidence, that there are 86,400 seconds in a day, that the sun is 864,000 miles across, and that 8,640,000,000 years pass by in one day and night of Brahma. These similarities are hints at relationships between the passage of time, the sun, and the ends of cycles brought on by the galactic center. These are also related to things measured with a number half their size: there are 43,200 seconds in a 12 hour night, 43,200 warriors in Valhalla, 43,200 stanzas in the "Rig Veda," and the Pyramid is a 1/43,200 scale model of the northern hemisphere of the earth.

The gematria of "Lord Jesus Christ" is 3168 and we can raise this number on an abacus (multiply it by ten) to get the 31,680 of the raised Jesus equal to the perimeter of squares and circles around the earth in regard to the New Jerusalem. The ancient texts are telling us that the raised Jesus—the winter solstice sun raised to the throne of the Most High at the galactic center—is linked to the new earth of the next pole shift. The earth's 24,883.2 mile circumference "raised" one level on an abacus to 248,832 equals the New Jerusalem's 12 gates * 12 foundations * 12 angels * 12 jewels * 12 pearls. These are clues, designed to make the wise seek patterns and relationships.

Many Christians believe that our world has had its surface features flooded and recreated before but that this upcoming event will be different; that the new Earth or New Jerusalem will be a final, separate, different, 1500 mile wide cube (or pyramid) for us to live in. Others make the argument that if a pole shift destroys our civilization then every chemical plant, every nuclear reactor, every toxic waste dump, every oil refinery, and a great many other bad things—will all be smashed and washed away, polluting the ground and the oceans so overwhelmingly that for the first time the planet will be rendered uninhabitable. Due to our advanced ability to create pollutants, we may need a new home away from Earth. Either way, Revelation 21:2 clarifies the world we will live in is the bride: "And I saw the holy city, new Jerusalem, coming down out of heaven from God, made ready as a bride adorned for her husband."

God the Father is the galactic center, the groom / the son is Jesus the winter solstice sun, and the bride is the Earth. The Earth has not "prepared herself" until after the pole shift and such disasters are clearly described in Matthew 24:29 as coming "immediately after the tribulation," which has not ended yet when Jesus comes on October 14, 2019. The same tribulation events are described as "Before the great and awesome day of the LORD" in Joel 2:31. The end of the tribulation is the start of the pole shift. The end of the pole shift and Judgment Day are both a week later on December 28, 2019.

So why does Jesus return on October 14? This failure for all events to line up on the same day was unexpected and troubling to this author. I should have realized from Isaiah 66:7 that Jesus returns and is symbolically reborn before the Earth has the birth pangs of a pole shift: "Before she travailed, she brought forth; Before her pain came, she gave birth to a boy." But early on I had not yet made that connection; years ago I remember approaching many Bible scholars with a conversation opener like: "I know you don't think anyone

2019

October	November	December
10/14		12/21 12/28

Jesus returns then 75 days judgment/wrath

Seven year tribulation ends
Weeklong Pole Shift begins

Judgment Day
Pole Shift Ends

can predict the exact timing of the end because in Matthew 24:36 'no one knows the day or the hour' but I think we can figure it out, and I have two different dates for the Second Coming and Judgment Day—why would Jesus come back and then not do anything for a few months? Why would Judgment Day not be the day Jesus arrives, which I always thought would be a really eventful day? Is there any good reason why I might be coming up with two dates that are months apart?" Now most of the very knowledgeable people I asked had no insights on this, but eventually one said: "Yes—if the two dates are exactly seventy-five days apart."

I thought for a few seconds and did some math in my head. "My two dates are exactly seventy-five days apart." He now had my complete attention. "Please do tell me more."

"In the book of Daniel," he said, "there are 1260 days, and 1290 days, and 1335 days. Between these different numbers there are thirty days of judgment and forty-five days of wrath."

More research led to several relevant quotes on this subject. Jewish rabbis tell us "Moses appeared to the Israelites, then disappeared, and eventually appeared once more, and the same peculiarity we have in connection with Messiah; He will appear, disappear, and appear again."[24] A more specific commentary in the Jewish Encyclopedia says "Like Moses, the Messiah will disappear for 90 or 45 days after his appearance."[25] Obviously there was disagreement on the exact timing. The 90 days could include the 75 days from birth to Judgment Day plus the preceding first half of the month of Tishri, starting with the traditional Tishri 1 date for the reign of a king, when astronomically Jesus is first seen in the womb of Virgo during the Great Sign of Revelations 12:1-2.

Several Christian writers seem to agree with the delay between my two dates as well: "No general resurrection or general judgment will immediately follow Christ's return."[26] "These additional 30 days and 45 days, which total a time of 75 more days, indicate that there will be an interim period between the second advent and the commencement of the millennial kingdom… Judgment of the nations follows the second advent and precedes the entrance of the saints into the kingdom."[27]

I was happy to be given the scriptural basis for my 75-day difference between my two astronomically determined dates, despite viewing the entire seven year tribulation as bad times and only the pole shift at the very end as God's wrath. Matthew 24:7-8 tells us "nation will rise against nation, and kingdom against kingdom, and in various places there will be famines and earthquakes. But all these things are merely the beginning of birth pangs." These are the initial signs of distress we see starting in 2012 as we approach the beginning of the tribulation. Regional wars, (maybe even World War III) scarce rain, hunger, major famine, and increasing earthquakes are bad enough—but far worse events will follow the return of Jesus in October 2019 as divine judgment and wrath begin in earnest. We may assume that the physical forces building up to a pole shift in December are already causing obvious problems by October.

Going back several topics to the astronomical realities in the fall of 2019, we covered the alignments through mid-October and how they fit perfectly with the descriptions in Revelations. Moving on to Revelations 12:4 "And his tail swept away a third of the stars of heaven and threw them to the earth. And the dragon stood before the woman who was about to give birth, so that when she gave birth he might devour her child." After the dragon stands near the woman as she is about to give birth, she eventually is finally giving birth in Revelations 12:5-6 "And she gave birth to a son, a male child, who is to rule all the nations with a rod of iron; and her child was caught up to God and to His throne." At this point the astronomical symbolism for Jesus transitions from the morning star back to his normal solar association. We are no longer concerned with an upcoming birth, so we are no longer drawn to compare Jesus with Venus.

At the moment of Jesus' birth on October 14 the sun/son appears roughly equidistant from Satan (Draco) and God (the galactic core.) Next the son is being "caught up to God and to His throne," which makes sense, because the sun progressively appears to move towards the galactic center for the next ten weeks. This movement of the sun towards the galactic center fits well with the descriptions of Jesus gradually moving towards God to take the scroll, approach his right hand, and join him on the throne. Matthais Reinhard Hoffman's doctoral dissertation touches on this progress through the book of Revelations, pointing out that Revelations 5:7 "clearly describes the Lamb as 'coming and taking' the scroll, which seems to indicate a certain distance from the throne before." He adds that "The communal sharing of the throne becomes defined more precisely between chapters 5 and 22" and that "The sharp distinction of describing only God as sitting on the throne in Apc 4-5 becomes less emphasized until the distinction is nearly dissolved in Apc 22:3."[28]

Then when Jesus/the sun approaches the throne in late December in Revelations 12:7-10 "There was war in heaven, Michael and his angels waging war with the dragon. The dragon and his angels waged war, and they were not strong enough, and there was no longer a place found for them in heaven. And the great dragon was thrown down, the serpent of old who is called the devil and Satan, who deceives the whole world; he was thrown down to the earth, and his angels were thrown down with him. Then I heard a loud voice in heaven, saying, 'Now the salvation, and the power, and the kingdom of our God and the authority of His Christ have come.'"

These passages describe events beginning December 21, 2019. This is exactly seven years after the end of the Mayan calendar, and it is the night before Hanukkah. Hanukkah begins on 12/22/19, which on the Hebrew calendar is the 25th day of the ninth month of Kislev. Haggai 2:18-22 tells us "from the four and twentieth day of the ninth month... I am going to shake the heavens and the earth... I will overthrow the thrones of kingdoms and destroy the power of the kingdoms." Kislev 24 is also the anniversary of the laying of the foundation of the Lord's Temple. This means that the day before Hanukkah starts, on the winter solstice, December 21, 2019— the pole shift which lays the foundations of the new world begins. Matthew 24:20-22 tells us to "pray that your flight will not be in the winter, or on a Sabbath. For then there will be a great tribulation, such as has not occurred since the beginning of the world until now." *December 21, 2019 is the first day of winter, and it is Saturday, the Sabbath. It is the night before Hanukkah on the twenty-fourth day of the ninth Hebrew month. It is also exactly seven years after the end of the Mayan calendar.* This tells us the seven year tribulation begins with the last day of the Mayan calendar on 12/21/2012.

Before we continue to cover the final week of the pole shift or GREAT tribulation from December 21-28, 2019, we need to address the idea of a pre-tribulation rapture. Many Christians assume there will be a pre-tribulation rapture that happens as the tribulation starts; this would mean December 21, 2012 would be the date of the rapture. But if the Earth is the bride, and the pole shift is the bride preparing herself, then any rapture of the bride will not occur until the pole shift is done. In that case the rapture would be on Judgment Day, and everyone has to suffer through the tribulation.

This author was not taught to expect a post-tribulation rapture. There are many passages which could be interpreted to indicate a pre-tribulation rapture, and it seems sensible that the faithful would be saved before such horrors, for why would Jesus make his bride go through such terrible events? But perhaps the pre-tribulation rapture is wishful thinking based on the idea that the church is the bride.

1 Thessalonians 5:9 tells us "God has not destined us for wrath, but for obtaining salvation." Many of us, including yours truly, interpreted this to mean that anyone who is saved would no longer be present on Earth during God's wrath. But perhaps it merely

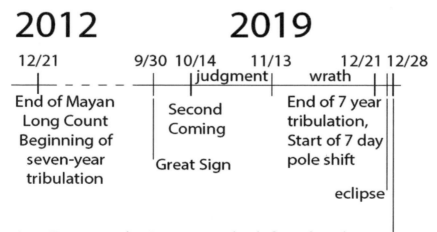

means that while salvation is what we were created for, sometimes people rebel and don't reach it. A general could tell a new soldier "You have not been trained for dying, but for obtaining victory." Yet not every soldier sees victory. As for the saved, they will still see salvation even if they do perish during God's wrath. They can also be present during the wrath, but be protected or hidden from it and not suffer the wrath. If they have not renounced God and taken the mark, the wrath is not directed at them. Luke 21:36 tells us "pray always, that ye may be accounted worthy to escape all these things that shall come to pass, and to stand before the Son of man." (KJB) John 17:15 also seems to indicate we will all be here on Earth during the tribulation and wrath, as Jesus says: "I do not ask You to take them out of the world, but to keep them from the evil one."

Those who believe in a pre-tribulation rapture assume that Jesus comes back twice in the end times, once before the tribulation to rescue the Church, taking them to heaven temporarily before returning seven years later. Other theories describe a mid-tribulation or pre-wrath rapture and require one or more "fly-by"'s in which Jesus comes near the Earth but does not come down to ground level. These all seem to conflict with the meaning of the Greek word "parousia" which is often translated into English as "coming." "Coming" is just a small part of the Greek concept. Parousia refers to the arrival of a visiting high official outside a city, at a point where the inhabitants show their respect by meeting him outside the city, and bringing him back to their city with them. This was a widespread tradition in the Middle East. Even today, if a famous visitor were coming to our house, we would probably not stand inside the door watching and waiting for them to knock; to show respect we would go out to their limousine and come back inside with them.

We mentioned such a parousia in Chapter One as the Roman historian Flavius Josephus described the arrival of Alexander the Great outside Jerusalem. Before Alexander came the high priest Jaddua had "a dream in which he was told to adorn the city, open its gates, command the populace to dress in white, and walk out to meet Alexander with the priests and the people. Upon seeing the resulting procession, Alexander advanced to meet the priests all by himself and saluted Jaddua. Parmenion then went up to Alexander and asked him why he did this and was told by Alexander that he had seen the same person in a dream when he was in Macedonia and had been exhorted by him to make no delay in invading Asia and told that he would be given dominion of Persia. Alexander next walked into the city with the priests, offered sacrifice at the Temple, and was shown the Book of Daniel and told that it indicates that a Greek would destroy the empire of the Persians."[29]

Of course, no less respect will be shown to Jesus at his parousia for that greatest of arrivals outside the New Jerusalem, the new home on the newly re-created Earth which He made for us when He was "at his father's house"—when the winter solstice sun is at the galactic center. We will greet him and welcome him at His own wedding. But parousia does involve his entrance, it is not a parousia if we meet him outside and go away with him. Parousia requires Jesus to completely descend, not to come close without landing. But a proper understanding of parousia (and the New Jerusalem) is far from the only support for the post-tribulational rapture. Let us review a few key passages:

Matthew 13:24-30 "Jesus presented another parable to them, saying, 'The kingdom of heaven may be compared to a man who sowed good seed in his field. But while his men were sleeping, his enemy came and sowed tares among the wheat, and went away. But when the wheat sprouted and bore grain, then the tares became evident also. The slaves of the landowner came and said to him, 'Sir, did you not sow good seed in your field? How then does it have tares?' And he said to them, 'An enemy has done this!' The slaves said to him, 'Do you want us, then, to go and gather them up?' But he said, 'No; for while you are gathering up the tares, you may uproot the wheat with them. Allow both to grow together until the harvest; and in the time of the harvest I will say to the reapers, "First gather up the tares and bind them in bundles to burn them up; but gather the wheat into my barn." The good wheat is not gathered first, the bad tares are burned first.

Matthew 13:36-43 is a great example of a "pesher," an interpretation, worded right into the text of the Bible itself. "His disciples came to Him and said, 'Explain to us the parable of the tares of the field.' And He said, 'The one who sows the good seed is the Son of Man, and the field is the world; and as for the good seed, these are the sons of the kingdom; and the tares are the sons of the evil one; and the enemy who sowed them is the devil, and the harvest is the end of the age; and the reapers are angels. So just as the tares are gathered up and burned with fire, so shall it be at the end of the age. The Son of Man will send forth His angels, and they will gather out of His kingdom all stumbling blocks, and those who commit lawlessness, and will throw them into the furnace of fire; in that place there will be weeping and gnashing of teeth. Then THE RIGHTEOUS WILL SHINE FORTH AS THE SUN in the kingdom of their Father. He who has ears, let him hear.'" The wise reader has initiated ears; he understands it is the lawless ones who are gathered for fire, *then* the righteous are rewarded.

1 Corinthians 15:51-52 "Behold, I tell you a mystery; we will not all sleep, but we will all be changed, in a moment, in the twinkling of an eye, at the last trumpet; for the trumpet will sound, and the dead will be raised imperishable, and we will be changed." This last trumpet is also what the seventh angel sounds in Revelations 11:15 when Christ has received his kingdom, after the tribulation.

Matthew 24:29-31 "But immediately after the tribulation of those days THE SUN WILL BE DARKENED, AND THE MOON WILL NOT GIVE ITS LIGHT, AND THE STARS WILL FALL from the sky, and the powers of the heavens will be shaken. And then the sign of the Son of Man will appear in the sky, and then all the tribes of the earth will mourn, and they will see the SON OF MAN COMING ON THE CLOUDS OF THE SKY with power and great glory. And He will send forth His angels with A GREAT TRUMPET and THEY WILL GATHER TOGETHER His elect from the four winds, from one end of the sky to the other." The great trumpet in Matthew 24 must be the same trumpet as in 1 Corinthians 15.

Joel 2:30-32 "I will display wonders in the sky and on the earth, Blood, fire and columns of smoke. The sun will be turned into darkness And the moon into blood Before the great and awesome day of the LORD comes. And it will come about that whoever calls on the name of the LORD Will be delivered; For on Mount Zion and in Jerusalem There will be those who escape, As the LORD has said, Even among the survivors whom the LORD calls." Surely the sun darkening in Matthew 24 after the tribulation is the same event which is before the day of the Lord in Joel 2.

Paul tells us the saints will be relieved only when Jesus is revealed in the wrath of heavenly fire with his angels in 2 Thessalonians 1:5-10 "This is a plain indication of God's righteous judgment so that you will be considered worthy of the kingdom of God, for which indeed you are suffering. For after all it is only just for God to repay with affliction those who afflict you, and to give relief to you who are afflicted and to us as well when the Lord Jesus will be revealed from heaven with His mighty angels in flaming fire, dealing out retribution to those who do not know God and to those who do not obey the gospel of our Lord Jesus. These will pay the penalty of eternal destruction, away from the presence of the Lord and from the glory of His power, when He comes to be glorified in His saints on that day."

Does a pre-tribulation rapture still make sense? Although that point of view is very popular in America today, it was not popular before the idea started about 200 years ago, and it is still not the dominant position outside the United States. Many great teachers have held the post-tribulation view, including Justin Martyr, Irenaeus, Tertullian, John Calvin, Martin Luther, Isaac Newton, and Adam Clarke—to name a few. There are good reasons to hold this post-tribulation view, despite its current lack of appeal. For one thing, Jesus warns us and describes early signs of the tribulation. We would not need such a description if we were not going to be here for these events:

Matthew 24:3 "And as He was sitting on the Mount of Olives, the disciples came to Him privately, saying, Tell us, when will these things be, and what will be the sign of Your coming, and of the end of the age?"

Matthew 24:6-8 "You will be hearing of wars and rumors of

wars. See that you are not frightened, for those things must take place, but that is not yet the end. For nation will rise against nation, and kingdom against kingdom, and in various places there will be famines and earthquakes. But all these things are merely the beginning of birth pangs." If the tribulation is going to occur after we are raptured, then why would Jesus have to warn us about such details?

We also know that halfway through the seven year tribulation the antichrist enters the rebuilt Temple and proclaims himself to be God. The following passage from 2 Thessalonians 2:1-4 tells us this is before the rapture: "With regard to the coming of our Lord Jesus Christ and our gathering together to Him, that you not be quickly shaken from your composure or be disturbed either by a spirit or a message or a letter as if from us, to the effect that the day of the Lord has come. Let no one in any way deceive you, for it will not come unless the apostasy comes first, and the man of lawlessness is revealed, the son of destruction, who opposes and exalts himself above every so-called god or object of worship, so that he takes his seat in the temple of God, displaying himself as being God." This passage indicates the Day of the Lord is not before the seven year tribulation.

Daniel 7:21-25 also tells us of the Antichrist "I kept looking, and that horn was waging war with the saints and overpowering them until the Ancient of Days came and judgment was passed... He will speak out against the Most High and wear down the saints of the Highest One, and he will intend to make alterations in times and in law; and they will be given into his hand for a time, times, and half a time" (three and a half years). These saints are not raptured away first, they endure the second half of the seven year tribulation on Earth, until judgment is passed.

Rumors regarding what is planned for these times have been circulating through many intelligence agencies in recent years and the details are far worse than you would imagine, even if you assume the Gerogia Guidestones' request to maintain humanity's population under 500,000,000 is significant. One source of mine who wants to be quoted as "HeKnowsTooMuch" tells me some early events, like the collapse of the dollar and economic chaos, were planned for around the end of December 2012 or early 2013. He says there are worse plans beyond that which will make the following images look hopeful by comparison. If there is economic collapse and social breakdown, someone has to step in to restore order (and seize power.) Have you heard rumors that our National Guard, police, and military forces have been focused on training for civil unrest, crowd control, and urban operations in recent years? There are many recently constructed detention facilities, and they weren't all built for nothing. The huge purchases of hollow point bullets and freeze-dried food for many government departments are also very significant. But "HeKnowsTooMuch" suspects that those in charge will bite off more than they can chew, and will not restore order and seize power so easily when they reemerge after hiding out through the initial chaos.

Another source I'll call "Black Ops Boss" or BOB independently verified everything "HeKnowsTooMuch" said (not that even the word of two such individuals truly verifies these details as facts) but BOB thinks the elite families can achieve their goals and he doesn't have any hope for the future. At a minimum, even if these stories are unfounded disinformation, such rumors are widespread amongst the crowd that does government dirty work under the radar. At the risk of sounding ridiculous and discrediting myself, I mention these details because the odds seem high, even from non-prophecy sources, that we should expect extremely bad events beginning approximately 12/21/2012. There are many additional details "HeKnowsTooMuch" would like me to describe here but they are not directly related to the scope of this book. Decide ahead of time how you might prepare, and how you should handle various possible developments.

Matthew 24:9 "Then they will deliver you to tribulation, and will kill you, and you will be hated by all nations because of My name." That doesn't sound like the faithful are avoiding the tribulation. "But the one who endures to the end, he will be saved." (Matthew 24:13) Luke 21:36 tells us to "But keep on the alert at all times, praying that you may have strength to escape all these things that are about to take place, and to stand before the Son of Man." This clarifies we will need strength to escape the terrible events and survive until the end. Suffering through such times will make some people think "my master is not coming for a long time" (Matthew 24:48) but we are warned only the evil servants think this, those who are enlightened are not expecting him before these tribulations. Revelations 2:10 clearly says "Do not fear what you are about to suffer. Be faithful until death, and I will give you the crown of life."

Matthew 24:15 " Therefore when you see the ABOMINATION OF DESOLATION which was spoken of through Daniel the prophet, standing in the holy place (let the reader understand)…" Here we are being given instructions on what we need to do when we see these tribulation signs. "Then those who are in Judea must flee to the mountains. Whoever is on the housetop must not go down to get the things out that are in his house. Whoever is in the field must not turn back to get his cloak." (Matthew 24:16-18) "…But pray that your flight will not be in the winter, or on a Sabbath. For then there will be a great tribulation, such as has not occurred since the beginning of the world until now." (Matthew 24:20-21) Jesus is telling us that on Saturday, the first day of winter in 2019, the GREAT tribulation of the pole shift begins. We should not try to gather our material possessions but we should run for high ground to avoid the tidal waves. Even then, just one week before Judgment Day, "Then if anyone says to you, 'Behold, here is the Christ,' or 'There He is,' do not believe him.'" (Matthew 24:23) Because even then it is not yet time for the rapture. In the northern hemisphere the week of the winter solstice has the shortest days of the year. "Unless those days had been cut short, no life would have been saved; but for the sake of the elect those days will be cut short." (Matthew 24:22) For whose sake? For the elect! The elect are still suffering on the Earth!

Jesus told us through his disciples: "But immediately after the tribulation of those days THE SUN WILL BE DARKENED, AND THE MOON WILL NOT GIVE ITS LIGHT, AND THE STARS WILL FALL from the sky, and the powers of the heavens will be shaken. And then the sign of the Son of Man will appear in the sky, and then all the tribes of the earth will mourn, and they will see the SON OF MAN COMING ON THE CLOUDS OF THE SKY with power and great glory. And He will send forth His angels with A GREAT TRUMPET and THEY WILL GATHER TOGETHER His elect from the four winds, from one end of the sky to the other." (Matthew 24:29-31) This clearly indicates Jesus gathers his elect after the dust clouds come, after the sun goes dark, after the pole shift makes the stars appear to fall—and after the tribulation. Jesus also tells us the rapture will be on the last day four times in the sixth chapter of John:

"This is the will of Him who sent Me, that of all that He has given Me I lose nothing, but raise it up on the last day." (John 6:39)

"For this is the will of My Father, that everyone who beholds the Son and believes in Him will have eternal life, and I Myself will raise him up on the last day". (John 6:40)

"No one can come to Me unless the Father who sent Me draws him; and I will raise him up on the last day." (John 6:44)

"He who eats My flesh and drinks My blood has eternal life, and I will raise him up on the last day." (John 6:54)

1 Thessalonians 4:15 says, "For this we say to you by the word of the Lord, that we who are alive and remain until the coming of the Lord, will not precede those who have fallen asleep." In John 11:21-24, Martha says to Jesus "if You had been here, my brother would not have died... [but] I know that he will rise again in the resurrection on the last day." Many things happen on that last day.

We know that December 28, 2019 is that last day, Judgment Day. We know the preceding week is the GREAT tribulation, following the seven year tribulation. Matthew 24:19-21 says "Woe to those who are pregnant and to those who are nursing babies in those days! But pray that your flight will not be in the winter, or on a Sabbath. For then there will be a great tribulation, such as has not occurred since the beginning of the world until now." This will start the night before Hanukkah begins, when Haggai 2:21 tells us God will "shake the heavens and the earth." This is December 21, 2019. It is Saturday, the Jewish Sabbath, and it is the first day of winter. It is also the last day of the seven year tribulation, and the first day of the pole shift. It may even mark the arrival of the galactic superwave. With all the radiation, death, and catastrophe going on at that time, pregnant women and babies are at great risk of death—but so is everybody else.

It sounds like God's glorious power has by this day reached out from the galactic center across 23,000 light-years of space. His holy spirit has finally reached our solar system with all the light and gravity waves and other forces necessary to crash and reboot the internal engines that control the normal function of the Sun and the Earth. The light of the sun goes out for three days while it appears to be near the galactic center, the dark rift of the Milky Way. Jesus was dead in the earth for parts of three days, and now the sun will appear to be dead for three days, just like the only sign we are told we will be given in Matthew 12:39-40 "An evil and adulterous generation craves for a sign; and yet no sign will be given to it but the sign of Jonah the prophet; for just as JONAH WAS THREE DAYS AND THREE NIGHTS IN THE BELLY OF THE SEA MONSTER, so will the Son of Man be three days and three nights in the heart of the earth."

The sun may appear dead for three days when in the "belly" of the Milky Way. It may be just as dark as when the sun is "underground" (between sunset and sunrise) and may seem like a 72 hour night. Could these 72 hours of darkness be the 72 companions of Set or the 72 Sanhedrin that conspire in the deaths of Osiris and Jesus? If the surface of the earth is shifting perhaps it simply is 72 hours of night, with a bright sun baking the opposite side of the planet for three days. We know Matthew is referring to a future occasion and the dates seem to be December 21-24, 2019. The sun appearing dead near the galactic center could also be what was seen in Revelations 5:6-8 "I saw between the throne (with the four living creatures) and the elders a Lamb standing, as if slain." The King James Bible reads: "in the midst of the throne... stood a Lamb as it had been slain." These will be scary times when, after years of famine, war, and persecution, civilization falls, the electricity and other utilities vanish, the earth is literally groaning beneath us as everything on the crust moves, there are earthquakes, volcanoes, and tidal waves, and for three of these terrible days we are in complete darkness. It may seem like the sun has been extinguished forever. It will feel like THE END and for most people it will be the end.

As the Maya described these events: the Hero Twins defeat Seven Macaw by shooting him out of his tree before they begin their attempts to resurrect their father, One Hunahpu, the winter solstice sun. The Hero Twins are the north and south poles leaving their posts (and they are also Venus and Jupiter.) Seven Macaw being shot off his tree axis is the same as our Satanic Draco falling from the northernmost point in the sky. The poles of the Earth move in an effort to resurrect the sun after the pole shift begins and Seven Macaw falls. One Hunahpu's head, the gameball, must move through the black hole goal ring at the center of the galaxy. The world tips over, there is a flood, and Bolon Yokte descends.

Could Bolon Yokte descending refer to the incoming cloud of cosmic dust from a galactic superwave? Could this be what is depicted in so many Mayan paintings where a black jaguar paw reaches out from behind the cosmic tree towards the scorpion? Could this be the "SON OF MAN COMING IN A CLOUD with power and great glory" as mentioned in Luke 21:27? If incoming cosmic dust makes our sun overheat and flare up like a T-Tauri star, then a significantly thicker corona could form. Isaiah 61:10 might be referencing the sun putting on a larger corona: "My soul will exult in my God; For He has clothed me with garments of salvation, He has wrapped me with a robe of righteousness, As a bridegroom decks himself with a garland." The NWT reads "like the bridegroom who, in a priestly way, puts on a headdress."

Isaiah 30:26 definitely tells us the sun will look bigger and brighter: "the light of the sun will be seven times brighter, like the light of seven days." A much larger corona could expand to eliminate the gap in the imperfect alignment between the sun and the galactic center. If this were to happen, and the edge of the sun were to overlap our line of sight with the galactic core as its ongoing gravity wave is still hitting us, the hot corona would suddenly scatter incoming graviton neutrinos and eliminate that huge gravitational tug. Do you remember our earlier example in which a hundred people are pulling you with ropes in a tug of war, and even one letting go might cause a noticeable jerk? Now imagine ten of them letting go simultaneously from the same side. You would lose balance and fall back the other way.

As British Cosmologist Fred Hoyle would tell us, the Mach Principle says that mass and gravity are dependent on everything else in the universe. If the component of gravity from the galactic center is suddenly scattered by the sun's corona and no longer reaches us, local solar system gravity increases, and the Earth would be jerked sunwards reflecting the new (very temporary) balance.[30]

If nothing else has already acted as the straw that broke the camel's back and sent Earth's crust in motion, a cosmic off switch capable of altering the planet's gravitational balance could certainly give us that final nudge. As the crust of the Earth starts moving, many stars appear to fall out of the sky. The stars near the North Pole (like Draco) have nowhere to go but down—away from their high spot near the celestial North Pole. Some hours later, Hanukkah begins, and the true meaning of the dreidel sinks in. A harmless holiday children's toy, this spinning top with four sides also represents the four cardinal directions and zodiac signs, and the wobbling precession of the Earth's axis, which ends its cycle by falling over. We should also consider the numerical values (gematria) of the four letters on the dreidel's sides, for "nun, gimmel, hey, shin" in gematria add up to 358, which is also the numerical equivalent of the Hebrew word "mashiach"— Messiah!

The drama of heavenly battle rages on even after the light of the new sun reappears on December 24. This should be in the middle of the pole shift, or as Matthew 19:28 says: "in the regeneration when the Son of Man will sit on His glorious throne." We know the throne the sun has reached is God's throne at the galactic center. In a few days Jupiter will line up behind the sun (from our point of view on Earth) but before Jupiter even reaches the sun to anoint or coronate Him (Jesus, the sun) as king, a solar eclipse should be visible over parts of the Middle East. There is rarely a better astronomical vision of the battle between darkness and light than the moon temporarily blotting out the sun. Of course, in an eclipse, light always wins, and the sun always reemerges. As the sun rises over Jerusalem on December 26 Israelis should observe the last minutes of the eclipse before the moon no longer covers the sun at all. I use the word should, because the above descriptions fit mainstream expectations for what should be visible on those dates—but if a pole shift began several days earlier, the surface of the globe would be in an unpredictable position, and all bets are off for where the eclipse is visible.

Until God begins to intervene directly; until Jesus is enthroned and given authority and kingdom, his powers are restrained. But eventually Jesus is empowered. And as Jesus is the sun, it is our sun that the galactic core eventually gives more active powers to. We know the galactic center will be in an active, bright blue Seyfert phase, because we are told in Ezekiel 1:26 that "over their heads there was something resembling a throne, like lapis lazuli in appearance; and on that which resembled a throne, high up, was a

A dreidel spinning at approximately fifty rotations per second starts to wobble as its axis begins an unstable counter-rotation like the precession of the Earth's axis.

figure with the appearance of a man." The King James Bible reads "above the firmament that was over their heads was the likeness of a throne, as the appearance of a sapphire stone: and upon the likeness of the throne was the likeness as the appearance of a man above upon it." We know the throne is at the galactic center. What most people don't know is that standing above the galactic center is the "13th zodiac constellation" of Ophiuchus.

It does not have an astronomical "sign" as it overlaps Sagittarius and Scorpio, but it is a major constellation on the band of the ecliptic/zodiac. Most important to us is that Ophiuchus is depicted as a man, and not just any man, but a man wrestling a serpent. He battles the serpent like Apollo's famous battle with Python at the navel of the world, or Horus' epic battle with Set, and may represent Jesus fighting Satan. He is also suffering a bite to his heel from Scorpio, the scorpion constellation associated with Death—and this all takes place right above the galactic center. Genesis 3:15 comments on Jesus and Satan fighting much like Ophiuchus astronomically depicts this: "He shall bruise you on the head, And you shall bruise him on the heel." We in the northern hemisphere rarely get to see Ophiuchus because at this point in the precessional cycle, the sun blinds us to the constellation when it is positioned high in our sky around December. This is how the great astronomer Johannes

Kepler drew Ophiuchus in 1604:

If the sun goes dark for three days we could, just as Ezekiel 1:26 tells us, suddenly see the sign of the son of man standing above the sapphire blue throne of the galactic center. Matthew 24:30 tells us "And then the sign of the Son of Man will appear in the sky, and then all the tribes of the earth will mourn, and they will see the SON OF MAN COMING ON THE CLOUDS OF THE SKY with power and great glory." And Matthew 16:27 tells us that "the Son of Man is going to come in the glory of His Father with His angels." (A few online references claim the "sign of the son of man" is Jupiter in Scorpio, and while Jupiter will be in Scorpio in late 2019, this happens almost every decade, and is not an important alignment.) We know one of these angels was Venus, and another will soon be Jupiter, for on December 27-28 Jupiter is behind the sun, and in Revelations 19:17 we are told: "I saw an angel standing in the sun."

By this point the galactic center's active Seyfert phase should be visible, eventually becoming brighter than anything else in the sky. We could start to see what various ancient peoples referred to as the Heart of Heaven, the seat of Brahma or the navel of Vishnu, the Blue Star Kachina, the Eye of Ra or the Eye of Horus, the Shekinah Glory, the Aztec's "Place of Light Where He-who-gives-light Hides Himself"[31] or the surprisingly modern description from the Fiote tribe of Africa's Loango Coast: "a huge star which, once, shone brighter from the sky than the Sun."[32] The burst of radiation and gravity waves could wreak havoc on the Sun and the Earth. We already know the sun will go dark and then light up again a few days later, probably with a reversed magnetic field and huge solar flares and coronal mass ejections, some of which could scorch the Earth.

As we are told in the Mayan "Chilam Balam": "When the Great Serpent was stolen, the firmament collapsed and the earth sank. The four gods, the Four Bacab leveled everything. At the moment when the leveling was finished, they were secured in their places... the fire of the sun was revived, his face approached and he burned the Earth..."

More than likely the sun will be far brighter than before when it first lights up again, and should also be spewing out the extra infrared, ultraviolet, and X-ray radiation typical of T-Tauri stars surrounded by the arriving dust cloud. This assumes that massive amounts of cosmic dust are pushed into our solar system by the wavefront from the galactic center, which also temporarily crashes the magnetospheres of the sun and planets, and prevents the formation of solar wind that normally keeps most dust away. On Earth, we should expect not only incoming clouds of acidic cosmic dust (described in the past as mist, spittle, poison, venom, and congealment) but also a crash and reversal of the planet's magnetic field, and a complete pole shift—a crustal displacement.

This pole shift will move the current polar locations of the Arctic and Antarctic to lower latitudes, where their ice will melt, and new ice ages will start new ice caps in new polar regions, quite possibly centered near Mongolia and Chile. The entire planet will experience massive tidal waves, earthquakes, volcanic eruptions, the end of technological civilization, darkness, and cold. Yes, cold—for just as the temperature tends to fall over a typical night without sunlight—often by about two or three degrees per hour—it might get pretty cold after three days without sunlight. These judgments/trumpets/seals/bowls of problems will kill off the overwhelming majority of the population (which was probably already devastated by World War III, famine, disease, and brutal dictatorship.) After an already nasty seven years of tribulation, those people who were left probably will not survive the maelstrom of cosmic and terrestrial disasters, and even if they do, they will probably never see electricity, doctors, grocery stores or many of the other benefits of civilization again. As for the natural disasters, a few of the most relevant Bible passages are quoted below:

Job 9:5-7 "It is God who removes the mountains, they know not how, When He overturns them in His anger; *Who shakes the earth out of its place, And its pillars tremble*; Who commands the sun not to shine, And sets a seal upon the stars."

Job 38:13-14 "That it might take hold of the ends of the earth, And the wicked be shaken out of it? It is changed like clay under the seal."

Job 38:37 The NWT reads: "*the water jars of heaven, who can tip [them] over, When the dust pours out* as into a molten mass"? The NASB reads: "Who can… tip the water jars of the heavens, When the dust hardens into a mass"?

Psalms 18:9 "He bowed the heavens also, and came down With thick darkness under His feet."

Psalms 46:2 "though the earth should change And though the mountains slip into the heart of the sea."

Isaiah 6:11-13 "Then I said, 'Lord, how long?' And He answered, 'Until cities are devastated and without inhabitant, Houses are without people And the land is utterly desolate, 'The LORD has removed men far away, And the forsaken places are many in the midst of the land. 'Yet there will be a tenth portion in it, And it will again be subject to burning."

Isaiah 13:13 "*I will make the heavens tremble, And the earth will be shaken from its place* At the fury of the LORD."

Isaiah 22:25 "*'In that day,' declares the LORD of hosts, 'the peg driven in a firm place will give way; it will even break off and fall, and the load hanging on it will be cut off.'*"

Isaiah 24:1-6 "*the LORD lays the earth waste, devastates it, distorts its surface and scatters its inhabitants… The earth will be completely laid waste* and completely despoiled, for the LORD has spoken this word. The earth mourns and withers, the world fades and withers, the exalted of the people of the earth fade away. The earth is also polluted by its inhabitants, for they transgressed laws, violated statutes, broke the everlasting covenant. Therefore, a curse devours the earth, and those who live in it are held guilty. Therefore, the inhabitants of the earth are burned, and few men are left."

Isaiah 24:18-20 "*the foundations of the earth shake. The earth is broken asunder, The earth is split through, The earth is shaken violently. The earth reels to and fro like a drunkard.*"

Isaiah 30:25-26 "*on the day of the great slaughter, when the towers fall. The light of the moon will be as the light of the sun, and the light of the sun will be seven times brighter*, like the light of seven days, on the day the LORD binds up the fracture of His people and heals the bruise He has inflicted."

Jeremiah 4:23-28 "I looked on the earth, and behold, it was

formless and void; And to the heavens, and they had no light. I looked on the mountains, and behold, they were quaking, And all the hills moved to and fro. I looked, and behold, there was no man, And all the birds of the heavens had fled. I looked, and behold, the fruitful land was a wilderness, And all its cities were pulled down Before the LORD, before His fierce anger. For thus says the LORD, 'The whole land shall be a desolation, Yet I will not execute a complete destruction.'"

Jeremiah 25:33 "Those slain by the LORD on that day will be from one end of the earth to the other. They will not be lamented, gathered or buried; they will be like dung on the face of the ground."

Ezekiel 32:7 "And when I extinguish you, I will cover the heavens and darken their stars; I will cover the sun with a cloud And the moon will not give its light."

Amos 9:6 "He who calls for the waters of the sea And pours them out on the face of the earth, The LORD is His name."

Zephaniah 2:5 *"Woe to the inhabitants of the seacoast… there will be no inhabitant."*

Luke 21:25-27 "There will be signs in sun and moon and stars, and on the earth dismay among nations, in perplexity at the roaring of the sea and the waves, men fainting from fear and the expectation of the things which are coming upon the world; for the powers of the heavens will be shaken. Then they will see THE SON OF MAN COMING IN A CLOUD with power and great glory."

Hebrews 12:26 *"YET ONCE MORE I WILL SHAKE NOT ONLY THE EARTH, BUT ALSO THE HEAVEN."*

Revelations 2:17 "To him who overcomes, to him I will give some of the hidden manna, and I will give him a white stone, and a new name written on the stone which no one knows but he who receives it." As when Abram became Abraham, Jacob became Israel, and Simon became Peter, such a God-given name change implies that Jesus and the sun have a new identity for an important new role. This is certainly the Mayan view: "For a king, accession to rulership was a kind of rebirth into a new identity." And they drew this as the sun emerging from the mouth of an animal like the cosmic caiman that represents the central bulge of the Milky Way.[33]

Revelations 6:12-13 "I looked when He broke the sixth seal, and *there was a great earthquake; and the sun became black as sackcloth made of hair, and the whole moon became like blood; and the stars of the sky fell to the earth,* as a fig tree casts its unripe figs when shaken by a great wind."

Revelations 8:5 *"Then the angel took the censer and filled it with the fire of the altar, and threw it to the earth;* and there followed peals of thunder and sounds and flashes of lightning and an earthquake."

Revelations 8:8 "The second angel sounded, and something like a great mountain burning with fire was thrown into the sea."

Revelations 8:10-11 "The third angel sounded, and a great star fell from heaven, burning like a torch, and it fell on a third of the rivers and on the springs of waters. The name of the star is called Wormwood; and a third of the waters became wormwood, and many men died from the waters, because they were made bitter."

Revelations 9:1-11 "Then the fifth angel sounded, and I saw a star from heaven which had fallen to the earth; and the key of the bottomless pit was given to him. *He opened the bottomless pit, and smoke went up out of the pit, like the smoke of a great furnace; and the sun and the air were darkened by the smoke* of the pit. Then out of the smoke came locusts upon the earth, and power was given them, as the scorpions of the earth have power… and their torment was like the torment of a scorpion when it stings a man… They have tails like scorpions, and stings; and in their tails is their power to hurt men for five months. They have as king over them, the angel of the abyss; his name in Hebrew is Abaddon, and in the Greek he has the name Apollyon."

Revelations 16:8 *"The fourth angel poured out his bowl upon the sun,* and it was given to it to scorch men with fire."

Revelations 16:18-20 "and there was a great earthquake, such as there had not been since man came to be upon the earth, so great an earthquake was it, and so mighty… and the cities of the nations fell… And every island fled away, and the mountains were not found."

Revelations 18:21 "Then a strong angel took up a stone like a great millstone and threw it into the sea, saying, 'So will Babylon, the great city, be thrown down with violence, and will not be found any longer.'"

Revelations 19:7-8 *"the marriage of the Lamb has come and His bride has made herself ready.* It was given to her to clothe herself in fine linen, bright and clean." The English words "has come" in 19:7 is a translation of the Greek "elthen," which indicates that the event is about to start, but has not started yet—which makes sense as the bride just became ready.

By December 28, Jesus/the sun has been coronated by Jupiter and the bride/Earth has prepared herself via pole shift with the "mikvah" ritual bathing/cleansing of the oceans flooding the nations and a set of new clothes/the new arrangement of the surface of the Earth. (As Job 38:14 reads in Young's Literal Translation: "To take hold on the skirts of the earth, And the wicked are shaken out of it, It turneth itself as clay of a seal And they station themselves as clothed.")

Revelations 19:17 "I saw an angel standing in the sun, and he cried out with a loud voice, saying to all the birds which fly in midheaven, 'Come, assemble for the great supper of God.'"

By the time this angel is standing in the sun, the destruction of the Earth as we knew it is almost complete. We have already established that the planet Venus is referred to as an angel. Matthew 13:38-40 tells us "the field is the world... the harvest is the end of the age; and the reapers are angels. So just as the tares are gathered up and burned with fire, so shall it be at the end of the age." If planets can be angels, and reapers are angels, then planets can be reapers of the final harvest. The king of planets—Jupiter—goes directly behind the sun from December 27-28, 2019. (Saturn does the same thing 17 days later, from January 13-14.) The first of these alignments of the largest planets behind the sun (with Jupiter) could be what Revelations 19:17 refers to with "an angel standing in the sun."

Backtracking slightly, Revelations 14:14 tells us there is "a white cloud, and sitting on the cloud was one like a son of man, having a golden crown on His head and a sharp sickle in His hand." The white cloud is probably the central bulge of the Milky Way, and the sun is at the center of the Milky Way, with the constellation Ophiuchus in the figure of a son of man wrestling a serpent and stepping on Scorpio with his heel. A lot of celestial bodies are gathered near the sun right now. The crown could be the larger than normal coronal crown emphasized by the solar eclipse that ends early on December 26. The sharp sickle in his hand could be Jupiter approaching the sun. With the dust cloud likely to be in our solar system at this point, all planets could have a visible tail of dust illuminating their magnetosphere, and Jupiter's could be briefly visible as sunset ends on December 26. It might look like a sickle.

Revelations 14:15 "And another angel came out of the temple, crying out with a loud voice to Him who sat on the cloud, 'Put in your sickle and reap, for the hour to reap has come, because the harvest of the earth is ripe.'" The moon emerges from in front of the sun on December 26 but the reaping has not yet taken place, as Jupiter has not yet touched the sun and empowered him with kingship. If Jupiter touching the sun is what finally brings Judgment Day then this sickle has not been put in to the sun yet. Of course the next day, on December 27, Jupiter finally touches the sun, and moves out from behind it (having now coronated the sun) on December 28.

As Jupiter appears to hover around the edge of the sun at the end of our week-long pole shift, we should also be reminded of one of the final traditions of an ancient Jewish wedding ceremony. After the bride and groom have spent a week together in the huppah, the bridal chamber, the invited guests waiting outside know the week is over and are ready for them to come out. When they are waiting outside for the door to open and for the wedding banquet to begin— it is customary that the groom's friend hovers near the door, waiting to hear a knock from inside as the groom will knock and then announce to his friend that the wedding couple is ready to come out and be officially introduced as man and wife. As John 3:29 tells us the "friend of the bridegroom, who stands and hears him, rejoices greatly because of the bridegroom's voice." With great fanfare the friend of the groom opens the door and the invited guests celebrate and cheer.

In theory Jupiter is Elijah, who comes before the Messiah and anoints him and acts as the friend of the bridegroom. But Moses, the friend or attendant of the bride, should also be present. Moses prepared the bride for the wedding, helping her get ready by providing us with the Old Testament. Since Moses' role is similar to Elijah's, and Elijah is Jupiter, perhaps Moses is Saturn. This second largest planet is most like Jupiter. As a friend and attendant of the bride (the Earth) the moon also comes to mind; but the moon has moved almost thirty degrees away from the sun since the eclipse ended two days before 12/28/2019. Moses' role as a wedding party attendant means that Elijah and Moses are in similar roles and Jupiter and Saturn are very similar. Saturn is also the only planet with visible rings, and such a ring-bearer would be appropriate at our heavenly wedding.

Sure enough a quick online search for any astronomical associations for Moses leads to "Moses, the Lawgiver on Mount Sinai, is Saturn in Capricorn." On December 28, 2019 Saturn is between Capricorn and Sagittarius but is much closer to Sagittarius. Not a perfect fit... Unless we consider that as far as astrologers are concerned Capricorn lasts from December 22 into January and therefore Saturn, on December 28, can be considered Saturn "in Capricorn." Further research shows that Saturn is probably "the queen of heaven" mentioned in Jeremiah 7:18 and 44:17 and especially 44:25, where there is an association with wedding vows. It makes sense that if Jupiter is traditionally the "King of Heaven" then the other bridal party attendant would be the queen. In Amos 5:26 Saturn is mentioned through its Assyrian/Persian name Kewan (or Kaiwan) and this may even be the original root of the European words for "queen." It may also be relevant that the two witnesses Jesus grants authority to in Revelations 11:3 are also called lampstands (planets) in verse 11:4.

We know Jesus is the sun. The sun appears to die and then a few days later is reborn brighter than we have ever seen it before. This is the transfiguration mentioned in Matthew 17:2-3 "He was transfigured before them; and His face shone like the sun, and His garments became as white as light. And behold, Moses and Elijah appeared to them, talking with Him." Of course the groom's best friends who helped prepare the wedding will be close to him, talking to him, and celebrating with him at his wedding banquet—just as it would be at many weddings today, where such close friends would be seated at the head table near the bride and groom.

Revelations 14:16 "Then He who sat on the cloud swung His sickle over the earth, and the earth was reaped." As our planet should be rotating off course at this point, having just suffered the fastest motion of the pole shift, it may very well look like the entire sky, sickle included, is being swung over us as we are reaped.

Revelations 14:17 "And another angel came out of the temple which is in heaven, and he also had a sharp sickle." Jupiter is the only planet emerging from the sun at this point, though Saturn is nearby and will also go behind the sun in early January. Perhaps the temple refers to a larger area in the sky than just the sun, like the Egyptian "Duat" region of the sky. Perhaps the temple is referring to an area around the sun including the dust cloud, the galactic center throne of God, and the sign of the Son of Man, in which case Saturn is in the area. Saturn is often represented as old man Time, holding a sickle, finishing things up as the Grim Reaper at the end of time. So two sickles are in the sky, the son of man holds one, (Jupiter/Elijah) and another angel nearby holds another sickle (Saturn/Moses.)

In Revelations 14:18 "Then another angel, the one who has power over fire, came out from the altar; and he called with a loud voice to him who had the sharp sickle, saying, 'Put in your sharp sickle and gather the clusters from the vine of the earth, because her grapes are ripe.'" The altar is the sun, and Jupiter has authority, and emerges from the sun 12/28/2019. (Assuming the sun's corona has not expanded considerably from the dusty T-Tauri phase, Jupiter comes out from behind the sun on December 28. If the sun has expanded, it is possible that other planets are close enough to be described this way too; for example Saturn will be just over ten degrees from the sun's normal edge by December 28, and Mercury, which could be the angel with power over fire, will only be about five and a half degrees from the sun.) These angels with sickles arrive for the final reaping of the harvest of men from the face of the Earth.

The angel standing in the sun is Jupiter on December 28. Jesus Christ is the winter solstice sun, just like One Hunahpu and Horus of the Two Horizons. In 33 A.D. the winter solstice sun's position in the sky was between Sagittarius and Capricorn. At that point Jesus had not yet paid the bride price, or proceeded to his father's house at the galactic center, or prepared a new place for his bride, and he had emptied himself certain divine abilities, so he could not tell us the day or the hour. But now the winter solstice sun has experienced two millennia of precession, he has gone to his father's house at the galactic center, and through a pole shift starting on the winter solstice a new home is built for the bride. The activity of the sun is crucial in initiating the pole shift, through which the Earth—the bride prepares herself. Then the weeklong pole shift finally ends; the bridegroom sun has prepared a new living space for his bride, and the earthly bride has washed herself and prepared new outer garments. The wedding ceremony, which traditionally was a week-long event, can be completed. The sun has returned and wears a golden crown, holding Jupiter as a sickle, with Saturn's sickle nearby. The Earth is reaped on that day. The royal scepter of Jupiter touches our sun-god Jesus and anoints him as king. Jupiter is "the scepter of Your kingdom" mentioned in Psalms 45:6 in the song celebrating the king's marriage, also "the scepter of His kingdom" in Hebrews 1:8.

The awakening sun responds to the energizing dust cloud by entering a T-Tauri stage, blasting away the veil of dust (apocalypse means removal of the veil) with massive flares and coronal mass ejections. As described in Hindu myth: "Vishnu begins the terrible last work by pouring his infinite energy into the sun… With its fierce, devouring rays he draws into himself the eyesight of every animate being… Finally, in the form of a great cloud, Vishnu sheds a torrential rain."[34] In the Bible, Revelations 1:7 tells us "Behold, He is coming with the clouds, and every eye will see Him." 2 Peter 3:7 also tells us: "by His word the present heavens and earth are being reserved for fire, kept for the day of judgment."

To those who are unfamiliar with Jupiter's portrayal through mythology, the idea that Jupiter is needed, like Elijah, to anoint the Messiah or crown him king may seem quite a stretch. But for citizens of the Roman Empire, like the Jews of the first century A.D., everyone knew that Jupiter was considered the most powerful planet, the lord of the heavens, and that Roman culture attributed to Jupiter power over any great changes in the heavens and on Earth. A good example of this concept is shown on an old Roman coin, one of which was listed for sale on the internet with the  description: "Emperor standing right, holding sceptre surmounted by eagle, receiving globe from Jupiter standing left, holding scepter."[35] So on this coin the Roman Emperor, associated with the sun, receives the Earth and power over it from Jupiter and his scepter, when they are near each other, touching. Likewise Jesus, associated with the Sun, will receive the Earth as a bride, with Jupiter acting as best man, when Jesus receives kingship at his wedding.

Not only is Jupiter known in astrology as the scepter, and as the King of Planets, but Jupiter is also associated with Melchizedek, the most outlandishly described priest in the Bible.

Hebrews 6:20-7:3 tells us that "Jesus has entered as a forerunner for us, having become a high priest forever according to the order of Melchizedek. For this Melchizedek, king of Salem, priest of the Most High God... was first of all, by the translation of his name, king of righteousness, and then also king of Salem, which is king of peace. Without father, without mother, without genealogy, having neither beginning of days nor end of life, but made like the Son of God, he remains a priest perpetually." One would think Christianity would put more emphasis on this character Melchizedek, who is "made like the Son of God," and is also fatherless, motherless, and "without genealogy, having neither beginning of days nor end of life." But the Bible says very little about him. Since Melech is the Hebrew word for king, and tzedek is the word for righteousness, his name could translate as King of Righteousness. But Zedek is the word for the planet Jupiter, so he also translates to King Jupiter, the king of planets. When we are told that Jesus has become a high priest "according to the order of Melchizedek," perhaps it means that King Jupiter anointed the sun as king.

Revelations 19:17-18 says "I saw an angel standing in the sun, and he cried out with a loud voice, saying to all the birds which fly in midheaven, 'Come, assemble for the great supper of God, so that you may eat the flesh of kings and the flesh of commanders and the flesh of mighty men and the flesh of horses and of those who sit on them and the flesh of all men, both free men and slaves, and small and great.'" Jupiter is the angel standing in the sun, and the corpses for vultures everywhere certainly indicates many dead.

Revelations 20 describes the odd fact that Satan will be cast into the Abyss, but only for a thousand years, after which he must be released to cause trouble again. Revelations 20:1-7 "Then I saw an angel coming down from heaven, holding the key of the abyss and a great chain in his hand. And he laid hold of the dragon, the serpent of old, who is the devil and Satan, and bound him for a thousand years; and he threw him into the abyss, and shut it and sealed it... until the thousand years were completed... When the thousand years are completed, Satan will be released from his prison." If these end times events are so all-encompassing and final, why would Satan need to be released again?

One possibility is that the thousand years is the duration of the galactic center's active (Seyfert) phase. Revelations 21:3 reads "Behold, the tabernacle of God is among men, and He will dwell among them." As the galactic center represents God, this new bright source of light at the throne of heaven could be viewed as God showing himself and being with us; as opposed to His normal hidden phase. Since the constellation Ophiuchus represents the Son of Man and the serpent, and the bright galactic center just below Ophiuchus hides the serpent in its light, we will see it (Satan) again when the galactic center reverts back its normal state as an invisible black hole. This would also explain Zechariah 14:4 "In that day His feet will stand on the Mount of Olives, which is in front of Jerusalem on the east." Ophiuchus will be in the east just above the sun, so the view from Jerusalem will have this constellation "standing" on the Mount of Olives.

Others assume "the millennium is an indefinitely long period of time, perhaps much longer than a literal thousand years."[36] The "millennium" could be the entire duration of a new world age. Satan being bound for a long time may only mean that after all hell is done breaking loose during a pole shift, the earth enjoys a very long period of rest—until the next pole shift. This idea is supported by ancient Jewish beliefs on the duration of the coming Messianic Kingdom: "There are various views regarding the duration of this kingdom, and there is considerable confusion in traditional literature on this point...." [Some think it lasts far longer than 1,000 years]... "even for 7,000 years. In the opinion of others its period is to equal the time from the creation of the world, or else from Noah, to the 'present' day."[37] 7,000 years, or the time from creation to today, would mean that the "Messianic kingdom" is simply a new golden age in the post-pole shift world of the new earth.

For those who have survived the disasters of late 2019, there is great happiness as the Earth and Sun return to their normal inactivity. Daniel 12:12-13 tells us "blessed is he who keeps waiting and attains to the 1,335 days! But as for you, go your way to the end; then you will enter into rest and rise again for your allotted portion at the end of the age." There are multiple fulfillments of this duration of 1335. Assuming the 1335 "days" are 45 "days" more than the 1290 "days" that (interpreted in the first case as years) got us to 1967, then 45 years later we reach 2012. By this point the seven year tribulation starts, the Earth's first birth pangs become obvious, and we can, with a healthy mix of fear and happiness, anticipate the end of the current system of things within seven years. That gives us hope that we can make it to the end and experience all these wondrous events like the Second Coming and the rapture.

But once we are in the second half of the seven year tribulation, there are additional time frames for which we should view the 1260, 1290, and 1335 counts as literal days. When the 1260 days end on October 14, 2019 it is the Second Coming. The next thirty days which bring us to day 1290 on November 13 encompass 30 days of judgment. The next forty-five days of wrath, including the pole shift, bring us to day 1335 on 12/28/2019: Judgment Day.

Revelations 19:9 says "Blessed are those who are invited to the marriage supper of the Lamb." In ancient Jewish weddings, the bride and groom spent seven days being alone together, during which the bride remains veiled. Then they come out of the special "Huppah" room and join their guests, the "children of the bridal chamber," for a very festive marriage feast, at which the bride is unveiled. In terms of the end times, there is a weeklong pole shift started by galactic core activity which also temporarily extinguishes the sunlight by blasting cosmic dust into our solar system. By December 28, 2019 the dust has led to T-Tauri conditions in the sun, Jupiter goes behind the sun's disk, the sun is king, and its built up energy trapped in the dust reaches a critical point and the sun sends out enormous solar flares that blow out the dust, unveiling our planet. This is the apocalypse, the "removal of the veil" of dust.

We have made many comparisons between the astronomical events of the end times and an ancient Jewish wedding ceremony without focusing on all the details of the wedding in order. Modern Jewish wedding ceremonies have undoubtedly incorporated some aspects of foreign cultural traditions during the thousands of years the Jews have spent outside their ancestral home. But many wedding traditions remain intact and are quite relevant to our interpretation of Bible prophecy. A comprehensive comparison of such wedding traditions with the astronomical events of late 2019 shows several impressive correlations.

After the marriage-to-be is arranged the groom pays the "mohar" ("the bride price") as a dowry. Jesus paid with his life in 33 A.D.

The groom typically went to his father's house to build a room or addition in which the married couple will live after the father of the groom says it is ready. This generally takes a maximum of two years. For our wedding in the sky involving the divine family the time frame is multiplied a thousand-fold; Christians have been waiting just under 2,000 years. (If this multiplication is valid, then the maximum allowable wait of 2,000 years means the Second Coming would have to occur by 2033 at the latest.) In this time the winter solstice sun/Jesus has, through precession, approached His father's house at the galactic center. This alignment has been ongoing since 1998, so there has been ample time to work on the new living quarters.

Because only the father of the groom decides when it is time for the groom to get his bride, the bride is expected to keep herself ready so that she is not caught unprepared when her groom does eventually surprise her "like a thief in the night." Of course, this surprise factor doesn't really apply to us or to the bride of a loving groom, for he traditionally sends a friend towards her (father's) house to make a ruckus, blow a trumpet, and otherwise attract attention to the fact that her groom is about to show up soon.

This corresponds to Elijah/John the Baptist, who must come before the Messiah; and it also corresponds to The Feast of Trumpets, the first of Tishri, the Jewish new year of Rosh Hashanah - which will be September 30, 2019, just two weeks before the arrival of the Messiah on October 14. The first of Tishri is the day Jews recognize kingship; it is a day of trumpet blasts, and the astronomical positions that day are fitting. Jupiter/the best man is close to the galactic center/Father's house (where the sun will be when He picks up His bride) announcing the soon to come arrival of the Sun/Jesus/ groom who is heading in that direction. The Sun is at Virgo's chest level, the Moon is at her feet, the royal/kingly constellation of Leo is above her head, and Venus/the Morningstar is near Spica at the level of her womb.

This fits Revelations 12:1-2 "And a great sign appeared in heaven: a woman clothed with the sun, and the moon under her feet, and on her head a crown of twelve stars; and she was with child; and she cried out, being in labor and in pain to give birth." The Second Coming will occur two weeks later on the Feast of Tabernacles, the Feast day when many Christian scholars expect it, when the morning star has dropped from the Virgin's womb to her feet, (is born) and the sun is at Spica, the bread of the Virgin, Bethulah-lehem. But Daniel tells us there are months of judgment and wrath before the pole shift/wedding and Judgment Day, leaving plenty of time for our astronomical wedding.

Kabbalat Panim: before a Jewish wedding starts, the bride and groom host separate celebrations, as they must stay apart and not see each other right before the ceremony. Astronomically, we can't see the Earth in the sky near the sun because we are on the Earth, so they do appear to be separate. The moon, the guard (shomeret) and attendant of the Earth/bride, appears to spend 12/18-12/21/2019 in Virgo, with the Virgin Bride. Of course the moon actually closely orbits the Earth. While the bride has only one attendant, the groom usually chooses two friends as witnesses, though one is higher ranking as the official shomer. Jupiter/Elijah/John the Baptist/the best man/shomer and Moses/Saturn are the two witnesses.

Jewish tradition tells us the bride is guided by Moses; this fits with the Christian idea that we are the bride and that Moses helped get us ready for Jesus. The Bible also clearly tells us Elijah and Moses are the witnesses and that John the Baptist represents Elijah. These are the two men who foreshadowed Jesus' future arrival, and they are represented by the two largest planets.

Jupiter is definitely associated with the scepter and kingship; Saturn has the rings that belong at any wedding and also is associated with Old Man Time and the end of an age, which is certainly appropriate for this wedding. These two witnesses/planets spend 12/18-12/21/2019 in the Huppah constellation of Sagittarius with the Sun/Jesus/the groom.

The Huppah is a wedding canopy supported above the altar on four poles. In this wedding it may be a region of the sky like the Egyptian Duat around the constellation Sagittarius; but it also sounds like the ancient definition of a new world by the four cardinal points of its orientation against the ecliptic.

Mikveh refers to the ritual bath of purification in which the bride to be symbolically washes away past associations. She traditionally does this no more than four days before the wedding. The Earth, which from 12/21 to 12/28/2019 will be undergoing a pole shift, will have oceans washing over continents. Our sinful civilization will be washed away and become a thing of the past. Aside from the mikveh, the bride's second main task to achieve before the wedding is to make new garments for herself. The Earth's new arrangement of land and sea, with continents in new positions, fulfills this requirement for new clothing.

Hakafot: before standing under the huppah at the altar where the groom (Jesus/sun) already waits for her, the bride circles the groom seven times. This represents the Earth/bride making seven annual orbits around the sun during the seven year tribulation, one of the clearest astronomical fulfillments of the wedding ceremony. At some Jewish weddings the bride does not have to walk alone to the altar at the end; the groom comes slightly towards her to meet her and escort her the rest of the way. This could refer to an expansion of the sun's corona after an incoming dust cloud initiates a reaction from the sun. This also sounds like the Greek concept of parousia and the Christian rapture.

The Badaken, or veiling, occurs next. The groom veils the bride himself, allegedly to make sure the identity of bride is correct; as he would not want to inadvertently marry someone else, like Jacob was tricked into marrying Leah when he thought he was marrying her sister Rachel. The veiling is the intrusion of the cosmic dust cloud into the solar system.

Kiddushin is the first of two portions of the actual wedding ceremony and starts with a blessing and a cup of wine. Immediately afterwards the bride and groom enter a seclusion room called "yichud." Yichud is an intermission giving the wedding couple a few minutes to calm down from any stresses built up during the wedding preparations, and to appreciate the specialness of just being alone together. Traditionally the groom gives the bride a ring in the yichud, and they must stay in the yichud together for eight minutes.

This eight minute window during which the bride receives the ring from the groom has an amazing astronomical correlation at just the right moment during our wedding in the sky in 2019. Halfway through the week of the pole shift that will take place from 12/21-12/28/2019, right in the midst of the wedding, there is a solar eclipse. As the Sun was already in Sagittarius/the huppah, and the Sun and Moon and Earth are now aligned on top of each other, we can say the Earth/bride has now entered the huppah and is with the Sun/groom. Depending on one's exact position on the Earth the eclipse will either occur late on the night of Christmas (for Americans) or early December 26 (for Israel.) The regions for which the eclipse will be visible, during a pole shift, seem uncertain.

Viewed from Earth, the moon appears slightly smaller than the sun, so when the moon covers most of the sun during an eclipse we see a circle of light from the edges of the solar disk which surrounds the moon. This is well known as the "Ring of Fire." The Sun/ groom/Jesus gives us on Earth/the bride this ring at just the right time in the midst of the astronomical wedding ceremony during the pole shift. And another incredible detail is that eclipses last no more than just over seven and one half minutes. The time requirement for the yichud is eight minutes because it represents receiving the Ring of Fire from the ultimate groom during an eclipse. Two valid witnesses must acknowledge the ring has been given to the bride; Jupiter and Saturn are still in the huppah/Sagittarius.

After the couple emerges from the yichud, the second portion of the wedding, the nissuin, begins with a reading of the Ketubah, the marriage contract, for which the two witnesses are also required. A plate is often smashed to represent the irreversability of the marriage. As the pieces can never be put back to the plate's prior condition, so the lives of the couple will never be the same from this point forward. It may also symbolize the destruction and replacement of the old earth-plane position.

A

second cup of wine is sipped and the Sheva B'rachot, or seven blessings, are recited. The seven blessings are: 1—general rejoicing, thanking God for creating 2—the world, 3—physical reality, 4—human spirituality; 5—a request to rebuild Jerusalem and the Holy Temple, 6—a request for the wedding couple's love to be as exclusive and special as that of Adam and Eve, and 7—a request that the Messiah will come to save the world. These blessings are rich with symbolic references to world-creation, the New Jerusalem, new Eden-like conditions, and the coming of Jesus.

After these blessings, as everyone knows, the groom stomps on a glass, repeatedly if necessary, until he smashes it. There are many guesses regarding the meaning of the breaking of the glass; the oldest is from the Kabbalah, which tells us that it symbolizes the breaking apart of the world at the beginning of the world (a concept we explored reviewing the first sentences of Genesis, and pole shifts) and that we are given the task of repairing the broken world, a concept known as "tikkun olam," or "repair of the world."

The modern Jewish wedding is now over, because our society doesn't want to publicly celebrate the act of consummating the marriage or make time to spend a week as guests before the dinner celebration. But in ancient times the newlyweds would retreat into a honeymoon chamber of the huppah for a week to consummate the marriage. After a week, the invited guests would look forward to wrapping things up and enjoying the big feast. Traditionally after the newlyweds spent a week in the huppah, the best man would hover outside the door of the bridal chamber waiting for the knock and voice from the groom inside which would announce to the best man that the bride and groom were ready to come out.

There are two important points here. First and most important, something astronomical can be expected to happen at this point which corresponds to the Sun/groom inseminating the Earth/bride. As there is both physical evidence of electric arcs scarring the surface of Earth, the Moon, and Mars; and there are ancient stories of the gods/planets throwing lightning bolts at each other, we should consider the possibility that the highly conductive dust cloud present at this point may encourage electrical discharges between the Sun and the planets. Many legends connect lightning with sacred sites and "hint that one party in the sacred marriage performed at the Temple was electrical current from the atmosphere."[38] This cosmic "lightning" may be what periodically boosts the strength of the Earth's disappearing magnetic field from its presently weak half-gauss strength to the range of 300 gauss found in the distant past.

The second comparison to the end of the bridal week is that with great fanfare and loud trumpet blasts, the best man would announce the emergence of the pair as they are finally, completely, and officially husband and wife. This corresponds to the Last Trumpet, the Rapture, the huge solar flare that blows away the cosmic dust and removes the veil, Judgment Day, and the end of the week-long pole shift. It also matches another event in the sky, as on 12/28/2019 Jupiter emerges from behind the Sun/groom/Jesus ("I am the door") after hovering by its edge for the better part of a day.

The modern Jewish wedding skips this week of consummation and goes straight from the breaking of the glass/world to the final celebration; a sit-down dinner party with music and dancing corresponding to the marriage supper of the Lamb. At any wedding, the guests celebrate the fact that out of the general population they were specially chosen to be present. An especially festive aspect of this celebration is dancing in large circles. The most popular and well known circular dance is the Horah, usually to the tune of the song "Hava Nagillah." The circular motion could easily represent renewed spinning of the Earth's axis, circular orbits, and/ or precession. The name of these circular dances, the "Horahs," is clearly derived from the Egyptian words for the Sun-god Horus.

This is a good point to mention a completely different way of timing Judgment Day through the Tree of Life. Looking at Genesis 3:22-23, just after God has found that mankind is eating from the tree of knowledge: "the LORD God said, 'Behold, the man has become like one of Us, knowing good and evil; and now, he might stretch out his hand, and take also from the tree of life, and eat, and live forever'— therefore the LORD God sent him out from the garden of Eden." This may be a reference to destroying an earlier civilization with a pole shift. Our technological progress may be the equivalent of eating from the tree of knowledge. We may be living in the material comforts of a relatively Edenic paradise today, before a pole shift makes the lives of whoever survives more difficult. And we do seem on the verge of fully understanding, and manipulating our DNA, which may be considered a tree of life.

Scientists from Osaka University in Japan have recently discovered that the C1q protein is directly responsible for the aging process. Unfortunately it is also part of our immune system, the complement system that helps the body clear away infections. Man has already learned to control the protein and block our cells' aging process. Eventually this discovery could be the key to near immortality. But forcing this protein into an inactive sleep mode also blocks the body's immune system, and the team at Osaka has not yet found a way to prevent aging while simultaneously allowing a normal immune response to continue. They will not find the answer in time because we are told we will not be allowed to eat from the tree of life.

But the tree of life also refers to a specific set of categories of wisdom described in the Kabbalah, the Jewish book of mysticism. These categories are arranged in a certain pattern of ten circles with twenty-two connecting lines between them. The initiated know these categories of wisdom well. They also know that some categories are more important than others and they know which subjects must be learned only after the others are mastered. A very basic and fundamental first step is to understand that "reverence for the sun is part of the Mysteries."[39] Understanding the deepest mysteries requires pulling some of these categories of hidden wisdom out of some of the others which are easier to grasp—pulling the sword

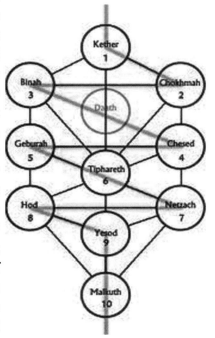

from the stone:

Anyone can grasp the basic wisdom in the sword's handle and the basic religious message in the categories in the stone (the church was founded on), but not everyone can use the wisdom in the handle to pull the hidden messages of the sword out of the Bible. The sword represents a great deal of "lost" wisdom, wisdom "buried" in stone, or built into stone monuments. It is the accumulated knowledge from past civilizations, including the astronomical causes and timing of pole shifts. We all understand the basics of the rock on which Jesus founded his church, (Matthew 16:18) Judaism's foundation stone on which Abraham was ready to sacrifice Isaac—on which God made his covenant with Abraham, on which Solomon's Temple was built, where the Dome of the Rock Mosque is today. But sometimes civilizations and religions often lose their focus, as our civilization has almost completely lost the knowledge of how the galactic center and the Sun periodically recreate the Earth.

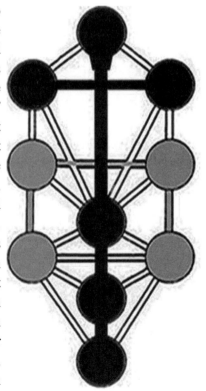

This is absolutely crucial to understanding the coming of the Messiah, the coming Kingdom, and the entire book of Revelations. Jesus alluded to this knowledge as "the stone which the builders rejected" from Psalms 118:22 and said that only the wise could understand what he meant. Only Arthur could remove the sword Excalibur from the stone, and this was the sign that he should be recognized as the one true king. English legends were based on this arrangement of categories of wisdom after the Knights Templar brought rediscovered knowledge back from the Holy Land, but this symbolism is not just a reference to King Arthur and the Holy Grail. Grail legends, both on the surface and in the hidden concepts, refer to Jesus Christ. Through his perfect mastery of all knowledge and wisdom Jesus stands out as the only rightful King, the only one who can pull the sword from the stone.

Likewise this arrangement in the sky—for each wisdom circle also represents a heavenly body—portends the pulling of the sword/axis from the stone/Earth, the timing of the coronation of Jesus as king, and our being kicked out of Eden. Knowledge of such things was almost completely lost to us in the destruction of the last pole shift, and the Bible describes the removal of this knowledge in the sword categories from our civilization well when God "drove the man out; and at the east of the garden of Eden He stationed the cherubim and the flaming sword which turned every direction to guard the way to the tree of life." (Genesis 3:24) Without being able to take hold of the sword to master its wisdom, we are denied the tree of life.

We have rediscovered the old understanding that each wisdom circle also represents a heavenly body. Knowing that the galactic center is represented by the top circle, that Saturn is represented below that, with Mars to Saturn's lower left, the sun below Saturn, Jupiter to Saturn's lower right, Mercury below Mars, the moon below the sun, Venus below Jupiter, and the Earth on the bottom—we have a potential arrangement of heavenly bodies which represents the tree of life.[40]

The odds of all these heavenly bodies being in close proximity, in a narrow field of view near the sun, are very low. This author estimates that such an arrangement might occur once in approximately five thousand years. It may have been referred to in Genesis 3:22, as something God could not allow mankind to reach before casting us out of Eden. It may be a reference to a point our current civilization will not be allowed to reach before destruction by pole shift. It may be the gathering at Ra's palace; in Egyptian myth, Ra summons his eye to punish mankind, he calls the other gods Shu, Tefnut, Geb, Nut, and Nun to gather at Ra's great palace to advise him in his actions against mankind. Could this assembly of Egyptian gods at the palace be a conjunction of planets near the galactic core? Could this also be represented by the assembly of gods Zeus calls together to judge the fate of Atlantis at the end of Plato's "Critias"? It may also be what is drawn on page 74 of the Dresden Codex version of the Mayan "Popul Vuh"—in which Venus is on the bottom, and "a cosmic Caiman, wearing the insignia of the planets Venus, Mars, Mercury and Jupiter, and itself probably representing the Milky Way, opens its mouth to pour forth a flood. The intention is clear— the world is destroyed by a deluge" during an alignment of planets overlapping the central bulge of the Milky Way, as the tipped over water jars of the new age of Aquarius are poured out.[41]

The odds of four of these planets being as close as they are to the sun portrayed in the Dresden Codex near the galactic center are very low, with odds of about one in 250. The planets are not in place for such an alignment when the Mayan Long Count ends in December 2012, but the planets do fit that Mayan description for about six

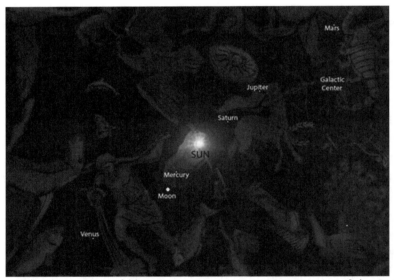

The night sky, as it would be seen January 25, 2020 at sunrise, if the Sun's light and the mass of the Earth didn't interfere with our view. While Stellarium images are not assuming that the Galactic Center will look like a giant supernova by late 2019, it may very well be the brightest object in the sky, the great throne of God. The Sun is on the horizon in the east, Saturn, Jupiter, the Galactic Center, and Mars are above the horizon, while Mercury, the Moon, Venus, and of course the Earth are below the horizon, all in a narrow field of view in a rare pattern corresponding to the Tree of Life. (I would like to thank Stellarium.org and its contributors for permission to reproduce their work, particularly Johan Meuris, who created the constellation art in this slightly modified Stellarium screenshot, in which I made the planets more visible and labeled them.)

weeks around the pole shift in December 2019. In fact there are seven astronomical bodies near the galactic center throne of God during the weeklong pole shift between the end of the seven year tribulation and Judgment Day. The five visible planets plus the Sun and Moon are the "seven lamps of fire burning before the throne" in Revelations 4:5. The kabalistic "Tree of Life" arrangement is an even more specific, more precisely defined version of these descriptions, and is far less likely, only occurring for a few days about every five thousand years.

So this author considers it no small coincidence that this rare tree of life alignment, with the sun on the horizon, and Mars, Jupiter, Saturn, and the Galactic Center above it; and Mercury, Venus, the Moon, and of course the Earth below the horizon—happens for the first time in thousands of years for a period of four days in January 2020. Interpreting this as a time our advanced civilization will not be allowed to reach intact, it is very interesting that this occurs just a few weeks after the end of the seven year tribulation, the pole shift, and Judgment Day in late December 2019.

With the idea of a pole shift from December 21-28, 2019 in mind, and knowing that these periodic and cyclical events have happened before, let us look at this "end" as a new beginning. We must hope that this will be the last such displacement of the Earth's crust over the interior, we must hope that mankind is saved once and for all, that God chooses to grant us access to the tree of life, and that our new beginning takes place in heaven. But our earlier translation of Genesis 1:1-2 may be relevant to anyone left on the Earth: "At a time when the earth became formless and void, God re-created and perfected the earth, and God's active force moved over the surface of the waters." And "Then God said, 'Let there be light'; and there was light…" (Genesis 1:3) Perhaps thousands of years from now, if there are descendants of those who survive the weeklong pole shift ending on Saturday, December 28, 2019 they will say of that day: "By the seventh day God completed His work which He had done, and He rested on the seventh day from all His work." (Genesis 2:2)

(Endnotes)

1 Lash, John. *The Skies in Memory*. As cited by Wilson, Colin and Rand Flem-Ath. *The Atlantis Blueprint: Unlocking the Ancient Mysteries of a Long-Lost Civilization*. New York: Delta Books, 2002, pp. 169-171

2 Lash, John. *The Skies in Memory*. As cited by Wilson, Colin and Rand Flem-Ath. Ibid., pp. 169-171

3 Lash, John. *The Skies in Memory*. As cited by Wilson, Colin and Rand Flem-Ath. Ibid., pp. 169-171

4 Campbell, Joseph. *The Mythic Image*. Princeton, NJ: Princeton University Press, 1981, p. 202

5 LaViolette, Paul. *Earth Under Fire: Humanity's Survival of the Ice Age.* Rochester, VT: Bear & Company, 2005, p. 256

6 Campbell, Joseph. *The Mythic Image*. Princeton, NJ: Princeton University Press, 1974, p. 202

7 S, Acharya. *Suns of God: Krishna, Buddha and Christ Unveiled*. Kempton, IL: Adventures Unlimited Press, 2004, p. 46

8 http://alignment2012.com/tonkins-error.html

9 http://www.the-big-meow.com/research/onfolio-files/httpedj. netmc2012truezone.htm

10 Montaigne, David. *Nostradamus, World War III,* 2002. St. Paul, MN: Llewellyn Books, 2002, p. 11

11 Leoni, Edgar. *Nostradamus and His Prophecies*. New York: Bell Publishing, 1982, p. 333

12 Leoni, Edgar. Ibid., p. 339

13 Leoni, Edgar. Ibid., p. 333

14 Leoni, Edgar. Ibid., p. 175

15 Leoni, Edgar. Ibid., p. 173

16 http://meteorshowersonline.com/showers/draconids.html

17 http://www.Biblenews1.com/planets/planets.html#Christ%20 in%20the%20Solar%20 System

18 Rylands, L. Gordon. *The Beginning of Gnostic Christianity*. London: Watts & Company, 1940, p. 186 as cited by S, Acharya. *Suns of God: Krishna, Buddha and Christ Unveiled*. Kempton, IL:

Adventures Unlimited Press, 2004, p. 136

19 Campbell, Joseph. *The Mythic Image*. Princeton, NJ: Princeton University Press, 1974, pp. 479-480

20 Lundy, John. *Monumental Christianity.* London: Swan Sonnenschein, 1889, p. 171

21 Herbermann, Charles, ed. *The Catholic Encyclopedia, vol. 2.* New York: The Encyclopedia Press, 1913, p. 734

22 Campbell, Joseph. *The Hero of a Thousand Faces.* London, Palladin Books, 1988, p. 145

23 Michell, John. *The New View Over Atlantis*. San Francisco, CA: Harper & Row, 1986, p. 178

24 *Midrash Numbers Rabbah* 11

25 Singer, Isidore. (Editor) *A Descriptive Record of the History, Religion, Literature, and Customs of the Jewish People from the Earliest Times to the Present Day, Volume 5*. New York: Funk and Wagnalls, 1906, p. 214

26 Hoyt, Herman. "A Dispensational Premillenial Response" a chapter in *The Meaning of the Millenium: Four Views*. Edited by Robert Clouse. Downers Grove, IL: InterVarsity Press, 1977, p. 144

27 LaHaye, Tim and Ed Hindson. *Exploring Bible Prophecy from Genesis to Revelation*. Eugene, OR: Harvest House, 2006, p. 266

28 Hoffman, Matthais Reinhard. "Angelomorphic Christology and the Book of Revelation" a revision of "The Destroyer and the Lamb" Doctoral Dissertation, Durham, NC: University of Durham, Mohr Siebeck, ISBN 3161487788, pp. 136-138

29 Josephus, Flavius. *Antiquities of the Jews*. Chicago, IL: Unabridged Books, 1981 10.219-27; 1.128-32

30 Hoyle, Fred. "Cosmology: Math Plus Mach Equals Far-Out Gravity." *Time Magazine*, June 26, 1964

31 Campbell, Joseph. *The Mythic Image*. Princeton, NJ: Princeton University Press, 1974, p. 153

32 de Santillana, Giorgio and Hertha von Dechend. *Hamlet's Mill: An Essay Investigating the Origins of Human Knowledge and its Transmission Through Myth*. Boston, MA: David R. Godine, 1969, p. 253

33 http://www.mayaexploration.org/pdf/MEC_Facebook_

Discussion_2010_Jenkins.pdf, p. 4, John Major Jenkins, 4/15/2010

34 Campbell, Joseph. *The Mythic Image*. Princeton, NJ: Princeton University Press, 1974, p. 134

35 http://probvs.net/probvs/R905/R905.html

36 Hoekema, Anthony. "An Amillenial Response," a chapter in *The Meaning of the Millenium: Four Views*. Edited by Robert Clouse. Downers Grove, IL: InterVarsity Press, 1977, p. 149.

37 Singer, Isidore. (Editor) *A Descriptive Record of the History, Religion, Literature, and Customs of the Jewish People from the Earliest Times to the Present Day, Volume 5*. New York: Funk and Wagnalls, 1906, p. 593

38 Michell, John. *The Dimensions of Paradise*. Rochester, VT: Inner Traditions, 2008, pp. 14-15

39 S, Acharya. *Suns of God: Krishna, Buddha and Christ Unveiled*. Kempton, IL: Adventures Unlimited Press, 2004, p. 66

40 Weidner, Jay and Vincent Bridges. *The Mysteries of the Great Cross of Hendaye: Alchemy and the End of Time*. Rochester, VT: Destiny Books, 2003, p. 258

41 Gilbert, Adrian and Maurice Cotterell. *The Mayan Prophecies*. New York: Barnes & Noble, 1996, p. 196

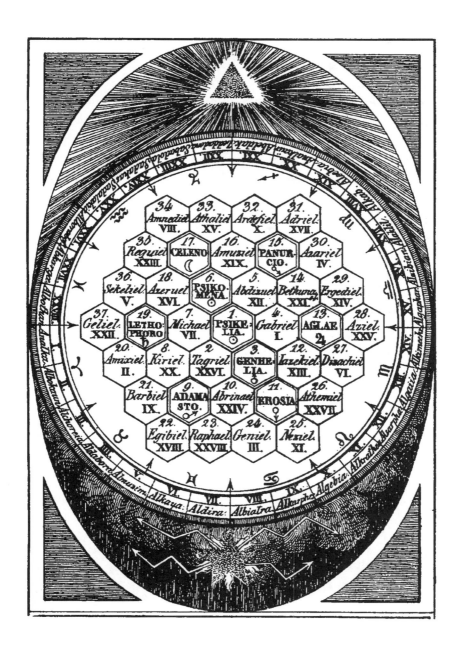

343

Selected Bibliography

Asimov, Isaac. *Asimov's Guide to the Bible: The Old Testament.* New York: Avon Books, 1968

Asimov, Isaac. *Asimov's Guide to the Bible: The New Testament.* New York: Avon Books, 1969

Campbell, Joseph. *The Mythic Image.* Princeton, NJ: Princeton University Press, 1974

Childress, David Hatcher. *Pirates & The Lost Templar Fleet: The Secret Naval War between the Knights Templar & the Vatican.* Kempton, IL: Adventures Unlimited Press, 2003

Childress, David Hatcher. *Technology of the Gods: The Incredible Sciences of the Ancients.* Kempton, IL: Adventures Unlimited Press, 2000

Creighton, Scott and Gary Osborn. *The Giza Prophecy: The Orion Code and the Secret Teachings of the Pyramids.* Rochester, VT: Bear & Company, 2012

Fideler, David R. *Jesus Christ, Sun of God: Ancient Cosmology and Early Christian Symbolism.* Wheaton, IL: Quest Books, 1993

Flem-Ath, Rand and Rose. *When the Sky Fell: In Search of Atlantis.* New York: St. Martin's Press, 1995

Gilbert, Adrian and Maurice Cotterell. *The Mayan Prophecies.* New York: Barnes & Noble, 1996

Hall, Manly P. *Freemasonry of the Ancient Egyptians.* Los Angeles, CA: Philosophical Research Society, 1937

Hapgood, Charles. *Earth's Shifting Crust: A Key to Some Basic Problems of Earth Science.* New York: Pantheon Books, 1958

Hapgood, Charles. *Maps of the Ancient Sea Kings.* Kempton, IL: Adventures Unlimited Press, 1996

Hapgood, Charles. *The Path of the Pole.* Kempton, IL: Adventures Unlimited Press, 1999

Hancock, Graham. *Fingerprints of the Gods.* New York: Three Rivers Press, 1995

Hancock, Graham and Robert Bauval. *The Message of the*

Sphinx: A Quest for the Hidden Legacy of Mankind. New York: Random House, 1996

Jenkins, John Major. *Maya Cosmogenesis 2012.* Santa Fe, NM: Bear & Company, 1998

LaHaye, Tim and Ed Hindson. *Exploring Bible Prophecy from Genesis to Revelation.* Eugene, OR: Harvest House, 2006

LaHaye, Tim. *Revelation Unveiled.* Grand Rapids, MI: Zondervan Press, 1999

LaViolette, Paul A. *Earth Under Fire: Humanity's Survival of the Ice Age.* Rochester, VT: Bear & Company, 2005

Michell, John. *The Dimensions of Paradise: Sacred Geometry, Ancient Science, and the Heavenly Order on Earth.* Rochester, VT: Inner Traditions, 2008

Michell, John. *The New View Over Atlantis.* San Francisco, CA: Harper & Row, 1986

S, Acharya. *Suns of God: Krishna, Buddha and Christ Unveiled.* Kempton, IL: Adventures Unlimited Press, 2004

de Santillana, Giorgio and Hertha von Dechend. *Hamlet's Mill: An Essay Investigating the Origins of Human Knowledge and its Transmission Through Myth.* Boston, MA: David R. Godine, 1969

Schoch, Robert. *Forgotten Civilization: The Role of Solar Outbursts in Our Past and Future.* Rochester, VT: Inner Traditions, 2012

Weidner, Jay and Vincent Bridges. *The Mysteries of the Great Cross of Hendaye: Alchemy and the End of Time.* Rochester, VT: Destiny Books, 2003

White, John. *Pole Shift.* Virginia Beach, VA: A.R.E. Press, 2007

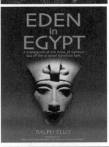

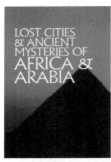

LOST CITIES & ANCIENT MYSTERIES OF AFRICA & ARABIA
by David Hatcher Childress

Childress continues his world-wide quest for lost cities and ancient mysteries. Join him as he discovers forbidden cities in the Empty Quarter of Arabia; "Atlantean" ruins in Egypt and the Kalahari desert; a mysterious, ancient empire in the Sahara; and more. This is the tale of an extraordinary life on the road: across war-torn countries, Childress searches for King Solomon's Mines, living dinosaurs, the Ark of the Covenant and the solutions to some of the fantastic mysteries of the past.
423 PAGES. 6x9 PAPERBACK. ILLUSTRATED. $14.95. CODE: AFA

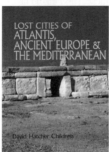

LOST CITIES OF ATLANTIS, ANCIENT EUROPE & THE MEDITERRANEAN
by David Hatcher Childress

Childress takes the reader in search of sunken cities in the Mediterranean; across the Atlas Mountains in search of Atlantean ruins; to remote islands in search of megalithic ruins; to meet living legends and secret societies. From Ireland to Turkey, Morocco to Eastern Europe, and around the remote islands of the Mediterranean and Atlantic, Childress takes the reader on an astonishing quest for mankind's past. Ancient technology, cataclysms, megalithic construction, lost civilizations and devastating wars of the past are all explored in this book.
524 PAGES. 6x9 PAPERBACK. ILLUSTRATED. $16.95. CODE: MED

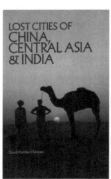

LOST CITIES OF CHINA, CENTRAL ASIA & INDIA
by David Hatcher Childress

Like a real life "Indiana Jones," maverick archaeologist David Childress takes the reader on an incredible adventure across some of the world's oldest and most remote countries in search of lost cities and ancient mysteries. Discover ancient cities in the Gobi Desert; hear fantastic tales of lost continents, vanished civilizations and secret societies bent on ruling the world; visit forgotten monasteries in forbidding snow-capped mountains with strange tunnels to mysterious subterranean cities! A unique combination of far-out exploration and practical travel advice, it will astound and delight the experienced traveler or the armchair voyager.
429 PAGES. 6x9 PAPERBACK. ILLUSTRATED. FOOTNOTES & BIBLIOGRAPHY. $14.95. CODE: CHI

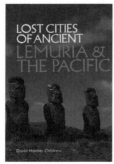

LOST CITIES OF ANCIENT LEMURIA & THE PACIFIC
by David Hatcher Childress

Was there once a continent in the Pacific? Called Lemuria or Pacifica by geologists, Mu or Pan by the mystics, there is now ample mythological, geological and archaeological evidence to "prove" that an advanced and ancient civilization once lived in the central Pacific. Maverick archaeologist and explorer David Hatcher Childress combs the Indian Ocean, Australia and the Pacific in search of the surprising truth about mankind's past. Contains photos of the underwater city on Pohnpei; explanations on how the statues were levitated around Easter Island in a clockwise vortex movement; tales of disappearing islands; Egyptians in Australia; and more.
379 PAGES. 6x9 PAPERBACK. ILLUSTRATED. FOOTNOTES & BIBLIOGRAPHY. $14.95. CODE: LEM

SUNKEN REALMS
A Survey of Underwater Ruins Around the World
By Karen Mutton

Australian researcher Karen Mutton begins by discussing some of the causes for sunken ruins: super-floods; volcanoes; earthquakes at the end of the last great flood; plate tectonics and other theories. From there she launches into a worldwide cataloging of underwater ruins by region. She begins with the many underwater cities in the Mediterranean, and then moves into northern Europe and the North Atlantic. Places covered in this book include: Tartessos; Cadiz; Morocco; Alexandria; The Bay of Naples; Libya; Phoenician and Egyptian sites; Roman era sites; Yarmuta, Lebanon; Cyprus; Malta; Thule & Hyperborea; Canary and Azore Islands; Bahamas; Cuba; Bermuda; Peru; Micronesia; Japan; Indian Ocean; Sri Lanka Land Bridge; Lake Titicaca; and inland lakes in Scotland, Russia, Iran, China, Wisconsin, Florida and more.

320 Pages. 6x9 Paperback. Illustrated. Bibliography. $20.00. Code: SRLM

TECHNOLOGY OF THE GODS
The Incredible Sciences of the Ancients
by David Hatcher Childress

Childress looks at the technology that was allegedly used in Atlantis and the theory that the Great Pyramid of Egypt was originally a gigantic power station. He examines tales of ancient flight and the technology that it involved; how the ancients used electricity; megalithic building techniques; the use of crystal lenses and the fire from the gods; evidence of various high tech weapons in the past, including atomic weapons; ancient metallurgy and heavy machinery; the role of modern inventors such as Nikola Tesla in bringing ancient technology back into modern use; impossible artifacts; and more.

356 PAGES. 6x9 PAPERBACK. ILLUSTRATED. BIBLIOGRAPHY. $16.95. CODE: TGOD

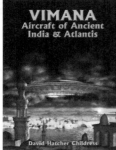

VIMANA AIRCRAFT OF ANCIENT INDIA & ATLANTIS
by David Hatcher Childress, introduction by Ivan T. Sanderson

In this incredible volume on ancient India, authentic Indian texts such as the *Ramayana* and the *Mahabharata* are used to prove that ancient aircraft were in use more than four thousand years ago. Included in this book is the entire Fourth Century BC manuscript *Vimaanika Shastra* by the ancient author Maharishi Bharadwaaja. Also included are chapters on Atlantean technology, the incredible Rama Empire of India and the devastating wars that destroyed it.

334 PAGES. 6x9 PAPERBACK. ILLUSTRATED. $15.95. CODE: VAA

LOST CONTINENTS & THE HOLLOW EARTH
I Remember Lemuria and the Shaver Mystery
by David Hatcher Childress & Richard Shaver

Shaver's rare 1948 book *I Remember Lemuria* is reprinted in its entirety, and the book is packed with illustrations from Ray Palmer's *Amazing Stories* magazine of the 1940s. Palmer and Shaver told of tunnels running through the earth—tunnels inhabited by the Deros and Teros, humanoids from an ancient spacefaring race that had inhabited the earth, eventually going underground, hundreds of thousands of years ago. Childress discusses the famous hollow earth books and delves deep into whatever reality may be behind the stories of tunnels in the earth. Operation High Jump to Antarctica in 1947 and Admiral Byrd's bizarre statements, tunnel systems in South America and Tibet, the underground world of Agartha, the belief of UFOs coming from the South Pole, more.

344 PAGES. 6x9 PAPERBACK. ILLUSTRATED. $16.95. CODE: LCHE

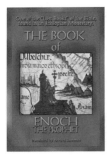

THE BOOK OF ENOCH
translated by Richard Laurence
This is a reprint of the Apocryphal *Book of Enoch the Prophet* which was first discovered in Abyssinia in the year 1773 by a Scottish explorer named James Bruce. One of the main influences from the book is its explanation of evil coming into the world with the arrival of the "fallen angels." Enoch acts as a scribe, writing up a petition on behalf of these fallen angels, or fallen ones, to be given to a higher power for ultimate judgment. Christianity adopted some ideas from Enoch, including the Final Judgment, the concept of demons, the origins of evil and the fallen angels, and the coming of a Messiah and ultimately, a Messianic kingdom.
224 PAGES. 6x9 PAPERBACK. ILLUSTRATED. INDEX. $16.95. CODE: BOE

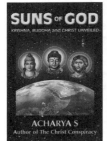

SUNS OF GOD
Krishna, Buddha and Christ Unveiled
by Acharya S
Over the past several centuries, the Big Three spiritual leaders have been the Lords Christ, Krishna and Buddha, whose stories and teachings are so remarkably similar as to confound and amaze those who encounter them. As classically educated archaeologist, historian, mythologist and linguist Acharya S thoroughly reveals, these striking parallels exist not because these godmen were "historical" personages who "walked the earth" but because they are personifications of the central focus of the famous and scandalous "mysteries." These mysteries date back thousands of years and are found globally, reflecting an ancient tradition steeped in awe and intrigue.
428 PAGES. 6x9 PAPERBACK. ILLUSTRATED. BIBLIOGRAPHY. INDEX. $18.95. CODE: SUNG

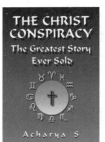

THE CHRIST CONSPIRACY
The Greatest Story Ever Sold
by Acharya S.
In this highly controversial and explosive book, archaeologist, historian, mythologist and linguist Acharya S. marshals an enormous amount of startling evidence to demonstrate that Christianity and the story of Jesus Christ were created by members of various secret societies, mystery schools and religions in order to unify the Roman Empire under one state religion. In developing such a fabrication, this multinational cabal drew upon a multitude of myths and rituals that existed long before the Christian era, and reworked them for centuries into the religion passed down to us today. Contrary to popular belief, Jesus was many characters rolled into one. These characters personified the ubiquitous solar myth, and their exploits were well known, as reflected by such popular deities as Mithras, Heracles/Hercules, Dionysos and many others throughout the Roman Empire and beyond.
436 PAGES. 6x9 PAPERBACK. ILLUSTRATED. $16.95. CODE: CHRC

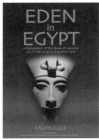

EDEN IN EGYPT
by Ralph Ellis
The story of Adam and Eve from the Book of Genesis is perhaps one of the best-known stories in circulation, even today, and yet nobody really knows where this tale came from or what it means. But even a cursory glance at the text will demonstrate the origins of this tale, for the river of Eden is described as having four branches. There is only one river in this part of the world that fits this description, and that is the Nile, with the four branches forming the Nile Delta. According to Ellis, Judaism was based upon the reign of the pharaoh Akhenaton, because the solitary Judaic god was known as Adhon while this pharaoh's solitary god was called Aton or Adjon. But what of the identities of Adam and Eve? Includes 16 page color section.
320 PAGES. 6x9 PAPERBACK. ILLUSTRATED. BIBLIOGRAPHY. INDEX. $20.00. CODE: EIE

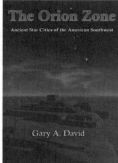

THE ORION ZONE
Ancient Star Cities of the American Southwest
by Gary A. David

This book on ancient star lore explores the mysterious location of Pueblos in the American Southwest, circa 1100 AD, that appear to be a mirror image of the major stars of the Orion constellation. Packed with maps, diagrams, astronomical charts, and photos of ruins and rock art, *The Orion Zone* explores this terrestrial-celestial relationship and its astounding global significance. Chapters include: Leaving Many Footprints—The Emergence and Migrations of the Anazazi; The Sky Over the Hopi Villages; Orion Rising in the Dark Crystal; The Cosmo-Magical Cities of the Anazazi; Windows Onto the Cosmos; To Calibrate the March of Time; They Came from Across the Ocean—The Patki (Water) Clan and the Snake Clan of the Hopi; Ancient and Mysterious Monuments; Beyond That Fiery Day; more.

346 pages. 6x9 Paperback. Illustrated. $19.95. Code: OZON

THE CRYSTAL SKULLS
Astonishing Portals to Man's Past
by David Hatcher Childress and Stephen S. Mehler

Childress introduces the technology and lore of crystals, and then plunges into the turbulent times of the Mexican Revolution form the backdrop for the rollicking adventures of Ambrose Bierce, the renowned journalist who went missing in the jungles in 1913, and F.A. Mitchell-Hedges, the notorious adventurer who emerged from the jungles with the most famous of the crystal skulls. Mehler shares his extensive knowledge of and experience with crystal skulls. Having been involved in the field since the 1980s, he has personally examined many of the most influential skulls, and has worked with the leaders in crystal skull research, including the inimitable Nick Nocerino, who developed a meticulous methodology for the purpose of examining the skulls.

294 pages. 6x9 Paperback. Illustrated. Bibliography. $18.95. Code: CRSK

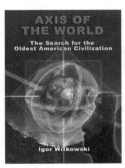

AXIS OF THE WORLD
The Search for the Oldest American Civilization
by Igor Witkowski

Polish author Witkowski's research reveals remnants of a high civilization that was able to exert its influence on almost the entire planet, and did so with full consciousness. Sites around South America show that this was not just one of the places influenced by this culture, but a place where they built their crowning achievements. Easter Island, in the southeastern Pacific, constitutes one of them. The Rongo-Rongo language that developed there points westward to the Indus Valley. Taken together, the facts presented by Witkowski provide a fresh, new proof that an antediluvian, great civilization flourished several millennia ago.

220 pages. 6x9 Paperback. Illustrated. References. $18.95. Code: AXOW

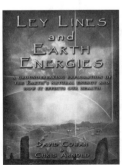

LEY LINE & EARTH ENERGIES
An Extraordinary Journey into the Earth's Natural Energy System
by David Cowan & Chris Arnold

The mysterious standing stones, burial grounds and stone circles that lace Europe, the British Isles and other areas have intrigued scientists, writers, artists and travellers through the centuries. How do ley lines work? How did our ancestors use Earth energy to map their sacred sites and burial grounds? How do ghosts and poltergeists interact with Earth energy? How can Earth spirals and black spots affect our health? This exploration shows how natural forces affect our behavior, how they can be used to enhance our health and well being.

368 PAGES. 6x9 PAPERBACK. ILLUSTRATED. $18.95. CODE: LLEE

ORDER FORM

10% Discount When You Order 3 or More Items!

One Adventure Place
P.O. Box 74
Kempton, Illinois 60946
United States of America
Tel.: 815-253-6390 • Fax: 815-253-6300
Email: auphq@frontiernet.net
http://www.adventuresunlimitedpress.com

ORDERING INSTRUCTIONS

✓ Remit by USD$ Check, Money Order or Credit Card

✓ Visa, Master Card, Discover & AmEx Accepted

✓ Paypal Payments Can Be Made To:
  info@wexclub.com

✓ Prices May Change Without Notice

✓ 10% Discount for 3 or more Items

SHIPPING CHARGES

United States

✓ Postal Book Rate { $4.00 First Item
                     50¢ Each Additional Item

✓ POSTAL BOOK RATE Cannot Be Tracked!

✓ Priority Mail { $5.00 First Item
                 $2.00 Each Additional Item

✓ UPS { $6.00 First Item
        $1.50 Each Additional Item

  NOTE: UPS Delivery Available to Mainland USA Only

Canada

✓ Postal Air Mail { $10.00 First Item
                    $2.50 Each Additional Item

✓ Personal Checks or Bank Drafts MUST BE
  US$ and Drawn on a US Bank

✓ Canadian Postal Money Orders OK

✓ Payment MUST BE US$

All Other Countries

✓ Sorry, No Surface Delivery!

✓ Postal Air Mail { $16.00 First Item
                    $6.00 Each Additional Item

✓ Checks and Money Orders MUST BE US$
  and Drawn on a US Bank or branch.

✓ Paypal Payments Can Be Made in US$ To:
  info@wexclub.com

SPECIAL NOTES

✓ RETAILERS: Standard Discounts Available

✓ BACKORDERS: We Backorder all Out-of-
  Stock Items Unless Otherwise Requested

✓ PRO FORMA INVOICES: Available on Request

ORDER ONLINE AT: www.adventuresunlimitedpress.com

Please check: ✓

☐ This is my first order   ☐ I have ordered before

Name

Address

City

State/Province   Postal Code

Country

Phone day   Evening

Fax   Email

Item Code	Item Description	Qty	Total

Please check: ✓

		Subtotal ▶	
☐ Postal-Surface		Less Discount-10% for 3 or more items ▶	
		Balance ▶	
☐ Postal-Air Mail	Illinois Residents 6.25% Sales Tax ▶		
(Priority in USA)		Previous Credit ▶	
☐ UPS		Shipping ▶	
(Mainland USA only)	Total (check/MO in USD$ only) ▶		

☐ Visa/MasterCard/Discover/American Express

Card Number

Expiration Date

10% Discount When You Order 3 or More Items!